本日も一日頑張りましょう。

ほんじつもいちにちがんばりましょう。
Honjitsu mo tsuitachi ganbarimashou.
Let's do our best today as well.

Variation 1	Variation 2
本日も全力で取り組みましょう。	Kyō mo shōjin shima shou.
ほんじつもぜんりょくでとりくみましょう。	ほんじつもぜんりょくでとりくみましょう。
Honjitsu mo zenryoku de torikumi ma shou.	Kyō mo shōjin shima shou.
Let's give our all today as well.	Let's do our best today as well.

Positive Response	Negative Response
はい、全力で取り組みます。	毎日同じ事を言われても疲れますよ。
はい、ぜんりょくでとりくみます。	まいにちおなじことをいわれてもつかれますよ。
Hai, zenryoku de torikumimasu.	Mainichi onaji koto o gen warete mo tsukaremasu yo.
Yes, I'll give it my all.	It's tiring to hear the same thing every day.

Conversation example person A	Conversation example person B
本日も一日頑張りましょう。	はい、今日も頑張ります！
ほんじつもいちにちがんばりましょう。	はい、きょうもがんばります！
Honjitsu mo ichi-nichi ganbari ma shou.	Hai, kyō mo ganbarimasu!
Let's do our best today as well.	Yes, I'll do my best today!

Cultural Context

Reflects Japanese work ethic and group mentality. Used daily in workplaces to boost morale.

安全第一で行動しましょう。

あんぜんだいいちでこうどうしましょう。

Anzendaiichi de kōdō shimashou.

Let's act with safety as our top priority.

Variation 1	Variation 2
安全を最優先に考えましょう。	Kyō mo shōjin shima shou.
あんぜんをさいゆうせんにかんがえましょう。	あんぜんをさいゆうせんにかんがえましょう。
Anzen o sai yūsen ni kangae ma shou.	Anzen o sai yūsen ni shima shou.
Let's prioritize safety above all else.	Let's prioritize safety.

Positive Response	Negative Response
もちろん、安全には細心の注意を払います。	そんなに言わなくても分かっていますよ。
もちろん、あんぜんにはさいしんのちゅういをはらいます。	そんなにいわなくてもわかっていますよ。
Mochiron, anzen ni wa saishin no chūi o haraimasu.	Son'nani iwanakute mo wakatte imasu yo.
Of course, I'll pay utmost attention to safety.	You don't need to say it so often, we already know.

Conversation example person A	Conversation example person B
今日の現場作業では、安全第一で行動しましょう。	了解です。安全確認を徹底します。
きょうのげんばさぎょうでは、あんぜんだいいちでこうどうしましょう。	りょうかいです。あんぜんかくにんをてっていします。
Kyō no genba sagyōde wa, anzen dai ichi de kōdō shima shou.	Ryōkaidesu. Anzen kakunin o tettei shimasu.
For today's on-site work, let's prioritize safety.	Understood. I'll thoroughly check for safety.

Cultural Context

Stems from Japan's focus on workplace safety. Common in industries with physical risks.

お客様の立場に立って考えましょう。

おきゃくさまのたちばにたってかんがえましょう。
Okyakusama no tachiba ni tatte kangaemashou.
Let's think from the customer's perspective.

Variation 1	Variation 2
顧客目線で物事を考えましょう。	Kyō mo shōjin shima shou.
こきゃくめせんでものごとをかんがえましょう。	こきゃくめせんでものごとをかんがえましょう。
Kokyaku mesen de monogoto o kangae ma shou.	Kokyaku shiten o wasurezu ni kōdō shima shou.
Let's think from the customer's perspective.	Let's act without forgetting the customer's perspective.

Positive Response	Negative Response
顧客満足を最優先に考えます。	現実的には難しいですよ。
こきゃくまんぞくをさいゆうせんにかんがえます。	げんじつてきにはむずかしいですよ。
Kokyaku manzoku o sai yūsen ni kangaemasu.	Genjitsu-teki ni wa muzukashīdesu yo.
I'll prioritize customer satisfaction.	That's difficult to do in reality.

Conversation example person A	Conversation example person B
新サービスの企画では、お客様の立場に立って考えましょう。	その通りですね。顧客ニーズを重視します。
しんさーびすのきかくでは、おきゃくさまのたちばにたってかんがえましょう。	そのとおりですね。こきゃくにーずをじゅうしします。
Shin sābisu no kikakude wa, okyakusama no tachiba ni tatte kangae ma shou.	Sono tōridesu ne. Kokyaku nīzu o jūshi shimasu.
When planning new services, let's think from the customer's perspective.	You're right. We'll focus on customer needs.

Cultural Context
Reflects Japan's customer-first mentality. Used in service industries and customer-facing roles.

健康管理に気をつけましょう。

けんこうかんりにきをつけましょう。

Kenkō kanri ni ki o tsukemashou.

Let's be mindful of our health.

Variation 1	Variation 2
自己の健康に留意しましょう。	Kyō mo shōjin shima shou.
じこのけんこうにりゅういしましょう。	じこのけんこうにりゅういしましょう。
Jiko no kenkō ni ryūi shima shou.	Jibun no taichō kanri ni ki o tsuke ma shou.
Let's be mindful of our own health.	Let's take care of our own health.

Positive Response	Negative Response
健康第一で仕事に取り組みます。	忙しすぎて気をつける余裕がありません。
けんこうだいいちでしごとにとりくみます。	いそがしすぎてきをつけるよゆうがありません。
Kenkō dai ichi de shigoto ni torikumimasu.	Isogashi sugite ki o tsukeru yoyū ga arimasen.
I'll work with health as my top priority.	I'm too busy to pay attention to that.

Conversation example person A	Conversation example person B
最近の残業続きで疲れていませんか？健康管理に気をつけましょう。	ありがとうございます。休息をしっかり取ります。
さいきんのざんぎょうつづきでつかれていませんか？けんこうかんりにきをつけましょう。	ありがとうございます。きゅうそくをしっかりとります。
Saikin no zangyō tsudzuki de tsukarete imasen ka? Kenkō kanri ni ki o tsuke ma shou.	Arigatōgozaimasu. Kyūsoku o shikkari torimasu.
Aren't you tired from all the recent overtime? Let's be mindful of our health.	Thank you. I'll make sure to get enough rest.

Cultural Context

Related to Japan's aging society and health consciousness. More common during flu seasons or health crises.

チームワークを大切にしましょう。

ちーむわーくをたいせつにしましょう。
Chīmuwāku o taisetsu ni shimashou.
Let's value teamwork.

Variation 1	Variation 2
協調性を大切にしましょう。	Kyō mo shōjin shima shou.
きょうちょうせいをたいせつにしましょう。	きょうちょうせいをたいせつにしましょう。
Kyōchō-sei o taisetsu ni shima shou.	Kyōchō-sei o jūshi shite kōdō shima shou.
Let's value cooperation.	Let's act with emphasis on cooperation.

Positive Response	Negative Response
協力し合って成果を出します。	個人の能力も重要だと思います。
きょうりょくしあってせいかをだします。	こじんののうりょくもじゅうようだとおもいます。
Kyōryoku shi atte seika o dashimasu.	Kojin no nōryoku mo jūyōda to omoimasu.
We'll collaborate to achieve results.	I think individual abilities are important too.

Conversation example person A	Conversation example person B
このプロジェクトは難しいですが、チームワークを大切にしましょう。	はい、協力して乗り越えていきましょう。
このぷろじぇくとはむずかしいですが、ちーむわーくをたいせつにしましょう。	はい、きょうりょくしてのりこえていきましょう。
Kono purojekuto wa muzukashīdesuga, chīmu wāku o taisetsu ni shima shou.	Hai, kyōryoku shite norikoete iki ma shou.
This project is challenging, but let's value our teamwork.	Yes, let's overcome this by working together.

Cultural Context
Reflects Japanese collectivist culture. Used in team-based work environments.

目標達成に向けて頑張りましょう。

もくひょうたっせいにむけてがんばりましょう。

Mokuhyō tassei ni mukete ganbarimashou.

Let's work hard towards achieving our goals.

Variation 1	Variation 2
目標実現に向けて努力しましょう。	Kyō mo shōjin shima shou.
もくひょうじつげんにむけてどりょくしましょう。	もくひょうじつげんにむけてどりょくしましょう。
Mokuhyō jitsugen ni mukete doryoku shima shou.	Mokuteki ishiki o motte maishin shima shou.
Let's strive towards achieving our goals.	Let's press forward with a sense of purpose.

Positive Response	Negative Response
目標を必ず達成します。	目標が高すぎて現実的ではありません。
もくひょうをかならずたっせいします。	もくひょうがたかすぎてげんじつてきではありません。
Mokuhyō o kanarazu tassei shimasu.	Mokuhyō ga taka sugite genjitsu-tekide wa arimasen.
I'll definitely achieve our goals.	The goal is too high and unrealistic.

Conversation example person A	Conversation example person B
四半期の目標達成に向けて頑張りましょう。	承知しました。全力で取り組みます。
しはんきのもくひょうたっせいにむけてがんばりましょう。	しょうちしました。ぜんりょくでとりくみます。
Shihanki no mokuhyō tassei ni mukete ganbari ma shou.	Shōchi shima shita. Zenryoku de torikumimasu.
Let's work hard towards achieving our quarterly goals.	Understood. I'll give it my all.

Cultural Context

Tied to Japan's goal-oriented work culture. Often used at the start of new projects or fiscal years.

効率的に業務を進めましょう。

こうりつてきにぎょうむをすすめましょう。
Kōritsu-teki ni gyōmu o susumemashou.
Let's proceed with our tasks efficiently.

Variation 1	Variation 2
業務の効率化を図りましょう。	Kyō mo shōjin shima shou.
ぎょうむのこうりつかをはかりましょう。	ぎょうむのこうりつかをはかりましょう。
Gyōmu no kōritsu-ka o hakari ma shou.	Sagyō no kōritsu-ka o hakari ma shou.
Let's work on improving work efficiency.	Let's work on improving operational efficiency.

Positive Response	Negative Response
効率的な方法を常に模索します。	効率だけを求めるとミスが増えます。
こうりつてきなほうほうをつねにもさくします。	こうりつだけをもとめるとみすがふえます。
Kōritsu-tekina hōhō o tsuneni mosaku shimasu.	Kōritsu dake o motomeru to misu ga fuemasu.
I'll always seek efficient methods.	Focusing only on efficiency can increase mistakes.

Conversation example person A	Conversation example person B
今月は案件が多いので、効率的に業務を進めましょう。	そうですね。優先順位をつけて進めていきます。
こんげつはあんけんがおおいので、こうりつてきにぎょうむをすすめましょう。	そうですね。ゆうせんじゅんいをつけてすすめていきます。
Kongetsu wa anken ga ōinode, kōritsu-teki ni gyōmu o susume ma shou.	Sōdesu ne. Yūsen jun'i o tsukete susumete ikimasu.
We have many projects this month, so let's work efficiently.	You're right. I'll prioritize tasks and proceed accordingly.

Cultural Context
Reflects Japan's focus on efficiency and productivity. Common in office environments.

コミュニケーションを大切にしましょう。

こみゅにけーしょんをたいせつにしましょう。
Komyunikēshon o taisetsu ni shimashou.
Let's value communication.

Variation 1	Variation 2
意思疎通を大切にしましょう。	Kyō mo shōjin shima shou.
いしそつうをたいせつにしましょう。	いしそつうをたいせつにしましょう。
Ishi sotsū o taisetsu ni shima shou.	Ishi sotsū o enkatsu ni shima shou.
Let's value clear communication.	Let's facilitate smooth communication.

Positive Response	Negative Response
オープンで明確なコミュニケーションを心がけます。	仕事が忙しくてそんな余裕はありません。
おーぷんでめいかくなこみゅにけーしょんをこころがけます。	しごとがいそがしくてそんなよゆうはありません。
Ōpun de meikakuna komyunikēshon o kokorogakemasu.	Shigoto ga isogashikute son'na yoyū wa arimasen.
I'll ensure open and clear communication.	I'm too busy with work to have time for that.

Conversation example person A	Conversation example person B
リモートワークが増えましたが、コミュニケーションを大切にしましょう。	はい、定期的に状況共有を行います。
りもーとわーくがふえましたが、こみゅにけーしょんをたいせつにしましょう。	はい、ていきてきにじょうきょうきょうゆうをおこないます。
Rimōto wāku ga fuemashitaga, komyunikēshon o taisetsu ni shima shou.	Hai, teiki-teki ni jōkyō kyōyū o okonaimasu.
Remote work has increased, but let's value communication.	Yes, I'll make sure to share updates regularly.

Cultural Context
Addresses the need for clear communication in hierarchical society. Used in diverse work environments to encourage open dialogue.

時間管理を意識しましょう。

じかんかんりをいしきしましょう。

Jikan kanri o ishiki shimashou.

Let's be conscious of time management.

Variation 1	Variation 2
時間の有効活用を心がけましょう。	Kyō mo shōjin shima shou.
じかんのゆうこうかつようをこころがけましょう。	じかんのゆうこうかつようをこころがけましょう。
Jikan no yūkō katsuyō o kokorogake ma shou.	Jikan o kōka-teki ni tsukau yō ni tsutome ma shou.
Let's make effective use of our time.	Let's strive to make effective use of time.

Positive Response	Negative Response
時間を有効活用し、生産性を高めます。	突発的な仕事が多くて難しいです。
じかんをゆうこうかつようし、せいさんせいをたかめます。	とっぱつてきなしごとがおおくてむずかしいです。
Jikan o yūkō katsuyō shi, seisan-sei o takamemasu.	Toppatsu-tekina shigoto ga ōkute muzukashīdesu.
I'll use time effectively to increase productivity.	It's difficult with so many unexpected tasks.

Conversation example person A	Conversation example person B
デッドラインが近いので、時間管理を意識しましょう。	了解です。スケジュールを見直します。
でっどらいんがちかいので、じかんかんりをいしきしましょう。	りょうかいです。すけじゅーるをみなおしします。
Deddo rain ga chikainode, jikan kanri o ishiki shima shou.	Ryōkaidesu. Sukejūru o minaoshimasu.
The deadline is approaching, so let's be conscious of time management.	Understood. I'll review the schedule.

Cultural Context

Reflects Japanese punctuality and efficiency. Often used in time-sensitive industries.

前向きな姿勢で臨みましょう。

まえむきなしせいでのぞみましょう。
Maemukina shisei de nozomimashou.
Let's approach our work with a positive attitude.

Variation 1	Variation 2
積極的な態度で臨みましょう。	Kyō mo shōjin shima shou.
せっきょくてきなたいどでのぞみましょう。	せっきょくてきなたいどでのぞみましょう。
Sekkyoku-tekina taido de nozomi ma shou.	Sekkyoku-tekina taido de torikumi ma shou.
Let's approach tasks with a positive attitude.	Let's tackle tasks with a proactive attitude.

Positive Response	Negative Response
ポジティブな態度で全ての課題に取り組みます。	現実を直視することも大切です。
ぽじてぃぶなたいどでするべてのかだいにとりくみます。	げんじつをちょくしすることもたいせつです。
Pojitibuna taido de subete no kadai ni torikumimasu.	Genjitsu o chokushi suru koto mo taisetsudesu.
I'll approach all challenges with a positive attitude.	It's also important to face reality.

Conversation example person A	Conversation example person B
困難な状況ですが、前向きな姿勢で臨みましょう。	そうですね。チャンスだと捉えて頑張ります。
こんなんなじょうきょうですが、まえむきなしせいでのぞみましょう。	そうですね。ちゃんすだととらえてがんばります。
Kon'nan'na jōkyōdesuga, maemukina shisei de nozomi ma shou.	Sōdesu ne. Chansuda to toraete ganbarimasu.
It's a difficult situation, but let's approach it with a positive attitude.	You're right. I'll see it as an opportunity and do my best.

Cultural Context
Encourages positive thinking in face of challenges. Used to motivate during difficult times.

品質向上に努めましょう。

ひんしつこうじょうにつとめましょう。

Hinshitsu kōjō ni tsutomemashou.

Let's strive for quality improvement.

Variation 1	Variation 2
品質改善に注力しましょう。	Kyō mo shōjin shima shou.
ひんしつかいぜんにちゅうりょくしましょう。	ひんしつかいぜんにちゅうりょくしましょう。
Hinshitsu kaizen ni chūryoku shima shou.	Shitsu no kaizen ni chūryoku shima shou.
Let's focus on quality improvement.	Let's focus on improving quality.

Positive Response	Negative Response
常に最高品質を目指します。	納期に間に合わなくなります。
つねにさいこうひんしつをめざします。	のうきにまにあわなくなります。
Tsuneni saikō hinshitsu o mezashimasu.	Nōki ni maniawanaku narimasu.
I'll always aim for the highest quality.	We won't be able to meet the deadlines.

Conversation example person A	Conversation example person B
お客様からのフィードバックを基に、品質向上に努めましょう。	承知しました。改善点を洗い出します。
おきゃくさまからのふぃーどばっくをもとに、ひんしつこうじょうにつとめましょう。	しょうちしました。かいぜんてんをあらいだします。
Okyakusama kara no fīdobakku o ki ni, hinshitsu kōjō ni tsutome ma shou.	Shōchi shima shita. Kaizen-ten o araidashimasu.
Based on customer feedback, let's strive for quality improvement.	Understood. I'll identify areas for improvement.

Cultural Context

Reflects Japan's reputation for high-quality products and services. Common in manufacturing and service industries.

新しいアイデアを歓迎しましょう。

あたらしいあいであをかんげいしましょう。

Atarashī aidea o kangei shimashou.

Let's welcome new ideas.

Variation 1	Variation 2
革新的な発想を歓迎しましょう。	Kyō mo shōjin shima shou.
かくしんてきなはっそうをかんげいしましょう。	かくしんてきなはっそうをかんげいしましょう。
Kakushin-tekina hassō o kangei shima shou.	Kakushin-tekina hassō o taisetsu ni shima shou.
Let's welcome innovative ideas.	Let's value innovative ideas.

Positive Response	Negative Response
革新的なアイデアを積極的に提案します。	今のやり方で十分だと思います。
かくしんてきなあいであをせっきょくてきにていあんします。	いまのやりかたでじゅうぶんだとおもいます。
Kakushin-tekina aidea o sekkyoku-teki ni teian shimasu.	Ima no yarikata de jūbunda to omoimasu.
I'll proactively suggest innovative ideas.	I think our current methods are sufficient.

Conversation example person A	Conversation example person B
部門会議では、新しいアイデアを歓迎しましょう。	はい、積極的に意見を出し合いましょう。
ぶもんかいぎでは、あたらしいあいであをかんげいしましょう。	はい、せっきょくてきにいけんをだしあいましょう。
Bumon kaigide wa, atarashī aidea o kangei shima shou.	Hai, sekkyoku-teki ni iken o dashiai ma shou.
In the department meeting, let's welcome new ideas.	Yes, let's actively share our opinions.

Cultural Context

Encourages innovation in traditionally conservative culture. Used to promote creativity and fresh thinking.

責任を持って行動しましょう。

せきにんをもってこうどうしましょう。

Sekininwomotte kōdō shimashou.

Let's act responsibly.

Variation 1	Variation 2
責任感を持って行動しましょう。	Kyō mo shōjin shima shou.
せきにんかんをもってこうどうしましょう。	せきにんかんをもってこうどうしましょう。
Sekinin-kan o motte kōdō shima shou.	Jikaku o motte torikumi ma shou.
Let's act with a sense of responsibility.	Let's work with a sense of responsibility.

Positive Response	Negative Response
自分の行動に責任を持ち、確実に遂行します。	責任を取らされるのが怖いです。
じぶんのこうどうにせきにんをもち、かくじつにすいこうします。	せきにんをとらされるのがこわいです。
Jibun no kōdō ni sekinin o mochi, kakujitsu ni suikō shimasu.	Sekinin o tora sa re ru no ga kowaidesu.
I'll take responsibility for my actions and execute them reliably.	I'm afraid of being held responsible.

Conversation example person A	Conversation example person B
各自の担当業務には、責任を持って行動しましょう。	了解しました。自分の役割をしっかり果たします。
かくじのたんとうぎょうむには、せきにんをもってこうどうしましょう。	りょうかいしました。じぶんのやくわりをしっかりはたします。
Kakuji no tantō gyōmu ni wa, sekinin o motte kōdō shima shou.	Ryōkai shima shita. Jibun no yakuwari o shikkari hatashimasu.
Let's act responsibly in our respective duties.	Understood. I'll fulfill my role diligently.

Cultural Context

Reflects Japanese sense of duty and responsibility. Used to reinforce individual accountability.

互いに協力し合いましょう。

たがいにきょうりょくしあいましょう。
Tagaini kyōryoku shi aimashou.
Let's cooperate with each other.

Variation 1	Variation 2
相互協力を心がけましょう。	Kyō mo shōjin shima shou.
そうごきょうりょくをこころがけましょう。	そうごきょうりょくをこころがけましょう。
Sōgo kyōryoku o kokorogake ma shou.	Tasukeai no seishin de kōdō shima shou.
Let's strive for mutual cooperation.	Let's act with a spirit of mutual assistance.

Positive Response	Negative Response
チームの一員として全力でサポートします。	自分の仕事で手一杯です。
ちーむのいちいんとしてぜんりょくでさぽーとします。	じぶんのしごとでていっぱいです。
Chīmu no ichiin to shite zenryoku de sapōto shimasu.	Jibun no shigoto de te ippaidesu.
I'll support the team with all my effort.	I'm already overwhelmed with my own work.

Conversation example person A	Conversation example person B
部署間の壁を越えて、互いに協力し合いましょう。	そうですね。横の連携を強化していきます。
ぶしょかんのかべをこえて、たがいにきょうりょくしあいましょう。	そうですね。よこのれんけいをきょうかしていきます。
Busho-kan no kabe o koete, tagaini kyōryoku shi gō ima shou.	Sōdesu ne. Yoko no renkei o kyōka shite ikimasu.
Let's cooperate with each other across departmental boundaries.	You're right. We'll strengthen cross-departmental collaboration.

Cultural Context
Emphasizes collective effort in Japanese society. Used to encourage teamwork and collaboration.

常に学ぶ姿勢を持ちましょう。

つねにまなぶしせいをもちましょう。
Tsuneni manabu shisei o mochimashou.
Let's maintain a learning attitude.

Variation 1	Variation 2
生涯学習の精神を持ちましょう。	Kyō mo shōjin shima shou.
しょうがいがくしゅうのせいしんをもちましょう。	しょうがいがくしゅうのせいしんをもちましょう。
Shōgai gakushū no seishin o mochi ma shou.	Keizoku-tekina jiko keihatsu o kokorogake ma shou.
Let's maintain a spirit of lifelong learning.	Let's be mindful of continuous self-improvement.

Positive Response	Negative Response
新しい知識とスキルの習得に努めます。	今の知識で十分だと思います。
あたらしいちしきとすきるのしゅうとくにつとめます。	いまのちしきでじゅうぶんだとおもいます。
Atarashī chishiki to sukiru no shūtoku ni tsutomemasu.	Ima no chishiki de jūbunda to omoimasu.
I'll strive to acquire new knowledge and skills.	I think my current knowledge is enough.

Conversation example person A	Conversation example person B
業界の変化が速いので、常に学ぶ姿勢を持ちましょう。	はい、最新の情報にアンテナを張ります。
ぎょうかいのへんかがはやいので、つねにまなぶしせいをもちましょう。	はい、さいしんのじょうほうにあんてなをはります。
Gyōkai no henka ga hayainode, tsuneni manabu shisei o mochi ma shou.	Hai, saishin no jōhō ni antena o harimasu.
The industry is changing rapidly, so let's maintain a constant learning attitude.	Yes, I'll keep my antenna up for the latest information.

Cultural Context

Reflects Japanese value of continuous improvement. Used to encourage lifelong learning and professional development.

挑戦することを恐れないでください。

ちょうせんすることをおそれないでください。

Chōsen suru koto o osorenaide kudasai.

Don't be afraid to take on challenges.

Variation 1	Variation 2
新たな挑戦を恐れずに。	Kyō mo shōjin shima shou.
あらたなちょうせんをおそれずに。	あらたなちょうせんをおそれずに。
Aratana chōsen o osorezu ni.	Atarashī koto ni kakan ni torikumi ma shou.
Don't be afraid of new challenges.	Let's tackle new things boldly.

Positive Response	Negative Response
新しい挑戦に積極的に取り組みます。	失敗するリスクが高すぎます。
あたらしいちょうせんにせっきょくてきにとりくみます。	しっぱいするりすくがたかすぎます。
Atarashī chōsen ni sekkyoku-teki ni torikumimasu.	Shippai suru risuku ga taka sugimasu.
I'll actively take on new challenges.	The risk of failure is too high.

Conversation example person A	Conversation example person B
新規プロジェクトは難しいかもしれませんが、挑戦することを恐れないでください。	ありがとうございます。積極的に取り組みます。
しんきぷろじぇくとはむずかしいかもしれませんが、ちょうせんすることをおそれないでください。	ありがとうございます。せっきょくてきにとりくみます。
Shinki purojekuto wa muzukashī kamo shiremasenga, chōsen suru koto o osorenaide kudasai.	Arigatōgozaimasu. Sekkyoku-teki ni torikumimasu.
The new project might be difficult, but don't be afraid to take on the challenge.	Thank you. I'll tackle it proactively.

Cultural Context

Encourages risk-taking in a traditionally risk-averse culture. Used to promote innovation and personal growth.

顧客満足度の向上を目指しましょう。

こきゃくまんぞくどのこうじょうをめざしましょう。
Kokakumanzoku-do no kōjō o mezashimashou.
Let's aim to improve customer satisfaction.

Variation 1	Variation 2
顧客満足の向上に努めましょう。	Kyō mo shōjin shima shou.
こきゃくまんぞくのこうじょうにつとめましょう。	こきゃくまんぞくのこうじょうにつとめましょう。
Kokyaku manzoku no kōjō ni tsutome ma shou.	Okyakusama no kitai o koeru kōdō o shima shou.
Let's work on improving customer satisfaction.	Let's act to exceed customer expectations.

Positive Response	Negative Response
お客様の期待を超えるサービスを提供します。	コストがかかりすぎて現実的ではありません。
おきゃくさまのきたいをこえるさーびすをていきょうします。	こすとがかかりすぎてげんじつてきではありません。
Okyakusama no kitai o koeru sābisu o teikyō shimasu.	Kosuto ga kakari sugite genjitsu-tekide wa arimasen.
I'll provide service that exceeds customer expectations.	It's not realistic due to the high costs involved.

Conversation example person A	Conversation example person B
今期は特に、顧客満足度の向上を目指しましょう。	了解です。顧客の声をよく聞いて改善します。
こんきはとくに、こきゃくまんぞくどのこうじょうをめざしましょう。	りょうかいです。こきゃくのこえをよくきいてかいぜんします。
Konki wa tokuni, kokyaku manzoku-do no kōjō o mezashi ma shou.	Ryōkaidesu. Kokyaku no koe o yoku kiite kaizen shimasu.
This term, let's aim for improving customer satisfaction in particular.	Understood. I'll listen carefully to customer feedback and make improvements.

Cultural Context
Reflects Japanese focus on customer service. Common in retail and service industries.

今日も笑顔で頑張りましょう。

きょうもえがおでがんばりましょう。

Kyō mo egao de ganbarimashou.

Let's work hard with a smile today as well.

Variation 1	Variation 2
明るい笑顔で一日を過ごしましょう。	Kyō mo shōjin shima shou.
あかるいえがおでいちにちをすごしましょう。	あかるいえがおでいちにちをすごしましょう。
Akarui egao de ichi-nichi o sugoshi ma shou.	Akarui hyōjō de ichi-nichi o sugoshi ma shou.
Let's spend the day with a bright smile.	Let's spend the day with a bright expression.

Positive Response	Negative Response
明るい笑顔で一日を過ごします。	無理に笑顔を作るのは疲れます。
あかるいえがおでいちにちをすごします。	むりにえがおをつくるのはつかれます。
Akarui egao de ichi-nichi o sugoshimasu.	Muri ni egao o tsukuru no wa tsukaremasu.
I'll spend the day with a bright smile.	Forcing a smile is tiring.

Conversation example person A	Conversation example person B
今日も笑顔で頑張りましょう。	はい、前向きに取り組みます！
きょうもえがおでがんばりましょう。	はい、まえむきにとりくみます！
Kyō mo egao de ganbari ma shou.	Hai, maemuki ni torikumimasu!
Let's do our best with a smile today as well.	Yes, I'll approach work positively!

Cultural Context

Emphasizes the importance of maintaining a positive demeanor. Often used in customer-facing roles.

効果的な時間の使い方を心がけましょう。

こうかてきなじかんのつかいかたをこころがけましょう。

Kōkatekina jikan no tsukaikata o kokorogakemashou.

Let's be mindful of using our time effectively.

Variation 1	Variation 2
時間を有効に使いましょう。	Kyō mo shōjin shima shou.
じかんをゆうこうにつかいましょう。	じかんをゆうこうにつかいましょう。
Jikan o yūkō ni tsukai ma shou.	Jikan no yūkō katsuyō o ishiki shite kōdō shima shou.
Let's use our time effectively.	Let's act with awareness of effective time use.

Positive Response	Negative Response
時間を最大限に活用し、成果を出します。	そんな余裕はありません。
じかんをさいだいげんにかつようし、せいかをだします。	そんなよゆうはありません。
Jikan o saidai-gen ni katsuyō shi, seika o dashimasu.	Son'na yoyū wa arimasen.
I'll maximize time usage to produce results.	I don't have the luxury for that.

Conversation example person A	Conversation example person B
締め切りが近いので、効果的な時間の使い方を心がけましょう。	承知しました。ムダな作業を省きます。
しめきりがちかいので、こうかてきなじかんのつかいかたをこころがけましょう。	しょうちしました。むだなさぎょうをはぶきます。
Shimekiri ga chikainode, kōka-tekina jikan no tsukaikata o kokorogake ma shou.	Shōchi shima shita. Mudana sagyō o habukimasu.
The deadline is approaching, so let's be mindful of using our time effectively.	Understood. I'll eliminate unnecessary tasks.

Cultural Context

Reflects Japanese efficiency-oriented culture. Used to promote productivity and time management.

継続は力なりを忘れずに。

けいぞくはちからなりをわすれずに。

Keizokuhachikaranari o wasurezu ni.

Remember, perseverance is power.

Variation 1	Variation 2
粘り強く取り組みましょう。	Kyō mo shōjin shima shou.
ねばりづよくとりくみましょう。	ねばりづよくとりくみましょう。
Nebaridzuyoku torikumi ma shou.	Nebaridzuyoku torikumu shisei o mochi tsudzuke ma shou.
Let's persevere in our efforts.	Let's maintain a persistent attitude.

Positive Response	Negative Response
継続的な努力で着実に成長します。	結果が出ないと続ける意味がありません。
けいぞくてきなどりょくでちゃくじつにせいちょうします。	けっかがでないとつづけるいみがありません。
Keizoku-tekina doryoku de chakujitsu ni seichō shimasu.	Kekka ga denai to tsudzukeru imi ga arimasen.
I'll grow steadily through continuous effort.	There's no point in continuing if we don't see results.

Conversation example person A	Conversation example person B
小さな改善の積み重ねが大切です。継続は力なりを忘れずに。	そうですね。毎日少しずつ頑張ります。
ちいさなかいぜんのつみかさねがたいせつです。けいぞくはちからなりをわすれずに。	そうですね。まいにちすこしずつがんばります。
Chīsana kaizen no tsumikasane ga taisetsudesu. Keizoku wa chikara nari o wasurezu ni.	Sōdesu ne. Mainichi sukoshi zutsu ganbarimasu.
Small, continuous improvements are important. Remember, persistence is power.	You're right. I'll do my best little by little every day.

Cultural Context

Emphasizes the value of persistence in Japanese culture. Used to encourage long-term commitment and effort.

小さな改善を積み重ねましょう。

ちいさなかいぜんをつみかさねましょう。

Chīsana kaizen o tsumikasanemashou.

Let's accumulate small improvements.

Variation 1	Variation 2
日々の小さな進歩を大切にしましょう。	Kyō mo shōjin shima shou.
ひびのちいさなしんぽをたいせつにしましょう。	ひびのちいさなしんぽをたいせつにしましょう。
Hibi no chīsana shinpo o taisetsu ni shima shou.	Sasaina kufū o taisetsu ni suru shūkan o tsuke ma shou.
Let's value small daily improvements.	Let's develop a habit of valuing small improvements.

Positive Response	Negative Response
日々の小さな改善を大切にします。	大きな変革が必要だと思います。
ひびのちいさなかいぜんをたいせつにします。	おおきなへんかくがひつようだとおもいます。
Hibi no chīsana kaizen o taisetsu ni shimasu.	Ōkina henkaku ga hitsuyōda to omoimasu.
I'll value small daily improvements.	I think we need major changes.

Conversation example person A	Conversation example person B
業務プロセスの見直しで、小さな改善を積み重ねましょう。	はい、日々の業務で改善点を探します。
ぎょうむぷろせすのみなおしで、ちいさなかいぜんをつみかさねましょう。	はい、ひびのぎょうむでかいぜんてんをさがします。
Gyōmu purosesu no minaoshi de, chīsana kaizen o tsumikasane ma shou.	Hai, hibi no gyōmu de kaizen-ten o sagashimasu.
In reviewing our work processes, let's accumulate small improvements.	Yes, I'll look for improvement points in daily operations.

Cultural Context

Reflects the concept of 'kaizen' or continuous improvement. Common in manufacturing and business settings.

周りへの感謝の気持ちを忘れずに。

まわりへのかんしゃのきもちをわすれずに。
Mawari e no kanshanokimochi o wasurezu ni.
Don't forget to be grateful to those around you.

Variation 1	Variation 2
周囲への感謝を忘れずに。	Kyō mo shōjin shima shou.
しゅういへのかんしゃをわすれずに。	しゅういへのかんしゃをわすれずに。
Shūi e no kansha o wasurezu ni.	Hoka-sha e no shai o tsuneni mochi tsudzuke ma shou.
Let's not forget to be grateful to those around us.	Let's always maintain gratitude towards others.

Positive Response	Negative Response
常に感謝の気持ちを持って行動します。	感謝されるべきなのは私の方です。
つねにかんしゃのきもちをもってこうどうします。	かんしゃされるべきなのはわたしのほうです。
Tsuneni kansha no kimochi o motte kōdō shimasu.	Kansha sa re rubekina no wa watashi no katadesu.
I'll always act with gratitude.	I'm the one who should be thanked.

Conversation example person A	Conversation example person B
チームの成功は皆の努力の賜物です。周りへの感謝の気持ちを忘れずに。	ありがとうございます。感謝の気持ちを持って働きます。
ちーむのせいこうはみなのどりょくのたまものです。まわりへのかんしゃのきもちをわすれずに。	ありがとうございます。かんしゃのきもちをもってはたらきます。
Chīmu no seikō wa mina no doryoku no tamamonodesu. Mawari e no kansha no kimochi o wasurezu ni.	Arigatōgozaimasu. Kansha no kimochi o motte hatarakimasu.
The team's success is thanks to everyone's efforts. Don't forget to be grateful to those around you.	Thank you. I'll work with a sense of gratitude.

Cultural Context

Emphasizes gratitude and harmony in Japanese society. Used to promote positive workplace relationships.

今日も安全運転で出勤しましょう。

きょうもあんぜんうんてんでしゅっきんしましょう。
Kyō mo anzen unten de shukkin shimashou.
Let's commute safely today as well.

Variation 1	Variation 2
交通安全に気をつけて出勤しましょう。	Kyō mo shōjin shima shou.
こうつうあんぜんにきをつけてしゅっきんしましょう。	こうつうあんぜんにきをつけてしゅっきんしましょう。
Kōtsū anzen ni ki o tsukete shukkin shima shou.	Kōtsū anzen ni ryūi shite tsūkin shima shou.
Let's commute with traffic safety in mind.	Let's commute with attention to traffic safety.

Positive Response	Negative Response
交通ルールを守り、安全に気をつけます。	急いでいるのでそんな余裕はありません。
こうつうるーるをまもり、あんぜんにきをつけます。	いそいでいるのでそんなよゆうはありません。
Kōtsū rūru o mamori, anzen ni ki o tsukemasu.	Isoide irunode son'na yoyū wa arimasen.
I'll follow traffic rules and be mindful of safety.	I'm in a hurry, I don't have time for that.

Conversation example person A	Conversation example person B
今日も安全運転で出勤しましょう。	はい、交通ルールを守って気をつけます。
きょうもあんぜんうんてんでしゅっきんしましょう。	はい、こうつうるーるをまもってきをつけます。
Kyō mo anzen unten de shukkin shima shou.	Hai, kōtsū rūru o mamotte ki o tsukemasu.
Let's commute safely today as well.	Yes, I'll be careful and follow traffic rules.

Cultural Context

Reflects concern for traffic safety in densely populated Japan. Common in companies with commuting employees.

報告・連絡・相談を徹底しましょう。

ほうこく・れんらく・そうだんをてっていしましょう。

Hōkoku renraku sōdan o tettei shimashou.

Let's thoroughly report, communicate, and consult.

Variation 1	Variation 2
情報共有を徹底しましょう。	Kyō mo shōjin shima shou.
じょうほうきょうゆうをてっていしましょう。	じょうほうきょうゆうをてっていしましょう。
Jōhō kyōyū o tettei shima shou.	Jōhō kyōyū o kakujitsu ni gyō ima shou.
Let's ensure thorough information sharing.	Let's ensure thorough information sharing.

Positive Response	Negative Response
密な情報共有を心がけます。	そんなことをしていたら仕事が進みません。
みつなじょうほうきょうゆうをこころがけます。	そんなことをしていたらしごとがすすみません。
Mitsuna jōhō kyōyū o kokorogakemasu.	Son'na koto o shite itara shigoto ga susumimasen.
I'll ensure thorough information sharing.	If we do that, we won't get any work done.

Conversation example person A	Conversation example person B
プロジェクトの進捗管理のため、報告・連絡・相談を徹底しましょう。	承知しました。密に情報共有を行います。
ぷろじぇくとのしんちょくかんりのため、ほうこく・れんらく・そうだんをてっていしましょう。	しょうちしました。みつにじょうほうきょうゆうをおこないます。
Purojekuto no shinchoku kanri no tame, hōkoku renraku sōdan o tettei shima shou.	Shōchi shima shita. Mitsu ni jōhō kyōyū o okonaimasu.
For project progress management, let's thoroughly implement reporting, communication, and consultation.	Understood. I'll share information closely.

Cultural Context

Emphasizes the importance of communication in hierarchical Japanese organizations. Used to prevent misunderstandings and errors.

今週も頑張っていきましょう。

こんしゅうもがんばっていきましょう。
Konshū mo ganbatte ikimashou.
Let's keep working hard this week too.

Variation 1	Variation 2
今週も努力を続けましょう。	Kyō mo shōjin shima shou.
こんしゅうもどりょくをつづけましょう。	こんしゅうもどりょくをつづけましょう。
Konshū mo doryoku o tsudzuke ma shou.	Konshū mo zenryoku de torikumi ma shou.
Let's continue our efforts this week as well.	Let's give our all this week as well.

Positive Response	Negative Response
今週も最高の成果を出せるよう努めます。	もう疲れ切っています。
こんしゅうもさいこうのせいかをだせるようつとめます。	もうつかれきっています。
Konshū mo saikō no seika o daseru yō tsutomemasu.	Mō tsukare kitte imasu.
I'll strive to produce the best results this week too.	I'm already exhausted.

Conversation example person A	Conversation example person B
新しい週の始まりです。今週も頑張っていきましょう。	はい、今週も全力で取り組みます。
あたらしいしゅうのはじまりです。こんしゅうもがんばっていきましょう。	はい、こんしゅうもぜんりょくでとりくみます。
Atarashī shū no hajimaridesu. Konshū mo ganbatte iki ma shou.	Hai, konshū mo zenryoku de torikumimasu.
It's the start of a new week. Let's do our best this week as well.	Yes, I'll give it my all this week too.

Cultural Context

Reflects the Japanese work ethic of continuous effort. Used at the beginning of the work week to boost morale.

明るい挨拶を心がけましょう。

あかるいあいさつをこころがけましょう。

Akarui aisatsu o kokorogakemashou.

Let's make an effort to greet each other cheerfully.

Variation 1	Variation 2
爽やかな挨拶を意識しましょう。	Kyō mo shōjin shima shou.
さわやかなあいさつをいしきしましょう。	さわやかなあいさつをいしきしましょう。
Sawayakana aisatsu o ishiki shima shou.	Akarui koe de aisatsu suru yō ni shima shou.
Let's be mindful of giving cheerful greetings.	Let's make a point to greet with a cheerful voice.

Positive Response	Negative Response
元気な挨拶で職場の雰囲気を明るくします。	形式的な挨拶は意味がないと思います。
げんきなあいさつでしょくばのふんいきをあかるくします。	けいしきてきなあいさつはいみがないとおもいます。
Genkina aisatsu de shokuba no fun'iki o akaruku shimasu.	Keishiki-tekina aisatsu wa imi ga nai to omoimasu.
I'll brighten the workplace atmosphere with energetic greetings.	I think formal greetings are meaningless.

Conversation example person A	Conversation example person B
オフィスの雰囲気づくりのため、明るい挨拶を心がけましょう。	そうですね。笑顔で挨拶を交わしていきます。
おふぃすのふんいきづくりのため、あかるいあいさつをこころがけましょう。	そうですね。えがおであいさつをかわしていきます。
Ofisu no fun'iki-dzukuri no tame, akarui aisatsu o kokorogake ma shou.	Sōdesu ne. Egao de aisatsu o kawashite ikimasu.
To create a positive office atmosphere, let's make an effort to greet each other cheerfully.	You're right. I'll exchange greetings with a smile.

Cultural Context

Emphasizes the importance of proper etiquette in Japanese society. Used to promote a positive workplace atmosphere.

整理整頓を心がけましょう。

せいりせいとんをこころがけましょう。
Seiri seiton o kokorogakemashou.
Let's keep our workspace tidy and organized.

Variation 1	Variation 2
清潔な環境維持に努めましょう。	Kyō mo shōjin shima shou.
せいけつなかんきょういじにつとめましょう。	せいけつなかんきょういじにつとめましょう。
Seiketsuna kankyō iji ni tsutome ma shou.	Shokuba no seiketsu-sa o tamochi ma shou.
Let's strive to maintain a clean environment.	Let's maintain a clean and organized workplace.

Positive Response	Negative Response
常に整理整頓を心がけ、効率的に働きます。	忙しくてそんな時間はありません。
つねにせいりせいとんをこころがけ、こうりつてきにはたらきます。	いそがしくてそんなじかんはありません。
Tsuneni seiri seiton o kokorogake, kōritsu-teki ni hatarakimasu.	Isogashikute son'na toki wa arimasen.
I'll always keep things organized for efficient work.	I'm too busy to have time for that.

Conversation example person A	Conversation example person B
作業効率を上げるため、整理整頓を心がけましょう。	了解です。毎日の終業時に片付けを行います。
さぎょうこうりつをあげるため、せいりせいとんをこころがけましょう。	りょうかいです。まいにちのしゅうぎょうじにかたづけをおこないます。
Sagyō kōritsu o ageru tame, seiri seiton o kokorogake ma shou.	Ryōkaidesu. Mainichi no shūgyō-ji ni katadzuke o okonaimasu.
To improve work efficiency, let's keep our workspace tidy.	Understood. I'll clean up at the end of each workday.

Cultural Context
Reflects Japanese values of cleanliness and order. Common in office and manufacturing environments.

今月の目標を達成しましょう。

こんげつのもくひょうをたっせいしましょう。
Kongetsu no mokuhyō o tassei shimashou.
Let's achieve this month's goals.

Variation 1	Variation 2
今月の目的を実現しましょう。	Kyō mo shōjin shima shou.
こんげつのもくてきをじつげんしましょう。	こんげつのもくてきをじつげんしましょう。
Kongetsu no mokuteki o jitsugen shima shou.	Gekkan mokuhyō no kansui o mezashi ma shou.
Let's accomplish this month's objectives.	Let's aim to accomplish this month's goals.

Positive Response	Negative Response
全力を尽くして目標達成に邁進します。	無理な目標ばかりで達成できません。
ぜんりょくをつくしてもくひょうたっせいにまいしんします。	むりなもくひょうばかりでたっせいできません。
Zenryoku o tsukushite mokuhyō tassei ni maishin shimasu.	Murina mokuhyō bakari de tassei dekimasen.
I'll do my utmost to achieve this month's goals.	We can't achieve these unrealistic goals.

Conversation example person A	Conversation example person B
残り1週間ですが、今月の目標を達成しましょう。	はい、ラストスパートで頑張ります。
のこり1しゅうかんですが、こんげつのもくひょうをたっせいしましょう。	はい、らすとすぱーとでがんばります。
Nokori 1-shūkandesuga, kongetsu no mokuhyō o tassei shima shou.	Hai, rasutosupāto de ganbarimasu.
We have one week left, let's achieve this month's goals.	Yes, I'll give it my all in this final sprint.

Cultural Context
Reflects goal-oriented Japanese work culture. Used to motivate employees towards monthly targets.

常に改善の余地を探しましょう。

つねにかいぜんのよちをさがしましょう。
Tsuneni kaizen no yochi o sagashimashou.
Let's always look for room for improvement.

Variation 1	Variation 2
継続的に向上の機会を見出しましょう。	Kyō mo shōjin shima shou.
けいぞくてきにこうじょうのきかいをみいだしましょう。	けいぞくてきにこうじょうのきかいをみいだしましょう。
Keizoku-teki ni kōjō no kikai o miidashi ma shou.	Keizoku-tekina kōjō o kokorogake ma shou.
Let's continuously look for opportunities to improve.	Let's always look for ways to improve.

Positive Response	Negative Response
常により良い方法を追求し続けます。	現状で十分だと思います。
つねにようりょしいほうほうをついきゅうしつづけます。	げんじょうでじゅうぶんだとおもいます。
Tsune ni yori yoi hōhō o tsuikyū shi tsudzukemasu.	Genjō de jūbunda to omoimasu.
I'll constantly seek better methods.	I think the current situation is fine.

Conversation example person A	Conversation example person B
現状に満足せず、常に改善の余地を探しましょう。	承知しました。問題意識を持って業務に取り組みます。
げんじょうにまんぞくせず、つねにかいぜんのよちをさがしましょう。	しょうちしました。もんだいいしきをもってぎょうむにとりくみます。
Genjō ni manzoku sezu, tsuneni kaizen no yochi o sagashi ma shou.	Shōchi shima shita. Mondai ishiki o motte gyōmu ni torikumimasu.
Let's not be satisfied with the status quo, but always look for room for improvement.	Understood. I'll approach my work with a problem-solving mindset.

Cultural Context
Embodies the 'kaizen' philosophy of continuous improvement. Used to encourage innovative thinking and efficiency.

今日も一日無事故で行きましょう。

きょうもいちにちむじこでいきましょう。
Kyōmoichinichi mujiko de ikimashou.
Let's go through another day without accidents.

Variation 1	Variation 2
本日も安全第一で過ごしましょう。	Kyō mo shōjin shima shou.
ほんじつもあんぜんだいいちですごしましょう。	ほんじつもあんぜんだいいちですごしましょう。
Honjitsu mo anzen dai ichi de sugoshi ma shou.	Kyō mo anzen o sai yūsen ni kōdō shima shou.
Let's prioritize safety throughout today as well.	Let's prioritize safety in our actions today.

Positive Response	Negative Response
安全第一で慎重に行動します。	毎日言われなくても分かっています。
あんぜんだいいちでしんちょうにこうどうします。	まいにちいわれなくてもわかっています。
Anzen dai ichi de shinchō ni kōdō shimasu.	Mainichi gen warenakute mo wakatte imasu.
I'll act cautiously with safety as the top priority.	We know that without being told every day.

Conversation example person A	Conversation example person B
安全第一です。今日も一日無事故で行きましょう。	はい、安全確認を徹底します。
あんぜんだいいちです。きょうもいちにちむじこでいきましょう。	はい、あんぜんかくにんをてっていします。
Anzen dai ichidesu. Kyō mo ichi-nichi mujiko de iki ma shou.	Hai, anzen kakunin o tettei shimasu.
Safety first. Let's go through today without any accidents.	Yes, I'll thoroughly check for safety.

Cultural Context
Reflects strong emphasis on workplace safety in Japan. Common in construction and manufacturing industries.

新しい挑戦を恐れないでください。

あたらしいちょうせんをおそれないでください。

Atarashī chōsen o osorenaide kudasai.

Don't be afraid of new challenges.

Variation 1	Variation 2
新たな試みに勇気を持って臨んでください。	Kyō mo shōjin shima shou.
あらたなこころみにゆうきをもってのぞんでください。	あらたなこころみにゆうきをもってのぞんでください。
Aratana kokoromi ni yūki o motte nozonde kudasai.	Michi no ryōiki ni sekkyoku-teki ni chōsen shima shou.
Please have the courage to take on new challenges.	Let's actively take on new challenges.

Positive Response	Negative Response
新しい挑戦を成長の機会として捉えます。	失敗したら責任を取らされそうで怖いです。
あたらしいちょうせんをせいちょうのきかいとしてとらえます。	しっぱいしたらせきにんをとらされそうでこわいです。
Atarashī chōsen o seichō no kikai to shite toraemasu.	Shippai shitara sekinin o tora sa re-sōde kowaidesu.
I'll see new challenges as opportunities for growth.	I'm afraid I'll be held responsible if I fail.

Conversation example person A	Conversation example person B
困難に見えるかもしれませんが、新しい挑戦を恐れないでください。	ありがとうございます。積極的に取り組んでいきます。
こんなんにみえるかもしれませんが、あたらしいちょうせんをおそれないでください。	ありがとうございます。せっきょくてきにとりくんでいきます。
Kon'nan ni mieru kamo shiremasenga, atarashī chōsen o osorenaide kudasai.	Arigatōgozaimasu. Sekkyoku-teki ni torikunde ikimasu.
It may seem difficult, but don't be afraid of new challenges.	Thank you. I'll tackle it proactively.

Cultural Context

Encourages risk-taking in a traditionally conservative culture. Used to promote innovation and personal growth.

顧客の声に耳を傾けましょう。

こきゃくのこえにみみをかたむけましょう。
Kokyaku no koe ni mimi o katamukemashou.
Let's listen to our customers' voices.

Variation 1	Variation 2
お客様のニーズに注意を払いましょう。	Kyō mo shōjin shima shou.
おきゃくさまのにーずにちゅういをはらいましょう。	おきゃくさまのにーずにちゅういをはらいましょう。
Okyakusama no nīzu ni chūi o harai ma shou.	Okyakusama no nīzu o tekikaku ni haaku shima shou.
Let's pay attention to customer needs.	Let's accurately grasp our customers' needs.

Positive Response	Negative Response
お客様の声を真摯に受け止め、改善に活かします。	顧客の要求は現実離れしています。
おきゃくさまのこえをしんしにうけとめ、かいぜんにいかします。	こきゃくのようきゅうはげんじつばなれしています。
Okyakusama no koe o shinshi ni uketome, kaizen ni ikashimasu.	Kokyaku no yōkyū wa genjitsubanare shite imasu.
I'll sincerely listen to customers and use their feedback for improvement.	The customers' demands are unrealistic.

Conversation example person A	Conversation example person B
サービス改善のため、顧客の声に耳を傾けましょう。	はい、顧客の意見を真摯に受け止めます。
さーびすかいぜんのため、こきゃくのこえにみみをかたむけましょう。	はい、こきゃくのいけんをしんしにうけとめます。
Sābisu kaizen no tame, kokyaku no koe ni mimi o katamuke ma shou.	Hai, kokyaku no iken o shinshi ni uketomemasu.
To improve our service, let's listen carefully to customer feedback.	Yes, I'll take customer opinions seriously.

Cultural Context

Reflects Japanese customer-centric business approach. Used in service industries to improve customer satisfaction.

今日も一日集中して頑張りましょう。

きょうもいちにちしゅうちゅうしてがんばりましょう。
Kyōmoichinichi shūchū shite ganbarimashou.
Let's stay focused and work hard today as well.

Variation 1	Variation 2
本日も終日集中力を保ちましょう。	Kyō mo shōjin shima shou.
ほんじつもしゅうじつしゅうちゅうりょくをたもちましょう。	ほんじつもしゅうじつしゅうちゅうりょくをたもちましょう。
Honjitsu mo hinemosu shūchū-ryoku o tamochi ma shou.	Honjitsu mo zen shinkei o shūchū sa sete hataraki ma shou.
Let's maintain our focus throughout the day.	Let's work with full concentration today as well.

Positive Response	Negative Response
集中力を維持し、生産性の高い一日にします。	毎日集中し続けるのは無理です。
しゅうちゅうりょくをいじし、せいさんせいのたかいいちにちにします。	まいにちしゅうちゅうしつづけるのはむりです。
Shūchū-ryoku o iji shi, seisan-sei no takai ichi-nichi ni shimasu.	Mainichi shūchū shi tsudzukeru no wa muridesu.
I'll maintain focus for a highly productive day.	It's impossible to stay focused every single day.

Conversation example person A	Conversation example person B
今日も一日集中して頑張りましょう。	はい、全力で業務に取り組みます。
きょうもいちにちしゅうちゅうしてがんばりましょう。	はい、ぜんりょくでぎょうむにとりくみます。
Kyō mo ichi-nichi shūchū shite ganbari ma shou.	Hai, zenryoku de gyōmu ni torikumimasu.
Let's stay focused and do our best today as well.	Yes, I'll tackle my work with all my effort.

Cultural Context

Emphasizes the value of focus and hard work in Japanese culture. Used to encourage productivity.

目標を常に意識しましょう。

もくひょうをつねにいしきしましょう。
Mokuhyō o tsuneni ishiki shimashou.
Let's always be conscious of our goals.

Variation 1	Variation 2
目的を絶えず念頭に置きましょう。	Kyō mo shōjin shima shou.
もくてきをたえずねんとうにおきましょう。	もくてきをたえずねんとうにおきましょう。
Mokuteki o taezu nentō ni zhìKi ma shou.	Mokuteki ishiki o jizoku sa se ma shou.
Let's always keep our goals in mind.	Let's constantly keep our goals in mind.

Positive Response	Negative Response
目標を常に念頭に置いて行動します。	現実的な目標を立ててほしいです。
もくひょうをつねにねんとうにおいてこうどうします。	げんじつてきなもくひょうをたててほしいです。
Mokuhyō o tsuneni nentō ni oite kōdō shimasu.	Genjitsu-tekina mokuhyō o tatete hoshīdesu.
I'll always act with our goals in mind.	I wish we had more realistic goals.

Conversation example person A	Conversation example person B
日々の業務に追われがちですが、目標を常に意識しましょう。	そうですね。大局を見失わないようにします。
ひびのぎょうむにおわれがちですが、もくひょうをつねにいしきしましょう。	そうですね。たいきょくをみうしなわないようにします。
Hibi no gyōmu ni tsui ware-gachidesuga, mokuhyō o tsuneni ishiki shima shou.	Sōdesu ne. Taikyoku o miushinawanai yō ni shimasu.
We tend to get caught up in daily tasks, but let's always keep our goals in mind.	You're right. I'll make sure not to lose sight of the big picture.

Cultural Context
Reflects goal-oriented Japanese work culture. Used to keep employees aligned with company objectives.

今週も事故のない一週間にしましょう。

こんしゅうもじこのないいっしゅうかんにしましょう。
Konshū mo jiko no nai isshūkan ni shimashou.
Let's make this week another accident-free week.

Variation 1	Variation 2
今週も安全な七日間を過ごしましょう。	Kyō mo shōjin shima shou.
こんしゅうもあんぜんななのかかんをすごしましょう。	こんしゅうもあんぜんななのかかんをすごしましょう。
Konshū mo anzen'na nanokakan o sugoshi ma shou.	Konshū mo anzen unten o tettei shima shou.
Let's have a safe week without accidents.	Let's ensure a week without accidents.

Positive Response	Negative Response
安全意識を高く持ち、無事故を達成します。	そんなに言われなくても気をつけています。
あんぜんいしきをたかくもち、むじこをたっせいします。	そんなにいわれなくてもきをつけています。
Anzen ishiki o takaku mochi, mujiko o tassei shimasu.	Son'nani gen warenakute mo ki o tsukete imasu.
I'll maintain high safety awareness to achieve zero accidents.	We're being careful without being told so often.

Conversation example person A	Conversation example person B
安全週間です。今週も事故のない一週間にしましょう。	了解しました。安全に細心の注意を払います。
あんぜんしゅうかんです。こんしゅうもじこのないいっしゅうかんにしましょう。	りょうかいしました。あんぜんにさいしんのちゅういをはらいます。
Anzen shūkandesu. Konshū mo jiko no nai ichi-shūkan ni shima shou.	Ryōkai shima shita. Anzen ni saishin no chūi o haraimasu.
It's safety week. Let's make this another accident-free week.	Understood. I'll pay utmost attention to safety.

Cultural Context

Emphasizes workplace safety consciousness. Common in industries with higher accident risks.

今日も元気に頑張りましょう。

きょうもげんきにがんばりましょう。
Kyō mo genki ni ganbarimashō.
Let's work energetically today as well.

Variation 1	Variation 2
本日も活力を持って努力しましょう。	Kyō mo shōjin shima shou.
ほんじつもかつりょくをもってどりょくしましょう。	ほんじつもかつりょくをもってどりょくしましょう。
Honjitsu mo katsuryoku o motte doryoku shima shou.	Honjitsu mo katsuryoku ni michite shigoto ni nozomi ma shou.
Let's work hard with energy today as well.	Let's approach work with energy today.

Positive Response	Negative Response
活力に満ちた一日を過ごします。	毎日元気でいるのは難しいです。
かつりょくにみちたいちにちをすごします。	まいにちげんきでいるのはむずかしいです。
Katsuryoku ni michita ichi-nichi o sugoshimasu.	Mainichi genkide iru no wa muzukashīdesu.
I'll spend an energetic day.	It's difficult to be energetic every day.

Conversation example person A	Conversation example person B
今日も元気に頑張りましょう。	はい、前向きな気持ちで臨みます。
きょうもげんきにがんばりましょう。	はい、まえむきなきもちでのぞみます。
Kyō mo genki ni ganbari ma shou.	Hai, maemukina kimochi de nozomimasu.
Let's work energetically today as well.	Yes, I'll approach work with a positive attitude.

Cultural Context

Reflects the Japanese work ethic of maintaining a positive attitude. Used to start the workday on a good note.

常に前を向いて進みましょう。

つねにまえをむいてすすみましょう。

Tsuneni mae o muite susumimashou.

Let's always move forward with a positive outlook.

Variation 1	Variation 2
絶えず未来に目を向けて前進しましょう。	Kyō mo shōjin shima shou.
たえずみらいにめをむけてぜんしんしましょう。	たえずみらいにめをむけてぜんしんしましょう。
Taezu mirai ni me o mukete zenshin shima shou.	Mirai shikō de kōdō shima shou.
Let's always move forward with our eyes on the future.	Let's always move forward with a future-oriented mindset.

Positive Response	Negative Response
前向きな姿勢で困難を乗り越えます。	時には立ち止まって考えることも大切です。
まえむきなしせいでこんなんをのりこえます。	ときにはたちどまってかんがえることもたいせつです。
Maemukina shisei de kon'nan o norikoemasu.	Tokiniha tachidomatte kangaeru koto mo taisetsudesu.
I'll overcome difficulties with a positive attitude.	Sometimes it's important to stop and think.

Conversation example person A	Conversation example person B
困難があっても、常に前を向いて進みましょう。	はい、前向きに取り組んでいきます。
こんなんがあっても、つねにまえをむいてすすみましょう。	はい、まえむきにとりくんでいきます。
Kon'nan ga atte mo, tsuneni mae o muite susumi ma shou.	Hai, maemuki ni torikunde ikimasu.
Even in the face of difficulties, let's always move forward.	Yes, I'll tackle things with a positive attitude.

Cultural Context

Encourages perseverance in face of challenges. Used to motivate during difficult times.

今日も一日生産性高く働きましょう。

きょうもいちにちせいさんせいたかくはたらきましょう。
Kyōmoichinichi seisan-sei takaku hatarakimashou.
Let's work productively today as well.

Variation 1	Variation 2
本日も効率的に業務を遂行しましょう。	Kyō mo shōjin shima shou.
ほんじつもこうりつてきにぎょうむをすいこうしましょう。	ほんじつもこうりつてきにぎょうむをすいこうしましょう。
Honjitsu mo kōritsu-teki ni gyōmu o suikō shima shou.	Honjitsu mo kōritsu-tekina gyōmu suikō o kokorogake ma shou.
Let's work efficiently throughout the day.	Let's strive for high productivity today as well.

Positive Response	Negative Response
効率的に仕事を進め、高い成果を出します。	質を犠牲にしてまで生産性を上げたくありません。
こうりつてきにしごとをすすめ、たかいせいかをだします。	しつをぎせいにしてまでせいさんせいをあげたくありません。
Kōritsu-teki ni shigoto o susume, takai seika o dashimasu.	Shitsu o gisei ni shite made seisan-sei o agetaku arimasen.
I'll work efficiently to produce high results.	I don't want to increase productivity at the expense of quality.

Conversation example person A	Conversation example person B
今日のタスクは多いですが、効率的に進めましょう。	今日も一日生産性高く働きましょう。
きょうのたすくはおおいですが、こうりつてきにすすめましょう。	きょうもいちにちせいさんせいたかくはたらきましょう。
Kyō no tasuku wa ōidesuga, kōritsu-teki ni susume ma shou.	Kyō mo ichi-nichi seisan-sei takaku hataraki ma shou.
We have many tasks today, but let's proceed efficiently.	Let's work with high productivity today as well.

Cultural Context
Reflects Japan's focus on high productivity. Common in office and manufacturing environments.

チームの和を大切にしましょう。

ちーむのわをたいせつにしましょう。
Chīmu no wa o taisetsu ni shimashou.
Let's value team harmony.

Variation 1	Variation 2
団結力を重視しましょう。	Kyō mo shōjin shima shou.
だんけつりょくをじゅうししましょう。	だんけつりょくをじゅうししましょう。
Danketsu-ryoku o jūshi shima shou.	Busho-nai no kyōchō-sei o jūshi shima shou.
Let's value team unity.	Let's value team harmony.

Positive Response	Negative Response
チームの団結力を高め、協力して目標達成を目指します。	個人の能力も重要だと思います。
ちーむのだんけつりょくをたかめ、きょうりょくしてもくひょうたっせいをめざします。	こじんののうりょくもじゅうようだとおもいます。
Chīmu no danketsu-ryoku o takame, kyōryoku shite mokuhyō tassei o mezashimasu.	Kojin no nōryoku mo jūyōda to omoimasu.
I'll enhance team unity and cooperate to achieve our goals.	I think individual abilities are important too.

Conversation example person A	Conversation example person B
チームの和を大切にしましょう。お互いを尊重し合いましょう。	そうですね。良好な人間関係が仕事の質を高めます。
ちーむのわをたいせつにしましょう。おたがいをそんちょうしあいましょう。	そうですね。りょうこうなにんげんかんけいがしごとのしつをたかめます。
Chīmu no wa o taisetsu ni shima shou. Otagai o sonchō shi gō ima shou.	Sōdesu ne. Ryōkōna ningen kankei ga shigoto no shitsu o takamemasu.
Let's value team harmony. Let's respect each other.	You're right. Good relationships improve the quality of our work.

Cultural Context
Emphasizes harmony in group settings, a key aspect of Japanese culture. Used to promote teamwork.

今日も一日ミスのない仕事を心がけましょう。

きょうもいちにちみすのないしごとをこころがけましょう。

Kyōmoichinichi misu no nai shigoto o kokorogakemashou.

Let's aim for error-free work today as well.

Variation 1	Variation 2
本日も正確な業務遂行を目指しましょう。	Kyō mo shōjin shima shou.
ほんじつもせいかくなぎょうむすいこうをめざしましょう。	ほんじつもせいかくなぎょうむすいこうをめざしましょう。
Honjitsu mo seikakuna gyōmu suikō o mezashi ma shou.	Kyō mo gyōmu o tadashiku suikō suru yō tsutome ma shou.
Let's aim for error-free work throughout the day.	Let's strive to carry out our duties accurately today.

Positive Response	Negative Response
細心の注意を払い、正確な仕事をします。	人間なのでミスは避けられません。
さいしんのちゅういをはらい、せいかくなしごとをします。	にんげんなのでみすはさけられません。
Saishin no chūi o harai, seikakuna shigoto o shimasu.	Ningen'nanode misu wa yoke raremasen.
I'll pay close attention to do accurate work.	As humans, mistakes are unavoidable.

Conversation example person A	Conversation example person B
慎重に作業を進めて、今日も一日ミスのない仕事を心がけましょう。	了解です。確認を徹底して進めます。
しんちょうにさぎょうをすすめて、きょうもいちにちみすのないしごとをこころがけましょう。	りょうかいです。かくにんをてっていしてすすめます。
Shinchō ni sagyō o susumete, kyō mo ichi-nichi misu no nai shigoto o kokorogake ma shou.	Ryōkaidesu. Kakunin o tettei shite susumemasu.
Let's proceed carefully and aim for error-free work today.	Understood. I'll proceed with thorough checks.

Cultural Context

Reflects Japanese pursuit of perfection in work. Used to encourage attention to detail and quality.

常に向上心を持ちましょう。

つねにこうじょうしんをもちましょう。

Tsuneni kōjōshin o mochimashou.

Let's always have a spirit of improvement.

Variation 1	Variation 2
絶えず成長への意欲を維持しましょう。	Kyō mo shōjin shima shou.
たえずせいちょうへのいよくをいじしましょう。	たえずせいちょうへのいよくをいじしましょう。
Taezu seichō e no iyoku o iji shima shou.	Taema nai seichō o tsuikyū shima shou.
Let's always maintain a desire for growth.	Let's constantly strive for improvement.

Positive Response	Negative Response
自己成長のための努力を惜しみません。	現状に満足しています。
じこせいちょうのためのどりょくをおしみません。	げんじょうにまんぞくしています。
Jiko seichō no tame no doryoku o oshimimasen.	Genjō ni manzoku shite imasu.
I'll spare no effort for self-improvement.	I'm satisfied with the current situation.

Conversation example person A	Conversation example person B
新しい技術が登場していますね。常に向上心を持ちましょう。	はい、積極的に学んでいきたいと思います。
あたらしいぎじゅつがとうじょうしていますね。つねにこうじょうしんをもちましょう。	はい、せっきょくてきにまなんでいきたいとおもいます。
Atarashī gijutsu ga tōjō shite imasu ne. Tsuneni kōjōshin o mochi ma shou.	Hai, sekkyoku-teki ni gakunde ikitai to omoimasu.
New technologies are emerging. Let's always maintain a desire for improvement.	Yes, I'd like to learn proactively.

Cultural Context

Embodies the Japanese concept of continuous self-improvement. Used to encourage professional growth.

今週も安全第一で頑張りましょう。

こんしゅうもあんぜんだいいちでがんばりましょう。
Konshū mo anzendaiichi de ganbarimashou.
Let's work hard this week with safety as our top priority.

Variation 1	Variation 2
今週も安全を最優先に努力しましょう。	Kyō mo shōjin shima shou.
こんしゅうもあんぜんをさいゆうせんにどりょくしましょう。	こんしゅうもあんぜんをさいゆうせんにどりょくしましょう。
Konshū mo anzen o sai yūsen ni doryoku shima shou.	Konshū mo anzen o sai yūsen ni gyōmu ni torikumi ma shou.
Let's prioritize safety in our efforts this week.	Let's prioritize safety this week as well.

Positive Response	Negative Response
安全を最優先に考え、慎重に行動します。	安全ばかり気にしていたら仕事が進みません。
あんぜんをさいゆうせんにかんがえ、しんちょうにこうどうします。	あんぜんばかりきにしていたらしごとがすすみません。
Anzen o sai yūsen ni kangae, shinchō ni kōdō shimasu.	Anzen bakari ki ni shite itara shigoto ga susumimasen.
I'll prioritize safety and act cautiously.	If we only focus on safety, we won't get any work done.

Conversation example person A	Conversation example person B
今週も安全第一で頑張りましょう。事故には十分注意してください。	承知しました。安全確認を徹底します。
こんしゅうもあんぜんだいいちでがんばりましょう。じこにはじゅうぶんちゅういしてください。	しょうちしました。あんぜんかくにんをてっていします。
Konshū mo anzen dai ichi de ganbari ma shou. Jiko ni wa jūbun chūi shite kudasai.	Shōchi shima shita. Anzen kakunin o tettei shimasu.
Let's do our best this week with safety as our top priority. Please be very careful to avoid accidents.	Understood. I'll thoroughly check for safety.

Cultural Context

Emphasizes the priority of safety in Japanese workplaces. Common in industries with physical risks.

今日も笑顔で接客しましょう。

きょうもえがおでせっきゃくしましょう。
Kyō mo egao de sekkyaku shimashou.
Let's serve our customers with a smile today as well.

Variation 1	Variation 2
本日も親切な対応を心がけましょう。	Kyō mo shōjin shima shou.
ほんじつもしんせつなたいおうをこころがけましょう。	ほんじつもしんせつなたいおうをこころがけましょう。
Honjitsu mo shinsetsuna taiō o kokorogake ma shou.	Kyō mo teineina ōtai o kokorogake ma shou.
Let's provide friendly customer service today.	Let's aim to provide kind and courteous service today.

Positive Response	Negative Response
お客様に最高のサービスと笑顔を提供します。	無理に笑顔を作るのは疲れます。
おきゃくさまにさいこうのさーびすとえがおをていきょうします。	むりにえがおをつくるのはつかれます。
Okyakusama ni saikō no sābisu to egao o teikyō shimasu.	Muri ni egao o tsukuru no wa tsukaremasu.
I'll provide the best service with a smile to customers.	Forcing a smile is tiring.

Conversation example person A	Conversation example person B
お客様との対応が多い一日ですね。今日も笑顔で接客しましょう。	はい、親切な対応を心がけます。
おきゃくさまとのたいおうがおおいいちにちですね。きょうもえがおでせっきゃくしましょう。	はい、しんせつなたいおうをこころがけます。
Okyakusama to no taiō ga ōi ichi-nichidesu ne. Kyō mo egao de sekkyaku shima shou.	Hai, shinsetsuna taiō o kokorogakemasu.
It's a day with many customer interactions. Let's serve customers with a smile today as well.	Yes, I'll make sure to respond kindly.

Cultural Context
Reflects the importance of customer service in Japan. Common in retail and hospitality industries.

常に謙虚な姿勢を忘れずに。

つねにけんきょなしせいをわすれずに。

Tsuneni kenkyona shisei o wasurezu ni.

Let's not forget to maintain a humble attitude.

Variation 1	Variation 2
絶えず謙遜の心を持ち続けましょう。	Kyō mo shōjin shima shou.
たえずけんそんのこころをもちつづけましょう。	たえずけんそんのこころをもちつづけましょう。
Taezu kenson no kokoro o mochi tsudzuke ma shou.	Tsuneni manabu shisei o mochi tsudzuke ma shou.
Let's always maintain a humble attitude.	Let's always maintain a humble attitude.

Positive Response	Negative Response
謙虚な態度で学び続けます。	自信を持つことも大切だと思います。
けんきょなたいどでまなびつづけます。	じしんをもつこともたいせつだとおもいます。
Kenkyona taido de manabi tsudzukemasu.	Jishin o motsu koto mo taisetsuda to omoimasu.
I'll continue learning with a humble attitude.	I think it's also important to have confidence.

Conversation example person A	Conversation example person B
どんな成果が出ても、常に謙虚な姿勢を忘れずに。	そうですね。傲慢にならないよう気をつけます。
どんなせいかがでても、つねにけんきょなしせいをわすれずに。	そうですね。ごうまんにならないようきをつけます。
Don'na seika ga dete mo, tsuneni kenkyona shisei o wasurezu ni.	Sōdesu ne. Gōman ni naranai yō ki o tsukemasu.
No matter what results we achieve, let's not forget to maintain a humble attitude.	You're right. I'll be careful not to become arrogant.

Cultural Context

Reflects the value of humility in Japanese culture. Used to promote respectful behavior in the workplace.

今日も一日無駄のない仕事をしましょう。

きょうもいちにちむだのないしごとをしましょう。

Kyōmoichinichi muda no nai shigoto o shimashou.

Let's work efficiently without waste today as well.

Variation 1	Variation 2
本日も効率的な業務遂行を心がけましょう。	Kyō mo shōjin shima shou.
ほんじつもこうりつてきなぎょうむすいこうをこころがけましょう。	ほんじつもこうりつてきなぎょうむすいこうをこころがけましょう。
Honjitsu mo kōritsu-tekina gyōmu suikō o kokorogake ma shou.	Honjitsu mo kōritsu-tekina jikan katsuyō o kokorogake ma shou.
Let's strive for efficient work throughout the day.	Let's work efficiently without waste today.

Positive Response	Negative Response
効率的に仕事を進め、時間を有効活用します。	効率ばかり求めるとミスが増えます。
こうりつてきにしごとをすすめ、じかんをゆうこうかつようします。	こうりつばかりもとめるとみすがふえます。
Kōritsu-teki ni shigoto o susume, jikan o yūkō katsuyō shimasu.	Kōritsu bakari motomeru to misu ga fuemasu.
I'll work efficiently and make the most of my time.	Focusing only on efficiency can increase mistakes.

Conversation example person A	Conversation example person B
タイトなスケジュールですが、今日も一日無駄のない仕事をしましょう。	了解です。時間を有効に使います。
たいとなすけじゅーるですが、きょうもいちにちむだのないしごとをしましょう。	りょうかいです。じかんをゆうこうにつかいます。
Taitona sukejūrudesuga, kyō mo ichi-nichi muda no nai shigoto o shima shou.	Ryōkaidesu. Jikan o yūkō ni tsukaimasu.
We have a tight schedule, but let's work efficiently without waste today.	Understood. I'll use time effectively.

Cultural Context

Emphasizes efficiency and productivity in Japanese work culture. Used to encourage focused, purposeful work.

チームの目標を再確認しましょう。

ちーむのもくひょうをさいかくにんしましょう。
Chīmu no mokuhyō o sai kakunin shimashou.
Let's reconfirm our team goals.

Variation 1	Variation 2
私たちの組織の目的を再確認しましょう。	Kyō mo shōjin shima shou.
わたしたちのそしきのもくてきをさいかくにんしましょう。	わたしたちのそしきのもくてきをさいかくにんしましょう。
Watashi-tachi no soshiki no mokuteki o sai kakunin shima shou.	Busho no mokuteki o saido kyōyū shima shou.
Let's reaffirm the purpose of our organization.	Let's reconfirm our team's goals.

Positive Response	Negative Response
チームの目標を常に意識し、全員で達成を目指します。	目標が現実離れしていて意味がありません。
ちーむのもくひょうをつねにいしき、ぜんいんでたっせいをめざします。	もくひょうがげんじつばなれしていていみがありません。
Chīmu no mokuhyō o tsuneni ishiki shi, zen'in de tassei o mezashimasu.	Mokuhyō ga genjitsubanare shite ite imi ga arimasen.
I'll always be aware of our team goals and aim for achievement together.	The goals are unrealistic and meaningless.

Conversation example person A	Conversation example person B
半期が終わりましたね。チームの目標を再確認しましょう。	はい、目標達成に向けて頑張ります。
はんきがおわりましたね。ちーむのもくひょうをさいかくにんしましょう。	はい、もくひょうたっせいにむけてがんばります。
Hanki ga owarimashita ne. Chīmu no mokuhyō o sai kakunin shima shou.	Hai, mokuhyō tassei ni mukete ganbarimasu.
The half-year has ended. Let's reconfirm our team's goals.	Yes, I'll work hard towards achieving our goals.

Cultural Context
Reflects the importance of shared goals in Japanese group-oriented culture. Used to align team efforts.

今日も一日気を引き締めて頑張りましょう。

きょうもいちにちきをひきしめてがんばりましょう。
Kyōmoichinichi ki o hikishimete ganbarimashou.
Let's stay focused and work hard today as well.

Variation 1	Variation 2
本日も緊張感を持って努力しましょう。	Kyō mo shōjin shima shou.
ほんじつもきんちょうかんをもってどりょくしましょう。	ほんじつもきんちょうかんをもってどりょくしましょう。
Honjitsu mo kinchō-kan o motte doryoku shima shou.	Honjitsu mo kinchō-kan o motte gyōmu ni nozomi ma shou.
Let's stay focused and work hard today.	Let's approach work with focus today.

Positive Response	Negative Response
集中力を保ち、最善を尽くします。	毎日緊張していては疲れます。
しゅうちゅうりょくをたもち、さいぜんをつくします。	まいにちきんちょうしていてはつかれます。
Shūchū-ryoku o tamochi, saizen o tsukushimasu.	Mainichi kinchō shite ite wa tsukaremasu.
I'll maintain focus and do my best.	It's tiring to be tense every day.

Conversation example person A	Conversation example person B
重要な会議がありますね。今日も一日気を引き締めて頑張りましょう。	はい、全力で取り組みます。
じゅうようなかいぎがありますね。きょうもいちにちきをひきしめてがんばりましょう。	はい、ぜんりょくでとりくみます。
Jūyōna kaigi ga arimasu ne. Kyō mo ichi-nichi ki o hikishimete ganbari ma shou.	Hai, zenryoku de torikumimasu.
We have an important meeting today. Let's stay focused and do our best.	Yes, I'll give it my all.

Cultural Context

Encourages maintaining focus and dedication throughout the day. Used to promote consistent effort.

常に顧客目線で考えましょう。

つねにこきゃくめせんでかんがえましょう。

Tsuneni kokyaku mesen de kangaemashou.

Let's always think from the customer's perspective.

Variation 1	Variation 2
絶えずお客様の立場に立って思考しましょう。	Kyō mo shōjin shima shou.
たえずおきゃくさまのたちばにたってしこうしましょう。	たえずおきゃくさまのたちばにたってしこうしましょう。
Taezu okyakusama no tachiba ni tatte shikō shima shou.	Okyakusama no shiten o tsuneni ishiki shima shou.
Let's always think from the customer's perspective.	Let's always think from the customer's perspective.

Positive Response	Negative Response
お客様のニーズを最優先に考えます。	会社の利益も考えるべきです。
おきゃくさまのにーずをさいゆうせんにかんがえます。	かいしゃのりえきもかんがえるべきです。
Okyakusama no nīzu o sai yūsen ni kangaemasu.	Kaisha no rieki mo kangaerubekidesu.
I'll prioritize customer needs.	We should also consider the company's profits.

Conversation example person A	Conversation example person B
新製品の開発では、常に顧客目線で考えましょう。	そうですね。顧客ニーズを最優先します。
しんせいひんのかいはつでは、つねにこきゃくめせんでかんがえましょう。	そうですね。こきゃくにーずをさいゆうせんします。
Shin seihin no kaihatsude wa, tsuneni kokyaku mesen de kangae ma shou.	Sōdesu ne. Kokyaku nīzu o sai yūsen shimasu.
In developing new products, let's always think from the customer's perspective.	You're right. We'll prioritize customer needs.

Cultural Context

Reflects Japan's customer-first business philosophy. Used in service-oriented industries.

今週も一週間無事故で頑張りましょう。

こんしゅうもいっしゅうかんむじこでがんばりましょう。
Konshū mo isshūkan mujiko de ganbarimashou.
Let's work hard this week without any accidents.

Variation 1	Variation 2
今週も安全に留意して努力しましょう。	Kyō mo shōjin shima shou.
こんしゅうもあんぜんにりゅういしてどりょくしましょう。	こんしゅうもあんぜんにりゅういしてどりょくしましょう。
Konshū mo anzen ni ryūi shite doryoku shima shou.	Konshū mo jiko bōshi o tettei shima shou.
Let's work safely throughout the week.	Let's work safely without accidents this week.

Positive Response	Negative Response
安全意識を高く持ち、無事故を継続します。	毎週言われなくても分かっています。
あんぜんいしきをたかくもち、むじこをけいぞくします。	まいしゅういわれなくてもわかっています。
Anzen ishiki o takaku mochi, mujiko o keizoku shimasu.	Maishū gen warenakute mo wakatte imasu.
I'll maintain high safety awareness to continue zero accidents.	We know that without being told every week.

Conversation example person A	Conversation example person B
今週も一週間無事故で頑張りましょう。安全確認を忘れずに。	承知しました。常に安全を意識します。
こんしゅうもいっしゅうかんむじこでがんばりましょう。あんぜんかくにんをわすれずに。	しょうちしました。つねにあんぜんをいしきします。
Konshū mo ichi-shūkan mujiko de ganbari ma shou. Anzen kakunin o wasurezu ni.	Shōchi shima shita. Tsuneni anzen o ishiki shimasu.
Let's work hard this week without any accidents. Don't forget to check for safety.	Understood. I'll always be conscious of safety.

Cultural Context
Emphasizes ongoing safety consciousness. Common in industries with potential safety risks.

今日も一日丁寧な仕事を心がけましょう。

きょうもいちにちていねいなしごとをこころがけましょう。
Kyōmoichinichi teineina shigoto o kokorogakemashou.
Let's aim for careful and thorough work today as well.

Variation 1	Variation 2
本日も細心の注意を払って業務に当たりましょう。	Kyō mo shōjin shima shou.
ほんじつもさいしんのちゅういをはらってぎょうむにあたりましょう。	ほんじつもさいしんのちゅういをはらってぎょうむにあたりましょう。
Honjitsu mo saishin no chūi o haratte gyōmu ni atari ma shou.	Honjitsu mo saishin no chūi o haratte gyōmu ni torikumi ma shou.
Let's be attentive to details in our work today.	Let's be thorough in our work today.

Positive Response	Negative Response
細部まで注意を払い、質の高い仕事をします。	丁寧すぎると効率が落ちます。
さいぶまでちゅういをはらい、しつのたかいしごとをします。	ていねいすぎるとこうりつがおちます。
Saibu made chūi o harai,-shitsu no takai shigoto o shimasu.	Teinei sugiruto kōritsu ga ochimasu.
I'll pay attention to details for high-quality work.	Being too careful decreases efficiency.

Conversation example person A	Conversation example person B
締め切りが近いですが、今日も一日丁寧な仕事を心がけましょう。	はい、品質を落とさないよう注意します。
しめきりがちかいですが、きょうもいちにちていねいなしごとをこころがけましょう。	はい、ひんしつをおとさないようちゅういします。
Shimekiri ga chikaidesuga, kyō mo ichi-nichi teineina shigoto o kokorogake ma shou.	Hai, hinshitsu o otosanai yō chūi shimasu.
The deadline is approaching, but let's aim for careful work today as well.	Yes, I'll be careful not to compromise on quality.

Cultural Context
Reflects Japanese attention to detail and quality. Used to encourage careful, thorough work.

常に効率的な仕事を意識しましょう。

つねにこうりつてきなしごとをいしきしましょう。
Tsuneni kōritsu-tekina shigoto o ishiki shimashou.
Let's always be conscious of working efficiently.

Variation 1	Variation 2
絶えず生産性の高い業務を心がけましょう。	Kyō mo shōjin shima shou.
たえずせいさんせいのたかいぎょうむをこころがけましょう。	たえずせいさんせいのたかいぎょうむをこころがけましょう。
Taezu seisan-sei no takai gyōmu o kokorogake ma shou.	Seisan-sei no kōjō o tsuneni ishiki shima shou.
Let's always be conscious of working efficiently.	Let's always be conscious of working efficiently.

Positive Response	Negative Response
最適な方法を常に探求し、効率を高めます。	質も大切だと思います。
さいてきなほうほうをつねにたんきゅうし、こうりつをたかめます。	しつもたいせつだとおもいます。
Saitekina hōhō o tsuneni tankyū shi, kōritsu o takamemasu.	Shitsu mo taisetsuda to omoimasu.
I'll always seek the best methods to improve efficiency.	I think quality is important too.

Conversation example person A	Conversation example person B
業務量が増えていますね。常に効率的な仕事を意識しましょう。	そうですね。ムダを省いて進めていきます。
ぎょうむりょうがふえていますね。つねにこうりつてきなしごとをいしきしましょう。	そうですね。むだをはぶいてすすめていきます。
Gyōmu-ryō ga fuete imasu ne. Tsuneni kōritsu-tekina shigoto o ishiki shima shou.	Sōdesu ne. Muda o shō ite susumete ikimasu.
Our workload is increasing. Let's always be conscious of working efficiently.	You're right. I'll proceed by eliminating waste.

Cultural Context
Emphasizes the value of efficiency in Japanese work culture. Used to promote productive work habits.

今日も一日前向きに頑張りましょう。

きょうもいちにちまえむきにがんばりましょう。
Kyōmoichinichi maemuki ni ganbarimashō.
Let's work positively today as well.

Variation 1	Variation 2
本日も積極的な姿勢で努力しましょう。	Kyō mo shōjin shima shou.
ほんじつもせっきょくてきなしせいでどりょくしましょう。	ほんじつもせっきょくてきなしせいでどりょくしましょう。
Honjitsu mo sekkyoku-tekina shisei de doryoku shima shou.	Honjitsu mo sekkyoku-tekina shisei de gyōmu ni nozomi ma shou.
Let's maintain a positive attitude throughout the day.	Let's approach work positively today.

Positive Response	Negative Response
前向きな姿勢で困難を乗り越えます。	現実を直視することも必要です。
まえむきなしせいでこんなんをのりこえます。	げんじつをちょくしすることもひつようです。
Maemukina shisei de kon'nan o norikoemasu.	Genjitsu o chokushi suru koto mo hitsuyōdesu.
I'll overcome difficulties with a positive attitude.	It's also necessary to face reality.

Conversation example person A	Conversation example person B
難しい案件もありますが、今日も一日前向きに頑張りましょう。	はい、前向きに取り組んでいきます。
むずかしいあんけんもありますが、きょうもいちにちまえむきにがんばりましょう。	はい、まえむきにとりくんでいきます。
Muzukashī anken mo arimasuga, kyō mo ichi-nichi maemuki ni ganbari ma shou.	Hai, maemuki ni torikunde ikimasu.
We have some difficult cases, but let's stay positive and do our best today.	Yes, I'll tackle things with a positive attitude.

Cultural Context
Encourages maintaining a positive attitude. Used to boost morale and productivity.

チーム一丸となって目標達成を目指しましょう。

ちーむいちがんとなってもくひょうたっせいをめざしましょう。
Chīmu ichigantonatte mokuhyō tassei o mezashimashou.
Let's aim for our goals as a united team.

Variation 1	Variation 2
団結して目的の実現に向けて邁進しましょう。	Kyō mo shōjin shima shou.
だんけつしてもくてきのじつげんにむけてまいしんしましょう。	だんけつしてもくてきのじつげんにむけてまいしんしましょう。
Danketsu shite mokuteki no jitsugen ni mukete maishin shima shou.	Busho zentai de mokuhyō kansui o mezashi ma shou.
Let's work together as a team to achieve our goals.	Let's aim for goal achievement as a united team.

Positive Response	Negative Response
全員で力を合わせて必ず目標を達成します。	個人の目標も大切にしたいです。
ぜんいんでちからをあわせてかならずもくひょうをたっせいします。	こじんのもくひょうもたいせつにしたいです。
Zen'in de chikara o awasete kanarazu mokuhyō o tassei shimasu.	Kojin no mokuhyō mo taisetsu ni shitaidesu.
We'll definitely achieve our goals by working together as a team.	I want to value my personal goals too.

Conversation example person A	Conversation example person B
今月の目標は高いですが、チーム一丸となって目標達成を目指しましょう。	了解です。全員で協力して頑張ります。
こんげつのもくひょうはたかいですが、ちーむいちがんとなってもくひょうたっせいをめざしましょう。	りょうかいです。ぜんいんできょうりょくしてがんばります。
Kongetsu no mokuhyō wa takaidesuga, chīmu ichigan to natte mokuhyō tassei o mezashi ma shou.	Ryōkaidesu. Zen'in de kyōryoku shite ganbarimasu.
This month's goal is high, but let's aim for it as a united team.	Understood. We'll all cooperate and do our best.

Cultural Context
Reflects the importance of teamwork in Japanese culture. Used to encourage collective effort towards goals.

今日も一日気持ちの良い挨拶を心がけましょう。

きょうもいちにちきもちのよいあいさつをこころがけましょう。
Kyōmoichinichi kimochi no yoi aisatsu o kokorogakemashou.
Let's make an effort to greet each other pleasantly today as well.

Variation 1	Variation 2
本日も爽やかな挨拶を意識しましょう。	Kyō mo shōjin shima shou.
ほんじつもさわやかなあいさつをいしきしましょう。	ほんじつもさわやかなあいさつをいしきしましょう。
Honjitsu mo sawayakana aisatsu o ishiki shima shou.	Kyō mo kimochi no yoi aisatsu o kokorogake ma shou.
Let's be mindful of giving pleasant greetings today.	Let's be mindful of offering pleasant greetings today.

Positive Response	Negative Response
明るい挨拶で職場の雰囲気を良くします。	形式的な挨拶に意味はないと思います。
あかるいあいさつでしょくばのふんいきをよくします。	けいしきてきなあいさつにいみはないとおもいます。
Akarui aisatsu de shokuba no fun'iki o yoku shimasu.	Keishiki-tekina aisatsu ni imi wa nai to omoimasu.
I'll improve the workplace atmosphere with cheerful greetings.	I think formal greetings are meaningless.

Conversation example person A	Conversation example person B
オフィスの雰囲気作りのため、今日も一日気持ちの良い挨拶を心がけましょう。	はい、笑顔で挨拶を心がけます。
おふぃすのふんいきづくりのため、きょうもいちにちきもちのよいあいさつをこころがけましょう。	はい、えがおであいさつをこころがけます。
Ofisu no fun'iki-tsukuri no tame, kyō mo ichi-nichi kimochi no yoi aisatsu o kokorogake ma shou.	Hai, egao de aisatsu o kokorogakemasu.
To create a good office atmosphere, let's make an effort to greet each other pleasantly today.	Yes, I'll make sure to greet with a smile.

Cultural Context
Emphasizes the importance of proper etiquette in Japanese society. Used to promote a positive workplace atmosphere.

常に新しいアイデアを歓迎しましょう。

つねにあたらしいあいであをかんげいしましょう。
Tsuneni atarashī aidea o kangei shimashou.
Let's always welcome new ideas.

Variation 1	Variation 2
絶えず革新的な発想を受け入れましょう。	Kyō mo shōjin shima shou.
たえずかくしんてきなはっそうをうけいれましょう。	たえずかくしんてきなはっそうをうけいれましょう。
Taezu kakushin-tekina hassō o ukeire ma shou.	Kakushin-tekina teian o sekkyoku-teki ni ukeire ma shou.
Let's always welcome new ideas.	Let's always welcome new ideas.

Positive Response	Negative Response
革新的なアイデアを積極的に提案します。	現状のやり方で十分だと思います。
かくしんてきなあいであをせっきょくてきにていあんします。	げんじょうのやりかたでじゅうぶんだとおもいます。
Kakushin-tekina aidea o sekkyoku-teki ni teian shimasu.	Genjō no yarikata de jūbunda to omoimasu.
I'll actively propose innovative ideas.	I think our current methods are sufficient.

Conversation example person A	Conversation example person B
業務改善のため、常に新しいアイデアを歓迎しましょう。	そうですね。積極的に提案していきます。
ぎょうむかいぜんのため、つねにあたらしいあいであをかんげいしましょう。	そうですね。せっきょくてきにていあんしていきます。
Gyōmu kaizen no tame, tsuneni atarashī aidea o kangei shima shou.	Sōdesu ne. Sekkyoku-teki ni teian shite ikimasu.
For business improvement, let's always welcome new ideas.	You're right. I'll make proposals proactively.

Cultural Context
Encourages innovation in a traditionally conservative culture. Used to promote creativity and fresh thinking.

今週も一週間事故なく過ごしましょう。

こんしゅうもいっしゅうかんじこなくすごしましょう。
Konshū mo isshūkan jiko naku sugoshimashou.
Let's spend this week without any accidents.

Variation 1	Variation 2
今週も安全に留意して七日間を過ごしましょう。	Kyō mo shōjin shima shou.
こんしゅうもあんぜんにりゅういしてなのかかんをすごしましょう。	こんしゅうもあんぜんにりゅういしてなのかかんをすごしましょう。
Konshū mo anzen ni ryūi shite nana-kakan o sugoshi ma shou.	Konshū mo anzen ishiki o takaku tamochi ma shou.
Let's spend the week safely without accidents.	Let's maintain high safety awareness this week.

Positive Response	Negative Response
安全を最優先に考え、無事故を継続します。	毎週同じことを言われても効果はありません。
あんぜんをさいゆうせんにかんがえ、むじこをけいぞくします。	まいしゅうおなじことをいわれてもこうかはありません。
Anzen o sai yūsen ni kangae, mujiko o keizoku shimasu.	Maishū onaji koto o gen warete mo kōka wa arimasen.
I'll prioritize safety to continue zero accidents.	Saying the same thing every week doesn't have any effect.

Conversation example person A	Conversation example person B
今週も一週間事故なく過ごしましょう。安全第一で行動してください。	承知しました。常に注意を払います。
こんしゅうもいっしゅうかんじこなくすごしましょう。あんぜんだいいちでこうどうしてください。	しょうちしました。つねにちゅういをはらいます。
Konshū mo ichi-shūkan jiko naku sugoshi ma shou. Anzen dai ichi de kōdō shite kudasai.	Shōchi shima shita. Tsuneni chūi o haraimasu.
Let's spend this week without any accidents. Please act with safety as the top priority.	Understood. I'll always be cautious.

Cultural Context
Reflects ongoing safety consciousness in Japanese workplaces. Used in industries with potential safety risks.

今日も一日感謝の気持ちを忘れずに。

きょうもいちにちかんしゃのきもちをわすれずに。

Kyōmoichinichi kanshanokimochi o wasurezu ni.

Let's not forget to be grateful today as well.

Variation 1	Variation 2
本日も感謝の心を持ち続けましょう。	Kyō mo shōjin shima shou.
ほんじつもかんしゃのこころをもちつづけましょう。	ほんじつもかんしゃのこころをもちつづけましょう。
Honjitsu mo kansha no kokoro o mochi tsudzuke ma shou.	Honjitsu mo shūi e no kansha o wasurezu ni sugoshi ma shou.
Let's maintain a grateful attitude throughout the day.	Let's not forget to be grateful today.

Positive Response	Negative Response
周りの支援に感謝しながら仕事に取り組みます。	感謝されるべきなのは私の方です。
まわりのしえんにかんしゃしながらしごとにとりくみます。	かんしゃされるべきなのはわたしのほうです。
Mawari no shien ni kansha shinagara shigoto ni torikumimasu.	Kansha sa re rubekina no wa watashi no katadesu.
I'll work with gratitude for the support around me.	I'm the one who should be thanked.

Conversation example person A	Conversation example person B
お客様や同僚への感謝を忘れずに、今日も一日感謝の気持ちを忘れずに。	はい、感謝の気持ちを持って仕事に臨みます。
おきゃくさまやどうりょうへのかんしゃをわすれずに、きょうもいちにちかんしゃのきもちをわすれずに。	はい、かんしゃのきもちをもってしごとにのぞみます。
Okyakusama ya dōryō e no kansha o wasurezu ni, kyō mo ichi-nichi kansha no kimochi o wasurezu ni.	Hai, kansha no kimochi o motte shigoto ni nozomimasu.
Let's not forget to be grateful to our customers and colleagues. Remember to maintain a sense of gratitude today.	Yes, I'll approach work with a sense of gratitude.

Cultural Context

Emphasizes the importance of gratitude in Japanese culture. Used to promote positive workplace relationships.

常に質の高い仕事を目指しましょう。

つねにしつのたかいしごとをめざしましょう。
Tsuneni shitsu no takai shigoto o mezashimashou.
Let's always aim for high-quality work.

Variation 1	Variation 2
絶えず卓越した業務遂行を心がけましょう。	Kyō mo shōjin shima shou.
たえずたくえつしたぎょうむすいこうをこころがけましょう。	たえずたくえつしたぎょうむすいこうをこころがけましょう。
Taezu takuetsu shita gyōmu suikō o kokorogake ma shou.	Kō hinshitsuna seika-mono o tsuneni tsuikyū shima shou.
Let's always aim for high-quality work.	Let's always aim for high-quality work.

Positive Response	Negative Response
最高品質の仕事を提供し続けます。	納期に間に合わなくなります。
さいこうひんしつのしごとをていきょうしつづけます。	のうきにまにあわなくなります。
Saikō hinshitsu no shigoto o teikyō shi tsudzukemasu.	Nōki ni maniawanaku narimasu.
I'll consistently deliver the highest quality work.	We won't be able to meet the deadlines.

Conversation example person A	Conversation example person B
どんな業務でも、常に質の高い仕事を目指しましょう。	了解です。妥協せずに取り組みます。
どんなぎょうむでも、つねにしつのたかいしごとをめざしましょう。	りょうかいです。だきょうせずにとりくみます。
Don'na gyōmu demo, tsuneni shitsu no takai shigoto o mezashi ma shou.	Ryōkaidesu. Dakyō sezu ni torikumimasu.
No matter what task, let's always aim for high-quality work.	Understood. I'll work without compromising.

Cultural Context

Reflects Japan's reputation for high-quality work. Used to encourage excellence in all tasks.

今日も一日コミュニケーションを大切にしましょう。

きょうもいちにちこみゅにけーしょんをたいせつにしましょう。

Kyōmoichinichi komyunikēshon o taisetsu ni shimashou.

Let's value communication today as well.

Variation 1	Variation 2
本日も円滑な意思疎通を重視しましょう。	Kyō mo shōjin shima shou.
ほんじつもえんかつないしそつうをじゅうししましょう。	ほんじつもえんかつないしそつうをじゅうししましょう。
Honjitsu mo enkatsuna ishi sotsū o jūshi shima shou.	Honjitsu mo enkatsuna jōhō kōkan o kokorogake ma shou.
Let's value communication throughout the day.	Let's value communication today as well.

Positive Response	Negative Response
オープンで効果的なコミュニケーションを心がけます。	仕事が忙しくてそんな余裕はありません。
おーぷんでこうかてきなこみゅにけーしょんをこころがけます。	しごとがいそがしくてそんなよゆうはありません。
Ōpun de kōka-tekina komyunikēshon o kokorogakemasu.	Aite kara no hentō shigoto ga isogashikute son'na yoyū wa arimasen.
I'll maintain open and effective communication.	I'm too busy with work to have time for that.

Conversation example person A	Conversation example person B
リモートワークが増えていますが、今日も一日コミュニケーションを大切にしましょう。	はい、こまめに連絡を取り合います。
りもーとわーくがふえていますが、きょうもいちにちこみゅにけーしょんをたいせつにしましょう。	はい、こまめにれんらくをとりあいます。
Rimōto wāku ga fuete imasuga, kyō mo ichi-nichi komyunikēshon o taisetsu ni shima shou.	Hai, komame ni renraku o toriaimasu.
Remote work is increasing, but let's value communication today as well.	Yes, I'll keep in touch frequently.

Cultural Context

Addresses the need for clear communication in hierarchical Japanese society. Used to promote open dialogue.

チームの強みを生かして頑張りましょう。

ちーむのつよみをいかしてがんばりましょう。

Chīmu no tsuyomi o ikashite ganbarimashou.

Let's work hard utilizing our team's strengths.

Variation 1	Variation 2
組織の強みを活かして頑張りましょう。	Kyō mo shōjin shima shou.
そしきのつよみをいかしてがんばりましょう。	そしきのつよみをいかしてがんばりましょう。
Soshiki no tsuyomi o ikashite ganbari ma shou.	Busho no chōsho o saidai-gen ni katsuyō shima shou.
Let's work hard by leveraging our organization's strengths.	Let's leverage our team's strengths.

Positive Response	Negative Response
チームの長所を最大限に活用します。	個人の能力も重要だと思います。
ちーむのちょうしょをさいだいげんにかつようします。	こじんののうりょくもじゅうようだとおもいます。
Chīmu no chōsho o saidai-gen ni katsuyō shimasu.	Kojin no nōryoku mo jūyōda to omoimasu.
I'll maximize our team's strengths.	I think individual abilities are important too.

Conversation example person A	Conversation example person B
各自の得意分野を活かし、チームの強みを生かして頑張りましょう。	そうですね。お互いの長所を認め合って進めます。
かくじのとくいぶんやをいかし、ちーむのつよみをいかしてがんばりましょう。	そうですね。おたがいのちょうしょをみとめあってすすめます。
Kakuji no tokui bun'ya o ikashi, chīmu no tsuyomi o ikashite ganbari ma shou.	Sōdesu ne. Otagai no chōsho o mitome atte susumemasu.
Let's utilize each person's strengths and work hard using our team's advantages.	You're right. We'll proceed by recognizing each other's strengths.

Cultural Context

Reflects the value of leveraging collective strengths in Japanese group-oriented culture. Used to encourage effective teamwork.

今日も一日ポジティブな姿勢で臨みましょう。

きょうもいちにちぽじてぃぶなしせいでのぞみましょう。

Kyōmoichinichi pojitibuna shisei de nozomimashou.

Let's approach today with a positive attitude.

Variation 1	Variation 2
本日も前向きな態度で取り組みましょう。	Kyō mo shōjin shima shou.
ほんじつもまえむきなたいどでとりくみましょう。	ほんじつもまえむきなたいどでとりくみましょう。
Honjitsu mo maemukina taido de torikumi ma shou.	Honjitsu mo maemukina taido de gyōmu ni torikumi ma shou.
Let's approach the day with a positive attitude.	Let's approach work with a positive attitude today.

Positive Response	Negative Response
前向きな態度で全ての課題に取り組みます。	現実を直視することも大切です。
まえむきなたいどですべてのかだいにとりくみます。	げんじつをちょくしすることもたいせつです。
Maemukina taido de subete no kadai ni torikumimasu.	Genjitsu o chokushi suru koto mo taisetsudesu.
I'll approach all tasks with a positive attitude.	It's also important to face reality.

Conversation example person A	Conversation example person B
おはようございます。今日も一日ポジティブな姿勢で臨みましょう。	はい、前向きに頑張ります！
おはようございます。きょうもいちにちぽじてぃぶなしせいでのぞみましょう。	はい、まえむきにがんばります！
Ohayōgozaimasu. Kyō mo ichi-nichi pojitibuna shisei de nozomi ma shou.	Hai, maemuki ni ganbarimasu!
Good morning. Let's approach today with a positive attitude.	Yes, I'll do my best with a positive mindset!

Cultural Context

Encourages maintaining a positive attitude in the face of challenges. Used to promote resilience and optimism.

常に顧客満足度を意識しましょう。

つねにこきゃくまんぞくどをいしきしましょう。
Tsuneni kokakumanzoku-do o ishiki shimashou.
Let's always be conscious of customer satisfaction.

Variation 1	Variation 2
絶えずお客様の満足を考慮しましょう。	Kyō mo shōjin shima shou.
たえずおきゃくさまのまんぞくをこうりょしましょう。	たえずおきゃくさまのまんぞくをこうりょしましょう。
Taezu okyakusama no manzoku o kōryo shima shou.	Okyakusama no manzoku o sai yūsen ni kangae ma shou.
Let's always be conscious of customer satisfaction.	Let's always be conscious of customer satisfaction.

Positive Response	Negative Response
お客様の期待を超えるサービスを提供します。	コストがかかりすぎて現実的ではありません。
おきゃくさまのきたいをこえるさーびすをていきょうします。	こすとがかかりすぎてげんじつてきではありません。
Okyakusama no kitai o koeru sābisu o teikyō shimasu.	Kosuto ga kakari sugite genjitsu-tekide wa arimasen.
I'll provide service that exceeds customer expectations.	It's not realistic due to the high costs involved.

Conversation example person A	Conversation example person B
新製品の開発では、常に顧客満足度を意識しましょう。	そうですね。顧客の声をしっかり反映させます。
しんせいひんのかいはつでは、つねにこきゃくまんぞくどをいしきしましょう。	そうですね。こきゃくのこえをしっかりはんえいさせます。
Shin seihin no kaihatsude wa, tsuneni kokyaku manzoku-do o ishiki shima shou.	Sōdesu ne. Kokyaku no koe o shikkari han'ei sa semasu.
In developing new products, let's always be conscious of customer satisfaction.	You're right. We'll make sure to reflect customer feedback.

Cultural Context

Reflects Japan's customer-centric business approach. Used in service industries to maintain high standards of customer service.

今週も一週間健康に気をつけて頑張りましょう。

こんしゅうもいっしゅうかんけんこうにきをつけてがんばりましょう。

Konshū mo isshūkan kenkō ni kiwotsukete ganbarimashou.

Let's work hard this week while taking care of our health.

Variation 1	Variation 2
今週も体調管理に留意して努力しましょう。	Kyō mo shōjin shima shou.
こんしゅうもたいちょうかんりにりゅういしてどりょくしましょう。	こんしゅうもたいちょうかんりにりゅういしてどりょくしましょう。
Konshū mo taichō kanri ni ryūi shite doryoku shima shou.	Konshū mo taichō kanri ni ryūi shite gyōmu ni hagemi ma shou.
Let's work hard while taking care of our health this week.	Let's take care of our health while working hard this week.

Positive Response	Negative Response
健康管理を徹底し、最高のパフォーマンスを発揮します。	忙しすぎて気をつける余裕がありません。
けんこうかんりをてっていし、さいこうのぱふぉーまんすをはっきします。	いそがしすぎてきをつけるよゆうがありません。
Kenkō kanri o tettei shi, saikō no pafōmansu o hakki shimasu.	Isogashi sugite ki o tsukeru yoyū ga arimasen.
I'll maintain my health to perform at my best.	I'm too busy to pay attention to that.

Conversation example person A	Conversation example person B
忙しい時期ですが、今週も一週間健康に気をつけて頑張りましょう。	ありがとうございます。休憩もしっかり取ります。
いそがしいじきですが、こんしゅうもいっしゅうかんけんこうにきをつけてがんばりましょう。	ありがとうございます。きゅうけいもしっかりとります。
Isogashī jikidesuga, konshū mo ichi-shūkan kenkō ni ki o tsukete ganbari ma shou.	Arigatōgozaimasu. Kyūkei mo shikkari torimasu.
It's a busy period, but let's take care of our health and do our best this week.	Thank you. I'll make sure to take proper breaks.

Cultural Context

Emphasizes the importance of health consciousness in Japanese work culture. More common during health crises or flu seasons.

今日も一日丁寧な対応を心がけましょう。

きょうもいちにちていねいなたいおうをこころがけましょう。

Kyōmoichinichi teineina taiō o kokorogakemashou.

Let's aim for polite and careful responses today as well.

Variation 1	Variation 2
本日も誠実な応対を意識しましょう。	Kyō mo shōjin shima shou.
ほんじつもせいじつなおうたいをいしきしましょう。	ほんじつもせいじつなおうたいをいしきしましょう。
Honjitsu mo seijitsuna ōtai o ishiki shima shou.	Honjitsu mo komayakana kikubari o wasurezu ni kōdō shima shou.
Let's be mindful of providing courteous service today.	Let's be mindful of providing attentive service today.

Positive Response	Negative Response
常に丁寧で親切な対応を心がけます。	効率が落ちて仕事が進みません。
つねにていねいでしんせつなたいおうをこころがけます。	こうりつがおちてしごとがすすみません。
Tsuneni teineide shinsetsuna taiō o kokorogakemasu.	Kōritsu ga ochite shigoto ga susumimasen.
I'll always strive for polite and kind interactions.	Work won't progress if we're too careful about everything.

Conversation example person A	Conversation example person B
今日も一日丁寧な対応を心がけましょう。特に新規のお客様には注意が必要です。	了解しました。お客様第一で対応します。
きょうもいちにちていねいなたいおうをこころがけましょう。とくにしんきのおきゃくさまにはちゅういがひつようです。	りょうかいしました。おきゃくさまだいいちでたいおうします。
Kyō mo ichi-nichi teineina taiō o kokorogake ma shou. Tokuni shinki no okyakusama ni wa chūi ga hitsuyōdesu.	Ryōkai shima shita. Okyakusama dai ichi de taiō shimasu.
Let's be mindful of providing courteous service throughout the day. We need to be especially careful with new customers.	Understood. I'll prioritize customer service.

Cultural Context

Reflects Japanese emphasis on politeness and respect. Used in customer-facing roles to ensure high-quality service.

常に改善点を見つける努力をしましょう。

つねにかいぜんてんをみつけるどりょくをしましょう。

Tsuneni kaizen-ten o mitsukeru doryoku o shimashou.

Let's always make an effort to find points for improvement.

Variation 1	Variation 2
絶えず向上の機会を探索しましょう。	Kyō mo shōjin shima shou.
たえずこうじょうのきかいをたんさくしましょう。	たえずこうじょうのきかいをたんさくしましょう。
Taezu kōjō no kikai o tansaku shima shou.	Keizoku-tekina gyōmu kaizen o kokorogake ma shou.
Let's always strive to find areas for improvement.	Let's always strive to find areas for improvement.

Positive Response	Negative Response
継続的な改善のために常に注意を払います。	現状で十分だと思います。
けいぞくてきなかいぜんのためにつねにちゅういをはらいます。	げんじょうでじゅうぶんだとおもいます。
Keizoku-tekina kaizen no tame ni tsuneni chūi o haraimasu.	Genjō de jūbunda to omoimasu.
I'll always be attentive for continuous improvement.	I think the current situation is fine.

Conversation example person A	Conversation example person B
現状に満足せず、常に改善点を見つける努力をしましょう。	そうですね。日々の業務を見直していきます。
げんじょうにまんぞくせず、つねにかいぜんてんをみつけるどりょくをしましょう。	そうですね。ひびのぎょうむをみなおしていきます。
Genjō ni manzoku sezu, tsuneni kaizen-ten o mitsukeru doryoku o shima shou.	Sōdesu ne. Hibi no gyōmu o minaoshite ikimasu.
Let's not be satisfied with the status quo and always strive to find areas for improvement.	You're right. I'll review our daily operations.

Cultural Context

Embodies the 'kaizen' philosophy of continuous improvement. Used to encourage proactive problem-solving and efficiency.

今日も一日時間を大切に使いましょう。

きょうもいちにちじかんをたいせつにつかいましょう。

Kyōmoichinichi jikan o taisetsu ni tsukaimashou.

Let's use our time wisely today as well.

Variation 1	Variation 2
本日も時間の有効活用を心がけましょう。	Kyō mo shōjin shima shou.
ほんじつもじかんのゆうこうかつようをこころがけましょう。	ほんじつもじかんのゆうこうかつようをこころがけましょう。
Honjitsu mo jikan no yūkō katsuyō o kokorogake ma shou.	Honjitsu mo jikan no yūkō katsuyō o ishiki shima shou.
Let's make the most of our time today.	Let's make the most of our time today.

Positive Response	Negative Response
時間を効果的に活用し、生産性を最大化します。	突発的な仕事が多くて難しいです。
じかんをこうかてきにかつようし、せいさんせいをさいだいかします。	とっぱつてきなしごとがおおくてむずかしいです。
Jikan o kōka-teki ni katsuyō shi, seisan-sei o saidai-ka shimasu.	Toppatsu-tekina shigoto ga ōkute muzukashīdesu.
I'll use time effectively to maximize productivity.	It's difficult with so many unexpected tasks.

Conversation example person A	Conversation example person B
今日も一日時間を大切に使いましょう。効率的に仕事を進めることが重要です。	はい、無駄な時間を減らすよう心がけます。
きょうもいちにちじかんをたいせつにつかいましょう。こうりつてきにしごとをすすめることがじゅうようです。	はい、むだなじかんをへらすようこころがけます。
Kyō mo ichi-nichi jikan o taisetsu ni tsukai ma shou. Kōritsu-teki ni shigoto o susumeru koto ga jūyōdesu.	Hai, mudana jikan o herasu yō kokorogakemasu.
Let's value our time today. It's important to work efficiently.	Yes, I'll try to reduce wasted time.

Cultural Context

Reflects Japanese value of time efficiency. Used to promote productive use of work hours.

チームの目標を再確認して頑張りましょう。

ちーむのもくひょうをさいかくにんしてがんばりましょう。

Chīmu no mokuhyō o sai kakunin shite ganbarimashou.

Let's reconfirm our team goals and work hard.

Variation 1	Variation 2
組織の目標を再確認し、全員で頑張りましょう。	Kyō mo shōjin shima shou.
そしきのもくひょうをさいかくにんし、ぜんいんでがんばりましょう。	そしきのもくひょうをさいかくにんし、ぜんいんでがんばりましょう。
Soshiki no mokuhyō o sai kakunin shi, zen'in de ganbari ma shou.	Busho no mokuteki o saido kyōyū shite torikumi ma shou.
Let's reaffirm our organizational goals and work hard together.	Let's reconfirm our team's goals and work hard.

Positive Response	Negative Response
目標を常に意識し、その達成に全力を尽くします。	目標が現実離れしていて意味がありません。
もくひょうをつねにいしき、そのたっせいにぜんりょくをつくします。	もくひょうがげんじつばなれしていていみがありません。
Mokuhyō o tsuneni ishiki shi, sono tassei ni zenryoku o tsukushimasu.	Mokuhyō ga genjitsubanare shite ite imi ga arimasen.
I'll always be mindful of our goals and give my all to achieve them.	The goals are unrealistic and meaningless.

Conversation example person A	Conversation example person B
月末が近づいてきました。チームの目標を再確認して頑張りましょう。	承知しました。目標達成に向けて全力を尽くします。
げつまつがちかづいてきました。ちーむのもくひょうをさいかくにんしてがんばりましょう。	しょうちしました。もくひょうたっせいにむけてぜんりょくをつくします。
Getsumatsu ga chikadzuite kimashita. Chīmu no mokuhyō o sai kakunin shite ganbari ma shou.	Shōchi shima shita. Mokuhyō tassei ni mukete zenryoku o tsukushimasu.
The end of the month is approaching. Let's reconfirm our team goals and do our best.	Understood. I'll give my all towards achieving our goals.

Cultural Context

Emphasizes the importance of shared goals in Japanese group-oriented culture. Used to align and motivate team efforts.

今日も一日安全運転で頑張りましょう。

きょうもいちにちあんぜんうんてんでがんばりましょう。

Kyōmoichinichi anzen unten de ganbarimashou.

Let's drive safely and work hard today as well.

Variation 1	Variation 2
本日も交通安全に留意して努力しましょう。	Kyō mo shōjin shima shou.
ほんじつもこうつうあんぜんにりゅういしてどりょくしましょう。	ほんじつもこうつうあんぜんにりゅういしてどりょくしましょう。
Honjitsu mo kōtsū anzen ni ryūi shite doryoku shima shou.	Honjitsu mo kōtsū anzen ni ryūi shite kōdō shima shou.
Let's drive safely and work hard today.	Let's drive safely today as well.

Positive Response	Negative Response
交通ルールを厳守し、安全運転を徹底します。	急いでいるのでそんな余裕はありません。
こうつうるーるをげんしゅし、あんぜんうんてんをてっていします。	いそいでいるのでそんなよゆうはありません。
Kōtsū rūru o genshu shi, anzen unten o tettei shimasu.	Isoide irunode son'na yoyū wa arimasen.
I'll strictly follow traffic rules and ensure safe driving.	I'm in a hurry, I don't have time for that.

Conversation example person A	Conversation example person B
外回りの多い一日ですね。今日も一日安全運転で頑張りましょう。	はい、交通ルールを守り、安全第一で行動します。
そとまわりのおおいいちにちですね。きょうもいちにちあんぜんうんてんでがんばりましょう。	はい、こうつうるーるをまもり、あんぜんだいいちでこうどうします。
Sotomawari no ōi ichi-nichidesu ne. Kyō mo ichi-nichi anzen unten de ganbari ma shou.	Hai, kōtsū rūru o mamori, anzen dai ichi de kōdō shimasu.
It's a day with many outside appointments. Let's drive safely and do our best today.	Yes, I'll follow traffic rules and prioritize safety.

Cultural Context

Reflects concern for traffic safety in Japan. Common in companies with employees who drive for work.

常に効率的な仕事の仕方を考えましょう。

つねにこうりつてきなしごとのしかたをかんがえましょう。

Tsuneni kōritsu-tekina shigoto no shikata o kangaemashou.

Let's always think about efficient ways of working.

Variation 1	Variation 2
絶えず生産性の高い業務方法を模索しましょう。	Kyō mo shōjin shima shou.
たえずせいさんせいのたかいぎょうむほうほうをもさくしましょう。	たえずせいさんせいのたかいぎょうむほうほうをもさくしましょう。
Taezu seisan-sei no takai gyōmu hōhō o mosaku shima shou.	Gyōmu no seisan-sei kōjō o tsuneni ishiki shima shou.
Let's always think about efficient ways of working.	Let's always think about efficient ways of working.

Positive Response	Negative Response
常により良い仕事の方法を追求します。	質も大切だと思います。
つねにようりょしいしごとのほうほうをついきゅうします。	しつもたいせつだとおもいます。
Tsune ni yori yoi shigoto no hōhō o tsuikyū shimasu.	Shitsu mo taisetsuda to omoimasu.
I'll always pursue better ways of working.	I think quality is important too.

Conversation example person A	Conversation example person B
業務量が増えていますね。常に効率的な仕事の仕方を考えましょう。	そうですね。無駄な作業を見直していきます。
ぎょうむりょうがふえていますね。つねにこうりつてきなしごとのしかたをかんがえましょう。	そうですね。むだなさぎょうをみなおしていきます。
Gyōmu-ryō ga fuete imasu ne. Tsuneni kōritsu-tekina shigoto no shikata o kangae ma shou.	Sōdesu ne. Mudana sagyō o minaoshite ikimasu.
Our workload is increasing. Let's always think about efficient ways of working.	You're right. I'll review and eliminate unnecessary tasks.

Cultural Context

Emphasizes the value of efficiency in Japanese work culture. Used to encourage innovative approaches to tasks.

今週も一週間事故ゼロを目指しましょう。

こんしゅうもいっしゅうかんじこぜろをめざしましょう。
Konshū mo isshūkan jiko zero o mezashimashou.
Let's aim for zero accidents this week as well.

Variation 1	Variation 2
今週も無事故を目標に七日間を過ごしましょう。	Kyō mo shōjin shima shou.
こんしゅうもむじこをもくひょうになのかかんをすごしましょう。	こんしゅうもむじこをもくひょうになのかかんをすごしましょう。
Konshū mo mujiko o mokuhyō ni nana-kakan o sugoshi ma shou.	Konshū mo mujiko mu saigai o tettei shima shou.
Let's aim for zero accidents this week.	Let's aim for zero accidents this week.

Positive Response	Negative Response
安全意識を高く保ち、無事故を達成します。	毎週言われなくても分かっています。
あんぜんいしきをたかくたもち、むじこをたっせいします。	まいしゅういわれなくてもわかっています。
Anzen ishiki o takaku tamochi, mujiko o tassei shimasu.	Maishū gen warenakute mo wakatte imasu.
I'll maintain high safety awareness to achieve zero accidents.	We know that without being told every week.

Conversation example person A	Conversation example person B
今週も一週間事故ゼロを目指しましょう。安全は全てに優先します。	はい、常に注意を怠らず作業します。
こんしゅうもいっしゅうかんじこぜろをめざしましょう。あんぜんはすべてにゆうせんします。	はい、つねにちゅういをおこたらずさぎょうします。
Konshū mo ichi-shūkan jiko zero o mezashi ma shou. Anzen wa subete ni yūsen shimasu.	Hai, tsuneni chūi o okotarazu sagyō shimasu.
Let's aim for zero accidents this week. Safety takes precedence over everything.	Yes, I'll work with constant vigilance.

Cultural Context
Reflects strong emphasis on workplace safety in Japan. Common in industries with higher accident risks.

今日も一日礼儀正しく行動しましょう。

きょうもいちにちれいぎただしくこうどうしましょう。
Kyōmoichinichi reigi tadashiku kōdō shimashou.
Let's act politely today as well.

Variation 1	Variation 2
本日も丁寧な態度で過ごしましょう。	Kyō mo shōjin shima shou.
ほんじつもていねいなたいどですごしましょう。	ほんじつもていねいなたいどですごしましょう。
Honjitsu mo teineina taido de sugoshi ma shou.	Honjitsu mo tekisetsuna manā o kokorogake ma shou.
Let's behave politely throughout the day.	Let's act politely today as well.

Positive Response	Negative Response
常に礼儀正しく、思いやりのある行動を心がけます。	形式的な礼儀に意味はないと思います。
つねにれいぎただしく、おもいやりのあるこうどうをこころがけます。	けいしきてきなれいぎにいみはないとおもいます。
Tsuneni reigi tadashiku, omoiyari no aru kōdō o kokorogakemasu.	Keishiki-tekina reigi ni imi wa nai to omoimasu.
I'll always act politely and considerately.	I think formal manners are meaningless.

Conversation example person A	Conversation example person B
お客様との面談が多い日です。今日も一日礼儀正しく行動しましょう。	承知しました。お客様に失礼のないよう気をつけます。
おきゃくさまとのめんだんがおおいひです。きょうもいちにちれいぎただしくこうどうしましょう。	しょうちしました。おきゃくさまにしつれいのないようきをつけます。
Okyakusama to no mendan ga ōi hidesu. Kyō mo ichi-nichi reigi tadashiku kōdō shima shou.	Shōchi shima shita. Okyakusama ni shitsurei no nai yō ki o tsukemasu.
We have many customer meetings today. Let's act politely throughout the day.	Understood. I'll be careful not to be discourteous to customers.

Cultural Context

Emphasizes the importance of proper etiquette in Japanese society. Used to maintain a respectful work environment.

常に前向きな姿勢を保ちましょう。

つねにまえむきなしせいをたもちましょう。

Tsuneni maemukina shisei o tamochimashou.

Let's always maintain a positive attitude.

Variation 1	Variation 2
絶えず積極的な態度を維持しましょう。	Kyō mo shōjin shima shou.
たえずせっきょくてきなたいどをいじしましょう。	たえずせっきょくてきなたいどをいじしましょう。
Taezu sekkyoku-tekina taido o iji shima shou.	Sekkyoku-tekina taido o iji shi tsudzuke ma shou.
Let's always maintain a positive attitude.	Let's always maintain a positive attitude.

Positive Response	Negative Response
どんな状況でも前向きな態度を維持します。	現実を直視することも必要です。
どんなじょうきょうでもまえむきなたいどをいじします。	げんじつをちょくしすることもひつようです。
Don'na jōkyō demo maemukina taido o iji shimasu.	Genjitsu o chokushi suru koto mo hitsuyōdesu.
I'll maintain a positive attitude in any situation.	It's also necessary to face reality.

Conversation example person A	Conversation example person B
困難な状況が続いていますが、常に前向きな姿勢を保ちましょう。	はい、どんな状況でも前向きに取り組みます。
こんなんなじょうきょうがつづいていますが、つねにまえむきなしせいをたもちましょう。	はい、どんなじょうきょうでもまえむきにとりくみます。
Kon'nan'na jōkyō ga tsudzuite imasuga, tsuneni maemukina shisei o tamochi ma shou.	Hai, don'na jōkyō demo maemuki ni torikumimasu.
Despite the ongoing difficult situation, let's maintain a positive attitude.	Yes, I'll approach every situation positively.

Cultural Context

Encourages maintaining a positive attitude in the face of challenges. Used to promote resilience and optimism.

今日も一日ムダを省いて仕事をしましょう。

きょうもいちにちむだをはぶいてしごとをしましょう。

Kyōmoichinichi muda o habuite shigoto o shimashou.

Let's work efficiently without waste today as well.

Variation 1	Variation 2
本日も効率的な業務遂行を心がけましょう。	Kyō mo shōjin shima shou.
ほんじつもこうりつてきなぎょうむすいこうをこころがけましょう。	ほんじつもこうりつてきなぎょうむすいこうをこころがけましょう。
Honjitsu mo kōritsu-tekina gyōmu suikō o kokorogake ma shou.	Kyō mo gyōmu o kōka-teki ni susumeru yō tsutome ma shou.
Let's work efficiently without waste today.	Let's endeavor to carry out our work efficiently today.

Positive Response	Negative Response
効率的に仕事を進め、無駄を最小限に抑えます。	効率ばかり求めるとミスが増えます。
こうりつてきにしごとをすすめ、むだをさいしょうげんにおさえます。	こうりつばかりもとめるとみすがふえます。
Kōritsu-teki ni shigoto o susume, muda o saishō-gen ni osaemasu.	Kōritsu bakari motomeru to misu ga fuemasu.
I'll work efficiently to minimize waste.	Focusing only on efficiency can increase mistakes.

Conversation example person A	Conversation example person B
今日も一日ムダを省いて仕事をしましょう。効率化が重要です。	そうですね。業務プロセスを見直していきます。
きょうもいちにちむだをはぶいてしごとをしましょう。こうりつかがじゅうようです。	そうですね。ぎょうむぷろせすをみなおしていきます。
Kyō mo ichi-nichi muda o shō ite shigoto o shima shou. Kōritsu-ka ga jūyōdesu.	Sōdesu ne. Gyōmu purosesu o minaoshite ikimasu.
Let's work without waste today. Efficiency is crucial.	You're right. I'll review our work processes.

Cultural Context

Reflects Japanese focus on efficiency and waste reduction. Used to promote lean working practices.

チーム全体の成長を意識しましょう。

ちーむぜんたいのせいちょうをいしきしましょう。
Chīmu zentai no seichō o ishiki shimashou.
Let's be conscious of the growth of the entire team.

Variation 1	Variation 2
組織全体の向上を目指しましょう。	Kyō mo shōjin shima shou.
そしきぜんたいのこうじょうをめざしましょう。	そしきぜんたいのこうじょうをめざしましょう。
Soshiki zentai no kōjō o mezashi ma shou.	Busho zentai no hatten o tsuneni kangae ma shou.
Let's aim for the growth of the entire organization.	Let's always be conscious of the entire team's growth.

Positive Response	Negative Response
チーム全体の成長に貢献できるよう努めます。	個人の成長も大切だと思います。
ちーむぜんたいのせいちょうにこうけんできるようつとめます。	こじんのせいちょうもたいせつだとおもいます。
Chīmu zentai no seichō ni kōken dekiru yō tsutomemasu.	Kojin no seichō mo taisetsuda to omoimasu.
I'll strive to contribute to the overall growth of the team.	I think personal growth is important too.

Conversation example person A	Conversation example person B
個人の成長も大切ですが、チーム全体の成長を意識しましょう。	はい、お互いに学び合える環境を作ります。
こじんのせいちょうもたいせつですが、ちーむぜんたいのせいちょうをいしきしましょう。	はい、おたがいにまなびあえるかんきょうをつくります。
Kojin no seichō mo taisetsudesuga, chīmu zentai no seichō o ishiki shima shou.	Hai, otagai ni manabi aeru kankyō o tsukurimasu.
While individual growth is important, let's be conscious of the entire team's growth.	Yes, I'll create an environment where we can learn from each other.

Cultural Context
Emphasizes collective growth in Japanese group-oriented culture. Used to encourage mutual support and development.

今日も一日気配りを忘れずに。

きょうもいちにちきくばりをわすれずに。

Kyōmoichinichi kikubari o wasurezu ni.

Let's not forget to be considerate today as well.

Variation 1	Variation 2
本日も周囲への配慮を心がけましょう。	Kyō mo shōjin shima shou.
ほんじつもしゅういへのはいりょをこころがけましょう。	ほんじつもしゅういへのはいりょをこころがけましょう。
Honjitsu mo shūi e no hairyo o kokorogake ma shou.	Kyō mo mawari no hito e no kikubari o wasurenai yō ni shima shou.
Let's be mindful of those around us today.	Let's not forget to be considerate of those around us today.

Positive Response	Negative Response
周りへの配慮を忘れず、思いやりを持って行動します。	そんなことを気にしていたら仕事が進みません。
まわりへのはいりょをわすれず、おもいやりをもってこうどうします。	そんなことをきにしていたらしごとがすすみません。
Mawari e no hairyo o wasurezu, omoiyari o motte kōdō shimasu.	Son'na koto o ki ni shite itara shigoto ga susumimasen.
I'll act with consideration and thoughtfulness for others.	If we worry about that, we won't get any work done.

Conversation example person A	Conversation example person B
今日も一日気配りを忘れずに。小さな変化にも注意しましょう。	承知しました。周囲の状況をよく観察します。
きょうもいちにちきくばりをわすれずに。ちいさなへんかにもちゅういしましょう。	しょうちしました。しゅういのじょうきょうをよくかんさつします。
Kyō mo ichi-nichi kikubari o wasurezu ni. Chīsana henka ni mo chūi shima shou.	Shōchi shima shita. Shūi no jōkyō o yoku kansatsu shimasu.
Let's not forget to be attentive today. Pay attention to small changes.	Understood. I'll carefully observe the surrounding situation.

Cultural Context

Reflects Japanese value of considerate behavior. Used to promote a harmonious work environment.

常に顧客の期待を超える仕事をしましょう。

つねにこきゃくのきたいをこえるしごとをしましょう。
Tsuneni kokyaku no kitai o koeru shigoto o shimashou.
Let's always strive to exceed customer expectations.

Variation 1	Variation 2
絶えずお客様の予想以上の成果を目指しましょう。	Kyō mo shōjin shima shou.
たえずおきゃくさまのよそういじょうのせいかをめざしましょう。	たえずおきゃくさまのよそういじょうのせいかをめざしましょう。
Taezu okyakusama no yosō ijō no seika o mezashi ma shou.	Okyakusama no sōtei ijō no seika o mezashi ma shou.
Let's always strive to exceed customer expectations.	Let's always strive to exceed customer expectations.

Positive Response	Negative Response
お客様の期待以上の価値を提供します。	現実的な期待に応えるのが精一杯です。
おきゃくさまのきたいいじょうのかちをていきょうします。	げんじつてきなきたいにこたえるのがせいいっぱいです。
Okyakusama no kitai ijō no kachi o teikyō shimasu.	Genjitsu-tekina kitai ni kotaeru no ga sei ippaidesu.
I'll provide value that exceeds customer expectations.	Meeting realistic expectations is already challenging enough.

Conversation example person A	Conversation example person B
常に顧客の期待を超える仕事をしましょう。それが私たちの強みになります。	はい、顧客満足度の向上に努めます。
つねにこきゃくのきたいをこえるしごとをしましょう。それがわたしたちのつよみになります。	はい、こきゃくまんぞくどのこうじょうにつとめます。
Tsuneni kokyaku no kitai o koeru shigoto o shima shou. Sore ga watashi-tachi no tsuyomi ni narimasu.	Hai, kokyaku manzoku-do no kōjō ni tsutomemasu.
Let's always strive to exceed customer expectations. That will become our strength.	Yes, I'll work on improving customer satisfaction.

Cultural Context
Reflects Japanese emphasis on exceptional customer service. Used to encourage going above and beyond in service industries.

今週も一週間整理整頓を心がけましょう。

こんしゅうもいっしゅうかんせいりせいとんをこころがけましょう。

Konshū mo isshūkan seiri seiton o kokorogakemashou.

Let's keep our workspace tidy and organized this week as well.

Variation 1	Variation 2
今週も七日間清潔な環境維持に努めましょう。	Kyō mo shōjin shima shou.
こんしゅうもなのかかんせいけつなかんきょういじにつとめましょう。	こんしゅうもなのかかんせいけつなかんきょういじにつとめましょう。
Konshū mo nanokakan seiketsuna kankyō iji ni tsutome ma shou.	Konshū mo shokuba no seiketsu-sa o iji shima shou.
Let's keep our workspace tidy throughout the week.	Let's keep our workplace tidy this week as well.

Positive Response	Negative Response
整理整頓を徹底し、効率的な職場環境を維持します。	忙しくてそんな時間はありません。
せいりせいとんをてってし、こうりつてきなしょくばかんきょうをいじします。	いそがしくてそんなじかんはありません。
Seiri seiton o tettei shi, kōritsu-tekina shokuba kankyō o iji shimasu.	Isogashikute son'na toki wa arimasen.
I'll maintain a clean and efficient workplace.	I'm too busy to have time for that.

Conversation example person A	Conversation example person B
今週も一週間整理整頓を心がけましょう。清潔な職場は効率を上げます。	了解です。毎日少しずつ整理していきます。
こんしゅうもいっしゅうかんせいりせいとんをこころがけましょう。せいけつなしょくばはこうりつをあげます。	りょうかいです。まいにちすこしずつせいりしていきます。
Konshū mo ichi-shūkan seiri seiton o kokorogake ma shou. Seiketsuna shokuba wa kōritsu o agemasu.	Ryōkaidesu. Mainichi sukoshi zutsu seiri shite ikimasu.
Let's keep our workplace tidy this week. A clean workplace increases efficiency.	Understood. I'll organize a little every day.

Cultural Context

Reflects Japanese values of cleanliness and order. Used to maintain an organized and efficient workplace.

今日も一日集中力を保って頑張りましょう。

きょうもいちにちしゅうちゅうりょくをたもってがんばりましょう。

Kyōmoichinichi shūchū-ryoku o tamotte ganbarimashou.

Let's maintain our concentration and work hard today as well.

Variation 1	Variation 2
本日も終日注意力を維持して努力しましょう。	Kyō mo shōjin shima shou.
ほんじつもしゅうじつちゅういりょくをいじしてどりょくしましょう。	ほんじつもしゅうじつちゅういりょくをいじしてどりょくしましょう。
Honjitsu mo hinemosu chūi-ryoku o iji shite doryoku shima shou.	Honjitsu mo chūi-ryoku o jizoku sa sete gyōmu ni hagemi ma shou.
Let's maintain our focus and work hard throughout the day.	Let's maintain our focus throughout the day.

Positive Response	Negative Response
高い集中力を維持し、生産性の高い一日を過ごします。	毎日集中し続けるのは無理です。
たかいしゅうちゅうりょくをいじし、せいさんせいのたかいいちにちをすごします。	まいにちしゅうちゅうしつづけるのはむりです。
Takai shūchū-ryoku o iji shi, seisan-sei no takai ichi-nichi o sugoshimasu.	Mainichi shūchū shi tsudzukeru no wa muridesu.
I'll maintain high concentration for a productive day.	It's impossible to stay focused every single day.

Conversation example person A	Conversation example person B
今日も一日集中力を保って頑張りましょう。質の高い仕事を目指しましょう。	はい、集中して業務に取り組みます。
きょうもいちにちしゅうちゅうりょくをたもってがんばりましょう。しつのたかいしごとをめざしましょう。	はい、しゅうちゅうしてぎょうむにとりくみます。
Kyō mo ichi-nichi shūchū-ryoku o tamotte ganbari ma shou. Shitsu no takai shigoto o mezashi ma shou.	Hai, shūchū shite gyōmu ni torikumimasu.
Let's maintain our concentration and do our best today. Let's aim for high-quality work.	Yes, I'll focus on my tasks.

Cultural Context

Emphasizes the value of focus and dedication in Japanese work culture. Used to encourage sustained effort throughout the day.

常に新しい知識の習得に努めましょう。

つねにあたらしいちしきのしゅうとくにつとめましょう。
Tsuneni atarashī chishiki no shūtoku ni tsutomemashou.
Let's always strive to acquire new knowledge.

Variation 1	Variation 2
絶えず最新の情報を学ぶ姿勢を持ちましょう。	Kyō mo shōjin shima shou.
たえずさいしんのじょうほうをまなぶしせいをもちましょう。	たえずさいしんのじょうほうをまなぶしせいをもちましょう。
Taezu saishin no jōhō o manabu shisei o mochi ma shou.	Keizoku-tekina gakushū o kokorogake ma shou.
Let's always strive to acquire new knowledge.	Let's always strive to acquire new knowledge.

Positive Response	Negative Response
継続的に学び、スキルアップに取り組みます。	今の知識で十分だと思います。
けいぞくてきにまなび、すきるあっぷにとりくみます。	いまのちしきでじゅうぶんだとおもいます。
Keizoku-teki ni manabi, sukiru appu ni torikumimasu.	Ima no chishiki de jūbunda to omoimasu.
I'll continuously learn and work on improving my skills.	I think my current knowledge is enough.

Conversation example person A	Conversation example person B
業界の変化が速いですね。常に新しい知識の習得に努めましょう。	そうですね。日々の学習を欠かさず行います。
ぎょうかいのへんかがはやいですね。つねにあたらしいちしきのしゅうとくにつとめましょう。	そうですね。ひびのがくしゅうをかかさずおこないます。
Gyōkai no henka ga hayaidesu ne. Tsuneni atarashī chishiki no shūtoku ni tsutome ma shou.	Sōdesu ne. Hibi no gakushū o kakasazu okonaimasu.
Our industry is changing rapidly. Let's always strive to acquire new knowledge.	You're right. I'll make sure to learn something new every day.

Cultural Context

Reflects Japanese value of continuous learning. Used to encourage ongoing professional development.

今日も一日明るい職場づくりに努めましょう。

きょうもいちにちあかるいしょくばづくりにつとめましょう。

Kyōmoichinichi akarui shokuba-dzukuri ni tsutomemashou.

Let's work on creating a positive workplace environment today as well.

Variation 1	Variation 2
今日も笑顔で、良い雰囲気の職場を作りましょう。	Kyō mo shōjin shima shou.
きょうもえがおで、よいふんいきのしょくばをつくりましょう。	きょうもえがおで、よいふんいきのしょくばをつくりましょう。
Kyō mo egao de, yoi fun'iki no shokuba o tsukuri ma shou.	Honjitsu mo kakki aru shokuba kankyō no sōshutsu o mezashi ma shou.
Let's create a positive workplace atmosphere with smiles today.	Let's work towards creating a positive workplace today.

Positive Response	Negative Response
積極的にコミュニケーションを取り、明るい雰囲気を作ります。	仕事の雰囲気よりも成果が大切です。
せっきょくてきにこみゅにけーしょんをとり、あかるいふんいきをつくります。	しごとのふんいきよりもせいかがたいせつです。
Sekkyoku-teki ni komyunikēshon o tori, akarui fun'iki o tsukurimasu.	Shigoto no fun'iki yori mo seika ga taisetsudesu.
I'll actively communicate to create a positive atmosphere.	Results are more important than the work atmosphere.

Conversation example person A	Conversation example person B
今日も一日明るい職場づくりに努めましょう。笑顔を忘れずに。	はい、良好なコミュニケーションを心がけます。
きょうもいちにちあかるいしょくばづくりにつとめましょう。えがおをわすれずに。	はい、りょうこうなこみゅにけーしょんをこころがけます。
Kyō mo ichi-nichi akarui shokuba-dzukuri ni tsutome ma shou. Egao o wasurezu ni.	Hai, ryōkōna komyunikēshon o kokorogakemasu.
Let's work on creating a bright workplace atmosphere today. Don't forget to smile.	Yes, I'll make an effort to maintain good communication.

Cultural Context

Emphasizes the importance of a positive work environment in Japanese culture. Used to promote workplace harmony and satisfaction.

チームの和を大切に協力し合いましょう。

ちーむのわをたいせつにきょうりょくしあいましょう。
Chīmu no wa o taisetsu ni kyōryoku shi aimashou.
Let's value team harmony and cooperate with each other.

Variation 1	Variation 2
団結力を重視して互いに助け合いましょう。	Kyō mo shōjin shima shou.
だんけつりょくをじゅうししてたがいにたすけあいましょう。	だんけつりょくをじゅうししてたがいにたすけあいましょう。
Danketsu-ryoku o jūshi shite tagaini tasukeai ma shou.	Busho-nai no kyōchō-sei o jūshi shite kōdō shima shou.
Let's value team harmony and cooperate with each other.	Let's value team harmony and cooperate with each other.

Positive Response	Negative Response
チームの団結力を高め、互いに支え合います。	個人の能力も重要だと思います。
ちーむのだんけつりょくをたかめ、たがいにささえあいます。	こじんののうりょくもじゅうようだとおもいます。
Chīmu no danketsu-ryoku o takame, tagaini sasae aimasu.	Kojin no nōryoku mo jūyōda to omoimasu.
I'll enhance team unity and support each other.	I think individual abilities are important too.

Conversation example person A	Conversation example person B
今週は忙しくなりそうです。チームの和を大切に協力し合いましょう。	承知しました。チームワークを大切にします。
こんしゅうはいそがしくなりそうです。ちーむのわをたいせつにきょうりょくしあいましょう。	しょうちしました。ちーむわーくをたいせつにします。
Konshū wa isogashiku nari-sōdesu. Chīmu no wa o taisetsu ni kyōryoku shi gō ima shou.	Shōchi shima shita. Chīmu wāku o taisetsu ni shimasu.
This week looks busy. Let's value team harmony and cooperate with each other.	Understood. I'll value teamwork.

Cultural Context

Reflects the value of harmony and cooperation in Japanese group-oriented culture. Used to encourage effective teamwork.

今日も一日謙虚な姿勢で仕事に臨みましょう。

きょうもいちにちけんきょなしせいでしごとにのぞみましょう。
Kyōmoichinichi kenkyona shisei de shigoto ni nozomimashou.
Let's approach our work with humility today as well.

Variation 1	Variation 2
本日も控えめな態度で業務に取り組みましょう。	Kyō mo shōjin shima shou.
ほんじつもひかえめなたいどでぎょうむにとりくみましょう。	ほんじつもひかえめなたいどでぎょうむにとりくみましょう。
Honjitsu mo hikaemena taido de gyōmu ni torikumi ma shou.	Honjitsu mo kenkyo-sa o wasurezu ni gyōmu ni torikumi ma shou.
Let's approach our work with humility today.	Let's approach work with humility today.

Positive Response	Negative Response
謙虚な態度で学び続け、成長を目指します。	自信を持つことも大切だと思います。
けんきょなたいどでまなびつづけ、せいちょうをめざします。	じしんをもつこともたいせつだとおもいます。
Kenkyona taido de manabi tsudzuke, seichō o mezashimasu.	Jishin o motsu koto mo taisetsuda to omoimasu.
I'll continue learning with a humble attitude and aim for growth.	I think it's also important to have confidence.

Conversation example person A	Conversation example person B
今日も一日謙虚な姿勢で仕事に臨みましょう。常に学ぶ気持ちを持ちましょう。	はい、謙虚に学ぶ姿勢を忘れません。
きょうもいちにちけんきょなしせいでしごとにのぞみましょう。つねにまなぶきもちをもちましょう。	はい、けんきょにまなぶしせいをわすれません。
Kyō mo ichi-nichi kenkyona shisei de shigoto ni nozomi ma shou. Tsuneni manabu kimochi o mochi ma shou.	Hai, kenkyo ni manabu shisei o wasuremasen.
Let's approach our work with humility today. Always maintain a learning attitude.	Yes, I won't forget to maintain a humble learning attitude.

Cultural Context

Reflects the value of humility in Japanese culture. Used to promote respectful behavior and openness to learning.

常に顧客の立場に立って考えましょう。

つねにこきゃくのたちばにたってかんがえましょう。
Tsuneni kokyaku no tachiba ni tatte kangaemashou.
Let's always think from the customer's perspective.

Variation 1	Variation 2
絶えずお客様の視点から物事を捉えましょう。	Kyō mo shōjin shima shou.
たえずおきゃくさまのしてんからものごとをとらえましょう。	たえずおきゃくさまのしてんからものごとをとらえましょう。
Taezu okyakusama no shiten kara monogoto o torae ma shou.	Okyakusama no shiten o tsuneni ishiki shite kōdō shima shou.
Let's always think from the customer's perspective.	Let's always think from the customer's perspective.

Positive Response	Negative Response
お客様の視点を常に意識し、最適な解決策を提供します。	会社の利益も考えるべきです。
おきゃくさまのしてんをつねにいしき、さいてきなかいけつさくをていきょうします。	かいしゃのりえきもかんがえるべきです。
Okyakusama no shiten o tsuneni ishiki shi, saitekina kaiketsu-saku o teikyō shimasu.	Kaisha no rieki mo kangaerubekidesu.
I'll always consider the customer's perspective and provide optimal solutions.	We should also consider the company's profits.

Conversation example person A	Conversation example person B
新サービスの開発では、常に顧客の立場に立って考えましょう。	はい、顧客ニーズを最優先に考えます。
しんさーびすのかいはつでは、つねにこきゃくのたちばにたってかんがえましょう。	はい、こきゃくにーずをさいゆうせんにかんがえます。
Shin sābisu no kaihatsude wa, tsuneni kokyaku no tachiba ni tatte kangae ma shou.	Hai, kokyaku nīzu o sai yūsen ni kangaemasu.
When developing new services, let's always think from the customer's perspective.	Yes, I'll prioritize customer needs.

Cultural Context
Reflects Japan's customer-first business philosophy. Used in service-oriented industries to improve customer satisfaction.

今週も一週間気を引き締めて頑張りましょう。

こんしゅうもいっしゅうかんきをひきしめてがんばりましょう。

Konshū mo isshūkan ki o hikishimete ganbarimashou.

Let's stay focused and work hard this week as well.

Variation 1	Variation 2
今週も気を抜かず、全力で取り組みましょう。	Kyō mo shōjin shima shou.
こんしゅうもきをぬかず、ぜんりょくでとりくみましょう。	こんしゅうもきをぬかず、ぜんりょくでとりくみましょう。
Konshū mo ki o nukazu, zenryoku de torikumi ma shou.	Konshū mo kinchō-kan o jizoku sa sete gyōmu ni nozomi ma shou.
Let's stay focused and give our best effort this week as well.	Let's stay focused and work hard this week.

Positive Response	Negative Response
高い意識を持ち続け、最高の成果を出します。	毎週緊張していては疲れます。
たかいいしきをもちつづけ、さいこうのせいかをだします。	まいしゅうきんちょうしていてはつかれます。
Takai ishiki o mochi tsudzuke, saikō no seika o dashimasu.	Maishū kinchō shite ite wa tsukaremasu.
I'll maintain high awareness and produce the best results.	It's tiring to be tense every week.

Conversation example person A	Conversation example person B
今週も一週間気を引き締めて頑張りましょう。重要な案件が多いですね。	了解です。気を抜かずに取り組みます。
こんしゅうもいっしゅうかんきをひきしめてがんばりましょう。じゅうようなあんけんがおおいですね。	りょうかいです。きをぬかずにとりくみます。
Konshū mo ichi-shūkan ki o hikishimete ganbari ma shou. Jūyōna anken ga ōidesu ne.	Ryōkaidesu. Ki o nukazu ni torikumimasu.
Let's stay focused and do our best this week. We have many important projects.	Understood. I'll work diligently without letting my guard down.

Cultural Context

Encourages maintaining focus and dedication throughout the week. Used to promote consistent effort.

今日も一日感謝の気持ちを持って仕事をしましょう。

きょうもいちにちかんしゃのきもちをもってしごとをしましょう。
Kyōmoichinichi kanshanokimochi o motte shigoto o shimashou.
Let's work with a sense of gratitude today as well.

Variation 1	Variation 2
本日も感謝の心を忘れずに業務に励みましょう。	Kyō mo shōjin shima shou.
ほんじつもかんしゃのこころをわすれずにぎょうむにはげみましょう。	ほんじつもかんしゃのこころをわすれずにぎょうむにはげみましょう。
Honjitsu mo kansha no kokoro o wasurezu ni gyōmu ni hagemi ma shou.	Honjitsu mo shūi e no kansha o wasurezu ni gyōmu ni torikumi ma shou.
Let's work with a grateful attitude today.	Let's work with a sense of gratitude today.

Positive Response	Negative Response
感謝の心を忘れず、前向きに仕事に取り組みます。	感謝されるべきなのは私の方です。
かんしゃのこころをわすれず、まえむきにしごとにとりくみます。	かんしゃされるべきなのはわたしのほうです。
Kansha no kokoro o wasurezu, maemuki ni shigoto ni torikumimasu.	Kansha sa re rubekina no wa watashi no katadesu.
I'll work positively with a grateful heart.	I'm the one who should be thanked.

Conversation example person A	Conversation example person B
今日も一日感謝の気持ちを持って仕事をしましょう。周りの支えがあってこそです。	そうですね。感謝の気持ちを忘れずに頑張ります。
きょうもいちにちかんしゃのきもちをもってしごとをしましょう。まわりのささえがあってこそです。	そうですね。かんしゃのきもちをわすれずにがんばります。
Kyō mo ichi-nichi kansha no kimochi o motte shigoto o shima shou. Mawari no sasae ga atte kosodesu.	Sōdesu ne. Kansha no kimochi o wasurezu ni ganbarimasu.
Let's work with a sense of gratitude today. We're here thanks to the support of those around us.	You're right. I'll work hard, never forgetting to be grateful.

Cultural Context
Emphasizes the importance of gratitude in Japanese culture. Used to promote positive attitudes and relationships at work.

常に効果的なコミュニケーションを心がけましょう。

つねにこうかてきなこみゅにけーしょんをこころがけましょう。
Tsuneni kōkatekina komyunikēshon o kokorogakemashou.
Let's always strive for effective communication.

Variation 1	Variation 2
絶えず有効な意思疎通を意識しましょう。	Kyō mo shōjin shima shou.
たえずゆうこうないしそつうをいしきしましょう。	たえずゆうこうないしそつうをいしきしましょう。
Taezu yūkōna ishi sotsū o ishiki shima shou.	Enkatsuna ishi sotsū o tsuneni ishiki shima shou.
Let's always strive for effective communication.	Let's always strive for effective communication.

Positive Response	Negative Response
明確で効果的なコミュニケーションを実践します。	仕事が忙しくてそんな余裕はありません。
めいかくでこうかてきなこみゅにけーしょんをじっせんします。	しごとがいそがしくてそんなよゆうはありません。
Meikakude kōka-tekina komyunikēshon o jissen shimasu.	Shigoto ga isogashikute son'na yoyū wa arimasen.
I'll practice clear and effective communication.	I'm too busy with work to have time for that.

Conversation example person A	Conversation example person B
リモートワークが増えていますが、常に効果的なコミュニケーションを心がけましょう。	はい、密に情報共有を行っていきます。
りもーとわーくがふえていますが、つねにこうかてきなこみゅにけーしょんをこころがけましょう。	はい、みつにじょうほうきょうゆうをおこなっていきます。
Rimōto wāku ga fuete imasuga, tsuneni kōka-tekina komyunikēshon o kokorogake ma shou.	Hai, mitsu ni jōhō kyōyū o okonatte ikimasu.
As remote work increases, let's always strive for effective communication.	Yes, I'll make sure to share information closely.

Cultural Context
Addresses the need for clear communication in Japanese workplace hierarchy. Used to promote effective information sharing.

今日も一日笑顔を忘れずに頑張りましょう。

きょうもいちにちえがおをわすれずにがんばりましょう。

Kyōmoichinichi egao o wasurezu ni ganbarimashou.

Let's not forget to smile and work hard today as well.

Variation 1	Variation 2
本日も明るい表情を保って努力しましょう。	Kyō mo shōjin shima shou.
ほんじつもあかるいひょうじょうをたもってどりょくしましょう。	ほんじつもあかるいひょうじょうをたもってどりょくしましょう。
Honjitsu mo akarui hyōjō o tamotte doryoku shima shou.	Honjitsu mo akarui hyōjō de gyōmu ni nozomi ma shou.
Let's work hard with a smile on our face today.	Let's work with a smile throughout the day.

Positive Response	Negative Response
笑顔を絶やさず、前向きに仕事に取り組みます。	無理に笑顔を作るのは疲れます。
えがおをたやさず、まえむきにしごとにとりくみます。	むりにえがおをつくるのはつかれます。
Egao o tayasazu, maemuki ni shigoto ni torikumimasu.	Muri ni egao o tsukuru no wa tsukaremasu.
I'll work positively with a constant smile.	Forcing a smile is tiring.

Conversation example person A	Conversation example person B
今日も一日笑顔を忘れずに頑張りましょう。笑顔は最高のコミュニケーションツールです。	はい、明るい雰囲気作りを心がけます。
きょうもいちにちえがおをわすれずにがんばりましょう。えがおはさいこうのこみゅにけーしょんつーるです。	はい、あかるいふんいきづくりをこころがけます。
Kyō mo ichi-nichi egao o wasurezu ni ganbari ma shou. Egao wa saikō no komyunikēshon tsūrudesu.	Hai, akarui fun'iki-tsukuri o kokorogakemasu.
Let's not forget to smile as we do our best today. A smile is the best communication tool.	Yes, I'll make an effort to create a cheerful atmosphere.

Cultural Context

Emphasizes the importance of maintaining a positive demeanor. Often used in customer-facing roles.

チームの目標達成に向けて一丸となりましょう。

ちーむのもくひょうたっせいにむけていちがんとなりましょう。
Chīmu no mokuhyō tassei ni mukete ichigan to narimashou.
Let's unite as one towards achieving our team goals.

Variation 1	Variation 2
私たちの目標達成に向けて、力を合わせて頑張りましょう。	Kyō mo shōjin shima shou.
わたしたちのもくひょうたっせいにむけて、ちからをあわせてがんばりましょう。	わたしたちのもくひょうたっせいにむけて、ちからをあわせてがんばりましょう。
Watashi-tachi no mokuhyō tassei ni mukete,-ryoku o awasete ganbari ma shou.	Busho zentai de mokuteki kansui o mezashi ma shou.
Let's work together and do our best to achieve our organization's goals.	Let's unite as a team to achieve our goals.

Positive Response	Negative Response
チーム全員で力を合わせ、目標達成に邁進します。	個人の目標も大切にしたいです。
ちーむぜんいんでちからをあわせ、もくひょうたっせいにまいしんします。	こじんのもくひょうもたいせつにしたいです。
Chīmu zen'in de chikara o awase, mokuhyō tassei ni maishin shimasu.	Kojin no mokuhyō mo taisetsu ni shitaidesu.
We'll all work together as a team to achieve our goals.	I want to value my personal goals too.

Conversation example person A	Conversation example person B
四半期の終わりが近づいています。チームの目標達成に向けて一丸となりましょう。	承知しました。チーム一丸となって頑張ります。
しはんきのおわりがちかづいています。ちーむのもくひょうたっせいにむけていちがんとなりましょう。	しょうちしました。ちーむいちがんとなってがんばります。
Shihanki no owari ga chikadzuite imasu. Chīmu no mokuhyō tassei ni mukete ichigan to nari ma shou.	Shōchi shima shita. Chīmu ichigan to natte ganbarimasu.
The end of the quarter is approaching. Let's unite towards achieving our team goals.	Understood. I'll work hard as part of the united team.

Cultural Context
Reflects the importance of teamwork in Japanese culture. Used to encourage collective effort towards shared goals.

今日も一日創意工夫を心がけましょう。

きょうもいちにちそういくふうをこころがけましょう。
Kyōmoichinichi sōi kufū o kokorogakemashou.
Let's be creative and innovative today as well.

Variation 1	Variation 2
今日も新しい発想を生み出す努力をしましょう。	Kyō mo shōjin shima shou.
きょうもあたらしいはっそうをうみだすどりょくをしましょう。	きょうもあたらしいはっそうをうみだすどりょくをしましょう。
Kyō mo atarashī hassō o umidasu doryoku o shima shou.	Honjitsu mo kakushin-tekina aidea no sōshutsu o mezashi ma shou.
Let's strive to come up with fresh ideas today as well.	Let's be innovative and creative today.

Positive Response	Negative Response
常に創造的な解決策を探求します。	今のやり方で十分だと思います。
つねにそうぞうてきなかいけつさくをたんきゅうします。	いまのやりかたでじゅうぶんだとおもいます。
Tsuneni sōzō-tekina kaiketsu-saku o tankyū shimasu.	Ima no yarikata de jūbunda to omoimasu.
I'll always seek creative solutions.	I think our current methods are sufficient.

Conversation example person A	Conversation example person B
今日も一日創意工夫を心がけましょう。新しいアイデアが生産性を高めます。	はい、常に改善点を探していきます。
きょうもいちにちそういくふうをこころがけましょう。あたらしいあいであがせいさんせいをたかめます。	はい、つねにかいぜんてんをさがしていきます。
Kyō mo ichi-nichi sōi kufū o kokorogake ma shou. Atarashī aidea ga seisan-sei o takamemasu.	Hai, tsuneni kaizen-ten o sagashite ikimasu.
Let's be innovative today. New ideas increase productivity.	Yes, I'll always look for areas of improvement.

Cultural Context
Encourages innovation and problem-solving. Used to promote creative thinking in traditionally conservative work environments.

常に品質向上を意識しましょう。

つねにひんしつこうじょうをいしきしましょう。
Tsuneni hinshitsu kōjō o ishiki shimashou.
Let's always be conscious of improving quality.

Variation 1	Variation 2
常に仕事の質を高める工夫をしていきましょう。	Kyō mo shōjin shima shou.
つねにしごとのしつをたかめるくふうをしていきましょう。	つねにしごとのしつをたかめるくふうをしていきましょう。
Tsuneni shigoto no shitsu o takameru kufū o shite iki ma shou.	Keizoku-tekina hinshitsu kaizen o kokorogake ma shou.
Let's continuously think of ways to improve the quality of our work.	Let's always be conscious of improving quality.

Positive Response	Negative Response
品質の継続的な向上に取り組みます。	納期に間に合わなくなります。
ひんしつのけいぞくてきなこうじょうにとりくみます。	のうきにまにあわなくなります。
Hinshitsu no keizoku-tekina kōjō ni torikumimasu.	Nōki ni maniawanaku narimasu.
I'll work on continuous quality improvement.	We won't be able to meet the deadlines.

Conversation example person A	Conversation example person B
お客様からの評価が上がってきていますね。常に品質向上を意識しましょう。	そうですね。さらなる品質向上に努めます。
おきゃくさまからのひょうかがあがってきていますね。つねにひんしつこうじょうをいしきしましょう。	そうですね。さらなるひんしつこうじょうにつとめます。
Okyakusama kara no hyōka ga agatte kite imasu ne. Tsuneni hinshitsu kōjō o ishiki shima shou.	Sōdesu ne. Saranaru hinshitsu kōjō ni tsutomemasu.
Customer evaluations are improving. Let's always be conscious of improving quality.	You're right. I'll strive for even better quality.

Cultural Context
Reflects Japan's reputation for high-quality products and services. Used to encourage continuous improvement in all tasks.

今週も一週間時間管理を徹底しましょう。

こんしゅうもいっしゅうかんじかんかんりをてっていしましょう。
Konshū mo isshūkan jikan kanri o tettei shimashou.
Let's thoroughly manage our time this week as well.

Variation 1	Variation 2
今週も効率よく時間を使いましょう。	Kyō mo shōjin shima shou.
こんしゅうもこうりつよくじかんをつかいましょう。	こんしゅうもこうりつよくじかんをつかいましょう。
Konshū mo kōritsu yoku jikan o tsukai ma shou.	Konshū mo kōritsu-tekina jikan katsuyō o ishiki shima shou.
Let's use our time efficiently this week as well.	Let's manage our time effectively this week.

Positive Response	Negative Response
時間を効果的に活用し、生産性を最大化します。	突発的な仕事が多くて難しいです。
じかんをこうかてきにかつようし、せいさんせいをさいだいかします。	とっぱつてきなしごとがおおくてむずかしいです。
Jikan o kōka-teki ni katsuyō shi, seisan-sei o saidai-ka shimasu.	Toppatsu-tekina shigoto ga ōkute muzukashīdesu.
I'll use time effectively to maximize productivity.	It's difficult with so many unexpected tasks.

Conversation example person A	Conversation example person B
今週も一週間時間管理を徹底しましょう。効率的な仕事が成果につながります。	了解です。タイムマネジメントに気をつけます。
こんしゅうもいっしゅうかんじかんかんりをてっていしましょう。こうりつてきなしごとがせいかにつながります。	りょうかいです。たいむまねじめんとにきをつけます。
Konshū mo ichi-shūkan jikan kanri o tettei shima shou. Kōritsu-tekina shigoto ga seika ni tsunagarimasu.	Ryōkaidesu. Taimu manejimento ni ki o tsukemasu.
Let's thoroughly manage our time this week. Efficient work leads to results.	Understood. I'll be careful with time management.

Cultural Context

Reflects Japanese value of punctuality and efficiency. Used to promote effective use of work hours.

今日も一日前向きな姿勢で仕事に取り組みましょう。

きょうもいちにちまえむきなしせいでしごとにとりくみましょう。
Kyōmoichinichi maemukina shisei de shigoto ni torikumimashou.
Let's approach our work with a positive attitude today as well.

Variation 1	Variation 2
本日も積極的な態度で業務に臨みましょう。	Kyō mo shōjin shima shou.
ほんじつもせっきょくてきなたいどでぎょうむにのぞみましょう。	ほんじつもせっきょくてきなたいどでぎょうむにのぞみましょう。
Honjitsu mo sekkyoku-tekina taido de gyōmu ni nozomi ma shou.	Kyō mo maemukina shisei de shigoto ni torikumi ma shou.
Let's approach our work with a positive attitude today.	Let's approach our work with a positive attitude today.

Positive Response	Negative Response
前向きな態度で全ての課題に挑戦します。	現実を直視することも大切です。
まえむきなたいどですべてのかだいにちょうせんします。	げんじつをちょくしすることもたいせつです。
Maemukina taido de subete no kadai ni chōsen shimasu.	Genjitsu o chokushi suru koto mo taisetsudesu.
I'll tackle all challenges with a positive attitude.	It's also important to face reality.

Conversation example person A	Conversation example person B
今日も一日前向きな姿勢で仕事に取り組みましょう。ポジティブな態度が周りにも良い影響を与えます。	はい、前向きに取り組み、良い雰囲気を作ります。
きょうもいちにちまえむきなしせいでしごとにとりくみましょう。ぽじてぃぶなたいどがまわりにもよいえいきょうをあたえます。	はい、まえむきにとりくみ、よいふんいきをつくります。
Kyō mo ichi-nichi maemukina shisei de shigoto ni torikumi ma shou. Pojitibuna taido ga mawari ni mo yoi eikyō o ataemasu.	Hai, maemuki ni torikumi, yoi fun'iki o tsukurimasu.
Let's approach our work with a positive attitude today. A positive attitude has a good influence on those around us.	Yes, I'll work positively and create a good atmosphere.

Cultural Context
Encourages maintaining a positive attitude towards work. Used to promote resilience and motivation.

常に効率的な仕事の進め方を考えましょう。

つねにこうりつてきなしごとのすすめかたをかんがえましょう。

Tsuneni kōritsu-tekina shigoto no susumekata o kangaemashou.

Let's always think about efficient ways to proceed with our work.

Variation 1	Variation 2
絶えず生産性の高い業務方法を模索しましょう。	Kyō mo shōjin shima shou.
たえずせいさんせいのたかいぎょうむほうほうをもさくしましょう。	たえずせいさんせいのたかいぎょうむほうほうをもさくしましょう。
Taezu seisan-sei no takai gyōmu hōhō o mosaku shima shou.	Gyōmu kōritsu no kōjō o tsuneni ishiki shima shou.
Let's always think about efficient ways of working.	Let's always think about efficient ways of working.

Positive Response	Negative Response
常により効率的な方法を追求し、実践します。	質も大切だと思います。
つねにようこうりつてきなほうほうをついきゅうし、じっせんします。	しつもたいせつだとおもいます。
Tsune ni yori kōritsu-tekina hōhō o tsuikyū shi, jissen shimasu.	Shitsu mo taisetsuda to omoimasu.
I'll always pursue and implement more efficient methods.	I think quality is important too.

Conversation example person A	Conversation example person B
業務量が増えていますね。常に効率的な仕事の進め方を考えましょう。	そうですね。作業の無駄を省いていきます。
ぎょうむりょうがふえていますね。つねにこうりつてきなしごとのすすめかたをかんがえましょう。	そうですね。さぎょうのむだをはぶいていきます。
Gyōmu-ryō ga fuete imasu ne. Tsuneni kōritsu-tekina shigoto no susumekata o kangae ma shou.	Sōdesu ne. Sagyō no muda o shō ite ikimasu.
Our workload is increasing. Let's always think about efficient ways of working.	You're right. I'll work on eliminating waste in our operations.

Cultural Context

Emphasizes the value of efficiency in Japanese work culture. Used to encourage innovative and productive work methods.

今日も一日ベストを尽くしましょう。

きょうもいちにちべすとをつくしましょう。
Kyōmoichinichi besuto o tsukushimashou.
Let's do our best today as well.

Variation 1	Variation 2
本日も最善の努力を払いましょう。	Kyō mo shōjin shima shou.
ほんじつもさいぜんのどりょくをはらいましょう。	ほんじつもさいぜんのどりょくをはらいましょう。
Honjitsu mo saizen no doryoku o harai ma shou.	Kyō mo besuto o tsukushi ma shou.
Let's do our best today.	Let's give our best effort today.

Positive Response	Negative Response
全力を尽くし、最高の結果を出します。	毎日100%の力を出すのは無理です。
ぜんりょくをつくし、さいこうのけっかをだします。	まいにちひゃくぱーせんとのちからをだすのはむりです。
Zenryoku o tsukushi, saikō no kekka o dashimasu.	Mainichi hyaku pāsento no chikara o dasu no wa muridesu.
I'll give my all to produce the best results.	It's impossible to give 100% every day.

Conversation example person A	Conversation example person B
今日も一日ベストを尽くしましょう。一日一日の積み重ねが大切です。	はい、今日も全力で取り組みます。
きょうもいちにちべすとをつくしましょう。いちにちいちにちのつみかさねがたいせつです。	はい、きょうもぜんりょくでとりくみます。
Kyō mo ichi-nichi besuto o tsukushi ma shou. Ichi-nichi ichi-nichi no tsumikasane ga taisetsudesu.	Hai, kyō mo zenryoku de torikumimasu.
Let's give our best today. Each day's effort accumulates and is important.	Yes, I'll give it my all today too.

Cultural Context

Reflects Japanese work ethic of giving one's all. Used to encourage maximum effort in daily tasks.

常に新しい課題に挑戦する姿勢を持ちましょう。

つねにあたらしいかだいにちょうせんするしせいをもちましょう。
Tsuneni atarashī kadai ni chōsen suru shisei o mochimashou.
Let's always maintain an attitude of taking on new challenges.

Variation 1	Variation 2
新たな課題に対して前向きに取り組む姿勢を維持しましょう。	Kyō mo shōjin shima shou.
あらたなかだいにたいしてまえむきにとりくむしせいをいじしましょう。	あらたなかだいにたいしてまえむきにとりくむしせいをいじしましょう。
Aratana kadai ni taishite maemuki ni torikumu shisei o iji shima shou.	Keizoku-tekina jiko seichō o mezashi ma shou.
Let's maintain a positive attitude towards tackling new issues.	Let's always maintain an attitude of taking on new challenges.

Positive Response	Negative Response
新しい課題を成長の機会として積極的に取り組みます。	失敗するリスクが高すぎます。
あたらしいかだいをせいちょうのきかいとしてせっきょくてきにとりくみます。	しっぱいするりすくがたかすぎます。
Atarashī kadai o seichō no kikai to shite sekkyoku-teki ni torikumimasu.	Shippai suru risuku ga taka sugimasu.
I'll actively tackle new challenges as opportunities for growth.	The risk of failure is too high.

Conversation example person A	Conversation example person B
業界の変化が激しいですね。常に新しい課題に挑戦する姿勢を持ちましょう。	承知しました。積極的に新しいことに取り組みます。
ぎょうかいのへんかがはげしいですね。つねにあたらしいかだいにちょうせんするしせいをもちましょう。	しょうちしました。せっきょくてきにあたらしいことにとりくみます。
Gyōkai no henka ga hageshīdesu ne. Tsuneni atarashī kadai ni chōsen suru shisei o mochi ma shou.	Shōchi shima shita. Sekkyoku-teki ni atarashī koto ni torikumimasu.
Our industry is changing rapidly. Let's always maintain an attitude of taking on new challenges.	Understood. I'll actively take on new challenges.

Cultural Context
Encourages proactive problem-solving and personal growth. Used to promote a dynamic and adaptive work environment.

今週も一週間、仕事の質にこだわりましょう。

こんしゅうもいっしゅうかん、しごとのしつにこだわりましょう。

Konshū mo isshūkan, shigoto no shitsu ni kodawarimashou.

Let's focus on the quality of our work this week as well.

Variation 1	Variation 2
今週一週間、仕事の効率と質の向上に力を入れていきましょう。	Kyō mo shōjin shima shou.
こんしゅういっしゅうかん、しごとのこうりつとしつのこうじょうにちからをいれていきましょう。	こんしゅういっしゅうかん、しごとのこうりつとしつのこうじょうにちからをいれていきましょう。
Konshū ichi-shūkan, shigoto no kōritsu to shitsu no kōjō ni chikara o irete iki ma shou.	Konshū mo kō hinshitsuna seika-mono no teikyō o kokorogake ma shou.
This week, let's focus on improving both the efficiency and quality of our work.	Let's focus on the quality of our work this week.

Positive Response	Negative Response
高品質の仕事を consistently 提供し続けます。	納期に間に合わなくなります。
こうひんしつのしごとをこんしすてんとりーていきょうしつづけます。	のうきにまにあわなくなります。
Kō hinshitsu no shigoto o consistently teikyō shi tsudzukemasu.	Nōki ni maniawanaku narimasu.
I'll consistently deliver high-quality work.	We won't be able to meet the deadlines.

Conversation example person A	Conversation example person B
今週も一週間、仕事の質にこだわりましょう。質の高い仕事が信頼につながります。	はい、常に最高品質を目指して頑張ります。
こんしゅうもいっしゅうかん、しごとのしつにこだわりましょう。しつのたかいしごとがしんらいにつながります。	はい、つねにさいこうひんしつをめざしてがんばります。
Konshū mo ichi-shūkan, shigoto no shitsu ni kodawari ma shou. Shitsu no takai shigoto ga shinrai ni tsunagarimasu.	Hai, tsuneni saikō hinshitsu o mezashite ganbarimasu.
Let's focus on the quality of our work this week. High-quality work leads to trust.	Yes, I'll always strive for the highest quality.

Cultural Context

Reflects Japanese emphasis on quality and attention to detail. Used to encourage maintaining high standards throughout the week.

今日も一日、細心の注意を払って仕事をしましょう。

きょうもいちにち、さいしんのちゅういをはらってしごとをしましょう。

Kyōmoichinichi, saishin no chūi o haratte shigoto o shimashou.

Let's work with utmost care and attention today as well.

Variation 1	Variation 2
本日も慎重な態度で業務に取り組みましょう。	Kyō mo shōjin shima shou.
ほんじつもしんちょうなたいどでぎょうむにとりくみましょう。	ほんじつもしんちょうなたいどでぎょうむにとりくみましょう。
Honjitsu mo shinchōna taido de gyōmu ni torikumi ma shou.	Honjitsu mo shinchō ni gyōmu o suikō shima shou.
Let's pay close attention to detail in our work today.	Let's carry out our work with utmost care today.

Positive Response	Negative Response
細部まで注意を払い、正確な仕事をします。	そんなに慎重になると仕事が進みません。
さいぶまでちゅういをはらい、せいかくなしごとをします。	そんなにしんちょうになるとしごとがすすみません。
Saibu made chūi o harai, seikakuna shigoto o shimasu.	Son'nani shinchō ni naru to shigoto ga susumimasen.
I'll pay attention to details for accurate work.	Being that cautious will slow down our work.

Conversation example person A	Conversation example person B
今日も一日、細心の注意を払って仕事をしましょう。小さなミスが大きな問題につながることもあります。	了解です。慎重に作業を進めていきます。
きょうもいちにち、さいしんのちゅういをはらってしごとをしましょう。ちいさなみすがおおきなもんだいにつながることもあります。	りょうかいです。しんちょうにさぎょうをすすめていきます。
Kyō mo ichi-nichi, soshin no chūi o haratte shigoto o shima shou. Chīsana misu ga ōkina mondai ni tsunagaru koto mo arimasu.	Ryōkaidesu. Shinchō ni sagyō o susumete ikimasu.
Let's work with utmost care today. Small mistakes can lead to big problems.	Understood. I'll proceed with work carefully.

Cultural Context

Emphasizes meticulous attention to detail in Japanese work culture. Used to promote careful and thorough work practices.

常に自己啓発の意識を持ちましょう。

つねにじこけいはつのいしきをもちましょう。
Tsuneni jiko keihatsu no ishiki o mochimashou.
Let's always maintain a mindset of self-improvement.

Variation 1	Variation 2
絶えず自己成長の姿勢を維持しましょう。	Kyō mo shōjin shima shou.
たえずじこせいちょうのしせいをいじしましょう。	たえずじこせいちょうのしせいをいじしましょう。
Taezu jiko seichō no shisei o iji shima shou.	Keizoku-tekina jiko seichō o kokorogake ma shou.
Let's always have the mindset of self-improvement.	Let's always be conscious of self-improvement.

Positive Response	Negative Response
はい、積極的に学び続けます。	仕事以外の時間まで使いたくありません。
はい、せっきょくてきにまなびつづけます。	しごといがいのじかんまでつかいたくありません。
Hai, sekkyoku-teki ni manabi tsudzukemasu.	Shigoto igai no jikan made tsukaitaku arimasen.
Yes, I'll continue to learn proactively.	I don't want to use my time outside of work for that.

Conversation example person A	Conversation example person B
業界の動向が変化していますね。常に自己啓発の意識を持ちましょう。	はい、積極的に新しい知識を吸収していきます。
ぎょうかいのどうこうがへんかしていますね。つねにじこけいはつのいしきをもちましょう。	はい、せっきょくてきにあたらしいちしきをきゅうしゅうしていきます。
Gyōkai no dōkō ga henka shite imasu ne. Tsuneni jiko keihatsu no ishiki o mochi ma shou.	Hai, sekkyoku-teki ni atarashī chishiki o kyūshū shite ikimasu.
The industry trends are changing. Let's always have a mindset of self-improvement.	Yes, I'll actively absorb new knowledge.

Cultural Context

Reflects Japanese value of continuous self-improvement. Used to encourage ongoing personal and professional development.

今日も一日、チームの和を大切にしましょう。

きょうもいちにち、ちーむのわをたいせつにしましょう。
Kyōmoichinichi, chīmu no wa o taisetsu ni shimashou.
Let's value team harmony today as well.

Variation 1	Variation 2
本日も、団結を重視しましょう。	Kyō mo shōjin shima shou.
ほんじつも、だんけつをじゅうししましょう。	ほんじつも、だんけつをじゅうししましょう。
Honjitsu mo, danketsu o jūshi shima shou.	Honjitsu mo busho no danketsu o jūshi shima shou.
Let's prioritize team unity today as well.	Let's value team harmony today as well.

Positive Response	Negative Response
もちろん、協力して頑張りましょう。	個人の能力も重要だと思います。
もちろん、きょうりょくしてがんばりましょう。	こじんののうりょくもじゅうようだとおもいます。
Mochiron, kyōryoku shite ganbari ma shou.	Kojin no nōryoku mo jūyōda to omoimasu.
Of course, let's work together and do our best.	I think individual abilities are important too.

Conversation example person A	Conversation example person B
今日も一日、チームの和を大切にしましょう。良好な人間関係が仕事の質を高めます。	そうですね。協力し合える雰囲気づくりを心がけます。
きょうもいちにち、ちーむのわをたいせつにしましょう。りょうこうなにんげんかんけいがしごとのしつをたかめます。	そうですね。きょうりょくしあえるふんいきづくりをこころがけます。
Kyō mo ichi-nichi, chīmu no wa o taisetsu ni shima shou. Ryōkōna ningen kankei ga shigoto no shitsu o takamemasu.	Sōdesu ne. Kyōryoku shi aeru fun'iki-dzukuri o kokorogakemasu.
Let's value team harmony today. Good relationships improve the quality of our work.	You're right. I'll work on creating an atmosphere of cooperation.

Cultural Context
Emphasizes the importance of harmony in Japanese group-oriented culture. Used to promote positive team dynamics and cooperation.

今週も一週間、目標達成に向けて全力を尽くしましょう。

こんしゅうもいっしゅうかん、もくひょうたっせいにむけてぜんりょくをつくしましょう。
Konshū mo isshūkan, mokuhyō tassei ni mukete zenryoku o tsukushimashou.
Let's give our all towards achieving our goals this week as well.

Variation 1	Variation 2
今週も目的完遂に邁進しましょう。	Kyō mo shōjin shima shou.
こんしゅうももくてきかんすいにまいしんしましょう。	こんしゅうももくてきかんすいにまいしんしましょう。
Konshū mo mokuteki kansui ni maishin shima shou.	Konshū mo mokuhyō kansui ni mukete saizen o tsukushi ma shou.
Let's give our all towards achieving our goals this week too.	Let's give our all towards achieving our goals this week.

Positive Response	Negative Response
承知しました。全力で取り組みます。	モチベーションが上がりません。
しょうちしました。ぜんりょくでとりくみます。	もちべーしょんがあがりません。
Shōchi shima shita. Zenryoku de torikumimasu.	Mochibēshon ga agarimasen.
Understood. I'll give it my all.	I'm not feeling motivated.

Conversation example person A	Conversation example person B
今週も一週間、目標達成に向けて全力を尽くしましょう。	はい、チーム一丸となって頑張ります。
こんしゅうもいっしゅうかん、もくひょうたっせいにむけてぜんりょくをつくしましょう。	はい、ちーむいちがんとなってがんばります。
Konshū mo ichi-shūkan, mokuhyō tassei ni mukete zenryoku o tsukushi ma shou.	Hai, chīmu ichigan to natte ganbarimasu.
Let's give our all this week to achieve our goals.	Yes, we'll work hard as a united team.

Cultural Context

Reflects Japanese work ethic of giving one's all towards goals. Used to encourage sustained effort throughout the week.

議事を始めましょう。

ぎじをはじめましょう。
Giji o hajimemashou.
Let's start the meeting.

Variation 1	Variation 2
会議を開始しましょう。	Kyō mo shōjin shima shou.
かいぎをかいしましょう。	かいぎをかいしましょう。
Kaigi o kaishi shima shou.	Honjitsu mo kakushin-tekina aidea o tsuikyū shima shou.
Let's start the meeting.	Let's strive for innovative ideas today.

Positive Response	Negative Response
はい、効率的に進めましょう。	準備ができていません。
はい、こうりつてきにすすめましょう。	じゅんびができていません。
Hai, kōritsu-teki ni susume ma shou.	Junbi ga dekite imasen.
Yes, let's proceed efficiently.	I'm not prepared yet.

Conversation example person A	Conversation example person B
皆さんお揃いですね。議事を始めましょう。	了解しました。準備はできています。
みなさんおそろいですね。ぎじをはじめましょう。	りょうかいしました。じゅんびはできています。
Minasan osoroide sune. Giji o hajime ma shou.	Ryōkai shima shita. Junbi wa dekite imasu.
Everyone's here. Let's start the meeting.	Understood. We're ready to begin.

Cultural Context
Ensure all participants are mentally prepared and focused before starting.

本日の議題は以下の通りです。

ほんじつのぎだいはいかのとおり です。

Honjitsu no gidai wa ikanotōridesu.

Today's agenda is as follows.

Variation 1	Variation 2
今回の協議事項は次の通りです。	Kyō mo shōjin shima shou.
こんかいのきょうぎじこうはつぎのとおり です。	こんかいのきょうぎじこうはつぎのとおり です。
Konkai no kyōgi jikō wa tsugi no tōridesu.	Keizoku-tekina hinshitsu kaizen o kokorogake ma shou.
Today's agenda items are as follows.	Let's always be conscious of improving quality.

Positive Response	Negative Response
了解しました。集中して取り組みます。	追加の議題があります。
りょうかいしました。しゅうちゅうしてとりくみます。	ついかのぎだいがあります。
Ryōkai shima shita. Shūchū shite torikumimasu.	Tsuika no gidai ga arimasu.
Understood. I'll focus on these topics.	I have additional topics to discuss.

Conversation example person A	Conversation example person B
本日の議題は以下の通りです。	承知しました。議題を確認しました。
ほんじつのぎだいはいかのとおり です。	しょうちしました。ぎだいをかくにんしました。
Honjitsu no gidai wa ika no tōridesu.	Shōchi shima shita. Gidai o kakunin shima shita.
Today's agenda is as follows.	Understood. I've confirmed the agenda.

Cultural Context

Confirm that all agenda items are relevant and achievable within the meeting time.

前回の議事録を確認しましょう。

ぜんかいのぎじろくをかくにんしましょう。

Zenkai no gijiroku o kakunin shimashou.

Let's review the minutes from the last meeting.

Variation 1	Variation 2
先日の会議記録を検証しましょう。	Kyō mo shōjin shima shou.
せんじつのかいぎきろくをけんしょうしましょう。	せんじつのかいぎきろくをけんしょうしましょう。
Senjitsu no kaigi kiroku o kenshō shima shou.	Konshū mo kōritsu-tekina jikan katsuyō o ishiki shima shou.
Let's review the minutes from the last meeting.	Let's thoroughly manage our time this week.

Positive Response	Negative Response
はい、しっかり確認します。	議事録に誤りがあります。
はい、しっかりかくにんします。	ぎじろくにあやまりがあります。
Hai, shikkari kakunin shimasu.	Giji-roku ni ayamari ga arimasu.
Yes, I'll review it thoroughly.	There are errors in the minutes.

Conversation example person A	Conversation example person B
まず、前回の議事録を確認しましょう。	はい、前回の決定事項を再確認します。
まず、ぜんかいのぎじろくをかくにんしましょう。	はい、ぜんかいのけっていじこうをさいかくにんします。
Mazu, zenkai no giji-roku o kakunin shima shou.	Hai, zenkai no kettei jikō o sai kakunin shimasu.
First, let's review the minutes from the last meeting.	Yes, let's reconfirm the decisions made in the previous meeting.

Cultural Context

Be prepared to address any unresolved issues from the previous meeting.

進捗状況を報告してください。

しんちょくじょうきょうをほうこくしてください。

Shinchoku jōkyō o hōkoku shite kudasai.

Please report on the progress.

Variation 1	Variation 2
現在の進展具合をお知らせください。	Kyō mo shōjin shima shou.
げんざいのしんてんぐあいをおしらせください。	げんざいのしんてんぐあいをおしらせください。
Genzai no shinten guai o oshirase kudasai.	Honjitsu mo sekkyoku-tekina taido de gyōmu ni nozomi ma shou.
Please report on the current progress.	Let's approach our work with a positive attitude today.

Positive Response	Negative Response
はい、詳細にご報告いたします。	進展がありません。
はい、しょうさいにごほうこくいたします。	しんてんがありません。
Hai, shōsai ni go hōkoku itashimasu.	Shinten ga arimasen.
Yes, I'll report in detail.	There's been no progress.

Conversation example person A	Conversation example person B
では、各部署の進捗状況を報告してください。	承知しました。先週の活動内容をまとめました。
では、かくぶしょのしんちょくじょうきょうをほうこくしてください。	しょうちしました。せんしゅうのかつどうないようをまとめました。
Dewa, kaku busho no shinchoku jōkyō o hōkoku shite kudasai.	Shōchi shima shita. Senshū no katsudō naiyō o matomemashita.
Now, please report on the progress of each department.	Understood. I've summarized last week's activities.

Cultural Context
Encourage concise reporting to avoid lengthy, unfocused updates.

重要なポイントをまとめます。

じゅうようなぽいんとをまとめます。

Jūyōna pointo o matomemasu.

I'll summarize the key points.

Variation 1	Variation 2
核心的な事項を集約します。	Kyō mo shōjin shima shou.
かくしんてきなじこうをしゅうやくします。	かくしんてきなじこうをしゅうやくします。
Kakushin-tekina jikō o shūyaku shimasu.	Gyōmu no seisan-sei kōjō o tsuneni tsuikyū shima shou.
I'll summarize the key points.	Let's always think about efficient ways to work.

Positive Response	Negative Response
ありがとうございます。注意深く聞きます。	重要な点が抜けています。
ありがとうございます。ちゅういぶかくききます。	じゅうようなてんがぬけています。
Arigatōgozaimasu. Chūibukaku kikimasu.	Jūyōna ten ga nukete imasu.
Thank you. I'll listen carefully.	You're missing some crucial points.

Conversation example person A	Conversation example person B
ありがとうございます。重要なポイントをまとめます。	はい、お願いします。
ありがとうございます。じゅうようなぽいんとをまとめます。	はい、おねがいします。
Arigatōgozaimasu. Jūyōna pointo o matomemasu.	Hai, onegai shimasu.
Thank you. I'll summarize the key points.	Yes, please do.

Cultural Context

Ensure key points are clearly understood and agreed upon by all participants.

質問はありますか？

しつもんはありますか？
Shitsumon wa arimasu ka?
Are there any questions?

Variation 1	Variation 2
何か疑問点はございますか？	Kyō mo shōjin shima shou.
なにかぎもんてんはございますか？	なにかぎもんてんはございますか？
Nani ka gimon-ten wagozaimasu ka?	Honjitsu mo saizen no doryoku o harai ma shou.
Do you have any questions?	Let's give our best effort today.

Positive Response	Negative Response
はい、いくつか確認したい点があります。	質問が多すぎて時間が足りません。
はい、いくつかかくにんしたいてんがあります。	しつもんがおおすぎてじかんがたりません。
Hai, ikutsu ka kakunin shitai ten ga arimasu.	Shitsumon ga ō sugite jikan ga tarimasen.
Yes, I have a few points I'd like to clarify.	There are too many questions and not enough time.

Conversation example person A	Conversation example person B
以上が要点ですが、質問はありますか？	はい、予算に関して確認したい点があります。
いじょうがようてんですが、しつもんはありますか？	はい、よさんにかんしてかくにんしたいてんがあります。
Ijō ga yōtendesuga, shitsumon wa arimasu ka?	Hai, yosan ni kanshite kakunin shitai ten ga arimasu.
That covers the main points. Are there any questions?	Yes, I have a question regarding the budget.

Cultural Context
Create an environment where participants feel comfortable asking questions.

意見を聞かせてください。

いけんをきかせてください。

Iken o kika sete kudasai.

Please share your opinions.

Variation 1	Variation 2
ご見解をお聞かせください。	Kyō mo shōjin shima shou.
ごけんかいをおきかせください。	ごけんかいをおきかせください。
Go kenkai o o kikase kudasai.	Taezu aratana chōsen o motomeru taido o iji shima shou.
Please share your opinions.	Let's always maintain an attitude of taking on new challenges.

Positive Response	Negative Response
はい、私の考えを共有させていただきます。	意見を言うのは控えます。
はい、わたしのかんがえをきょうゆうさせていただきます。	いけんをいうのはひかえます。
Hai, watashi no kangae o kyōyū sa sete itadakimasu.	Iken o iu no wa hikaemasu.
Yes, I'll share my thoughts.	I'd rather not share my opinion.

Conversation example person A	Conversation example person B
この提案について、皆さんの意見を聞かせてください。	私は賛成です。効率的だと思います。
このていあんについて、みなさんのいけんをきかせてください。	わたしはさんせいです。こうりつてきだとおもいます。
Kono teian ni tsuite, minasan no iken o kika sete kudasai.	Watashi wa sanseidesu. Kōritsu-tekida to omoimasu.
Please share your thoughts on this proposal.	I agree. I think it's efficient.

Cultural Context

Encourage diverse perspectives and avoid domination by a few voices.

次のステップについて話し合いましょう。

つぎのすてっぷについてはなしあいましょう。

Tsugi no suteppu ni tsuite hanashiaimashou.

Let's discuss the next steps.

Variation 1	Variation 2
今後の展開について協議しましょう。	Kyō mo shōjin shima shou.
こんごのてんかいについてきょうぎしましょう。	こんごのてんかいについてきょうぎしましょう。
Kongo no tenkai ni tsuite kyōgi shima shou.	Konshū mo kō hinshitsuna seika-mono o tsuikyū shima shou.
Let's discuss the next steps.	Let's focus on the quality of our work this week.

Positive Response	Negative Response
はい、具体的な行動計画を立てましょう。	現状の問題を解決してからにしましょう。
はい、ぐたいてきなこうどうけいかくをたてましょう。	げんじょうのもんだいをかいけつしてからにしましょう。
Hai, gutai-tekina kōdō keikaku o tate ma shou.	Genjō no mondai o kaiketsu shite kara ni shima shou.
Yes, let's create a specific action plan.	Let's solve current issues before moving on.

Conversation example person A	Conversation example person B
では、次のステップについて話し合いましょう。	はい、具体的な行動計画を立てる必要がありますね。
では、つぎのすてっぷについてはなしあいましょう。	はい、ぐたいてきなこうどうけいかくをたてるひつようがありますね。
Dewa, tsugi no suteppu ni tsuite hanashiai ma shou.	Hai, gutai-tekina kōdō keikaku o tateru hitsuyō ga arimasu ne.
Now, let's discuss the next steps.	Yes, we need to create a specific action plan.

Cultural Context

Ensure that action items and responsibilities are clearly defined.

この件について決定を下す必要があります。

このけんについてけっていをくだすひつようがあります。

Kono-ken ni tsuite kettei o kudasu hitsuyō ga arimasu.

We need to make a decision on this matter.

Variation 1	Variation 2
この案件に関して結論を出す必要があります。	Kyō mo shōjin shima shou.
このあんけんにかんしてけつろんをだすひつようがあります。	このあんけんにかんしてけつろんをだすひつようがあります。
Kono anken ni kanshite ketsuron o dasu hitsuyō ga arimasu.	Kono anken ni tsuite ketsuron o deshi ma shou.
We need to make a decision on this matter.	Let's reach a conclusion on this matter.

Positive Response	Negative Response
承知しました。最善の決定ができるよう努めます。	もっと情報が必要です。
しょうちしました。さいぜんのけっていができるようつとめます。	もっとじょうほうがひつようです。
Shōchi shima shita. Saizen no kettei ga dekiru yō tsutomemasu.	Motto jōhō ga hitsuyōdesu.
Understood. I'll strive to make the best decision.	We need more information before deciding.

Conversation example person A	Conversation example person B
この件について決定を下す必要があります。時間内に結論を出しましょう。	同意します。全ての情報を考慮して決めましょう。
このけんについてけっていをくだすひつようがあります。じかんないにけつろんをだしましょう。	どういします。すべてのじょうほうをこうりょしてきめましょう。
Kono-ken ni tsuite kettei o kudasu hitsuyō ga arimasu. Jikan uchi ni ketsuron o dashi ma shou.	Dōi shimasu. Subete no jōhō o kōryo shite kime ma shou.
We need to make a decision on this matter. Let's reach a conclusion within the time limit.	I agree. Let's consider all the information before deciding.

Cultural Context
Be prepared with all necessary information to make an informed decision.

タイムラインを設定しましょう。

たいむらいんをせっていしましょう。
Taimu rain o settei shimashou.
Let's set a timeline.

Variation 1	Variation 2
期限を定めましょう。	Kyō mo shōjin shima shou.
きげんをさだめましょう。	きげんをさだめましょう。
Kigen o sadame ma shou.	Sukejūru o kumi ma shou.
Let's set a timeline.	Let's set up a schedule.

Positive Response	Negative Response
はい、現実的で達成可能なスケジュールを立てましょう。	スケジュールが厳しすぎます。
はい、げんじつてきでたっせいかのうなすけじゅーるをたてましょう。	すけじゅーるがきびしすぎます。
Hai, genjitsu-tekide tassei kanōna sukejūru o tate ma shou.	Sukejūru ga kibishi sugimasu.
Yes, let's set a realistic and achievable schedule.	The timeline is too tight.

Conversation example person A	Conversation example person B
プロジェクトのタイムラインを設定しましょう。	了解です。マイルストーンも決めましょう。
ぷろじぇくとのたいむらいんをせっていしましょう。	りょうかいです。まいるすとーんもきめましょう。
Purojekuto no taimu rain o settei shima shou.	Ryōkaidesu. Mairu sutōn mo kime ma shou.
Let's set a timeline for the project.	Understood. Let's also decide on the milestones.

Cultural Context
Consider potential obstacles and allow for some flexibility in the timeline.

責任者を決めましょう。

せきにんしゃをきめましょう。
Sekininsha o kimemashou.
Let's assign responsibilities.

Variation 1	Variation 2
担当者を指名しましょう。	Kyō mo shōjin shima shou.
たんとうしゃをしめいしましょう。	たんとうしゃをしめいしましょう。
Tantō-sha o shimei shima shou.	Tantō-sha o sen bima shou.
Let's designate a person in charge.	Let's assign a person in charge.

Positive Response	Negative Response
はい、適任者を選びましょう。	誰も引き受けたがらないでしょう。
はい、てきにんしゃをえらびましょう。	だれもひきうけたがらないでしょう。
Hai, tekinin-sha o sen bima shou.	Dare mo hikiuketa garanaide shou.
Yes, let's choose the right person for the job.	No one will want to take responsibility.

Conversation example person A	Conversation example person B
各タスクの責任者を決めましょう。	はい、適材適所で割り当てましょう。
かくたすくのせきにんしゃをきめましょう。	はい、てきざいてきしょでわりあてましょう。
Kaku tasuku no sekinin-sha o kime ma shou.	Hai, tekizai tekisho de wariate ma shou.
Let's assign responsible persons for each task.	Yes, let's assign tasks based on each person's strengths.

Cultural Context
Ensure the chosen person has the necessary authority and resources.

予算について検討する必要があります。

よさんについてけんとうするひつようがあります。

Yosan ni tsuite kentō suru hitsuyō ga arimasu.

We need to consider the budget.

Variation 1	Variation 2
資金配分を熟考する必要があります。	Kyō mo shōjin shima shou.
しきんはいぶんをじゅくこうするひつようがあります。	しきんはいぶんをじゅくこうするひつようがあります。
Shikin haibun o jukukō suru hitsuyō ga arimasu.	Hiyō no mitsumori o shima shou.
We need to consider the budget.	Let's estimate the costs.

Positive Response	Negative Response
はい、コスト効率の良い方法を探りましょう。	予算が足りません。
はい、こすとこうりつのよいほうほうをさぐりましょう。	よさんがたりません。
Hai, kosuto kōritsu no yoi hōhō o saguri ma shou.	Yosan ga tarimasen.
Yes, let's explore cost-effective methods.	The budget is insufficient.

Conversation example person A	Conversation example person B
次に、予算について検討する必要があります。	そうですね。コスト削減の可能性も探りましょう。
つぎに、よさんについてけんとうするひつようがあります。	そうですね。こすとさくげんのかのうせいもさぐりましょう。
Tsugi ni, yosan ni tsuite kentō suru hitsuyō ga arimasu.	Sōdesu ne. Kosuto sakugen no kanō-sei mo saguri ma shou.
Next, we need to discuss the budget.	You're right. Let's also explore possibilities for cost reduction.

Cultural Context

Have detailed financial information available for discussion.

リスクを評価しましょう。

りすくをひょうかしましょう。
Risuku o hyōka shimashou.
Let's assess the risks.

Variation 1	Variation 2
危険性を査定しましょう。	Kyō mo shōjin shima shou.
きけんせいをさていしましょう。	きけんせいをさていしましょう。
Kiken-sei o satei shima shou.	Kiken-sei o kakunin shima shou.
Let's assess the risks.	Let's assess the risks.

Positive Response	Negative Response
承知しました。慎重に分析します。	リスクが高すぎます。
しょうちしました。しんちょうにぶんせきします。	りすくがたかすぎます。
Shōchi shima shita. Shinchō ni bunseki shimasu.	Risuku ga taka sugimasu.
Understood. I'll analyze carefully.	The risks are too high.

Conversation example person A	Conversation example person B
このプロジェクトのリスクを評価しましょう。	承知しました。リスク管理計画も立てる必要がありますね。
このぷろじぇくとのりすくをひょうかしましょう。	しょうちしました。りすくかんりけいかくもたてるひつようがありますね。
Kono purojekuto no risuku o hyōka shima shou.	Shōchi shima shita. Risuku kanri keikaku mo tateru hitsuyō ga arimasu ne.
Let's assess the risks of this project.	Understood. We should also create a risk management plan.

Cultural Context
Consider both short-term and long-term risks, not just immediate ones.

代替案を提案してください。

だいたいあんをていあんしてください。

Daitaian o teian shite kudasai.

Please propose alternative solutions.

Variation 1	Variation 2
別の選択肢を提示してください。	Kyō mo shōjin shima shou.
べつのせんたくしをていじしてください。	べつのせんたくしをていじしてください。
Betsu no sentakushi o teiji shite kudasai.	Hoka no sentakushi o dashite kudasai.
Please propose alternative options.	Please suggest alternative options.

Positive Response	Negative Response
はい、いくつかの選択肢を用意しました。	良い案が思いつきません。
はい、いくつかのせんたくしをよういしました。	よいあんがおもいつきません。
Hai, ikutsu ka no sentakushi o yōi shima shita.	Yoi an ga omoitsukimasen.
Yes, I've prepared several options.	I can't think of any good alternatives.

Conversation example person A	Conversation example person B
もし現在の計画が実行できない場合の代替案を提案してください。	はい、バックアッププランを２つ用意しました。
もしげんざいのけいかくがじっこうできないばあいのだいたいあんをていあんしてください。	はい、ばっくあっぷぷらんをふたつよういしました。
Moshi genzai no keikaku ga jikkō dekinai baai no daitai-an o teian shite kudasai.	Hai, bakkuappu puran o 2-tsu yōi shima shita.
Please propose alternative plans in case the current plan can't be implemented.	Yes, I've prepared two backup plans.

Cultural Context

Encourage creative thinking and avoid dismissing ideas too quickly.

全員の合意を得たいと思います。

ぜんいんのごういをえたいとおもいます。

Zen'in no gōi o etai to omoimasu.

I'd like to reach a consensus.

Variation 1	Variation 2
皆様の同意を頂きたいと考えます。	Kyō mo shōjin shima shou.
みなさまのどういをいただきたいとかんがえます。	みなさまのどういをいただきたいとかんがえます。
Minasama no dōi o itadakitai to kangaemasu.	Minasan no sandō o etaidesu.
I'd like to get everyone's agreement.	I'd like to get everyone's agreement.

Positive Response	Negative Response
はい、建設的な議論を心がけます。	意見の相違が大きすぎます。
はい、けんせつてきなぎろんをこころがけます。	いけんのそういがおおきすぎます。
Hai, kensetsu-tekina giron o kokorogakemasu.	Iken no sōi ga ōki sugimasu.
Yes, I'll aim for constructive discussion.	The differences in opinions are too great.

Conversation example person A	Conversation example person B
この方針について、全員の合意を得たいと思います。	私は賛成です。他の方々の意見も聞きたいです。
このほうしんについて、ぜんいんのごういをえたいとおもいます。	わたしはさんせいです。ほかのかたがたのいけんもききたいです。
Kono hōshin ni tsuite, zen'in no gōi o etai to omoimasu.	Watashi wa sanseidesu. Hoka no katagata no iken mo kikitaidesu.
I'd like to get everyone's agreement on this policy.	I agree. I'd like to hear others' opinions as well.

Cultural Context

Be prepared for potential conflicts and have strategies to reach consensus.

この議論は時間外としましょう。

このぎろんはじかんがいとしましょう。
Kono giron wa jikangai to shimashou.
Let's take this discussion offline.

Variation 1	Variation 2
この討議は別の機会に持ち越しましょう。	Kyō mo shōjin shima shou.
このとうぎはべつのきかいにもちこししましょう。	このとうぎはべつのきかいにもちこししましょう。
Kono tōgi wa betsu no kikai ni mochikoshi ma shou.	Ko no hanashi wa gojitsu ni kai shima shou.
Let's continue this discussion offline.	Let's postpone this discussion.

Positive Response	Negative Response
了解です。次回の会議で続きを話し合いましょう。	今日中に解決したいです。
りょうかいです。じかいのかいぎでつづきをはなしあいましょう。	きょうじゅうにかいけつしたいです。
Ryōkaidesu. Jikai no kaigi de tsudzuki o hanashiai ma shou.	Kyō-chū ni kaiketsu shitaidesu.
Understood. Let's continue this at the next meeting.	I want to resolve this today.

Conversation example person A	Conversation example person B
この議論は複雑なので、時間外としましょう。	了解しました。別途時間を設けて話し合いましょう。
このぎろんはふくざつなので、じかんがいとしましょう。	りょうかいしました。べっとじかんをもうけてはなしあいましょう。
Kono giron wa fukuzatsunanode, jikan-gai to shima shou.	Ryōkai shima shita. Betto jikan o mōkete hanashiai ma shou.
This discussion is complex, so let's continue it outside of this meeting.	Understood. Let's set up a separate time to discuss this.

Cultural Context
Ensure there's a plan to continue the discussion at a later time.

次回の会議日程を決めましょう。

じかいのかいぎにっていをきめましょう。
Jikai no kaigi nittei o kimemashou.
Let's set the date for our next meeting.

Variation 1	Variation 2
次の集会の日取りを定めましょう。	Kyō mo shōjin shima shou.
つぎのしゅうかいのひどりをさだめましょう。	つぎのしゅうかいのひどりをさだめましょう。
Tsugi no shūkai no hi tori o sadame ma shou.	Tsugi no uchiawase no hi o kime ma shou.
Let's set the date for our next meeting.	Let's set the date for our next meeting.

Positive Response	Negative Response
はい、皆さんの都合を確認して決めましょう。	スケジュールが合いません。
はい、みなさんのつごうをかくにんしてきめましょう。	すけじゅーるがあいません。
Hai, minasan no tsugō o kakunin shite kime ma shou.	Sukejūru ga aimasen.
Yes, let's check everyone's schedule and decide.	My schedule doesn't allow for that.

Conversation example person A	Conversation example person B
では最後に、次回の会議日程を決めましょう。	来週の水曜日はいかがでしょうか。
ではさいごに、じかいのかいぎにっていをきめましょう。	らいしゅうのすいようびはいかがでしょうか。
Dewa saigo ni, jikai no kaigi nittei o kime ma shou.	Raishū no suiyōbi wa ikagadeshou ka.
Finally, let's set the date for our next meeting.	How about next Wednesday?

Cultural Context
Consider everyone's schedules and potential conflicts.

会議を終了します。

かいぎをしゅうりょうします。

Kaigi o shūryō shimasu.

This concludes our meeting.

Variation 1	Variation 2
協議を締めくくります。	Kyō mo shōjin shima shou.
きょうぎをしめくくります。	きょうぎをしめくくります。
Kyōgi o shimekukurimasu.	Kore de owari ni shimasu.
We'll conclude the meeting.	This concludes our meeting.

Positive Response	Negative Response
ありがとうございました。生産的な会議でした。	まだ議論すべき点があります。
ありがとうございました。せいさんてきなかいぎでした。	まだぎろんすべきてんがあります。
Arigatō go zaimashita. Seisan-tekina kaigi de shita.	Mada giron subeki ten ga arimasu.
Thank you. It was a productive meeting.	There are still points to be discussed.

Conversation example person A	Conversation example person B
以上で議題が終わりました。会議を終了します。	お疲れ様でした。フォローアップを行います。
いじょうでぎだいがおわりました。かいぎをしゅうりょうします。	おつかれさまでした。ふぉろーあっぷをおこないます。
Ijō de gidai ga owarimashita. Kaigi o shūryō shimasu.	Otsukaresama de shita. Forō appu o okonaimasu.
We've covered all agenda items. The meeting is adjourned.	Thank you for your hard work. I'll follow up on the discussed items.

Cultural Context

Summarize key decisions and action items before concluding.

現状分析から始めましょう。

げんじょうぶんせきからはじめましょう。
Genjō bunseki kara hajimemashou.
Let's start with an analysis of the current situation.

Variation 1	Variation 2
実情把握から着手しましょう。	Kyō mo shōjin shima shou.
じつじょうはあくからちゃくしゅしましょう。	じつじょうはあくからちゃくしゅしましょう。
Jitsujō haaku kara chakushu shima shou.	Mazu ima no jōkyō o kakunin shima shou.
Let's start with analyzing the current situation.	Let's start by assessing the current situation.

Positive Response	Negative Response
はい、客観的なデータを基に分析しましょう。	データが不足しています。
はい、きゃっかんてきなでーたをもとにぶんせきしましょう。	でーたがふそくしています。
Hai, kyakkan-tekina dēta o ki ni bunseki shima shou.	Dēta ga fusoku shite imasu.
Yes, let's analyze based on objective data.	We lack sufficient data.

Conversation example person A	Conversation example person B
新プロジェクトの計画を立てるにあたり、現状分析から始めましょう。	同意します。SWOT 分析を行いましょう。
しんぷろじぇくとのけいかくをたてるにあたり、げんじょうぶんせきからはじめましょう。	どういします。すわっとぶんせきをおこないましょう。
Shin purojekuto no keikaku o tateru ni atari, genjō bunseki kara hajime ma shou.	Dōi shimasu. SWOT bunseki o gyō ima shou.
Let's start with a current situation analysis for planning the new project.	I agree. Let's conduct a SWOT analysis.

Cultural Context
Ensure you have accurate and up-to-date data for the analysis.

目標を再確認しましょう。

もくひょうをさいかくにんしましょう。

Mokuhyō o sai kakunin shimashou.

Let's reconfirm our objectives.

Variation 1	Variation 2
目的を改めて確かめましょう。	Kyō mo shōjin shima shou.
もくてきをあらためてたしかめましょう。	もくてきをあらためてたしかめましょう。
Mokuteki o aratamete tashikame ma shou.	Mokuteki o aratamete kakunin shima shou.
Let's reconfirm our objectives.	Let's reconfirm our objectives.

Positive Response	Negative Response
はい、全員で共通認識を持ちましょう。	目標が現実的ではありません。
はい、ぜんいんできょうつうにんしきをもちましょう。	もくひょうがげんじつてきではありません。
Hai, zen'in de kyōtsū ninshiki o mochi ma shou.	Mokuhyō ga genjitsu-tekide wa arimasen.
Yes, let's ensure we all have a common understanding.	The goals are not realistic.

Conversation example person A	Conversation example person B
中間地点に来たので、目標を再確認しましょう。	はい、KPIの進捗も確認する必要がありますね。
ちゅうかんちてんにきたので、もくひょうをさいかくにんしましょう。	はい、けーぴーあいのしんちょくもかくにんするひつようがありますね。
Chūkan chiten ni kitanode, mokuhyō o sai kakunin shima shou.	Hai, kēpīai no shinchoku mo kakunin suru hitsuyō ga arimasu ne.
We're at the halfway point, so let's reconfirm our objectives.	Yes, we should also check the progress of our KPIs.

Cultural Context

Make sure goals are still relevant and aligned with current business needs.

KPI の進捗を確認します。

けーぴーあいのしんちょくをかくにんします。

Kēpīai no shinchoku o kakunin shimasu.

We'll check the progress of our KPIs.

Variation 1	Variation 2
核心的な業績指標の進展を確認します。	Kyō mo shōjin shima shou.
かくしんてきなぎょうせきしひょうのしんてんをかくにんします。	かくしんてきなぎょうせきしひょうのしんてんをかくにんします。
Kakushin-tekina gyōseki shihyō no shinten o kakunin shimasu.	Shuyō shihyō no tassei jōkyō o kakunin shimasu.
We'll verify the advancement of our core performance metrics.	We'll check the progress of our key performance indicators.

Positive Response	Negative Response
はい、詳細な報告を準備しました。	KPI が適切ではありません。
はい、しょうさいなほうこくをじゅんびしました。	けーぴーあいがてきせつではありません。
Hai, shōsaina hōkoku o junbi shima shita.	KPI ga tekisetsude wa arimasen.
Yes, I've prepared a detailed report.	The KPIs are not appropriate.

Conversation example person A	Conversation example person B
それでは、各部門の KPI の進捗を確認します。	販売部門の報告をさせていただきます。
それでは、かくぶもんのけーぴーあいのしんちょくをかくにんします。	はんばいぶもんのほうこくをさせていただきます。
Soredewa, kaku bumon no kēpīai no shinchoku o kakunin shimasu.	Hanbai bumon no hōkoku o sa sete itadakimasu.
Now, let's check the progress of KPIs for each department.	I'll report on the sales department's progress.

Cultural Context

Ensure KPIs are still relevant and accurately measure progress.

課題を洗い出しましょう。

かだいをあらいだしましょう。
Kadai o araidashimashou.
Let's identify the issues.

Variation 1	Variation 2
問題点を抽出しましょう。	Kyō mo shōjin shima shou.
もんだいてんをちゅうしゅつしましょう。	もんだいてんをちゅうしゅつしましょう。
Mondai-ten o chūshutsu shima shou.	Mondai-ten o rekkyo shima shou.
Let's identify the issues.	Let's list out the issues.

Positive Response	Negative Response
はい、問題点を明確にして改善策を考えましょう。	問題が多すぎて手に負えません。
はい、もんだいてんをめいかくにしてかいぜんさくをかんがえましょう。	もんだいがおおすぎててにおえません。
Hai, mondai-ten o meikaku ni shite kaizen-saku o kangae ma shou.	Mondai ga ō sugite te ni oemasen.
Yes, let's identify issues and think of improvements.	There are too many issues to handle.

Conversation example person A	Conversation example person B
現在直面している課題を洗い出しましょう。	はい、各部門から主要な問題点を挙げていきます。
げんざいちょくめんしているかだいをあらいだしましょう。	はい、かくぶもんからしゅようなもんだいてんをあげていきます。
Genzai chokumen shite iru kadai o araidashi ma shou.	Hai, kaku bumon kara shuyōna mondai-ten o agete ikimasu.
Let's identify the challenges we're currently facing.	Yes, let's list the main issues from each department.

Cultural Context
Encourage open and honest discussion about challenges.

優先順位を決める必要があります。

ゆうせんじゅんいをきめるひつようがあります。
Yūsen jun'i o kimeru hitsuyō ga arimasu.
We need to set priorities.

Variation 1	Variation 2
重要度を定める必要があります。	Kyō mo shōjin shima shou.
じゅうようどをさだめるひつようがあります。	じゅうようどをさだめるひつようがあります。
Jūyō-do o sadameru hitsuyō ga arimasu.	Jūyō-do o kime ma shou.
We need to set priorities.	We need to set priorities.

Positive Response	Negative Response
承知しました。重要度と緊急度を考慮しましょう。	全てが重要で優先順位をつけられません。
しょうちしました。じゅうようどときんきゅうどをこうりょしましょう。	すべてがじゅうようでゆうせんじゅんいをつけられません。
Shōchi shima shita. Jūyō-do to kinkyū-do o kōryo shima shou.	Subete ga jūyōde yūsen jun'i o tsuke raremasen.
Understood. Let's consider importance and urgency.	Everything is important, can't prioritize.

Conversation example person A	Conversation example person B
多くの課題がありますが、優先順位を決める必要があります。	そうですね。影響度と緊急度で評価しましょう。
おおくのかだいがありますが、ゆうせんじゅんいをきめるひつようがあります。	そうですね。えいきょうどときんきゅうどでひょうかしましょう。
Ōku no kadai ga arimasuga, yūsen jun'i o kimeru hitsuyō ga arimasu.	Sōdesu ne. Eikyō-do to kinkyū-do de hyōka shima shou.
We have many issues, but we need to prioritize them.	Agreed. Let's evaluate based on impact and urgency.

Cultural Context
Consider both urgency and importance when prioritizing.

フィードバックをお願いします。

ふぃーどばっくをおねがいします。

Fīdobakku o onegaishimasu.

Please provide your feedback.

Variation 1	Variation 2
意見や感想をお聞かせください。	Kyō mo shōjin shima shou.
いけんやかんそうをおきかせください。	いけんやかんそうをおきかせください。
Iken ya kansō o o kikase kudasai.	Go iken o o kikase kudasai.
Please provide your feedback.	Please provide your feedback.

Positive Response	Negative Response
はい、建設的な意見を出すよう心がけます。	建設的なフィードバックがありません。
はい、けんせつてきないけんをだすようこころがけます。	けんせつてきなふぃーどばっくがありません。
Hai, kensetsu-tekina iken o dasu yō kokorogakemasu.	Kensetsu-tekina fīdobakku ga arimasen.
Yes, I'll try to provide constructive feedback.	I don't have any constructive feedback.

Conversation example person A	Conversation example person B
新製品のプロトタイプについて、フィードバックをお願いします。	デザインは良いですが、使いやすさに改善の余地があります。
しんせいひんのぷろとたいぷについて、ふぃーどばっくをおねがいします。	でざいんはよいですが、つかいやすさにかいぜんのよちがあります。
Shin seihin no purototaipu ni tsuite, fīdobakku o onegai shimasu.	Dezain wa yoidesuga, tsukai yasu-sa ni kaizen no yochi ga arimasu.
Please provide feedback on the new product prototype.	The design is good, but there's room for improvement in usability.

Cultural Context

Create a safe environment for constructive feedback.

具体的な行動計画を立てましょう。

ぐたいてきなこうどうけいかくをたてましょう。

Gutaitekina kōdō keikaku o tatemashou.

Let's create a specific action plan.

Variation 1	Variation 2
詳細な実行案を策定しましょう。	Kyō mo shōjin shima shou.
しょうさいなじっこうあんをさくていしましょう。	しょうさいなじっこうあんをさくていしましょう。
Shōsaina jikkō-an o sakutei shima shou.	Jikkō no suteppu o kime ma shou.
Let's create a specific action plan.	Let's create a concrete action plan.

Positive Response	Negative Response
はい、実行可能な計画を立てましょう。	詳細が不明確です。
はい、じっこうかのうなけいかくをたてましょう。	しょうさいがふめいかくです。
Hai, jikkō kanōna keikaku o tate ma shou.	Shōsai ga fu meikakudesu.
Yes, let's create an actionable plan.	The details are unclear.

Conversation example person A	Conversation example person B
フィードバックを基に、具体的な行動計画を立てましょう。	承知しました。改善点ごとにタスクを割り当てます。
ふぃーどばっくをもとに、ぐたいてきなこうどうけいかくをたてましょう。	しょうちしました。かいぜんてんごとにたすくをわりあてます。
Fīdobakku o ki ni, gutai-tekina kōdō keikaku o tate ma shou.	Shōchi shima shita. Kaizen-ten-goto ni tasuku o wariatemasu.
Based on the feedback, let's create a specific action plan.	Understood. I'll assign tasks for each improvement point.

Cultural Context

Ensure plans are realistic and have clear ownership.

この提案についてどう思いますか？

このていあんについてどうおもいますか？
Kono teian ni tsuite dōomoimasuka?
What do you think about this proposal?

Variation 1	Variation 2
この案に関してどのようなご意見をお持ちですか？	Kyō mo shōjin shima shou.
このあんにかんしてどのようなごいけんをおもちですか？	このあんにかんしてどのようなごいけんをおもちですか？
Kono an ni kanshite dono yōna go iken o o mochidesu ka?	Kono an ni tsuite go iken wa arimasu ka?
What do you think about this proposal?	What do you think about this proposal?

Positive Response	Negative Response
興味深い提案だと思います。さらに詳しく聞かせてください。	実現可能性が低いと思います。
きょうみぶかいていあんだとおもいます。さらにくわしくきかせてください。	じつげんかのうせいがひくいとおもいます。
Kyōmibukai teianda to omoimasu. Sarani kuwashiku kika sete kudasai.	Jitsugen kanō-sei ga hikui to omoimasu.
I think it's an interesting proposal. Could you elaborate?	I think the feasibility is low.

Conversation example person A	Conversation example person B
マーケティング戦略の新しい提案についてどう思いますか？	斬新なアイデアだと思います。実行可能性を検討しましょう。
まーけてぃんぐせんりゃくのあたらしいていあんについてどうおもいますか？	ざんしんなあいであだとおもいます。じっこうかのうせいをけんとうしましょう。
Māketingu senryaku no atarashī teian ni tsuite dō omoimasu ka?	Zanshin'na aideada to omoimasu. Jikkō kanō-sei o kentō shima shou.
What do you think about this new marketing strategy proposal?	I think it's an innovative idea. Let's examine its feasibility.

Cultural Context
Encourage critical thinking and avoid groupthink.

実行可能性を検討しましょう。

じっこうかのうせいをけんとうしましょう。

Jikkō kanōsei o kentō shimashou.

Let's examine the feasibility.

Variation 1	Variation 2
遂行の見込みを吟味しましょう。	Kyō mo shōjin shima shou.
すいこうのみこみをぎんみしましょう。	すいこうのみこみをぎんみしましょう。
Suikō no mikomi o ginmi shima shou.	Jitsugen dekiru ka kakunin shima shou.
Let's examine the feasibility.	Let's examine the feasibility.

Positive Response	Negative Response
はい、リソースと制約を考慮しながら評価しましょう。	リソースが足りません。
はい、りそーすとせいやくをこうりょしながらひょうかしましょう。	りそーすがたりません。
Hai, risōsu to seiyaku o kōryo shinagara hyōka shima shou.	Risōsu ga tarimasen.
Yes, let's evaluate considering our resources and constraints.	We don't have enough resources.

Conversation example person A	Conversation example person B
この案の実行可能性を検討しましょう。リソースと時間を考慮する必要があります。	同意します。コスト分析も行いましょう。
このあんのじっこうかのうせいをけんとうしましょう。りそーすとじかんをこうりょするひつようがあります。	どういします。こすとぶんせきもおこないましょう。
Kono an no jikkō kanō-sei o kentō shima shou. Risōsu to jikan o kōryo suru hitsuyō ga arimasu.	Dōi shimasu. Kosuto bunseki mo gyō ima shou.
Let's assess the feasibility of this plan. We need to consider resources and time.	I agree. Let's also conduct a cost analysis.

Cultural Context

Consider all resources and constraints when assessing feasibility.

各部署の状況報告をお願いします。

かくぶしょのじょうきょうほうこくをおねがいします。

Kaku busho no jōkyō hōkoku o onegaishimasu.

Please provide status reports from each department.

Variation 1	Variation 2
各セクションの現況をご説明ください。	Kyō mo shōjin shima shou.
かくせくしょんのげんきょうをごせつめいください。	かくせくしょんのげんきょうをごせつめいください。
Kaku sekushon no genkyō o go setsumei kudasai.	Kaku chīmu no shinchoku o oshiete kudasai.
Please provide status reports from each department.	Please provide status updates from each department.

Positive Response	Negative Response
はい、各部署の最新情報を共有いたします。	他部署の情報が不足しています。
はい、かくぶしょのさいしんじょうほうをきょうゆういたします。	たぶしょのじょうほうがふそくしています。
Hai, kaku busho no saishin jōhō o kyōyū itashimasu.	Ta busho no jōhō ga fusoku shite imasu.
Yes, I'll share the latest information from each department.	We lack information from other departments.

Conversation example person A	Conversation example person B
では、各部署の状況報告をお願いします。	営業部門の報告をさせていただきます。
では、かくぶしょのじょうきょうほうこくをおねがいします。	えいぎょうぶもんのほうこくをさせていただきます。
Dewa, kaku busho no jōkyō hōkoku o onegai shimasu.	Eigyō bumon no hōkoku o sa sete itadakimasu.
Now, I'd like to request status reports from each department.	I'll report on the sales department's status.

Cultural Context

Ensure reports are concise and focused on key issues.

この方針で進めてよろしいでしょうか。

このほうしんですすめてよろしいでしょうか。

Kono hōshin de susumete yoroshīdeshou ka.

Is it okay to proceed with this policy?

Variation 1	Variation 2
この方向性で推進して問題ないでしょうか。	Kyō mo shōjin shima shou.
このほうこうせいですいしんしてもんだいないでしょうか。	このほうこうせいですいしんしてもんだいないでしょうか。
Kono hōkō-sei de suishin shite mondainaideshou ka.	Kono hōkō-sei de mondainaidesu ka.
Is it alright to proceed with this policy?	Is it okay to proceed with this approach?

Positive Response	Negative Response
はい、賛成です。早速実行に移しましょう。	再考が必要だと思います。
はい、さんせいです。さっそくじっこうにうつしましょう。	さいこうがひつようだとおもいます。
Hai, sanseidesu. Sassoku jikkō ni Utsuri shima shou.	Saikō ga hitsuyōda to omoimasu.
Yes, I agree. Let's start implementing it right away.	I think we need to reconsider.

Conversation example person A	Conversation example person B
以上の内容を踏まえ、この方針で進めてよろしいでしょうか。	はい、異議ありません。実行に移しましょう。
いじょうのないようをふまえ、このほうしんですすめてよろしいでしょうか。	はい、いぎありません。じっこうにうつしましょう。
Ijō no naiyō o fumae, kono hōshin de susumete yoroshīdeshou ka.	Hai, igi arimasen. Jikkō ni Utsuri shima shou.
Based on what we've discussed, shall we proceed with this policy?	Yes, I have no objections. Let's move forward with implementation.

Cultural Context

Confirm that all stakeholders are aligned before proceeding.

期限までに完了できますか？

きげんまでにかんりょうできますか？
Kigen made ni kanryō dekimasu ka?
Can we complete this by the deadline?

Variation 1	Variation 2
締切までに仕上げることは可能ですか？	Kyō mo shōjin shima shou.
しめきりまでにしあげることはかのうですか？	しめきりまでにしあげることはかのうですか？
Shimekiri made ni shiageru koto wa kanōdesu ka?	Shimekiri ni maniaimasu ka.
Can we complete this by the deadline?	Can you finish by the deadline?

Positive Response	Negative Response
はい、全力を尽くして期限内に完了させます。	無理なスケジュールです。
はい、ぜんりょくをつくしてきげんないにかんりょうさせます。	むりなすけじゅーるです。
Hai, zenryoku o tsukushite kigen-nai ni kanryō sa semasu.	Murina sukejūrudesu.
Yes, I'll do my best to complete it within the deadline.	The schedule is unrealistic.

Conversation example person A	Conversation example person B
現在の進捗状況を考えると、期限までに完了できますか？	厳しいですが、追加リソースがあれば可能です。
げんざいのしんちょくじょうきょうをかんがえると、きげんまでにかんりょうできますか？	きびしいですが、ついかりそーすがあればかのうです。
Genzai no shinchoku jōkyō o kangaeru to, kigen made ni kanryō dekimasu ka?	Kibishīdesuga, tsuika risōsu ga areba kanōdesu.
Given our current progress, can we complete this by the deadline?	It's tight, but possible with additional resources.

Cultural Context
Consider potential obstacles and have contingency plans.

追加リソースが必要かどうか検討しましょう。

ついかりそーすがひつようかどうかけんとうしましょう。
Tsuika risōsu ga hitsuyō ka dō ka kentō shimashou.
Let's consider whether we need additional resources.

Variation 1	Variation 2
補充資源の要否を考慮しましょう。	Kyō mo shōjin shima shou.
ほじゅうしげんのようひをこうりょしましょう。	ほじゅうしげんのようひをこうりょしましょう。
Hojū shigen no yō hi o kōryo shima shou.	Tsuika no jin'in ya yosan ga yōru ka kangae ma shou.
Let's consider whether additional resources are needed.	Let's consider if we need additional resources.

Positive Response	Negative Response
はい、現状のリソースを分析し、必要性を判断しましょう。	リソースの余裕がありません。
はい、げんじょうのりそーすをぶんせきし、ひつようせいをはんだんしましょう。	りそーすのよゆうがありません。
Hai, genjō no risōsu o bunseki shi, hitsuyō-sei o handan shima shou.	Risōsu no yoyū ga arimasen.
Yes, let's analyze current resources and determine the necessity.	We don't have any spare resources.

Conversation example person A	Conversation example person B
その場合、追加リソースが必要かどうか検討しましょう。	はい、人員と予算の両面から検討する必要がありますね。
そのばあい、ついかりそーすがひつようかどうかけんとうしましょう。	はい、じんいんとよさんのりょうめんからけんとうするひつようがありますね。
So no baai, tsuika risōsu ga hitsuyō ka dō ka kentō shima shou.	Hai, jin'in to yosan no ryōmen kara kentō suru hitsuyō ga arimasu ne.
In that case, let's consider whether we need additional resources.	Yes, we need to consider both personnel and budget aspects.

Cultural Context
Be realistic about resource needs and availability.

この問題の根本原因は何でしょうか。

このもんだいのこんぽんげんいんはなんでしょうか。
Kono mondai no konpon gen'in wa nanideshou ka.
What is the root cause of this problem?

Variation 1	Variation 2
この課題の本質的要因は何でしょうか。	Kyō mo shōjin shima shou.
このかだいのほんしつてきよういんはなんでしょうか。	このかだいのほんしつてきよういんはなんでしょうか。
Kono kadai no honshitsu-teki yōin wa nanideshou ka.	Kono mondai no hontō no riyū wa nanidesu ka.
What is the root cause of this problem?	What's the root cause of this issue?

Positive Response	Negative Response
徹底的に分析して、本質的な問題を特定しましょう。	原因が複雑すぎて特定できません。
てっていてきにぶんせきして、ほんしつてきなもんだいをとくていしましょう。	げんいんがふくざつすぎてとくていできません。
Tettei-teki ni bunseki shite, honshitsu-tekina mondai o tokutei shima shou.	Gen'in ga fukuzatsu sugite tokutei dekimasen.
Let's analyze thoroughly to identify the fundamental issue.	The cause is too complex to identify.

Conversation example person A	Conversation example person B
納期の遅れが発生していますが、この問題の根本原因は何でしょうか。	サプライチェーンの問題が主な原因だと考えられます。
のうきのおくれがはっせいしていますが、このもんだいのこんぽんげんいんはなんでしょうか。	さぷらいちぇーんのもんだいがおもながげんいんだとかんがえられます。
Nōki no okure ga hassei shite imasuga, kono mondai no konpon gen'in wa nanideshou ka.	Sapurai chēn no mondai ga omona gen'inda to kangae raremasu.
We're experiencing delays in delivery times. What's the root cause of this problem?	The main cause appears to be supply chain issues.

Cultural Context
Avoid jumping to conclusions without thorough analysis.

今後の展開について議論しましょう。

こんごのてんかいについてぎろんしましょう。

Kongo no tenkai ni tsuite giron shimashou.

Let's discuss future developments.

Variation 1	Variation 2
将来の進展に関して討議しましょう。	Kyō mo shōjin shima shou.
しょうらいのしんてんにかんしてとうぎしましょう。	しょうらいのしんてんにかんしてとうぎしましょう。
Shōrai no shinten ni kanshite tōgi shima shou.	Korekara no hōkō-sei o hanashiai ma shou.
Let's discuss future developments.	Let's discuss future developments.

Positive Response	Negative Response
はい、長期的な視点で戦略を立てましょう。	現状の問題解決が先決です。
はい、ちょうきてきなしてんでせんりゃくをたてましょう。	げんじょうのもんだいかいけつがせんけつです。
Hai, chōki-tekina shiten de senryaku o tate ma shou.	Genjō no mondai kaiketsu ga senketsudesu.
Yes, let's develop a strategy with a long-term perspective.	Solving current issues should come first.

Conversation example person A	Conversation example person B
問題の原因が分かったので、今後の展開について議論しましょう。	代替サプライヤーの検討を提案します。
もんだいのげんいんがわかったので、こんごのてんかいについてぎろんしましょう。	だいたいさぷらいやーのけんとうをていあんします。
Mondai no gen'in ga wakattanode, kongo no tenkai ni tsuite giron shima shou.	Daitai sapuraiyā no kentō o teian shimasu.
Now that we understand the cause, let's discuss future developments.	I suggest we consider alternative suppliers.

Cultural Context

Consider both short-term and long-term implications.

成功基準を定義する必要があります。

せいこうきじゅんをていぎするひつようがあります。

Seikō kijun o teigi suru hitsuyō ga arimasu.

We need to define success criteria.

Variation 1	Variation 2
達成指標を規定する必要があります。	Kyō mo shōjin shima shou.
たっせいしひょうをきていするひつようがあります。	たっせいしひょうをきていするひつようがあります。
Tassei shihyō o kitei suru hitsuyō ga arimasu.	Seikō no handan kijun o kime ma shou.
We need to define success criteria.	We need to define success criteria.

Positive Response	Negative Response
はい、具体的で測定可能な指標を設定しましょう。	明確な基準を設定するのは難しいです。
はい、ぐたいてきではかりかのうなしひょうをせっていしましょう。	めいかくなきじゅんをせっていするのはむずかしいです。
Hai, gutai-tekide sokutei kanōna shihyō o settei shima shou.	Meikakuna kijun o settei suru no wa muzukashīdesu.
Yes, let's set specific and measurable indicators.	It's difficult to set clear criteria.

Conversation example person A	Conversation example person B
このプロジェクトの成功基準を定義する必要があります。	同意します。具体的な数値目標を設定しましょう。
このぷろじぇくとのせいこうきじゅんをていぎするひつようがあります。	どういします。ぐたいてきなすうちもくひょうをせっていしましょう。
Kono purojekuto no seikō kijun o teigi suru hitsuyō ga arimasu.	Dōi shimasu. Gutai-tekina sūchi mokuhyō o settei shima shou.
We need to define the success criteria for this project.	I agree. Let's set specific numerical targets.

Cultural Context

Ensure criteria are measurable and aligned with overall goals.

この決定の影響を評価しましょう。

このけっていのえいきょうをひょうかしましょう。
Kono kettei no eikyō o hyōka shimashou.
Let's evaluate the impact of this decision.

Variation 1	Variation 2
この判断の波及効果を査定しましょう。	Kyō mo shōjin shima shou.
このはんだんのはきゅうこうかをさていしましょう。	このはんだんのはきゅうこうかをさていしましょう。
Kono handan no hakyū kōka o satei shima shou.	Kono handan ga dō eikyō suru ka kangae ma shou.
Let's evaluate the impact of this decision.	Let's evaluate the impact of this decision.

Positive Response	Negative Response
はい、短期的・長期的な影響を考慮しましょう。	影響範囲が広すぎて評価できません。
はい、たんきてき・ちょうきてきなえいきょうをこうりょしましょう。	えいきょうはんいがひろすぎてひょうかできません。
Hai, tanki-teki chōki-tekina eikyō o kōryo shima shou.	Eikyō han'i ga hiro sugite hyōka dekimasen.
Yes, let's consider both short-term and long-term impacts.	The impact is too broad to evaluate.

Conversation example person A	Conversation example person B
新しい方針を採用した場合、この決定の影響を評価しましょう。	はい、短期的および長期的な影響を分析する必要がありますね。
あたらしいほうしんをさいようしたばあい、このけっていのえいきょうをひょうかしましょう。	はい、たんきてきおよびちょうきてきなえいきょうをぶんせきするひつようがありますね。
Atarashī hōshin o saiyō shita baai, kono kettei no eikyō o hyōka shima shou.	Hai, tanki-teki oyobi chōki-tekina eikyō o bunseki suru hitsuyō ga arimasu ne.
If we adopt this new policy, let's evaluate its impact.	Yes, we need to analyze both short-term and long-term impacts.

Cultural Context
Consider impacts on all stakeholders, not just immediate ones.

他部門との連携が必要です。

たぶもんとのれんけいがひつようです。

Ta bumon to no renkei ga hitsuyōdesu.

We need to collaborate with other departments.

Variation 1	Variation 2
他セクションとの協調が不可欠です。	Kyō mo shōjin shima shou.
たせくしょんとのきょうちょうがふかけつです。	たせくしょんとのきょうちょうがふかけつです。
Ta sekushon to no kyōchō ga fukaketsudesu.	Hoka no chīmu to kyōryoku suru hitsuyō ga arimasu.
Collaboration with other departments is necessary.	We need to collaborate with other departments.

Positive Response	Negative Response
はい、効果的なコミュニケーション方法を考えましょう。	部門間の壁が高すぎます。
はい、こうかてきなこみゅにけーしょんほうほうをかんがえましょう。	ぶもんかんのかべがたかすぎます。
Hai, kōka-tekina komyunikēshon hōhō o kangae ma shou.	Bumon-kan no kabe ga taka sugimasu.
Yes, let's think about effective communication methods.	The barriers between departments are too high.

Conversation example person A	Conversation example person B
この計画を実行するには、他部門との連携が必要です。	承知しました。部門間の会議を設定します。
このけいかくをじっこうするには、たぶもんとのれんけいがひつようです。	しょうちしました。ぶもんかんのかいぎをせっていします。
Kono keikaku o jikkō suru ni wa, ta bumon to no renkei ga hitsuyōdesu.	Shōchi shima shita. Bumon-kan no kaigi o settei shimasu.
To execute this plan, we need cooperation with other departments.	Understood. I'll set up inter-departmental meetings.

Cultural Context

Identify potential barriers to collaboration and address them.

顧客のフィードバックを検討しましょう。

こきゃくのふぃーどばっくをけんとうしましょう。
Kokyaku no fīdobakku o kentō shimashou.
Let's consider customer feedback.

Variation 1	Variation 2
利用者の意見を考察しましょう。	Kyō mo shōjin shima shou.
りようしゃのいけんをこうさつしましょう。	りようしゃのいけんをこうさつしましょう。
Riyō-sha no iken o kōsatsu shima shou.	Okyakusama no iken o kakunin shima shou.
Let's consider customer feedback.	Let's review customer feedback.

Positive Response	Negative Response
はい、顧客の声を真摯に受け止め、改善に活かしましょう。	フィードバックが限られています。
はい、こきゃくのこえをしんしにうけとめ、かいぜんにいかしましょう。	ふぃーどばっくがかぎられています。
Hai, kokyaku no koe o shinshi ni uketome, kaizen ni ikashi ma shou.	Fīdobakku ga kiri rarete imasu.
Yes, let's sincerely consider customer feedback for improvements.	The feedback is limited.

Conversation example person A	Conversation example person B
最近の顧客満足度調査の結果が出ました。顧客のフィードバックを検討しましょう。	はい、特に改善が必要な点に注目しましょう。
さいきんのこきゃくまんぞくどちょうさのけっかがでました。こきゃくのふぃーどばっくをけんとうしましょう。	はい、とくにかいぜんがひつようなてんにちゅうもくしましょう。
Saikin no kokyaku manzoku-do chōsa no kekka ga demashita. Kokyaku no fīdobakku o kentō shima shou.	Hai, tokuni kaizen ga hitsuyōna ten ni chūmoku shima shou.
The results of our recent customer satisfaction survey are in. Let's review the customer feedback.	Yes, let's focus on areas that need improvement.

Cultural Context
Ensure feedback is representative and not biased.

マイルストーンを設定しましょう。

まいるすとーんをせっていしましょう。

Mairusutōn o settei shimashou.

Let's set milestones.

Variation 1	Variation 2
重要段階を定めましょう。	Kyō mo shōjin shima shou.
じゅうようだんかいをさだめましょう。	じゅうようだんかいをさだめましょう。
Jūyō dankai o sadame ma shou.	Chūkan mokuhyō o kime ma shou.
Let's set milestones.	Let's set milestones.

Positive Response	Negative Response
はい、達成可能な中間目標を立てましょう。	進捗が遅れています。
はい、たっせいかのうなちゅうかんもくひょうをたてましょう。	しんちょくがおくれています。
Hai, tassei kanōna chūkan mokuhyō o tate ma shou.	Shinchoku ga okurete imasu.
Yes, let's set achievable intermediate goals.	We're behind schedule.

Conversation example person A	Conversation example person B
プロジェクトの進捗を管理するため、マイルストーンを設定しましょう。	了解です。各フェーズの終了時期を決めましょう。
ぷろじぇくとのしんちょくをかんりするため、まいるすとーんをせっていしましょう。	りょうかいです。かくふぇーずのしゅうりょうじきをきめましょう。
Purojekuto no shinchoku o kanri suru tame, mairu sutōn o settei shima shou.	Ryōkaidesu. Kaku fēzu no shūryō jiki o kime ma shou.
To manage the project's progress, let's set milestones.	Understood. Let's decide on the completion dates for each phase.

Cultural Context

Make sure milestones are realistic and aligned with overall timeline.

実施計画を詳細化する必要があります。

じっしけいかくをしょうさいかするひつようがあります。

Jisshi keikaku o shōsai-ka suru hitsuyō ga arimasu.

We need to flesh out the implementation plan.

Variation 1	Variation 2
遂行案を精緻化する必要があります。	Kyō mo shōjin shima shou.
すいこうあんをせいちかするひつようがあります。	すいこうあんをせいちかするひつようがあります。
Suikō-an o seichi-ka suru hitsuyō ga arimasu.	Jikkō keikaku o motto gutai-teki ni shima shou.
We need to elaborate on the implementation plan.	We need to detail the implementation plan.

Positive Response	Negative Response
はい、具体的なアクションアイテムを洗い出しましょう。	時間がかかりすぎます。
はい、ぐたいてきなあくしょんあいてむをあらいだしましょう。	じかんがかかりすぎます。
Hai, gutai-tekina akushon aitemu o araidashi ma shou.	Jikan ga kakari sugimasu.
Yes, let's identify specific action items.	It will take too much time.

Conversation example person A	Conversation example person B
大枠の計画は決まりましたが、実施計画を詳細化する必要があります。	はい、具体的なアクションアイテムを列挙しましょう。
おおわくのけいかくはきまりましたが、じっしけいかくをしょうさいかするひつようがあります。	はい、ぐたいてきなあくしょんあいてむをれっきょしましょう。
Ōwaku no keikaku wa kimarimashitaga, jisshi keikaku o shōsai-ka suru hitsuyō ga arimasu.	Hai, gutai-tekina akushon aitemu o rekkyo shima shou.
We've agreed on the overall plan, but we need to elaborate on the implementation plan.	Yes, let's list specific action items.

Cultural Context

Ensure all necessary steps and resources are included in the plan.

この戦略の ROI を計算しましょう。

このせんりゃくのあーるおーあいをけいさんしましょう。

Kono senryaku no āruōai o keisan shimashou.

Let's calculate the ROI for this strategy.

Variation 1	Variation 2
この方策の投資収益率を算出しましょう。	Kyō mo shōjin shima shou.
このほうさくのとうししゅうえきりつをさんしゅつしましょう。	このほうさくのとうししゅうえきりつをさんしゅつしましょう。
Kono hōsaku no tōshi shūeki-ritsu o sanshutsu shima shou.	Kono keikaku no tōshi tai kōka o sanshutsu shima shou.
Let's calculate the ROI of this strategy.	Let's calculate the ROI of this strategy.

Positive Response	Negative Response
はい、投資対効果を慎重に分析しましょう。	正確な計算は困難です。
はい、とうしたいこうかをしんちょうにぶんせきしましょう。	せいかくなけいさんはこんなんです。
Hai, tōshi tai kōka o shinchō ni bunseki shima shou.	Seikakuna keisan wa kon'nandesu.
Yes, let's carefully analyze the return on investment.	Accurate calculation is difficult.

Conversation example person A	Conversation example person B
投資の妥当性を判断するため、この戦略の ROI を計算しましょう。	承知しました。予測売上と予測コストのデータを用意します。
とうしのだとうせいをはんだんするため、このせんりゃくのあーるおーあいをけいさんしましょう。	しょうちしました。よそくうりあげとよそくこすとのでーたをよういします。
Tōshi no datō-sei o handan suru tame, kono senryaku no āru ō ai o keisan shima shou.	Shōchi shima shita. Yosoku uriage to yosoku kosuto no dēta o yōi shimasu.
To determine the investment's validity, let's calculate the ROI of this strategy.	Understood. I'll prepare the projected sales and cost data.

Cultural Context

Consider both tangible and intangible benefits in ROI calculation.

プロジェクトの進捗状況を確認します。

ぷろじぇくとのしんちょくじょうきょうをかくにんします。

Purojekuto no shinchoku jōkyō o kakunin shimasu.

We'll check the project's progress status.

Variation 1	Variation 2
進行中の企画の状況を確認します。	Kyō mo shōjin shima shou.
しんこうちゅうのきかくのじょうきょうをかくにんします。	しんこうちゅうのきかくのじょうきょうをかくにんします。
Shinkō-chū no kikaku no jōkyō o kakunin shimasu.	Keikaku no susumi guai o kakunin shimasu.
I will verify the status of the ongoing plan.	We'll check the project progress.

Positive Response	Negative Response
はい、現状と課題を明確にして報告いたします。	遅れが生じています。
はい、げんじょうとかだいをめいかくにしてほうこくいたします。	おくれがしょうじています。
Hai, genjō to kadai o meikaku ni shite hōkoku itashimasu.	Okure ga shōjite imasu.
Yes, I'll report clearly on the current status and challenges.	We're experiencing delays.

Conversation example person A	Conversation example person B
では、各チームのプロジェクトの進捗状況を確認します。	開発チームの報告をさせていただきます。
では、かくちーむのぷろじぇくとのしんちょくじょうきょうをかくにんします。	かいはつちーむのほうこくをさせていただきます。
Dewa, kaku chīmu no purojekuto no shinchoku jōkyō o kakunin shimasu.	Kaihatsu chīmu no hōkoku o sa sete itadakimasu.
Now, let's check the progress status of each team's project.	I'll report on the development team's progress.

Cultural Context

Look for early warning signs of potential issues.

リソースの配分を見直す必要があります。

りそーすのはいぶんをみなおすひつようがあります。

Risōsu no haibun o minaosu hitsuyō ga arimasu.

We need to review resource allocation.

Variation 1	Variation 2
資源の割当を再考する必要があります。	Kyō mo shōjin shima shou.
しげんのわりあてをさいこうするひつようがあります。	しげんのわりあてをさいこうするひつようがあります。
Shigen no wariate o saikō suru hitsuyō ga arimasu.	Jin'in to yosan no wariate o sai kentō shima shou.
We need to review resource allocation.	We need to review resource allocation.

Positive Response	Negative Response
はい、効率的な資源活用方法を考えましょう。	余剰リソースがありません。
はい、こうりつてきなしげんかつようほうほうをかんがえましょう。	よじょうりそーすがありません。
Hai, kōritsu-tekina shigen katsuyō hōhō o kangae ma shou.	Yojō risōsu ga arimasen.
Yes, let's consider efficient resource utilization methods.	We don't have any excess resources.

Conversation example person A	Conversation example person B
現在の進捗状況を考えると、リソースの配分を見直す必要があります。	同意します。優先度の高いタスクにリソースを集中させましょう。
げんざいのしんちょくじょうきょうをかんがえると、りそーすのはいぶんをみなおすひつようがあります。	どういします。ゆうせんどのたかいたすくにりそーすをしゅうちゅうさせましょう。
Genzai no shinchoku jōkyō o kangaeru to, risōsu no haibun o minaosu hitsuyō ga arimasu.	Dōi shimasu. Yūsen-do no takai tasuku ni risōsu o shūchū sa se ma shou.
Given our current progress, we need to review the resource allocation.	I agree. Let's concentrate resources on high-priority tasks.

Cultural Context

Consider long-term implications of resource allocation decisions.

市場動向を分析しましょう。

しじょうどうこうをぶんせきしましょう。
Ichiba dōkō o bunseki shimashou.
Let's analyze market trends.

Variation 1	Variation 2
市況の傾向を解析しましょう。	Kyō mo shōjin shima shou.
しきょうのけいこうをかいせきしましょう。	しきょうのけいこうをかいせきしましょう。
Shikyō no keikō o kaiseki shima shou.	Gyōkai no keikō o shirabe ma shou.
Let's analyze market trends.	Let's analyze market trends.

Positive Response	Negative Response
はい、最新のデータを基に傾向を把握しましょう。	データが不足しています。
はい、さいしんのでーたをもとにけいこうをはあくしましょう。	でーたがふそくしています。
Hai, saishin no dēta o ki ni keikō o haaku shima shou.	Dēta ga fusoku shite imasu.
Yes, let's grasp trends based on the latest data.	We lack sufficient data.

Conversation example person A	Conversation example person B
次の戦略を立てる前に、市場動向を分析しましょう。	はい、競合他社の動きも把握する必要がありますね。
つぎのせんりゃくをたてるまえに、しじょうどうこうをぶんせきしましょう。	はい、きょうごうたしゃのうごきもはあくするひつようがありますね。
Tsugi no senryaku o tateru mae ni, ichiba dōkō o bunseki shima shou.	Hai, kyōgō tasha no ugoki mo haaku suru hitsuyō ga arimasu ne.
Before formulating our next strategy, let's analyze market trends.	Yes, we also need to understand our competitors' moves.

Cultural Context

Ensure analysis includes emerging trends, not just current state.

競合他社の動きを把握する必要があります。

きょうごうたしゃのうごきをはあくするひつようがあります。

Kyōgō tasha no ugoki o haaku suru hitsuyō ga arimasu.

We need to understand our competitors' movements.

Variation 1	Variation 2
競争相手の行動を理解する必要があります。	Kyō mo shōjin shima shou.
きょうそうあいてのこうどうをりかいするひつようがあります。	きょうそうあいてのこうどうをりかいするひつようがあります。
Kyōsō aite no kōdō o rikai suru hitsuyō ga arimasu.	Tasha no jōkyō o shiru hitsuyō ga arimasu.
We need to understand our competitors' moves.	We need to understand our competitors' moves.

Positive Response	Negative Response
はい、競合分析を詳細に行いましょう。	情報収集が困難です。
はい、きょうごうぶんせきをしょうさいにおこないましょう。	じょうほうしゅうしゅうがこんなんです。
Hai, kyōgō bunseki o shōsai ni gyō ima shou.	Jōhō shūshū ga kon'nandesu.
Yes, let's conduct a detailed competitor analysis.	Gathering information is challenging.

Conversation example person A	Conversation example person B
市場シェアを維持するために、競合他社の動きを把握する必要があります。	了解しました。競合分析レポートを作成します。
しじょうしぇあをいじするために、きょうごうたしゃのうごきをはあくするひつようがあります。	りょうかいしました。きょうごうぶんせきれぽーとをさくせいします。
Ichiba shea o iji suru tame ni, kyōgō tasha no ugoki o haaku suru hitsuyō ga arimasu.	Ryōkai shima shita. Kyōgō bunseki repōto o sakusei shimasu.
To maintain our market share, we need to understand our competitors' moves.	Understood. I'll create a competitive analysis report.

Cultural Context

Look beyond direct competitors to potential disruptors.

新しい技術の導入について検討しましょう。

あたらしいぎじゅつのどうにゅうについてけんとうしましょう。

Atarashī gijutsu no dōnyū ni tsuite kentō shimashou.

Let's consider introducing new technologies.

Variation 1	Variation 2
新規技術の採用について熟考しましょう。	Kyō mo shōjin shima shou.
しんきぎじゅつのさいようについてじゅくこうしましょう。	しんきぎじゅつのさいようについてじゅくこうしましょう。
Shinki gijutsu no saiyō ni tsuite jukukō shima shou.	Shin gijutsu no saiyō o kangae ma shou.
Let's consider introducing new technologies.	Let's consider adopting new technologies.

Positive Response	Negative Response
はい、最新技術のメリットとデメリットを評価しましょう。	コストが高すぎます。
はい、さいしんぎじゅつのめりっととでめりっとをひょうかしましょう。	こすとがたかすぎます。
Hai, saishin gijutsu no meritto to demeritto o hyōka shima shou.	Kosuto ga taka sugimasu.
Yes, let's evaluate the pros and cons of new technologies.	The cost is too high.

Conversation example person A	Conversation example person B
業務効率を上げるため、新しい技術の導入について検討しましょう。	AI や RPA の活用が有効だと思います。
ぎょうむこうりつをあげるため、あたらしいぎじつつのどうにゅうについてけんとうしましょう。	えーあいやあーるぴーえーのかつようがゆうこうだとおもいます。
Gyōmu kōritsu o ageru tame, atarashī gijutsu no dōnyū ni tsuite kentō shima shou.	Ēai ya āru pīē no katsuyō ga yūkōda to omoimasu.
To improve operational efficiency, let's consider introducing new technologies.	I think utilizing AI and RPA would be effective.

Cultural Context

Consider both benefits and potential disruptions of new technology.

コスト削減の可能性を探りましょう。

こすとさくげんのかのうせいをさぐりましょう。
Kosuto sakugen no kanōsei o sagurimashou.
Let's explore cost-cutting possibilities.

Variation 1	Variation 2
経費縮小の見込みを調査しましょう。	Kyō mo shōjin shima shou.
けいひしゅくしょうのみこみをちょうさしましょう。	けいひしゅくしょうのみこみをちょうさしましょう。
Keihi shukushō no mikomi o chōsa shima shou.	Keihi setsuyaku no hōhō o sagashi ma shou.
Let's explore cost-cutting possibilities.	Let's explore cost-saving opportunities.

Positive Response	Negative Response
はい、効率化できる領域を特定しましょう。	これ以上の削減は難しいです。
はい、こうりつかできるりょういきをとくていしましょう。	これいじょうのさくげんはむずかしいです。
Hai, kōritsu-ka dekiru ryōiki o tokutei shima shou.	Kore ijō no sakugen wa muzukashīdesu.
Yes, let's identify areas where we can improve efficiency.	Further cost reduction is difficult.

Conversation example person A	Conversation example person B
利益率を向上させるため、コスト削減の可能性を探りましょう。	承知しました。各部門の経費を見直してみます。
りえきりつをこうじょうさせるため、こすとさくげんのかのうせいをさぐりましょう。	しょうちしました。かくぶもんのけいひをみなおしてみます。
Rieki-ritsu o kōjō sa seru tame, kosuto sakugen no kanō-sei o saguri ma shou.	Shōchi shima shita. Kaku bumon no keihi o minaoshite mimasu.
To improve our profit margins, let's explore cost-reduction possibilities.	Understood. I'll review the expenses of each department.

Cultural Context
Ensure cost-cutting doesn't compromise quality or long-term growth.

品質管理プロセスを見直しましょう。

ひんしつかんりぷろせすをみなおしましょう。

Hinshitsu kanri purosesu o minaoshimashou.

Let's review our quality control processes.

Variation 1	Variation 2
品質保証手順を再検討しましょう。	Kyō mo shōjin shima shou.
ひんしつほしょうてじゅんをさいけんとうしましょう。	ひんしつほしょうてじゅんをさいけんとうしましょう。
Hinshitsu hoshō tejun o sai kentō shima shou.	Hinshitsu chekku no hōhō o sai kentō shima shou.
Let's review our quality control process.	Let's review our quality control process.

Positive Response	Negative Response
はい、より効果的な品質保証方法を考えましょう。	現行のプロセスで十分です。
はい、よりこうかてきなひんしつほしょうほうほうをかんがえましょう。	げんこうのぷろせすでじゅうぶんです。
Hai, yori kōka-tekina hinshitsu hoshō hōhō o kangae ma shou.	Genkō no purosesu de jūbundesu.
Yes, let's consider more effective quality assurance methods.	The current process is sufficient.

Conversation example person A	Conversation example person B
最近の不良品発生率の上昇を受けて、品質管理プロセスを見直しましょう。	はい、各工程のチェックポイントを再評価します。
さいきんのふりょうひんはっせいりつのじょうしょうをうけて、ひんしつかんりぷろせすをみなおしましょう。	はい、かくこうていのちぇっくぽいんとをさいひょうかします。
Saikin no fu ryōhin hassei-ritsu no jōshō o ukete, hinshitsu kanri purosesu o minaoshi ma shou.	Hai, kaku kōtei no chekku pointo o sai hyōka shimasu.
In light of the recent increase in defect rates, let's review our quality control process.	Yes, I'll re-evaluate the checkpoints at each stage of the process.

Cultural Context

Consider both efficiency and effectiveness in quality processes.

従業員の満足度を向上させる方法を考えましょう。

じゅうぎょういんのまんぞくどをこうじょうさせるほうほうをかんがえましょう。

Jūgyōin no manzoku-do o kōjō sa seru hōhō o kangaemashou.

Let's think about ways to improve employee satisfaction.

Variation 1	Variation 2
社員の満足感を高める策を検討しましょう。	Kyō mo shōjin shima shou.
しゃいんのまんぞくかんをたかめるさくをけんとうしましょう。	しゃいんのまんぞくかんをたかめるさくをけんとうしましょう。
Shain no manzoku-kan o takameru saku o kentō shima shou.	Shain no yaruki o takameru hōhō o kangae ma shou.
Let's think about ways to improve employee satisfaction.	Let's think of ways to improve employee satisfaction.

Positive Response	Negative Response
はい、従業員の声を聞きながら改善策を立てましょう。	予算が限られています。
はい、じゅうぎょういんのこえをききながらかいぜんさくをたてましょう。	よさんがかぎられています。
Hai, jūgyō-in no koe o kikinagara kaizen-saku o tate ma shou.	Yosan ga kiri rarete imasu.
Yes, let's develop improvement plans while listening to employees.	The budget is limited.

Conversation example person A	Conversation example person B
離職率が上がっているので、従業員の満足度を向上させる方法を考えましょう。	ワークライフバランスの改善が重要だと考えます。
りしょくりつがあがっているので、じゅうぎょういんのまんぞくどをこうじょうさせるほうほうをかんがえましょう。	わーくらいふばらんすのかいぜんがじゅうようだとかんがえます。
Rishoku-ritsu ga agatte irunode, jūgyō-in no manzoku-do o kōjō sa seru hōhō o kangae ma shou.	Wāku raifu baransu no kaizen ga jūyōda to kangaemasu.
As the turnover rate is increasing, let's think of ways to improve employee satisfaction.	I believe improving work-life balance is crucial.

Cultural Context
Look beyond surface-level issues to deeper cultural factors.

新規事業の可能性を探りましょう。

しんきじぎょうのかのうせいをさぐりましょう。

Shinki jigyō no kanōsei o sagurimashou.

Let's explore possibilities for new business ventures.

Variation 1	Variation 2
新たな事業展開の見込みを調査しましょう。	Kyō mo shōjin shima shou.
あらたなじぎょうてんかいのみこみをちょうさしましょう。	あらたなじぎょうてんかいのみこみをちょうさしましょう。
Aratana jigyō tenkai no mikomi o chōsa shima shou.	Atarashī bijinesu chansu o sagashi ma shou.
Let's explore possibilities for new business ventures.	Let's explore new business opportunities.

Positive Response	Negative Response
素晴らしいアイデアです。新しい成長機会を見つけられそうですね。	リスクが高すぎます。
すばらしいあいであです。あたらしいせいちょうきかいをみつけられそうですね。	りすくがたかすぎます。
Subarashī aideadesu. Atarashī seichō kikai o mitsuke rare-sōdesu ne.	Risuku ga taka sugimasu.
Great idea. We're likely to find new growth opportunities.	The risks are too high.

Conversation example person A	Conversation example person B
長期的な成長のため、新規事業の可能性を探りましょう。	はい、市場調査を行い、有望な分野を特定しましょう。
ちょうきてきなせいちょうのため、しんきじぎょうのかのうせいをさぐりましょう。	はい、しじょうちょうさをおこない、ゆうぼうなぶんやをとくていしましょう。
Chōki-tekina seichō no tame, shinki jigyō no kanō-sei o saguri ma shou.	Hai, ichiba chōsa o okonai, yūbōna bun'ya o tokutei shima shou.
For long-term growth, let's explore possibilities for new business ventures.	Yes, let's conduct market research and identify promising areas.

Cultural Context

Consider synergies with existing business as well as new opportunities.

環境への影響を考慮する必要があります。

かんきょうへのえいきょうをこうりょするひつようがあります。

Kankyō e no eikyō o kōryo suru hitsuyō ga arimasu.

We need to consider the environmental impact.

Variation 1	Variation 2
生態系への作用を勘案する必要があります。	Kyō mo shōjin shima shou.
せいたいけいへのさようをかんがんするひつようがあります。	せいたいけいへのさようをかんがんするひつようがあります。
Seitai-kei e no sayō o kan'an suru hitsuyō ga arimasu.	Kankyō e no hairyo ga hitsuyōdesu.
We need to consider the environmental impact.	We need to consider environmental impact.

Positive Response	Negative Response
同感です。持続可能な事業展開は重要ですね。	コストがかかりすぎます。
どうかんです。じぞくかのうなじぎょうてんかいはじゅうようですね。	こすとがかかりすぎます。
Dōkandesu. Jizoku kanōna jigyō tenkai wa jūyōdesu ne.	Kosuto ga kakari sugimasu.
I agree. Sustainable business development is crucial.	It's too costly.

Conversation example person A	Conversation example person B
新工場建設の計画では、環境への影響を考慮する必要があります。	同感です。環境アセスメントを実施しましょう。
しんこうじょうけんせつのけいかくでは、かんきょうへのえいきょうをこうりょするひつようがあります。	どうかんです。かんきょうあせすめんとをじっししましょう。
Shin kōjō kensetsu no keikakude wa, kankyō e no eikyō o kōryo suru hitsuyō ga arimasu.	Dōkandesu. Kankyō asesumento o jisshi shima shou.
In planning the new factory construction, we need to consider the environmental impact.	I agree. Let's conduct an environmental assessment.

Cultural Context

Look at both direct and indirect environmental impacts.

デジタル化戦略について話し合いましょう。

でじたるかせんりゃくについてはなしあいましょう。
Dejitaru-ka senryaku ni tsuite hanashiaimashou.
Let's discuss our digitalization strategy.

Variation 1	Variation 2
情報化方針について協議しましょう。	Kyō mo shōjin shima shou.
じょうほうかほうしんについてきょうぎしましょう。	じょうほうかほうしんについてきょうぎしましょう。
Jōhō-ka hōshin ni tsuite kyōgi shima shou.	IT katsuyō no hōshin o giron shima shou.
Let's discuss our digitalization strategy.	Let's discuss our digitalization strategy.

Positive Response	Negative Response
ぜひ進めましょう。競争力強化に不可欠ですね。	従業員のスキルが不足しています。
ぜひすすめましょう。きょうそうりょくきょうかにふかけつですね。	じゅうぎょういんのすきるがふそくしています。
Zehi susume ma shou. Kyōsō-ryoku kyōka ni fukaketsudesu ne.	Jūgyō-in no sukiru ga fusoku shite imasu.
Let's definitely proceed. It's essential for strengthening our competitiveness.	Our employees lack the necessary skills.

Conversation example person A	Conversation example person B
今後の成長に向けて、デジタル化戦略について話し合いましょう。	はい、具体的な施策を検討する必要がありますね。
こんごのせいちょうにむけて、でじたるかせんりゃくについてはなしあいましょう。	はい、ぐたいてきなしさくをけんとうするひつようがありますね。
Kongo no seichō ni mukete, dejitaru-ka senryaku ni tsuite hanashiai ma shou.	Hai, gutai-tekina shisaku o kentō suru hitsuyō ga arimasu ne.
Let's discuss our digitalization strategy for future growth.	Yes, we need to consider specific measures.

Cultural Context
Consider both technological and cultural aspects of digital transformation.

人材育成計画を立てる必要があります。

じんざいいくせいけいかくをたてるひつようがあります。

Jinzai ikusei keikakuwotateru hitsuyō ga arimasu.

We need to create a talent development plan.

Variation 1	Variation 2
人財開発構想を策定する必要があります。	Kyō mo shōjin shima shou.
じんざいかいはつこうそうをさくていするひつようがあります。	じんざいかいはつこうそうをさくていするひつようがあります。
Hito-zai kaihatsu kōsō o sakutei suru hitsuyō ga arimasu.	Shain kyōiku no hōshin o kimeru hitsuyō ga arimasu.
We need to create a talent development plan.	We need to create a talent development plan.

Positive Response	Negative Response
賛成です。社員の成長が会社の発展につながりますね。	時間とリソースが足りません。
さんせいです。しゃいんのせいちょうがかいしゃのはってんにつながりますね。	じかんとりそーすがたりません。
Sanseidesu. Shain no seichō ga kaisha no hatten ni tsunagarimasu ne.	Jikan to risōsu ga tarimasen.
I agree. Employee growth leads to company development.	We lack time and resources.

Conversation example person A	Conversation example person B
長期的な視点で、人材育成計画を立てる必要があります。	そうですね。各部門のニーズを踏まえて策定しましょう。
ちょうきてきなしてんで、じんざいいくせいけいかくをたてるひつようがあります。	そうですね。かくぶもんのにーずをふまえてさくていしましょう。
Chōki-tekina shiten de, jinzai ikusei keikaku o tateru hitsuyō ga arimasu.	Sōdesu ne. Kaku bumon no nīzu o fumaete sakutei shima shou.
We need to establish a long-term talent development plan.	Agreed. Let's create it based on each department's needs.

Cultural Context

Align development plans with both individual and organizational needs.

イノベーションを促進する方法を考えましょう。

いのべーしょんをそくしんするほうほうをかんがえましょう。

Inobēshon o sokushin suru hōhō o kangaemashou.

Let's think about ways to promote innovation.

Variation 1	Variation 2
革新を助長する手段を検討しましょう。	Kyō mo shōjin shima shou.
かくしんをじょちょうするしゅだんをけんとうしましょう。	かくしんをじょちょうするしゅだんをけんとうしましょう。
Kakushin o jochō suru shudan o kentō shima shou.	Atarashī aidea o umidasu hōhō o kangae ma shou.
Let's think about ways to promote innovation.	Let's think of ways to promote innovation.

Positive Response	Negative Response
良いですね。新しいアイデアが会社を前進させます。	組織文化が保守的です。
いいですね。あたらしいあいであがかいしゃをぜんしんさせます。	そしきぶんかがほしゅてきです。
Īdesu ne. Atarashī aidea ga kaisha o zenshin sa semasu.	Soshiki bunka ga hoshu-tekidesu.
That's good. New ideas will move the company forward.	Our organizational culture is conservative.

Conversation example person A	Conversation example person B
競争力強化のため、イノベーションを促進する方法を考えましょう。	社内ベンチャー制度の導入はどうでしょうか。
きょうそうりょくきょうかのため、いのべーしょんをそくしんするほうほうをかんがえましょう。	しゃないべんちゃーせいどのどうにゅうはどうでしょうか。
Kyōsō-ryoku kyōka no tame, inobēshon o sokushin suru hōhō o kangae ma shou.	Shanai benchā seido no dōnyū wa dōdeshou ka.
Let's think about ways to promote innovation to enhance our competitiveness.	How about introducing an intrapreneurship program?

Cultural Context

Consider both process improvements and cultural changes.

グローバル展開について議論しましょう。

ぐろーばるてんかいについてぎろんしましょう。

Gurōbaru tenkai ni tsuite giron shimashou.

Let's discuss global expansion.

Variation 1	Variation 2
世界規模の拡大について討議しましょう。	Kyō mo shōjin shima shou.
せかいきぼのかくだいについてとうぎしましょう。	せかいきぼのかくだいについてとうぎしましょう。
Sekai kibo no kakudai ni tsuite tōgi shima shou.	Kaigai shinshutsu ni tsuite hanashiai ma shou.
Let's discuss global expansion.	Let's discuss global expansion.

Positive Response	Negative Response
賛成です。国際市場での成長機会を探れそうですね。	リスクが高すぎます。
さんせいです。こくさいしじょうでのせいちょうきかいをさぐれそうですね。	りすくがたかすぎます。
Sanseidesu. Kokusai shijō de no seichō kikai o sagure-sōdesu ne.	Risuku ga taka sugimasu.
I agree. We can explore growth opportunities in international markets.	The risks are too high.

Conversation example person A	Conversation example person B
市場拡大のため、グローバル展開について議論しましょう。	各国の規制や文化の違いを十分研究する必要がありますね。
しじょうかくだいのため、ぐろーばるてんかいについてぎろんしましょう。	かっこくのきせいやぶんかのちがいをじゅうぶんけんきゅうするひつようがありますね。
Ichiba kakudai no tame, gurōbaru tenkai ni tsuite giron shima shou.	Kakkoku no kisei ya bunka no chigai o jūbun kenkyū suru hitsuyō ga arimasu ne.
Let's discuss global expansion to enlarge our market.	We need to thoroughly research the regulatory and cultural differences of each country.

Cultural Context

Consider cultural and regulatory differences in new markets.

サプライチェーンの最適化を検討しましょう。

さぷらいちぇーんのさいてきかをけんとうしましょう。
Sapuraichēn no saiteki-ka o kentō shimashou.
Let's consider optimizing our supply chain.

Variation 1	Variation 2
供給網の効率化を考察しましょう。	Kyō mo shōjin shima shou.
きょうきゅうもうのこうりつかをこうさつしましょう。	きょうきゅうもうのこうりつかをこうさつしましょう。
Kyōkyū-mō no kōritsu-ka o kōsatsu shima shou.	Chōtatsu kara haisō made no kōritsu-ka o kangae ma shou.
Let's consider optimizing our supply chain.	Let's consider optimizing our supply chain.

Positive Response	Negative Response
重要な課題ですね。効率化で競争力が高まりそうです。	複雑すぎて難しいです。
じゅうようなかだいですね。こうりつかできょうそうりょくがたかまりそうです。	ふくざつすぎてむずかしいです。
Jūyōna kadaidesu ne. Kōritsu-ka de kyōsō-ryoku ga takamari-sōdesu.	Fukuzatsu sugite muzukashīdesu.
That's an important issue. Efficiency improvements could enhance our competitiveness.	It's too complex and difficult.

Conversation example person A	Conversation example person B
コスト削減のため、サプライチェーンの最適化を検討しましょう。	同意します。在庫管理システムの見直しから始めましょう。
こすとさくげんのため、さぷらいちぇーんのさいてきかをけんとうしましょう。	どういします。ざいこかんりしすてむのみなおしからはじめましょう。
Kosuto sakugen no tame, sapurai chēn no saiteki-ka o kentō shima shou.	Dōi shimasu. Zaiko kanri shisutemu no minaoshi kara hajime ma shou.
Let's consider optimizing our supply chain to reduce costs.	I agree. Let's start by reviewing our inventory management system.

Cultural Context
Look at both efficiency and resilience in supply chain design.

ブランド戦略を再評価する必要があります。

ぶらんどせんりゃくをさいひょうかするひつようがあります。

Burando senryaku o sai hyōka suru hitsuyō ga arimasu.

We need to reassess our brand strategy.

Variation 1	Variation 2
企業イメージ戦略を見直す必要があります。	Kyō mo shōjin shima shou.
きぎょういめーじせんりゃくをみなおすひつようがあります。	きぎょういめーじせんりゃくをみなおすひつようがあります。
Kigyō imēji senryaku o minaosu hitsuyō ga arimasu.	Kaisha imēji senryaku o minaosu hitsuyō ga arimasu.
We need to reassess our brand strategy.	We need to reassess our brand strategy.

Positive Response	Negative Response
同意します。市場での位置づけを強化できそうですね。	現状で問題ありません。
どういします。しじょうでのいちづけをきょうかできそうですね。	げんじょうでもんだいありません。
Dōi shimasu. Shijō de no ichidzuke o kyōka deki-sōdesu ne.	Genjō de mondai arimasen.
I agree. We can strengthen our market positioning.	There's no problem with the current situation.

Conversation example person A	Conversation example person B
市場動向の変化に対応するため、ブランド戦略を再評価する必要があります。	その通りです。顧客調査を実施して、ブランドイメージを確認しましょう。
しじょうどうこうのへんかにたいおうするため、ぶらんどせんりゃくをさいひょうかするひつようがあります。	そのとおりです。こきゃくちょうさをじっしして、ぶらんどいめーじをかくにんしましょう。
Ichiba dōkō no henka ni taiō suru tame, burando senryaku o sai hyōka suru hitsuyō ga arimasu.	Sono tōridesu. Kokyaku chōsa o jisshi shite, burando imēji o kakunin shima shou.
We need to reassess our brand strategy to respond to market trends.	You're right. Let's conduct a customer survey to check our brand image.

Cultural Context

Consider both current perceptions and desired future positioning.

顧客満足度向上の施策を考えましょう。

こきゃくまんぞくどこうじょうのしさくをかんがえましょう。

Kokakumanzoku-do kōjō no shisaku o kangaemashou.

Let's think about measures to improve customer satisfaction.

Variation 1	Variation 2
顧客満足度改善の方策を検討しましょう。	Kyō mo shōjin shima shou.
こきゃくまんぞくどかいぜんのほうさくをけんとうしましょう。	こきゃくまんぞくどかいぜんのほうさくをけんとうしましょう。
Kokyaku manzoku-do kaizen no hōsaku o kentō shima shou.	Okyakusama no manzoku-do o ageru hōhō o kangae ma shou.
Let's consider measures to improve customer satisfaction.	Let's think of measures to improve customer satisfaction.

Positive Response	Negative Response
大切な取り組みですね。顧客との関係強化につながります。	コストがかかりすぎます。
たいせつなとりくみですね。こきゃくとのかんけいきょうかにつながります。	こすとがかかりすぎます。
Taisetsuna torikumidesu ne. Kokyaku to no kankei kyōka ni tsunagarimasu.	Kosuto ga kakari sugimasu.
That's an important initiative. It will lead to stronger customer relationships.	It's too costly.

Conversation example person A	Conversation example person B
顧客満足度向上の施策を考えましょう。私たちのサービス品質を見直す時期かもしれません。	賛成です。カスタマーサポートの強化から始めてはどうでしょうか。
こきゃくまんぞくどこうじょうのしさくをかんがえましょう。わたしたちのさーびすひんしつをみなおすじきかもしれません。	さんせいです。かすたまーさぽーとのきょうかからはじめてはどうでしょうか。
Kokyaku manzoku-do kōjō no shisaku o kangae ma shou. Watashi-tachi no sābisu hinshitsu o minaosu jiki kamo shiremasen.	Sanseidesu. Kasutamāsapōto no kyōka kara hajimete wa dōdeshou ka.
Let's think about measures to improve customer satisfaction. It might be time to review our service quality.	I agree. How about starting with strengthening our customer support?

Cultural Context

Look beyond immediate satisfaction to long-term loyalty drivers.

リスク管理体制を強化しましょう。

りすくかんりたいせいをきょうかしましょう。

Risuku kanri taisei o kyōka shimashou.

Let's strengthen our risk management system.

Variation 1	Variation 2
危機対応体勢を充実させましょう。	Kyō mo shōjin shima shou.
ききたいおうたいせいをじゅうじつさせましょう。	ききたいおうたいせいをじゅうじつさせましょう。
Kiki taiō taisei o jūjitsu sa se ma shou.	Kiki kanri no shikumi o kaizen shima shou.
Let's strengthen our risk management system.	Let's strengthen our risk management system.

Positive Response	Negative Response
賛成です。安定した事業運営に不可欠ですね。	現行の体制で十分です。
さんせいです。あんていしたじぎょううんえいにふかけつですね。	げんこうのたいせいでじゅうぶんです。
Sanseidesu. Antei shita jigyō un'ei ni fukaketsudesu ne.	Genkō no taisei de jūbundesu.
I agree. It's essential for stable business operations.	The current system is sufficient.

Conversation example person A	Conversation example person B
不確実性の高い環境下で、リスク管理体制を強化しましょう。	その通りです。各部門のリスク評価を定期的に行う仕組みを作りましょう。
ふかくじつせいのたかいかんきょうかで、りすくかんりたいせいをきょうかしましょう。	そのとおりです。かくぶもんのりすくひょうかをていきてきにおこなうしくみをつくりましょう。
Fu kakujitsu-sei no takai kankyō-ka de, risuku kanri taisei o kyōka shima shou.	Sono tōridesu. Kaku bumon no risuku hyōka o teiki-teki ni okonau shikumi o tsukuri ma shou.
Let's strengthen our risk management system in this highly uncertain environment.	You're right. Let's create a system to regularly assess risks in each department.

Cultural Context
Consider both known risks and potential emerging threats.

業務効率化の方法を探りましょう。

ぎょうむこうりつかのほうほうをさぐりましょう。

Gyōmu kōritsu-ka no hōhō o sagurimashou.

Let's explore ways to improve operational efficiency.

Variation 1	Variation 2
職務能率向上の手段を模索しましょう。	Kyō mo shōjin shima shou.
しょくむのうりつこうじょうのしゅだんをもさくしましょう。	しょくむのうりつこうじょうのしゅだんをもさくしましょう。
Shokumu nōritsu kōjō no shudan o mosaku shima shou.	Shigoto no nōritsu o ageru hōhō o sagashi ma shou.
Let's explore ways to improve operational efficiency.	Let's explore ways to improve operational efficiency.

Positive Response	Negative Response
良いアイデアです。生産性向上につながりそうですね。	これ以上の効率化は難しいです。
よいあいであです。せいさんせいこうじょうにつながりそうですね。	これいじょうのこうりつかはむずかしいです。
Ī aideadesu. Seisan-sei kōjō ni tsunagari-sōdesu ne.	Kore ijō no kōritsu-ka wa muzukashīdesu.
Good idea. It's likely to lead to productivity improvements.	Further efficiency improvements are difficult.

Conversation example person A	Conversation example person B
人手不足に対応するため、業務効率化の方法を探りましょう。	RPA導入を検討してみてはいかがでしょうか。
ひとでぶそくにたいおうするため、ぎょうむこうりつかのほうほうをさぐりましょう。	あーるぴーえーどうにゅうをけんとうしてみてはいかがでしょうか。
Hitode fusoku ni taiō suru tame, gyōmu kōritsu-ka no hōhō o saguri ma shou.	RPA dōnyū o kentō shite mite wa ikagadeshou ka.
Let's explore ways to improve operational efficiency to address labor shortages.	How about considering the introduction of RPA?

Cultural Context

Ensure efficiency improvements don't compromise quality or employee satisfaction.

社内コミュニケーションの改善策を考えましょう。

しゃないこみゅにけーしょんのかいぜんさくをかんがえましょう。

Shanai komyunikēshon no kaizen-saku o kangaemashou.

Let's think about ways to improve internal communication.

Variation 1	Variation 2
組織内対話の向上方法を検討しましょう。	Kyō mo shōjin shima shou.
そしきないたいわのこうじょうほうほうをけんとうしましょう。	そしきないたいわのこうじょうほうほうをけんとうしましょう。
Soshiki-nai taiwa no kōjō hōhō o kentō shima shou.	Shanai no jōhō kyōyū o yoku suru hōhō o kangae ma shou.
Let's consider ways to improve internal communication.	Let's think of ways to improve internal communication.

Positive Response	Negative Response
重要な課題ですね。チームワークの強化につながります。	改善の余地がありません。
じゅうようなかだいですね。ちーむわーくのきょうかにつながります。	かいぜんのよちがありません。
Jūyōna kadaidesu ne. Chīmu wāku no kyōka ni tsunagarimasu.	Kaizen no yochi ga arimasen.
That's an important issue. It will lead to stronger teamwork.	There's no room for improvement.

Conversation example person A	Conversation example person B
リモートワークの増加に伴い、社内コミュニケーションの改善策を考えましょう。	オンラインツールの活用を促進する研修を実施してはどうでしょうか。
りもーとわーくのぞうかにともない、しゃないこみゅにけーしょんのかいぜんさくをかんがえましょう。	おんらいんつーるのかつようをそくしんするけんしゅうをじっししてはどうでしょうか。
Rimōto wāku no zōka ni tomonai, shanai komyunikēshon no kaizen-saku o kangae ma shou.	Onrain tsūru no katsuyō o sokushin suru kenshū o jisshi shite wa dōdeshou ka.
With the increase in remote work, let's think about ways to improve internal communication.	How about conducting training to promote the use of online tools?

Cultural Context

Consider both formal and informal communication channels.

データ分析の結果を検討しましょう。

でーたぶんせきのけっかをけんとうしましょう。
Dēta bunseki no kekka o kentō shimashou.
Let's examine the results of our data analysis.

Variation 1	Variation 2
情報解析の成果を吟味しましょう。	Kyō mo shōjin shima shou.
じょうほうかいせきのせいかをぎんみしましょう。	じょうほうかいせきのせいかをぎんみしましょう。
Jōhō kaiseki no seika o ginmi shima shou.	Jōhō kaiseki no kekka o kakunin shima shou.
Let's examine the results of the data analysis.	Let's review the results of our data analysis.

Positive Response	Negative Response
賛成です。データに基づいた意思決定ができそうですね。	データの信頼性に問題があります。
さんせいです。でーたにもとづいたいしけっていができそうですね。	でーたのしんらいせいにもんだいがあります。
Sanseidesu. Dēta ni motodzuita ishi kettei ga deki-sōdesu ne.	Dēta no shinrai-sei ni mondai ga arimasu.
I agree. We can make data-driven decisions.	There are issues with data reliability.

Conversation example person A	Conversation example person B
マーケティング戦略の見直しのため、データ分析の結果を検討しましょう。	はい、顧客セグメントごとの傾向を詳しく見ていく必要がありますね。
まーけてぃんぐせんりゃくのみなおしのため、でーたぶんせきのけっかをけんとうしましょう。	はい、こきゃくせぐめんとごとのけいこうをくわしくみていくひつようがありますね。
Māketingu senryaku no minaoshi no tame, dēta bunseki no kekka o kentō shima shou.	Hai, kokyaku segumento-goto no keikō o kuwashiku mite iku hitsuyō ga arimasu ne.
Let's review the results of data analysis to revise our marketing strategy.	Yes, we need to look closely at the trends for each customer segment.

Cultural Context
Ensure data interpretation considers context and potential biases.

長期的な成長戦略について話し合いましょう。

ちょうきてきなせいちょうせんりゃくについてはなしあいましょう。

Chōki-tekina seichō senryaku ni tsuite hanashiaimashou.

Let's discuss long-term growth strategies.

Variation 1	Variation 2
持続的発展方針について協議しましょう。	Kyō mo shōjin shima shou.
じぞくてきはってんほうしんについてきょうぎしましょう。	じぞくてきはってんほうしんについてきょうぎしましょう。
Jizoku-teki hatten hōshin ni tsuite kyōgi shima shou.	Shōrai-tekina hatten keikaku o giron shima shou.
Let's discuss long-term growth strategies.	Let's discuss long-term growth strategies.

Positive Response	Negative Response
素晴らしいですね。持続可能な発展につながりそうです。	短期的な問題に集中すべきです。
すばらしいですね。じぞくかのうなはってんにつながりそうです。	たんきてきなもんだいにしゅうちゅうすべきです。
Subarashīdesu ne. Jizoku kanōna hatten ni tsunagari-sōdesu.	Tanki-tekina mondai ni shūchū subekidesu.
That's great. It's likely to lead to sustainable development.	We should focus on short-term issues.

Conversation example person A	Conversation example person B
市場の変化に対応するため、長期的な成長戦略について話し合いましょう。	新規事業への投資と既存事業の強化のバランスを考える必要がありますね。
しじょうのへんかにたいおうするため、ちょうきてきなせいちょうせんりゃくについてはなしあいましょう。	しんきじぎょうへのとうしときそんじぎょうのきょうかのばらんすをかんがえるひつようがありますね。
Ichiba no henka ni taiō suru tame, chōki-tekina seichō senryaku ni tsuite hanashiai ma shou.	Shinki jigyō e no tōshi to kizon jigyō no kyōka no baransu o kangaeru hitsuyō ga arimasu ne.
Let's discuss long-term growth strategies to adapt to market changes.	We need to consider the balance between investing in new businesses and strengthening existing ones.

Cultural Context

Balance short-term performance with long-term sustainability.

新製品開発のアイデアを出し合いましょう。

しんせいひんかいはつのあいであをだしあいましょう。

Shinseihinkaihatsu no aidea o dashiaimashou.

Let's brainstorm ideas for new product development.

Variation 1	Variation 2
新商品創造の構想を共有しましょう。	Kyō mo shōjin shima shou.
しんしょうひんそうぞうのこうそうをきょうゆうしましょう。	しんしょうひんそうぞうのこうそうをきょうゆうしましょう。
Shin shōhin sōzō no kōsō o kyōyū shima shou.	Shin shōhin no aidea o kyōyū shima shou.
Let's brainstorm ideas for new product development.	Let's brainstorm ideas for new product development.

Positive Response	Negative Response
楽しみですね。革新的な製品が生まれそうです。	リソースが足りません。
たのしみですね。かくしんてきなせいひんがうまれそうです。	りそーすがたりません。
Tanoshimidesu ne. Kakushin-tekina seihin ga umare-sōdesu.	Risōsu ga tarimasen.
That's exciting. We might create innovative products.	We don't have enough resources.

Conversation example person A	Conversation example person B
競争力強化のため、新製品開発のアイデアを出し合いましょう。	クロスファンクショナルなチームを作って、多角的な視点を取り入れましょう。
きょうそうりょくきょうかのため、しんせいひんかいはつのあいであをだしあいましょう。	くろすふぁんくしょなるなちーむをつくって、たかくてきなしてんをとりいれましょう。
Kyōsō-ryoku kyōka no tame, shin seihin kaihatsu no aidea o dashiai ma shou.	Kurosu fanku shonaruna chīmu o tsukutte, takaku-tekina shiten o toriire ma shou.
Let's brainstorm ideas for new product development to enhance our competitiveness.	Let's create a cross-functional team to incorporate diverse perspectives.

Cultural Context
Encourage wild ideas while also considering feasibility.

マーケティング戦略の効果を評価しましょう。

まーけてぃんぐせんりゃくのこうかをひょうかしましょう。

Māketingu senryaku no kōka o hyōka shimashou.

Let's evaluate the effectiveness of our marketing strategy.

Variation 1	Variation 2
販促方針の成果を査定しましょう。	Kyō mo shōjin shima shou.
はんそくほうしんのせいかをさていしましょう。	はんそくほうしんのせいかをさていしましょう。
Hansoku hōshin no seika o satei shima shou.	Hansoku katsudō no seika o kakunin shima shou.
Let's evaluate the effectiveness of our marketing strategy.	Let's evaluate the effectiveness of our marketing strategy.

Positive Response	Negative Response
重要ですね。効果的な戦略立案につながりそうです。	測定が難しいです。
じゅうようですね。こうかてきなせんりゃくりつあんにつながりそうです。	そくていがむずかしいです。
Jūyōdesu ne. Kōka-tekina senryaku ritsuan ni tsunagari-sōdesu.	Sokutei ga muzukashīdesu.
That's important. It could lead to more effective strategy planning.	It's difficult to measure.

Conversation example person A	Conversation example person B
今四半期のマーケティング戦略の効果を評価しましょう。改善点を見つける必要があります。	ROIを詳細に分析し、各チャネルの効果を比較する必要がありますね。
こんしはんきのまーけてぃんぐせんりゃくのこうかをひょうかしましょう。かいぜんてんをみつけるひつようがあります。	あーるおーあいをしょうさいにぶんせきし、かくちゃねるのこうかをひかくするひつようがありますね。
Ima shihanki no māketingu senryaku no kōka o hyōka shima shou. Kaizen-ten o mitsukeru hitsuyō ga arimasu.	Āru ō ai o shōsai ni bunseki shi, kaku chaneru no kōka o hikaku suru hitsuyō ga arimasu ne.
Let's evaluate the effectiveness of this quarter's marketing strategy. We need to identify areas for improvement.	We need to analyze the ROI in detail and compare the effectiveness of each channel.

Cultural Context
Look at both direct ROI and broader brand impact.

組織構造の見直しについて議論しましょう。

そしきこうぞうのみなおしについてぎろんしましょう。

Soshiki kōzō no minaoshi ni tsuite giron shimashou.

Let's discuss restructuring our organization.

Variation 1	Variation 2
機構改革について討議しましょう。	Kyō mo shōjin shima shou.
きこうかいかくについてとうぎしましょう。	きこうかいかくについてとうぎしましょう。
Kikō kaikaku ni tsuite tōgi shima shou.	Shanai taisei no sai hensei ni tsuite hanashiai ma shou.
Let's discuss reorganizing our organizational structure.	Let's discuss restructuring our organization.

Positive Response	Negative Response
良いタイミングですね。より効率的な体制が作れそうです。	混乱を招く可能性があります。
よいたいみんぐですね。よりこうりつてきなたいせいがつくれそうです。	こんらんをまねくかのうせいがあります。
Ī taimingudesu ne. Yori kōritsu-tekina taisei ga tsukure-sōdesu.	Konran o maneku kanō-sei ga arimasu.
Good timing. We can create a more efficient structure.	It might cause confusion.

Conversation example person A	Conversation example person B
業務効率化のため、組織構造の見直しについて議論しましょう。	フラットな組織構造への移行を検討してみてはいかがでしょうか。
ぎょうむこうりつかのため、そしきこうぞうのみなおしについてぎろんしましょう。	ふらっとなそしきこうぞうへのいこうをけんとうしてみてはいかがでしょうか。
Gyōmu kōritsu-ka no tame, soshiki kōzō no minaoshi ni tsuite giron shima shou.	Furattona soshiki kōzō e no ikō o kentō shite mite wa ikagadeshou ka.
Let's discuss reviewing our organizational structure for operational efficiency.	How about considering a transition to a flatter organizational structure?

Cultural Context

Consider both efficiency and employee satisfaction in restructuring.

業界のベストプラクティスを研究しましょう。

ぎょうかいのべすとぷらくてぃすをけんきゅうしましょう。

Gyōkai no besutopurakutisu o kenkyū shimashou.

Let's study industry best practices.

Variation 1	Variation 2
同業他社の成功例を調査しましょう。	Kyō mo shōjin shima shou.
どうぎょうたしゃのせいこうれいをちょうさしましょう。	どうぎょうたしゃのせいこうれいをちょうさしましょう。
Dōgyō tasha no seikō rei o chōsa shima shou.	Gyōkai no seikō jirei o shirabe ma shou.
Let's study industry best practices.	Let's study industry best practices.

Positive Response	Negative Response
素晴らしいアイデアです。競争力強化につながりそうですね。	我々の状況には適用できません。
すばらしいあいであです。きょうそうりょくきょうかにつながりそうですね。	われわれのじょうきょうにはてきようできません。
Subarashī aideadesu. Kyōsō-ryoku kyōka ni tsunagari-sōdesu ne.	Wareware no jōkyō ni wa tekiyō dekimasen.
Great idea. It's likely to enhance our competitiveness.	It's not applicable to our situation.

Conversation example person A	Conversation example person B
競争力向上のため、業界のベストプラクティスを研究しましょう。	同意します。ベンチマーキング調査を実施しましょう。
きょうそうりょくこうじょうのため、ぎょうかいのべすとぷらくてぃすをけんきゅうしましょう。	どういします。べんちまーきんぐちょうさをじっししましょう。
Kyōsō-ryoku kōjō no tame, gyōkai no besuto purakutisu o kenkyū shima shou.	Dōi shimasu. Benchi mākingu chōsa o jisshi shima shou.
Let's study industry best practices to improve our competitiveness.	I agree. Let's conduct a benchmarking study.

Cultural Context

Adapt best practices to fit your unique organizational context.

社会的責任について考えましょう。

しゃかいてきせきにんについてかんがえましょう。
Shakaitekisekinin ni tsuite kangaemashou.
Let's think about our social responsibility.

Variation 1	Variation 2
公共への貢献について検討しましょう。	Kyō mo shōjin shima shou.
こうきょうへのこうけんについてけんとうしましょう。	こうきょうへのこうけんについてけんとうしましょう。
Kōkyō e no kōken ni tsuite kentō shima shou.	Kigyō no shakai kōken ni tsuite kangae ma shou.
Let's think about our social responsibility.	Let's think about our social responsibility.

Positive Response	Negative Response
重要な課題ですね。持続可能な成長につながりそうです。	利益に直結しません。
じゅうようなかだいですね。じぞくかのうなせいちょうにつながりそうです。	りえきにちょっけつしません。
Jūyōna kadaidesu ne. Jizoku kanōna seichō ni tsunagari-sōdesu.	Rieki ni chokketsu shima sen.
That's an important issue. It could lead to sustainable growth.	It doesn't directly lead to profits.

Conversation example person A	Conversation example person B
企業の持続可能性のため、社会的責任について考えましょう。	SDGs への取り組みを強化する必要がありますね。
きぎょうのじぞくかのうせいのため、しゃかいてきせきにんについてかんがえましょう。	えすでぃーじーずへのとりくみをきょうかするひつようがありますね。
Kigyō no jizoku kanō-sei no tame, shakai-teki sekinin ni tsuite kangae ma shou.	Esudī jīzu e no torikumi o kyōka suru hitsuyō ga arimasu ne.
Let's think about our social responsibility for corporate sustainability.	We need to strengthen our efforts towards the SDGs.

Cultural Context
Look beyond compliance to proactive social impact.

IT インフラの更新計画を立てましょう。

あいてぃーいんふらのこうしんけいかくをたてましょう。

Aitīinfura no kōshin keikaku o tatemashou.

Let's create an IT infrastructure upgrade plan.

Variation 1	Variation 2
情報基盤の刷新案を策定しましょう。	Kyō mo shōjin shima shou.
じょうほうきばんのしっしんあんをさくていしましょう。	じょうほうきばんのしっしんあんをさくていしましょう。
Jōhō kiban no sasshin-an o sakutei shima shou.	Jōhō shisutemu no sasshin keikaku o tsukuri ma shou.
Let's create a plan to update our IT infrastructure.	Let's create an IT infrastructure update plan.

Positive Response	Negative Response
賛成です。業務効率化につながりそうですね。	コストが高すぎます。
さんせいです。ぎょうむこうりつかにつながりそうですね。	こすとがたかすぎます。
Sanseidesu. Gyōmu kōritsu-ka ni tsunagari-sōdesu ne.	Kosuto ga taka sugimasu.
I agree. It's likely to lead to operational efficiency.	The cost is too high.

Conversation example person A	Conversation example person B
セキュリティ強化のため、ITインフラの更新計画を立てましょう。	クラウドへの移行を含めた包括的な計画が必要ですね。
せきゅりてぃきょうかのため、あいてぃーいんふらのこうしんけいかくをたてましょう。	くらうどへのいこうをふくめたほうかつてきなけいかくがひつようですね。
Sekyuriti kyōka no tame, IT infura no kōshin keikaku o tate ma shou.	Kura udo e no ikō o fukumeta hōkatsu-tekina keikaku ga hitsuyōdesu ne.
Let's create an IT infrastructure upgrade plan to enhance security.	We need a comprehensive plan that includes migration to the cloud.

Cultural Context

Consider both current needs and future scalability.

人事評価システムの改善を検討しましょう。

じんじひょうかしすてむのかいぜんをけんとうしましょう。

Jinji hyōka shisutemu no kaizen o kentō shimashou.

Let's consider improving our performance evaluation system.

Variation 1	Variation 2
従業員査定制度の向上を考察しましょう。	Kyō mo shōjin shima shou.
じゅうぎょういんさていせいどのこうじょうをこうさつしましょう。	じゅうぎょういんさていせいどのこうじょうをこうさつしましょう。
Jūgyō-in satei seido no kōjō o kōsatsu shima shou.	Shain no hyōka hōhō no minaoshi o kangae ma shou.
Let's consider improving our personnel evaluation system.	Let's consider improving our performance appraisal system.

Positive Response	Negative Response
良いアイデアです。社員のモチベーション向上につながりそうですね。	現行のシステムで問題ありません。
よいあいであです。しゃいんのもちべーしょんこうじょうにつながりそうですね。	げんこうのしすてむでもんだいありません。
Ī aideadesu. Shain no mochibēshon kōjō ni tsunagari-sōdesu ne.	Genkō no shisutemu de mondai arimasen.
Good idea. It could lead to improved employee motivation.	There's no problem with the current system.

Conversation example person A	Conversation example person B
従業員のモチベーション向上のため、人事評価システムの改善を検討しましょう。	360度評価の導入を検討してみてはいかがでしょうか。
じゅうぎょういんのもちべーしょんこうじょうのため、じんじひょうかしすてむのかいぜんをけんとうしましょう。	さんびゃくろくじゅうどひょうかのどうにゅうをけんとうしてみてはいかがでしょうか。
Jūgyō-in no mochibēshon kōjō no tame, jinji hyōka shisutemu no kaizen o kentō shima shou.	San byaku roku jū-do hyōka no dōnyū o kentō shite mite wa ikagadeshou ka.
Let's consider improving our performance evaluation system to boost employee motivation.	How about considering the introduction of 360-degree feedback?

Cultural Context

Ensure alignment with organizational values and goals.

財務状況を詳しく分析しましょう。

ざいむじょうきょうをくわしくぶんせきしましょう。

Zaimu jōkyō o kuwashiku bunseki shimashou.

Let's analyze our financial situation in detail.

Variation 1	Variation 2
経理状態を綿密に解析しましょう。	Kyō mo shōjin shima shou.
けいりじょうたいをめんみつにかいせきしましょう。	けいりじょうたいをめんみつにかいせきしましょう。
Keiri jōtai o menmitsu ni kaiseki shima shou.	Keiei jōtai o komakaku shirabe ma shou.
Let's analyze our financial situation in detail.	Let's analyze our financial situation in detail.

Positive Response	Negative Response
重要ですね。健全な経営判断につながりそうです。	機密情報の開示が問題です。
じゅうようですね。けんぜんなけいえいはんだんにつながりそうです。	きみつじょうほうのかいじがもんだいです。
Jūyōdesu ne. Kenzen'na keiei handan ni tsunagari-sōdesu.	Kimitsu jōhō no kaiji ga mondaidesu.
That's important. It could lead to sound management decisions.	Disclosing confidential information is an issue.

Conversation example person A	Conversation example person B
今後の投資判断のため、財務状況を詳しく分析しましょう。	キャッシュフロー分析に重点を置く必要がありますね。
こんごのとうしはんだんのため、ざいむじょうきょうをくわしくぶんせきしましょう。	きゃっしゅふろーぶんせきにじゅうてんをおくひつようがありますね。
Kongo no tōshi handan no tame, zaimu jōkyō o kuwashiku bunseki shima shou.	Kyasshu furō bunseki ni jūten o oku hitsuyō ga arimasu ne.
Let's analyze our financial situation in detail for future investment decisions.	We need to focus on cash flow analysis.

Cultural Context

Look beyond surface numbers to underlying trends and risks.

新しい市場セグメントの開拓を検討しましょう。

あたらしいしじょうせぐめんとのかいたくをけんとうしましょう。
Atarashī ichiba segumento no kaitaku o kentō shimashou.
Let's consider exploring new market segments.

Variation 1	Variation 2
未開拓の顧客層の獲得を考えましょう。	Kyō mo shōjin shima shou.
みかいたくのこきゃくそうのかくとくをかんがえましょう。	みかいたくのこきゃくそうのかくとくをかんがえましょう。
Mi kaitaku no kokyaku-sō no kakutoku o kangae ma shou.	Shinki kokyaku-sō no kakutoku o kangae ma shou.
Let's consider exploring new market segments.	Let's consider exploring new market segments.

Positive Response	Negative Response
素晴らしいアイデアです。新たな成長機会が見つかりそうですね。	リスクが高すぎます。
すばらしいあいであです。あらたなせいちょうきかいがみつかりそうですね。	りすくがたかすぎます。
Subarashī aideadesu. Aratana seichō kikai ga mitsukari-sōdesu ne.	Risuku ga taka sugimasu.
Great idea. We might find new growth opportunities.	The risks are too high.

Conversation example person A	Conversation example person B
成長戦略の一環として、新しい市場セグメントの開拓を検討しましょう。	若年層向けの新製品ラインの開発はどうでしょうか。
せいちょうせんりゃくのいっかんとして、あたらしいしじょうせぐめんとのかいたくをけんとうしましょう。	わかねんそうむけのしんせいひんらいんのかいはつはどうでしょうか。
Seichō senryaku no ikkan to shite, atarashī ichiba segumento no kaitaku o kentō shima shou.	Wakanen-sō-muke no shin seihin rain no kaihatsu wa dōdeshou ka.
As part of our growth strategy, let's consider exploring new market segments.	How about developing a new product line for the younger generation?

Cultural Context
Consider both market potential and organizational fit.

生産性向上のための施策を考えましょう。

せいさんせいこうじょうのためのしさくをかんがえましょう。

Seisanseikōjō no tame no shisaku o kangaemashou.

Let's think about measures to improve productivity.

Variation 1	Variation 2
作業能率改善の方策を検討しましょう。	Kyō mo shōjin shima shou.
さぎょうのうりつかいぜんのほうさくをけんとうしましょう。	さぎょうのうりつかいぜんのほうさくをけんとうしましょう。
Sagyō nōritsu kaizen no hōsaku o kentō shima shou.	Kōritsu appu no hōhō o kangae ma shou.
Let's consider measures to improve productivity.	Let's think of measures to improve productivity.

Positive Response	Negative Response
賛成です。競争力強化につながりそうですね。	これ以上の改善は難しいです。
さんせいです。きょうそうりょくきょうかにつながりそうですね。	これいじょうのかいぜんはむずかしいです。
Sanseidesu. Kyōsō-ryoku kyōka ni tsunagari-sōdesu ne.	Kore ijō no kaizen wa muzukashīdesu.
I agree. It's likely to enhance our competitiveness.	Further improvements are difficult.

Conversation example person A	Conversation example person B
コスト競争力強化のため、生産性向上のための施策を考えましょう。	自動化技術の導入を検討する必要がありますね。
こすときょうそうりょくきょうかのため、せいさんせいこうじょうのためのしさくをかんがえましょう。	じどうかぎじゅつのどうにゅうをけんとうするひつようがありますね。
Kosuto kyōsō-ryoku kyōka no tame, seisan-sei kōjō no tame no shisaku o kangae ma shou.	Jidōka gijutsu no dōnyū o kentō suru hitsuyō ga arimasu ne.
Let's think about measures to improve productivity to enhance cost competitiveness.	We need to consider introducing automation technology.

Cultural Context

Balance productivity gains with employee well-being.

顧客ロイヤルティプログラムの効果を評価しましょう。

こきゃくろいやるてぃーぷろぐらむのこうかをひょうかしましょう。

Kokyaku roiyarutipuroguramu no kōka o hyōka shimashou.

Let's evaluate the effectiveness of our customer loyalty program.

Variation 1	Variation 2
利用者忠誠度施策の成果を査定しましょう。	Kyō mo shōjin shima shou.
りようしゃちゅうせいどしさくのせいかをさていしましょう。	りようしゃちゅうせいどしさくのせいかをさていしましょう。
Riyō-sha chūsei-do shisaku no seika o satei shima shou.	Jōren kyaku-muke sābisu no seika o kakunin shima shou.
Let's evaluate the effectiveness of our customer loyalty program.	Let's evaluate the effectiveness of our customer loyalty program.

Positive Response	Negative Response
良いですね。顧客との関係強化につながりそうです。	測定が困難です。
よいですね。こきゃくとのかんけいきょうかにつながりそうです。	そくていがこんなんです。
Īdesu ne. Kokyaku to no kankei kyōka ni tsunagari-sōdesu.	Sokutei ga kon'nandesu.
That's good. It could lead to stronger customer relationships.	Measurement is challenging.

Conversation example person A	Conversation example person B
顧客維持戦略の一環として、顧客ロイヤルティプログラムの効果を評価しましょう。	データ分析を通じて、プログラムの改善点を見つけましょう。
こきゃくいじせんりゃくのいっかんとして、こきゃくろいやるてぃぷろぐらむのこうかをひょうかしましょう。	でーたぶんせきをつうじて、ぷろぐらむのかいぜんてんをみつけましょう。
Kokyaku iji senryaku no ikkan to shite, kokyaku roiyaru ti puroguramu no kōka o hyōka shima shou.	Dēta bunseki o tsūjite, puroguramu no kaizen-ten o mitsuke ma shou.
As part of our customer retention strategy, let's evaluate the effectiveness of our customer loyalty program.	Let's find areas for improvement in the program through data analysis.

Cultural Context

Look at both short-term metrics and long-term customer value.

海外展開のリスクと機会を分析しましょう。

かいがいてんかいのりすくときかいをぶんせきしましょう。

Kaigai tenkai no risuku to kikai o bunseki shimashou.

Let's analyze the risks and opportunities of overseas expansion.

Variation 1	Variation 2
国際進出の危険性と可能性を解析しましょう。	Kyō mo shōjin shima shou.
こくさいしんしゅつのきけんせいとかのうせいをかいせきしましょう。	こくさいしんしゅつのきけんせいとかのうせいをかいせきしましょう。
Kokusai shinshutsu no kiken-sei to kanō-sei o kaiseki shima shou.	Kaigai shinshutsu no kiken-sei to kanō-sei o shirabe ma shou.
Let's analyze the risks and opportunities of overseas expansion.	Let's analyze the risks and opportunities of overseas expansion.

Positive Response	Negative Response
重要な課題ですね。グローバル戦略の立案に役立ちそうです。	情報が不足しています。
じゅうようなかだいですね。ぐろーばるせんりゃくのりつあんにやくだちそうです。	じょうほうがふそくしています。
Jūyōna kadaidesu ne. Gurōbaru senryaku no ritsuan ni yakudachi-sōdesu.	Jōhō ga fusoku shite imasu.
That's an important issue. It could help in formulating our global strategy.	We lack sufficient information.

Conversation example person A	Conversation example person B
事業拡大の可能性を探るため、海外展開のリスクと機会を分析しましょう。	PESTLE 分析を行い、各国の状況を詳細に調査する必要がありますね。
じぎょうかくだいのかのうせいをさぐるため、かいがいてんかいのりすくときかいをぶんせきしましょう。	ぺすてるぶんせきをおこない、かっこくのじょうきょうをしょうさいにちょうさするひつようがありますね。
Jigyō kakudai no kanō-sei o saguru tame, kaigai tenkai no risuku to kikai o bunseki shima shou.	Pesuteru bunseki o okonai, kakkoku no jōkyō o shōsai ni chōsa suru hitsuyō ga arimasu ne.
To explore the possibility of business expansion, let's analyze the risks and opportunities of overseas expansion.	We need to conduct a PESTEL analysis and investigate the situation in each country in detail.

Cultural Context

Consider both market-specific factors and global trends.

持続可能な事業モデルについて議論しましょう。

じぞくかのうなじぎょうもでるについてぎろんしましょう。
Jizoku kanōna jigyō moderu ni tsuite giron shimashou.
Let's discuss sustainable business models.

Variation 1	Variation 2
永続的な経営形態について討議しましょう。	Kyō mo shōjin shima shou.
えいぞくてきなけいえいけいたいについてとうぎしましょう。	えいぞくてきなけいえいけいたいについてとうぎしましょう。
Eizoku-tekina keiei keitai ni tsuite tōgi shima shou.	Chōki-teki ni tsudzuku jigyō no katachi ni tsuite hanashiai ma shou.
Let's discuss sustainable business models.	Let's discuss sustainable business models.

Positive Response	Negative Response
賛成です。長期的な成功につながりそうですね。	短期的な利益が減少します。
さんせいです。ちょうきてきなせいこうにつながりそうですね。	たんきてきなりえきがげんしょうします。
Sanseidesu. Chōki-tekina seikō ni tsunagari-sōdesu ne.	Tanki-tekina rieki ga genshō shimasu.
I agree. It's likely to lead to long-term success.	It will decrease short-term profits.

Conversation example person A	Conversation example person B
長期的な企業価値向上のため、持続可能な事業モデルについて議論しましょう。	循環型経済への移行を視野に入れた戦略が必要ですね。
ちょうきてきなきぎょうかちこうじょうのため、じぞくかのうなじぎょうもでるについてぎろんしましょう。	じゅんかんがたけいざいへのいこうをしやにいれたせんりゃくがひつようですね。
Chōki-tekina kigyō kachi kōjō no tame, jizoku kanōna jigyō moderu ni tsuite giron shima shou.	Junkan-gata keizai e no ikō o shiya ni ireta senryaku ga hitsuyōdesu ne.
To enhance long-term corporate value, let's discuss sustainable business models.	We need a strategy that considers the transition to a circular economy.

Cultural Context

Balance economic, social, and environmental considerations.

従業員のスキル向上プログラムを検討しましょう。

じゅうぎょういんのすきるこうじょうぷろぐらむをけんとうしましょう。

Jūgyōin no sukiru kōjō puroguramu o kentō shimashou.

Let's consider employee skill enhancement programs.

Variation 1	Variation 2
社員の能力開発計画を考察しましょう。	Kyō mo shōjin shima shou.
しゃいんののうりょくかいはつけいかくをこうさつしましょう。	しゃいんののうりょくかいはつけいかくをこうさつしましょう。
Shain no nōryoku kaihatsu keikaku o kōsatsu shima shou.	Shain no nōryoku kaihatsu keikaku o kangae ma shou.
Let's consider employee skill enhancement programs.	Let's consider employee skill development programs.

Positive Response	Negative Response
素晴らしいアイデアです。社員の成長が会社の発展につながりますね。	予算が足りません。
すばらしいあいであです。しゃいんのせいちょうがかいしゃのはってんにつながりますね。	よさんがたりません。
Subarashī aideadesu. Shain no seichō ga kaisha no hatten ni tsunagarimasu ne.	Yosan ga tarimasen.
Great idea. Employee growth leads to company development.	We don't have enough budget.

Conversation example person A	Conversation example person B
人材育成の一環として、従業員のスキル向上プログラムを検討しましょう。	オンライン学習プラットフォームの導入はどうでしょうか。
じんざいいくせいのいっかんとして、じゅうぎょういんのすきるこうじょうぷろぐらむをけんとうしましょう。	おんらいんがくしゅうぷらっとふぉーむのどうにゅうはどうでしょうか。
Jinrai ikusei no ikkan to shite, jūgyō-in no sukiru kōjō puroguramu o kentō shima shou.	Onrain gakushū purattofōmu no dōnyū wa dōdeshou ka.
As part of talent development, let's consider skill enhancement programs for employees.	How about introducing an online learning platform?

Cultural Context

Align skill development with both current and future organizational needs.

クロスファンクショナルな協力体制を強化しましょう。

くろすふぁんくしょなるなきょうりょくたいせいをきょうかしましょう。

Kurosufankushonaruna kyōryoku taisei o kyōka shimashou.

Let's strengthen cross-functional cooperation.

Variation 1	Variation 2
部門横断的な連携体制を充実させましょう。	Kyō mo shōjin shima shou.
ぶもんおうだんてきなれんけいたいせいをじゅうじつさせましょう。	ぶもんおうだんてきなれんけいたいせいをじゅうじつさせましょう。
Bumon ōdan-tekina renkei taisei o jūjitsu sa se ma shou.	Bumon o koeta kyōryoku no shikumi o kaizen shima shou.
Let's strengthen cross-functional collaboration.	Let's strengthen cross-functional collaboration.

Positive Response	Negative Response
良いですね。部門間の連携が強化されそうです。	部門間の対立が問題です。
よいですね。ぶもんかんのれんけいがきょうかされそうです。	ぶもんかんのたいりつがもんだいです。
Yoidesu ne. Bumon-kan no renkei ga kyōka sa re-sōdesu.	Bumon-kan no tairitsu ga mondaidesu.
That's good. It could strengthen interdepartmental collaboration.	Interdepartmental conflicts are an issue.

Conversation example person A	Conversation example person B
業務効率化のため、クロスファンクショナルな協力体制を強化しましょう。	部門間の定期的な情報共有会議を設けてはいかがでしょうか。
ぎょうむこうりつかのため、くろすふぁんくしょなるなきょうりょくたいせいをきょうかしましょう。	ぶもんかんのていきてきなじょうほうきょうゆうかいぎをもうけてはいかがでしょうか。
Gyōmu kōritsu-ka no tame, kurosu fanku shonaruna kyōryoku taisei o kyōka shima shou.	Bumon-kan no teiki-tekina jōhō kyōyū kaigi o mōkete wa ikagadeshou ka.
To improve operational efficiency, let's strengthen cross-functional cooperation.	How about setting up regular cross-departmental information sharing meetings?

Cultural Context

Address both structural and cultural barriers to collaboration.

顧客体験の改善策を考えましょう。

こきゃくたいけんのかいぜんさくをかんがえましょう。

Kokyaku taiken no kaizen-saku o kangaemashou.

Let's think about ways to improve customer experience.

Variation 1	Variation 2
利用者経験の向上方法を検討しましょう。	Kyō mo shōjin shima shou.
りようしゃけいけんのこうじょうほうほうをけんとうしましょう。	りようしゃけいけんのこうじょうほうほうをけんとうしましょう。
Riyō-sha keiken no kōjō hōhō o kentō shima shou.	Okyakusama no manzoku-do o ageru hōhō o kangae ma shou.
Let's consider ways to improve customer experience.	Let's think of ways to improve customer experience.

Positive Response	Negative Response
重要な課題ですね。顧客満足度の向上につながりそうです。	現状で十分です。
じゅうようなかだいですね。こきゃくまんぞくどのこうじょうにつながりそうです。	げんじょうでじゅうぶんです。
Jūyōna kadaidesu ne. Kokyaku manzoku-do no kōjō ni tsunagari-sōdesu.	Genjō de jūbundesu.
That's an important issue. It could lead to improved customer satisfaction.	The current situation is sufficient.

Conversation example person A	Conversation example person B
競争優位性確保のため、顧客体験の改善策を考えましょう。	カスタマージャーニーマップを作成し、各接点での改善を検討しましょう。
きょうそうゆういせいかくほのため、こきゃくたいけんのかいぜんさくをかんがえましょう。	かすたまーじゃーにーまっぷをさくせいし、かくせってんでのかいぜんをけんとうしましょう。
Kyōsō yūi-sei kakuho no tame, kokyaku taiken no kaizen-saku o kangae ma shou.	Kasutamā jānī mappu o sakusei shi, kaku setten de no kaizen o kentō shima shou.
To secure competitive advantage, let's think about ways to improve customer experience.	Let's create a customer journey map and consider improvements at each touchpoint.

Cultural Context

Consider the entire customer journey, not just individual touchpoints.

業務プロセスの自動化を検討しましょう。

ぎょうむぷろせすのじどうかをけんとうしましょう。

Gyōmu purosesu no jidō-ka o kentō shimashou.

Let's consider automating business processes.

Variation 1	Variation 2
職務手順の機械化を考察しましょう。	Kyō mo shōjin shima shou.
しょくむてじゅんのきかいかをこうさつしましょう。	しょくむてじゅんのきかいかをこうさつしましょう。
Shokumu tejun no kikai-ka o kōsatsu shima shou.	Shigoto no nagare no kikai-ka o kangae ma shou.
Let's consider automating business processes.	Let's consider automating business processes.

Positive Response	Negative Response
賛成です。効率化と品質向上につながりそうですね。	従業員の反発が予想されます。
さんせいです。こうりつかとひんしつこうじょうにつながりそうですね。	じゅうぎょういんのはんぱつがよそうされます。
Sanseidesu. Kōritsu-ka to hinshitsu kōjō ni tsunagari-sōdesu ne.	Jūgyō-in no hanpatsu ga yosō sa remasu.
I agree. It's likely to lead to efficiency and quality improvements.	Employee resistance is expected.

Conversation example person A	Conversation example person B
効率化とコスト削減のため、業務プロセスの自動化を検討しましょう。	RPA ツールの導入から始めてみてはいかがでしょうか。
こうりつかとこすとさくげんのため、ぎょうむぷろせすのじどうかをけんとうしましょう。	あーるぴーえーつーるのどうにゅうからはじめてみてはいかがでしょうか。
Kōritsu-ka to kosuto sakugen no tame, gyōmu purosesu no jidō-ka o kentō shima shou.	Āru pīē tsūru no dōnyū kara hajimete mite wa ikagadeshou ka.
To improve efficiency and reduce costs, let's consider automating business processes.	How about starting with the introduction of RPA tools?

Cultural Context

Balance efficiency gains with potential job displacement concerns.

新しい収益源を探りましょう。

あたらしいしゅうえきげんをさぐりましょう。

Atarashī shūeki-gen o sagurimashou.

Let's explore new revenue streams.

Variation 1	Variation 2
未開拓の利益獲得手段を模索しましょう。	Kyō mo shōjin shima shou.
みかいたくのりえきかくとくしゅだんをもさくしましょう。	みかいたくのりえきかくとくしゅだんをもさくしましょう。
Mi kaitaku no rieki kakutoku shudan o mosaku shima shou.	Aratana mōke kuchi o sagashi ma shou.
Let's explore new revenue streams.	Let's explore new revenue streams.

Positive Response	Negative Response
素晴らしいアイデアです。事業の多角化につながりそうですね。	リスクが高すぎます。
すばらしいあいであです。じぎょうのたかくかにつながりそうですね。	りすくがたかすぎます。
Subarashī aideadesu. Jigyō no takaku-ka ni tsunagari-sōdesu ne.	Risuku ga taka sugimasu.
Great idea. It could lead to business diversification.	The risks are too high.

Conversation example person A	Conversation example person B
事業の多角化のため、新しい収益源を探りましょう。	サブスクリプションモデルの導入を検討してみましょう。
じぎょうのたかくかのため、あたらしいしゅうえきげんをさぐりましょう。	さぶすくりぷしょんもでるのどうにゅうをけんとうしてみましょう。
Jigyō no takaku-ka no tame, atarashī shūeki-gen o saguri ma shou.	Sabusukuripushon moderu no dōnyū o kentō shite mimashou.
To diversify our business, let's explore new revenue streams.	Let's consider introducing a subscription model.

Cultural Context

Consider both immediate opportunities and long-term strategic fit.

コンプライアンス体制を強化する必要があります。

こんぷらいあんすたいせいをきょうかするひつようがあります。
Konpuraiansu taisei o kyōka suru hitsuyō ga arimasu.
We need to strengthen our compliance system.

Variation 1	Variation 2
法令順守体制を充実させる必要があります。	Kyō mo shōjin shima shou.
ほうれいじゅんしゅたいせいをじゅうじつさせるひつようがあります。	ほうれいじゅんしゅたいせいをじゅうじつさせるひつようがあります。
Hōrei junshu taisei o jūjitsu sa seru hitsuyō ga arimasu.	Hōrei junshu no shikumi o kaizen suru hitsuyō ga arimasu.
We need to strengthen our compliance system.	We need to strengthen our compliance system.

Positive Response	Negative Response
重要ですね。リスク管理の向上につながりそうです。	コストがかかりすぎます。
じゅうようですね。りすくかんりのこうじょうにつながりそうです。	こすとがかかりすぎます。
Jūyōdesu ne. Risuku kanri no kōjō ni tsunagari-sōdesu.	Kosuto ga kakari sugimasu.
That's important. It could lead to improved risk management.	It's too costly.

Conversation example person A	Conversation example person B
リスク管理の観点から、コンプライアンス体制を強化する必要があります。	定期的な社内研修と監査の実施が重要ですね。
りすくかんりのかんてんから、こんぷらいあんすたいせいをきょうかするひつようがあります。	ていきてきなしゃないけんしゅうとかんさのじっしがじゅうようですね。
Risuku kanri no kanten kara, konpuraiansu taisei o kyōka suru hitsuyō ga arimasu.	Teiki-tekina shanai kenshū to kansa no jisshi ga jūyōdesu ne.
From a risk management perspective, we need to strengthen our compliance system.	Regular internal training and audits are important.

Cultural Context
Look beyond mere compliance to ethical business practices.

従業員のモチベーション向上策を考えましょう。

じゅうぎょういんのもちべーしょんこうじょうさくをかんがえましょう。

Jūgyōin no mochibēshon kōjō-saku o kangaemashou.

Let's think about ways to improve employee motivation.

Variation 1	Variation 2
社員の意欲増進方法を検討しましょう。	Kyō mo shōjin shima shou.
しゃいんのいよくぞうしんほうほうをけんとうしましょう。	しゃいんのいよくぞうしんほうほうをけんとうしましょう。
Shain no iyoku zōshin hōhō o kentō shima shou.	Shain no yaruki o takameru hōhō o saguri ma shou.
Let's consider ways to improve employee motivation.	Let's explore ways to boost employee motivation.

Positive Response	Negative Response
良いアイデアです。生産性の向上につながりそうですね。	効果が見込めません。
よいあいであです。せいさんせいのこうじょうにつながりそうですね。	こうかがみこめません。
Ī aideadesu. Seisan-sei no kōjō ni tsunagari-sōdesu ne.	Kōka ga mikomemasen.
Good idea. It could lead to increased productivity.	We can't expect significant effects.

Conversation example person A	Conversation example person B
生産性向上のため、従業員のモチベーション向上策を考えましょう。	フレックスタイム制の導入はどうでしょうか。
せいさんせいこうじょうのため、じゅうぎょういんのもちべーしょんこうじょうさくをかんがえましょう。	ふれっくすたいむせいのどうにゅうはどうでしょうか。
Seisan-sei kōjō no tame, jūgyō-in no mochibēshon kōjō-saku o kangae ma shou.	Furekkusu taimu-sei no dōnyū wa dōdeshou ka.
To increase productivity, let's think about ways to improve employee motivation.	How about introducing a flextime system?

Cultural Context

Consider both extrinsic and intrinsic motivation factors.

市場シェア拡大の戦略を立てましょう。

しじょうしぇあかくだいのせんりゃくをたてましょう。
Ichiba shea kakudai no senryaku o tatemashou.
Let's develop a strategy to increase market share.

Variation 1	Variation 2
販売占有率増加の方針を策定しましょう。	Kyō mo shōjin shima shou.
はんばいせんゆうりつぞうかのほうしんをさくていしましょう。	はんばいせんゆうりつぞうかのほうしんをさくていしましょう。
Hanbai sen'yū-ritsu zōka no hōshin o sakutei shima shou.	Hanbai han'i o hirogeru keikaku o neri ma shou.
Let's develop a strategy to expand our market share.	Let's develop a strategy to increase our market share.

Positive Response	Negative Response
賛成です。成長機会の拡大につながりそうですね。	競争が激しすぎます。
さんせいです。せいちょうきかいのかくだいにつながりそうですね。	きょうそうがはげしすぎます。
Sanseidesu. Seichō kikai no kakudai ni tsunagari-sōdesu ne.	Kyōsō ga geki shi sugimasu.
I agree. It's likely to lead to expanded growth opportunities.	The competition is too fierce.

Conversation example person A	Conversation example person B
成長戦略の一環として、市場シェア拡大の戦略を立てましょう。	競合分析を行い、差別化ポイントを明確にする必要がありますね。
せいちょうせんりゃくのいっかんとして、しじょうしぇあかくだいのせんりゃくをたてましょう。	きょうごうぶんせきをおこない、さべつかぽいんとをめいかくにするひつようがありますね。
Seichō senryaku no ikkan to shite, shijō shea kakudai no senryaku o tate ma shou.	Kyōgō bunseki o okonai, sabetsuka pointo o meikaku ni suru hitsuyō ga arimasu ne.
As part of our growth strategy, let's develop a strategy to expand market share.	We need to conduct a competitive analysis and clarify our differentiation points.

Cultural Context
Balance market share growth with profitability considerations.

研究開発投資の方針を決定しましょう。

けんきゅうかいはつとうしのほうしんをけっていしましょう。

Kenkyū kaihatsu tōshi no hōshin o kettei shimashou.

Let's decide on our R&D investment policy.

Variation 1	Variation 2
技術革新への資金配分方針を定めましょう。	Kyō mo shōjin shima shou.
ぎじゅつかくしんへのしきんはいぶんほうしんをさだめましょう。	ぎじゅつかくしんへのしきんはいぶんほうしんをさだめましょう。
Gijutsu kakushin e no shikin haibun hōshin o sadame ma shou.	Shin gijutsu e no tōshi keikaku o tate ma shou.
Let's decide on our R&D investment policy.	Let's decide on our R&D investment policy.

Positive Response	Negative Response
重要な課題ですね。イノベーション創出につながりそうです。	リターンが不確実です。
じゅうようなかだいですね。いのべーしょんそうしゅつにつながりそうです。	りたーんがふかくじつです。
Jūyōna kadaidesu ne. Inobēshon sōshutsu ni tsunagari-sōdesu.	Ritān ga fu kakujitsudesu.
That's an important issue. It could lead to innovation creation.	The return on investment is uncertain.

Conversation example person A	Conversation example person B
将来の競争力確保のため、研究開発投資の方針を決定しましょう。	オープンイノベーションの推進も検討すべきですね。
しょうらいのきょうそうりょくかくほのため、けんきゅうかいはつとうしのほうしんをけっていしましょう。	おーぷんいのべーしょんのすいしんもけんとうすべきですね。
Shōrai no kyōsō-ryoku kakuho no tame, kenkyū kaihatsu tōshi no hōshin o kettei shima shou.	Ōpun inobēshon no suishin mo kentō subeki desu ne.
To secure future competitiveness, let's decide on our R&D investment policy.	We should also consider promoting open innovation.

Cultural Context
Align R&D priorities with overall business strategy.

企業文化の改革について話し合いましょう。

きぎょうぶんかのかいかくについてはなしあいましょう。

Kigyō bunka no kaikaku ni tsuite hanashiaimashou.

Let's discuss corporate culture reform.

Variation 1	Variation 2
組織風土の変革について協議しましょう。	Kyō mo shōjin shima shou.
そしきふうどのへんかくについてきょうぎしましょう。	そしきふうどのへんかくについてきょうぎしましょう。
Soshiki fūdo no henkaku ni tsuite kyōgi shima shou.	Kaisha no fun'iki o yoku suru hōhō o hanashiai ma shou.
Let's discuss reforming our corporate culture.	Let's discuss ways to improve our corporate culture.

Positive Response	Negative Response
素晴らしいアイデアです。組織の活性化につながりそうですね。	抵抗が大きいでしょう。
すばらしいあいであです。そしきのかっせいかにつながりそうですね。	ていこうがおおきいでしょう。
Subarashī aideadesu. Soshiki no kassei-ka ni tsunagari-sōdesu ne.	Teikō ga ōkīde shou.
Great idea. It could lead to organizational revitalization.	There will be significant resistance.

Conversation example person A	Conversation example person B
組織の活性化のため、企業文化の改革について話し合いましょう。	多様性と包括性を重視する文化づくりが必要ですね。
そしきのかっせいかのため、きぎょうぶんかのかいかくについてはなしあいましょう。	たようせいとほうかつせいをじゅうしするぶんかづくりがひつようですね。
Soshiki no kassei-ka no tame, kigyō bunka no kaikaku ni tsuite hanashiai ma shou.	Tayōsei to hōkatsu-sei o jūshi suru bunka-zukuri ga hitsuyōdesu ne.
To revitalize the organization, let's discuss reforming our corporate culture.	We need to create a culture that values diversity and inclusivity.

Cultural Context

Recognize that cultural change is a long-term process requiring consistent effort.

事業継続計画を見直す必要があります。

じぎょうけいぞくけいかくをみなおすひつようがあります。
Jigyō keizoku keikaku o minaosu hitsuyō ga arimasu.
We need to review our business continuity plan.

Variation 1	Variation 2
業務存続策を再検討する必要があります。	Kyō mo shōjin shima shou.
ぎょうむそんぞくさくをさいけんとうするひつようがあります。	ぎょうむそんぞくさくをさいけんとうするひつようがあります。
Gyōmu sonzoku-saku o sai kentō suru hitsuyō ga arimasu.	Kinkyū-ji no taiō-saku o sai kakunin shima shou.
We need to review our business continuity plan.	We need to review our business continuity plan.

Positive Response	Negative Response
賛成です。リスク管理の強化につながりそうですね。	現行の計画で十分です。
さんせいです。りすくかんりのきょうかにつながりそうですね。	げんこうのけいかくでじゅうぶんです。
Sanseidesu. Risuku kanri no kyōka ni tsunagari-sōdesu ne.	Genkō no keikaku de jūbundesu.
I agree. It's likely to lead to strengthened risk management.	The current plan is sufficient.

Conversation example person A	Conversation example person B
リスク管理の観点から、事業継続計画を見直す必要があります。	パンデミックや自然災害など、様々なシナリオを想定する必要がありますね。
りすくかんりのかんてんから、じぎょうけいぞくけいかくをみなおすひつようがあります。	ぱんでみっくやしぜんさいがいなど、さまざまなしなりおをそうていするひつようがありますね。
Risuku kanri no kanten kara, jigyō keizoku keikaku o minaosu hitsuyō ga arimasu.	Pandemikku ya shizen saigai nado, samazama na shinario o sōtei suru hitsuyō ga arimasu ne.
From a risk management perspective, we need to review our business continuity plan.	We need to consider various scenarios, such as pandemics and natural disasters.

Cultural Context
Consider a wide range of potential disruptions, not just obvious risks.

技術革新への対応策を考えましょう。

ぎじゅつかくしんへのたいおうさくをかんがえましょう。
Gijutsu kakushin e no taiō-saku o kangaemashou.
Let's think about how to respond to technological innovations.

Variation 1	Variation 2
先端技術への適応方法を検討しましょう。	Kyō mo shōjin shima shou.
せんたんぎじゅつへのてきおうほうほうをけんとうしましょう。	せんたんぎじゅつへのてきおうほうほうをけんとうしましょう。
Sentan gijutsu e no tekiō hōhō o kentō shima shou.	Atarashī gijutsu ni dō taisho suru ka kangae ma shou.
Let's consider strategies to respond to technological innovations.	Let's think about how to respond to technological innovations.

Positive Response	Negative Response
重要ですね。競争力の維持・向上につながりそうです。	コストが高すぎます。
じゅうようですね。きょうそうりょくのいじ・こうじょうにつながりそうです。	こすとがたかすぎます。
Jūyōdesu ne. Kyōsō-ryoku no iji kōjō ni tsunagari-sōdesu.	Kosuto ga taka sugimasu.
That's important. It could lead to maintaining and enhancing our competitiveness.	The cost is too high.

Conversation example person A	Conversation example person B
市場競争力維持のため、技術革新への対応策を考えましょう。	AI や IoT の活用を積極的に検討する必要がありますね。
しじょうきょうそうりょくいじのため、ぎじゅつかくしんへのたいおうさくをかんがえましょう。	えーあいやあいおーてぃーのかつようをせっきょくてきにけんとうするひつようがありますね。
Shijō kyōsō-ryoku iji no tame, gijutsu kakushin e no taiō-saku o kangae ma shou.	Ēai ya aiō tī no katsuyō o sekkyoku-teki ni kentō suru hitsuyō ga arimasu ne.
To maintain market competitiveness, let's think about strategies to respond to technological innovations.	We need to actively consider utilizing AI and IoT.

Cultural Context
Balance early adoption advantages with implementation risks.

パートナーシップ戦略を立案しましょう。

ぱーとなーしっぷせんりゃくをりつあんしましょう。

Pātonāshippu senryaku o ritsuan shimashou.

Let's formulate a partnership strategy.

Variation 1	Variation 2
協力関係構築の方針を策定しましょう。	Kyō mo shōjin shima shou.
きょうりょくかんけいこうちくのほうしんをさくていしましょう。	きょうりょくかんけいこうちくのほうしんをさくていしましょう。
Kyōryoku kankei kōchiku no hōshin o sakutei shima shou.	Tasha to no kyōryoku kankei o kizuku keikaku o tate ma shou.
Let's formulate a partnership strategy.	Let's create a partnership strategy.

Positive Response	Negative Response
良いアイデアです。新たな成長機会の創出につながりそうですね。	適切なパートナーが見つかりません。
よいあいであです。あらたなせいちょうきかいのそうしゅつにつながりそうですね。	てきせつなぱーとなーがみつかりません。
Ī aideadesu. Aratana seichō kikai no sōshutsu ni tsunagari-sōdesu ne.	Tekisetsuna pātonā ga mitsukarimasen.
Good idea. It could lead to creating new growth opportunities.	We can't find suitable partners.

Conversation example person A	Conversation example person B
事業拡大のため、パートナーシップ戦略を立案しましょう。	異業種との協業も視野に入れるべきですね。
じぎょうかくだいのため、ぱーとなーしっぷせんりゃくをりつあんしましょう。	いぎょうしゅとのきょうぎょうもしやにいれるべきですね。
Jigyō kakudai no tame, pātonāshippu senryaku o ritsuan shima shou.	Igyōshu to no kyōgyō mo shiya ni ireru beki desu ne.
For business expansion, let's develop a partnership strategy.	We should also consider collaborations with different industries.

Cultural Context

Consider both strategic fit and cultural compatibility in partnerships.

経費削減の余地を探りましょう。

けいひさくげんのよちをさぐりましょう。

Keihi sakugen no yochi o sagurimashou.

Let's look for opportunities to reduce expenses.

Variation 1	Variation 2
支出縮小の可能性を模索しましょう。	Kyō mo shōjin shima shou.
ししゅつしゅくしょうのかのうせいをもさくしましょう。	ししゅつしゅくしょうのかのうせいをもさくしましょう。
Shishutsu shukushō no kanō-sei o mosaku shima shou.	Kosuto o heraseru bubun o mitsuke ma shou.
Let's explore possibilities for cost reduction.	Let's look for areas where we can cut costs.

Positive Response	Negative Response
賛成です。収益性の向上につながりそうですね。	これ以上の削減は難しいです。
さんせいです。しゅうえきせいのこうじょうにつながりそうですね。	これいじょうのさくげんはむずかしいです。
Sanseidesu. Shūeki-sei no kōjō ni tsunagari-sōdesu ne.	Kore ijō no sakugen wa muzukashīdesu.
I agree. It's likely to lead to improved profitability.	Further cost reductions are difficult.

Conversation example person A	Conversation example person B
利益率改善のため、経費削減の余地を探りましょう。	固定費の見直しから始めてみてはいかがでしょうか。
りえきりつかいぜんのため、けいひさくげんのよちをさぐりましょう。	こていひのみなおしからはじめてみてはいかがでしょうか。
Rieki-ritsu kaizen no tame, keihi sakugen no yochi o saguri ma shou.	Koteihihi no minaoshi kara hajimete mite wa ikagadeshou ka.
To improve profit margins, let's explore areas for cost reduction.	How about starting with reviewing our fixed costs?

Cultural Context

Ensure cost-cutting doesn't compromise long-term growth potential.

人材採用戦略を見直しましょう。

じんざいさいようせんりゃくをみなおしましょう。
Jinzai saiyō senryaku o minaoshimashou.
Let's review our recruitment strategy.

Variation 1	Variation 2
社員獲得方針を再検討しましょう。	Kyō mo shōjin shima shou.
しゃいんかくとくほうしんをさいけんとうしましょう。	しゃいんかくとくほうしんをさいけんとうしましょう。
Shain kakutoku hōshin o sai kentō shima shou.	Hito no yatoi-kata o sai kentō shima shou.
Let's review our recruitment strategy.	Let's revise our recruitment strategy.

Positive Response	Negative Response
重要な課題ですね。優秀な人材の確保につながりそうです。	人材市場が厳しいです。
じゅうようなかだいですね。ゆうしゅうなじんざいのかくほにつながりそうです。	じんざいしじょうがきびしいです。
Jūyōna kadaidesu ne. Yūshūna jinzai no kakuho ni tsunagari-sōdesu.	Jinzai shijō ga kibishīdesu.
That's an important issue. It could lead to securing excellent talent.	The job market is tough.

Conversation example person A	Conversation example person B
優秀な人材確保のため、人材採用戦略を見直しましょう。	ダイバーシティ推進の観点も取り入れる必要がありますね。
ゆうしゅうなじんざいかくほのため、じんざいさいようせんりゃくをみなおしましょう。	だいばーしてぃすいしんのかんてんもとりいれるひつようがありますね。
Yūshūna jinzai kakuho no tame, jinzai saiyō senryaku o minaoshi ma shou.	Daibāshiti suishin no kanten mo toriireru hitsuyō ga arimasu ne.
To secure talented personnel, let's review our recruitment strategy.	We need to incorporate the perspective of promoting diversity as well.

Cultural Context
Consider both immediate skill needs and long-term cultural fit.

製品ポートフォリオの最適化を検討しましょう。

せいひんぽーとふぉりおのさいてきかをけんとうしましょう。

Seihin pōtoforio no saiteki-ka o kentō shimashou.

Let's consider optimizing our product portfolio.

Variation 1	Variation 2
商品構成の改善を考察しましょう。	Kyō mo shōjin shima shou.
しょうひんこうせいのかいぜんをこうさつしましょう。	しょうひんこうせいのかいぜんをこうさつしましょう。
Shōhin kōsei no kaizen o kōsatsu shima shou.	Shōhin rain'nappu no minaoshi o kangae ma shou.
Let's consider optimizing our product portfolio.	Let's consider optimizing our product portfolio.

Positive Response	Negative Response
素晴らしいアイデアです。効率的な資源配分につながりそうですね。	既存製品への影響が懸念されます。
すばらしいあいであです。こうりつてきなしげんはいぶんにつながりそうですね。	きそんせいひんへのえいきょうがけねんされます。
Subarashī aideadesu. Kōritsu-tekina shigen haibun ni tsunagari-sōdesu ne.	Kizon seihin e no eikyō ga kenen sa remasu.
Great idea. It could lead to efficient resource allocation.	We're concerned about the impact on existing products.

Conversation example person A	Conversation example person B
経営資源の効率的配分のため、製品ポートフォリオの最適化を検討しましょう。	各製品のライフサイクルと市場性を分析する必要がありますね。
けいえいしげんのこうりつてきはいぶんのため、せいひんぽーとふぉりおのさいてきかをけんとうしましょう。	かくせいひんのらいふさいくるとしじょうせいをぶんせきするひつようがありますね。
Keiei shigen no kōritsu-teki haibun no tame, seihin pōtoforio no saiteki-ka o kentō shima shou.	Kaku seihin no raifu saikuru to shijō-sei o bunseki suru hitsuyō ga arimasu ne.
To efficiently allocate management resources, let's consider optimizing our product portfolio.	We need to analyze the life cycle and marketability of each product.

Cultural Context

Balance profitability with market positioning and future potential.

営業プロセスの効率化を図りましょう。

えいぎょうぷろせすのこうりつかをはかりましょう。
Eigyō purosesu no kōritsu-ka o hakarimashou.
Let's work on streamlining our sales process.

Variation 1	Variation 2
販売手順の能率向上を目指しましょう。	Kyō mo shōjin shima shou.
はんばいてじゅんののうりつこうじょうをめざしましょう。	はんばいてじゅんののうりつこうじょうをめざしましょう。
Hanbai tejun no nōritsu kōjō o mezashi ma shou.	Hanbai hōhō o yori kōka-teki ni shima shou.
Let's aim to streamline our sales process.	Let's work on making our sales process more efficient.

Positive Response	Negative Response
賛成です。売上向上と顧客満足度アップにつながりそうですね。	顧客との関係に影響します。
さんせいです。うりあげこうじょうとこきゃくまんぞくどあっぷにつながりそうですね。	こきゃくとのかんけいにえいきょうします。
Sanseidesu. Uriage kōjō to kokyaku manzoku-do appu ni tsunagari-sōdesu ne.	Kokyaku to no kankei ni eikyō shimasu.
I agree. It's likely to lead to increased sales and customer satisfaction.	It will affect our relationships with customers.

Conversation example person A	Conversation example person B
売上向上のため、営業プロセスの効率化を図りましょう。	CRM システムの導入を検討してみてはいかがでしょうか。
うりあげこうじょうのため、えいぎょうぷろせすのこうりつかをはかりましょう。	しーあーるえむしすてむのどうにゅうをけんとうしてみてはいかがでしょうか。
Uriage kōjō no tame, eigyō purosesu no kōritsu-ka o hakari ma shou.	Shīāru emu shisutemu no dōnyū o kentō shite mite wa ikagadeshou ka.
To increase sales, let's work on improving the efficiency of our sales process.	How about considering the introduction of a CRM system?

Cultural Context

Ensure efficiency improvements don't compromise customer relationships.

情報セキュリティ対策を強化しましょう。

じょうほうせきゅりてぃたいさくをきょうかしましょう。

Jōhō sekyuriti taisaku o kyōka shimashou.

Let's strengthen our information security measures.

Variation 1	Variation 2
機密保護策を充実させましょう。	Kyō mo shōjin shima shou.
きみつほごさくをじゅうじつさせましょう。	きみつほごさくをじゅうじつさせましょう。
Kimitsu hogo-saku o jūjitsu sa se ma shou.	Dēta hogo no shikumi o kaizen shima shou.
Let's strengthen our information security measures.	Let's strengthen our information security measures.

Positive Response	Negative Response
重要ですね。顧客信頼の向上につながりそうです。	コストが高すぎます。
じゅうようですね。こきゃくしんらいのこうじょうにつながりそうです。	こすとがたかすぎます。
Jūyōdesu ne. Kokyaku shinrai no kōjō ni tsunagari-sōdesu.	Kosuto ga taka sugimasu.
That's important. It could lead to improved customer trust.	The cost is too high.

Conversation example person A	Conversation example person B
データ保護のため、情報セキュリティ対策を強化しましょう。	従業員向けのセキュリティ教育も重要ですね。
でーたほごのため、じょうほうせきゅりてぃたいさくをきょうかしましょう。	じゅうぎょういんむけのせきゅりてぃきょういくもじゅうようですね。
Dēta hogo no tame, jōhō sekyuriti taisaku o kyōka shima shou.	Jūgyōin-muke no sekyuriti kyōiku mo jūyōdesu ne.
To protect data, let's strengthen our information security measures.	Employee security education is also important.

Cultural Context

Consider both technological solutions and employee awareness training.

顧客データの活用方法を検討しましょう。

こきゃくでーたのかつようほうほうをけんとうしましょう。

Kokyaku dēta no katsuyō hōhō o kentō shimashou.

Let's consider how to utilize customer data.

Variation 1	Variation 2
利用者情報の利用法を考察しましょう。	Kyō mo shōjin shima shou.
りようしゃじょうほうのりようほうをこうさつしましょう。	りようしゃじょうほうのりようほうをこうさつしましょう。
Riyō-sha jōhō no riyō-hō o kōsatsu shima shou.	Okyakusama no jōhō o dō tsukau ka kangae ma shou.
Let's consider how to utilize customer data.	Let's consider how to utilize customer data.

Positive Response	Negative Response
良いアイデアです。マーケティング効果の向上につながりそうですね。	プライバシーの問題があります。
よいあいであです。まーけてぃんぐこうかのこうじょうにつながりそうですね。	ぷらいばしーのもんだいがあります。
Ī aideadesu. Māketingu kōka no kōjō ni tsunagari-sōdesu ne.	Puraibashī no mondai ga arimasu.
Good idea. It could lead to improved marketing effectiveness.	There are privacy concerns.

Conversation example person A	Conversation example person B
マーケティング効果向上のため、顧客データの活用方法を検討しましょう。	プライバシー保護に配慮しながら、パーソナライゼーションを進めるべきですね。
まーけてぃんぐこうかこうじょうのため、こきゃくでーたのかつようほうほうをけんとうしましょう。	ぷらいばしーほごにはいりょしながら、ぱーそならいぜーしょんをすすめるべきですね。
Māketingu kōka kōjō no tame, kokyaku dēta no katsuyō hōhō o kentō shima shou.	Puraibashī hogo ni hairyo shinagara, pāsonaraizēshon o susumeru beki desu ne.
To improve marketing effectiveness, let's consider how to utilize customer data.	We should advance personalization while being mindful of privacy protection.

Cultural Context
Balance data utilization with privacy concerns and regulations.

働き方改革の推進策を議論しましょう。

はたらきかたかいかくのすいしんさくをぎろんしましょう。
Hataraki-kata kaikaku no suishin-saku o giron shimashou.
Let's discuss measures to promote work style reform.

Variation 1	Variation 2
労働環境改善の促進方法を討議しましょう。	Kyō mo shōjin shima shou.
ろうどうかんきょうかいぜんのそくしんほうほうをとうぎしましょう。	ろうどうかんきょうかいぜんのそくしんほうほうをとうぎしましょう。
Rōdō kankyō kaizen no sokushin hōhō o tōgi shima shou.	Shigoto no yarikata o kaizen suru hōhō o hanashiai ma shou.
Let's discuss measures to promote work style reform.	Let's discuss strategies to promote work style reform.

Positive Response	Negative Response
賛成です。従業員満足度と生産性の向上につながりそうですね。	生産性低下が心配です。
さんせいです。じゅうぎょういんまんぞくどとせいさんせいのこうじょうにつながりそうですね。	せいさんせいていかがしんぱいです。
Sanseidesu. Jūgyō-in manzoku-do to seisan-sei no kōjō ni tsunagari-sōdesu ne.	Seisan-sei teika ga shinpaidesu.
I agree. It's likely to lead to improved employee satisfaction and productivity.	We're worried about decreased productivity.

Conversation example person A	Conversation example person B
従業員の満足度向上のため、働き方改革の推進策を議論しましょう。	リモートワークの拡大と柔軟な勤務体系の導入を検討しましょう。
じゅうぎょういんのまんぞくどこうじょうのため、はたらきかたかいかくのすいしんさくをぎろんしましょう。	りもーとわーくのかくだいとじゅうなんなきんむたいけいのどうにゅうをけんとうしましょう。
Jūgyō-in no manzoku-do kōjō no tame, hatarakikata kaikaku no suishin-saku o giron shima shou.	Rimōto wāku no kakudai to jūnan na kinmu taikei no dōnyū o kentō shimashou.
To improve employee satisfaction, let's discuss measures to promote work style reform.	Let's consider expanding remote work and introducing flexible working arrangements.

Cultural Context
Consider both productivity and employee well-being in reform efforts.

事業拡大のための M&A 戦略を立てましょう。

じぎょうかくだいのためのえむあんどえーせんりゃくをたてましょう。

Jigyō kakudai no tame no M& A senryaku o tatemashou.

Let's develop an M&A strategy for business expansion.

Variation 1	Variation 2
業務拡張のための合併買収方針を策定しましょう。	Kyō mo shōjin shima shou.
ぎょうむかくちょうのためのがっぺいばいしゅうほうしんをさくていしましょう。	ぎょうむかくちょうのためのがっぺいばいしゅうほうしんをさくていしましょう。
Gyōmu kakuchō no tame no gappei baishū hōshin o sakutei shima shou.	Kaisha baishū ni yoru seichō keikaku o kangae ma shou.
Let's develop an M&A strategy for business expansion.	Let's develop an M&A strategy for business expansion.

Positive Response	Negative Response
素晴らしいアイデアです。急速な成長につながる可能性がありますね。	リスクが高すぎます。
すばらしいあいであです。きゅうそくなせいちょうにつながるかのうせいがありますね。	りすくがたかすぎます。
Subarashī aideadesu. Kyūsokuna seichō ni tsunagaru kanō-sei ga arimasu ne.	Risuku ga taka sugimasu.
Great idea. It has the potential to lead to rapid growth.	The risks are too high.

Conversation example person A	Conversation example person B
急速な成長のため、事業拡大のための M&A 戦略を立てましょう。	シナジー効果の高い企業を特定する必要がありますね。
きゅうそくなせいちょうのため、じぎょうかくだいのためのえむあんどえーせんりゃくをたてましょう。	しなじーこうかのたかいきぎょうをとくていするひつようがありますね。
Kyūsokuna seichō no tame, jigyō kakudai no tame no emu andoē senryaku o tate ma shou.	Shinajī kōka no takai kigyō o tokutei suru hitsuyō ga arimasu ne.
For rapid growth, let's develop an M&A strategy for business expansion.	We need to identify companies with high synergy potential.

Cultural Context
Consider both financial and cultural aspects of potential acquisitions.

地域社会への貢献策を考えましょう。

ちいきしゃかいへのこうけんさくをかんがえましょう。

Chiiki shakai e no kōken-saku o kangaemashou.

Let's think about ways to contribute to the local community.

Variation 1	Variation 2
地元への還元方法を検討しましょう。	Kyō mo shōjin shima shou.
ちもとへのかんげんほうほうをけんとうしましょう。	ちもとへのかんげんほうほうをけんとうしましょう。
Jimoto e no kangen hōhō o kentō shima shou.	Jimoto ni yakudatsu katsudō o keikaku shima shou.
Let's consider ways to contribute to the local community.	Let's think about ways to contribute to the local community.

Positive Response	Negative Response
重要な課題ですね。企業イメージの向上につながりそうです。	直接的な利益につながりません。
じゅうようなかだいですね。きぎょういめーじのこうじょうにつながりそうです。	ちょくせつてきなりえきにつながりません。
Jūyōna kadaidesu ne. Kigyō imēji no kōjō ni tsunagari-sōdesu.	Chokusetsu-tekina rieki ni tsunagarimasen.
That's an important issue. It could lead to improved corporate image.	It doesn't lead to direct profits.

Conversation example person A	Conversation example person B
企業の社会的責任を果たすため、地域社会への貢献策を考えましょう。	地域のニーズに合ったボランティア活動を計画してはどうでしょうか。
きぎょうのしゃかいてきせきにんをはたすため、ちいきしゃかいへのこうけんさくをかんがえましょう。	ちいきのにーずにあったぼらんてぃあかつどうをけいかくしてはどうでしょうか。
Kigyō no shakai-teki sekinin o hatasu tame, chiiki shakai e no kōken-saku o kangae ma shou.	Chiiki no nīzu ni atta borantia katsudō o keikaku shite wa dōdeshou ka.
To fulfill our corporate social responsibility, let's think about ways to contribute to the local community.	How about planning volunteer activities that meet local needs?

Cultural Context

Align community initiatives with overall business strategy.

中期経営計画の進捗を確認しましょう。

ちゅうきけいえいけいかくのしんちょくをかくにんしましょう。

Chūki keiei keikaku no shinchoku o kakunin shimashou.

Let's check the progress of our mid-term business plan.

Variation 1	Variation 2
中長期事業構想の進展を点検しましょう。	Kyō mo shōjin shima shou.
ちゅうちょうきじぎょうこうそうのしんてんをてんけんしましょう。	ちゅうちょうきじぎょうこうそうのしんてんをてんけんしましょう。
Chū chōki jigyō kōsō no shinten o tenken shima shou.	San kara go nen no jigyō keikaku no susumi guai o mi ma shou.
Let's check the progress of our medium-term management plan.	Let's check the progress of our medium-term business plan.

Positive Response	Negative Response
賛成です。目標達成に向けた調整ができそうですね。	目標が現実的ではありません。
さんせいです。もくひょうたっせいにむけたちょうせいができそうですね。	もくひょうがげんじつてきではありません。
Sanseidesu. Mokuhyō tassei ni muketa chōsei ga deki-sōdesu ne.	Mokuhyō ga genjitsu-tekide wa arimasen.
I agree. We can make adjustments towards achieving our goals.	The goals are not realistic.

Conversation example person A	Conversation example person B
目標達成に向けて、中期経営計画の進捗を確認しましょう。	KPI の達成状況を詳細に分析する必要がありますね。
もくひょうたっせいにむけて、ちゅうきけいえいけいかくのしんちょくをかくにんしましょう。	けーぴーあいのたっせいじょうきょうをしょうさいにぶんせきするひつようがありますね。
Mokuhyō tassei ni mukete, chūki keiei keikaku no shinchoku o kakunin shima shou.	Kēpīai no tassei jōkyō o shōsai ni bunseki suru hitsuyō ga arimasu ne.
To achieve our goals, let's check the progress of our medium-term management plan.	We need to analyze the achievement status of our KPIs in detail.

Cultural Context

Look for early indicators of potential issues or needed adjustments.

社内研修プログラムの効果を評価しましょう。

しゃないけんしゅうぷろぐらむのこうかをひょうかしましょう。
Shanai kenshū puroguramu no kōka o hyōka shimashou.
Let's evaluate the effectiveness of our internal training programs.

Variation 1	Variation 2
社内教育の成果を確認しましょう。	Kyō mo shōjin shima shou.
しゃないきょういくのせいかをかくにんしましょう。	しゃないきょういくのせいかをかくにんしましょう。
Shanai kyōiku no seika o kakunin shima shou.	Shain kyōiku no seika o kakunin shima shou.
Let's assess the effectiveness of our internal training programs.	Let's evaluate the effectiveness of our internal training programs.

Positive Response	Negative Response
良いですね。より効果的な人材育成につながりそうです。	効果の測定が難しいです。
いいですね。よりこうかてきなじんざいいくせいにつながりそうです。	こうかのそくていがむずかしいです。
Īdesu ne. Yori kōka-tekina jinzai ikusei ni tsunagari-sōdesu.	Kōka no sokutei ga muzukashīdesu.
That's good. It could lead to more effective human resource development.	It's difficult to measure the effectiveness.

Conversation example person A	Conversation example person B
人材育成の観点から、社内研修プログラムの効果を評価しましょう。	参加者からのフィードバックを分析し、改善点を見つけましょう。
じんざいいくせいのかんてんから、しゃないけんしゅうぷろぐらむのこうかをひょうかしましょう。	さんかしゃからのふぃーどばっくをぶんせきし、かいぜんてんをみつけましょう。
Jinzai ikusei no kanten kara, shanai kenshū puroguramu no kōka o hyōka shima shou.	Sankasha kara no fīdobakku o bunseki shi, kaizen-ten o mitsuke mashou.
From a talent development perspective, let's evaluate the effectiveness of our internal training programs.	Let's analyze feedback from participants and identify areas for improvement.

Cultural Context
Consider both immediate skill improvements and long-term career development.

次世代リーダーの育成計画を立てましょう。

じせだいりーだーのいくせいけいかくをたてましょう。

Jisedai rīdā no ikusei keikaku o tatemashou.

Let's create a development plan for next-generation leaders.

Variation 1	Variation 2
将来の幹部候補の養成方針を決めましょう。	Kyō mo shōjin shima shou.
しょうらいのかんぶこうほのようせいほうしんをきめましょう。	しょうらいのかんぶこうほのようせいほうしんをきめましょう。
Shōrai no kanbu kōho no yōsei hōshin o kime ma shou.	Shōrai no kanbu kōho o sodateru hōhō o kangae ma shou.
Let's create a development plan for our future leaders.	Let's create a development plan for future leaders.

Positive Response	Negative Response
素晴らしい提案です。会社の未来を支える重要な取り組みですね。	今はその余裕がありません。
すばらしいていあんです。かいしゃのみらいをささえるじゅうようなとりくみですね。	いまはそのよゆうがありません。
Subarashī teiandesu. Kaisha no mirai o sasaeru jūyōna torikumidesu ne.□	Ima wa sono yoyū ga arimasen.
Excellent proposal. It's a crucial initiative to support the company's future.	We don't have the capacity for that right now.

Conversation example person A	Conversation example person B
次世代リーダーの育成計画を立てましょう。	はい、長期的な視点で考えていきましょう。
じせだいりーだーのいくせいけいかくをたてましょう。	はい、ちょうきてきなしてんでかんがえていきましょう。
Ji sedai rīdā no ikusei keikaku o tate ma shou.	Hai, chōki-tekina shiten de kangaete iki ma shou.
Let's create a development plan for next-generation leaders.	Yes, let's think about it from a long-term perspective.

Cultural Context

Consider the importance of seniority and long-term commitment in Japanese corporate culture when planning leadership development.

お世話になっております。

おせわになっております。

Osewa ni natte orimasu.

Thank you for your continued support.

Variation 1	Variation 2
いつもお力添えいただき、ありがとうございます。	Kyō mo shōjin shima shou.
いつもおちからぞえいただき、ありがとうございます。	いつもおちからぞえいただき、ありがとうございます。
Itsumo o chikarazoe itadaki, arigatōgozaimasu.	Itsumo go shien itadakimashite, kansha mōshiagemasu.
Thank you for your continued support.	Thank you for your continued support.

Positive Response	Negative Response
こちらこそ、いつもお世話になっております。	それほどお世話になっていませんが。
こちらこそ、いつもおせわになっております。	それほどおせわになっていませんが。
Kochira koso, itsumo osewa ni natte orimasu.	Sorehodo osewa ni natte imasenga.
The pleasure is ours. Thank you for your continued support.	I don't think I've been of much help to you.

Conversation example person A	Conversation example person B
いつもお世話になっております。今回の件についてご相談させていただきたいのですが。	お世話になっております。どのようなことでしょうか？
いつもおせわになっております。こんかいのけんについてごそうだんさせていただきたいのですが。	おせわになっております。どのようなことでしょうか？
Itsumo osewa ni natte orimasu. Konkai no kudan ni tsuite go sōdan sa sete itadakitai nodesuga.	Osewa ni natte orimasu. Do no yōna kotodeshou ka?
Thank you for your continued support. I'd like to consult with you about a matter.	It's my pleasure. What can I help you with?

Cultural Context

Use only with people you have an ongoing relationship with. Not suitable for first-time contacts.

ご連絡いただき、ありがとうございます。

ごれんらくいただき、ありがとうございます。

Go renraku itadaki, arigatōgozaimasu.

Thank you for your message.

Variation 1	Variation 2
お知らせいただき、感謝申し上げます。	Kyō mo shōjin shima shou.
おしらせいただき、かんしゃもうしあげます。	おしらせいただき、かんしゃもうしあげます。
Oshirase itadaki, kansha mōshiagemasu.	Go renraku itadakimashite, arigatōgozaimasu.
Thank you for contacting us.	Thank you for letting me know.

Positive Response	Negative Response
こちらこそ、迅速なご対応感謝いたします。	連絡が遅すぎます。
こちらこそ、じんそくなごたいおうかんしゃいたします。	れんらくがおそすぎます。
Kochira koso, jinsokuna go taiō kansha itashimasu.	Renraku ga oso sugimasu.
Thank you for your prompt response. We appreciate it.	Your contact is too late.

Conversation example person A	Conversation example person B
先日の件について、ご連絡いただき、ありがとうございます。	こちらこそ、迅速なご対応感謝いたします。
せんじつのけんについて、ごれんらくいただき、ありがとうございます。	こちらこそ、じんそくなごたいおうかんしゃいたします。
Senjitsu no kudan ni tsuite, go renraku itadaki, arigatōgozaimasu.	Kochira koso, jinsokuna go taiō kansha itashimasu.
Thank you for contacting me about the matter from the other day.	Thank you for your prompt response as well.

Cultural Context

Avoid using if you initiated the contact. Use when responding to someone's message.

お返事が遅くなり、申し訳ございません。

おへんじがおそくなり、もうしわけございません。
O henji ga osoku nari, mōshiwakegozaimasen.
I apologize for the delayed response.

Variation 1	Variation 2
回答が遅れてしまい、大変失礼いたしました。	Kyō mo shōjin shima shou.
かいとうがおくれてしまい、たいへんしつれいいたしました。	かいとうがおくれてしまい、たいへんしつれいいたしました。
Kaitō ga okurete shimai, taihen shitsurei itashimashita.	Henshin ga okurete, taihen shitsurei itashimashita.
I apologize for the delay in my response.	I apologize for the delay in my response.

Positive Response	Negative Response
お気遣いありがとうございます。問題ございません。	もっと早く返信してください。
おきづかいありがとうございます。もんだいございません。	もっとはやくへんしんしてください。
O kidzukai arigatōgozaimasu. Mondai go zaimasen.	Motto hayaku henshin shite kudasai.
Thank you for your concern. No problem at all.	Please respond more quickly next time.

Conversation example person A	Conversation example person B
お返事が遅くなり、申し訳ございません。先週は出張で少々バタバタしております まして。	いえいえ、お気になさらないでください。お忙 しいのは重々承知しております。
おへんじがおそくなり、もうしわけございません。せんしゅうはしゅっち ょうですこしばたばたしておりまして。	いえいえ、おきになさらないでください。おい そがしいのはじゅうじゅうしょうちしております。
O henji ga osoku nari, mōshiwake go zaimasen. Senshū wa shutchō de shōshō batabata shite orimashite.	Ieie, oki ni nasaranaide kudasai. O isogashī no wa jūjū shōchi shite orimasu.
I apologize for the late reply. I was a bit busy with a business trip last week.	No worries at all. I completely understand that you're busy.

Cultural Context
Use only when there's a significant delay. Overuse can make you seem unreliable.

ご確認いただけますでしょうか。

ごかくにんいただけますでしょうか。

Go kakunin itadakemasudeshou ka.

Could you please confirm this?

Variation 1	Variation 2
お手数ですが、ご覧いただけますか。	Kyō mo shōjin shima shou.
おてすうですが、ごらんいただけますか。	おてすうですが、ごらんいただけますか。
Otesūdesuga, goran itadakemasu ka.	Otesūdesuga, go kakunin o onegai dekimasu ka.
Could you please check this?	Could you please confirm this?

Positive Response	Negative Response
承知いたしました。すぐに確認いたします。	確認する時間がありません。
しょうちいたしました。すぐにかくにんいたします。	かくにんするじかんがありません。
Shōchi itashimashita. Sugu ni kakunin itashimasu.	Kakunin suru jikan ga arimasen.
Understood. I'll check it right away.	I don't have time to check.

Conversation example person A	Conversation example person B
添付の資料をご確認いただけますでしょうか。	はい、確認いたしました。特に問題はございません。
てんぷのしりょうをごかくにんいただけますでしょうか。	はい、かくにんいたしました。とくにもんだいはございません。
Tenpu no shiryō o go kakunin itadakemasudeshou ka.	Hai, kakunin itashimashita. Tokuni mondai wa go zaimasen.
Could you please check the attached document?	Yes, I've checked it. There are no particular issues.

Cultural Context

Implies the recipient might have missed something. Use carefully to avoid seeming accusatory.

よろしくお願いいたします。

よろしくおねがいいたします。

Yoroshikuonegaītashimasu.

Thank you in advance for your cooperation.

Variation 1	Variation 2
お力添えいただけますと幸いです。	Kyō mo shōjin shima shou.
おちからぞえいただけますとさいわいです。	おちからぞえいただけますとさいわいです。
O chikarazoe itadakemasuto saiwaidesu.	Otesū o okake shimasuga, dōzo yoroshiku onegai shimasu.
Thank you in advance for your cooperation.	Thank you in advance for your cooperation.

Positive Response	Negative Response
こちらこそ、よろしくお願いいたします。	具体的に何をすればいいのですか。
こちらこそ、よろしくおねがいいたします。	ぐたいてきになにをすればいいのですか。
Kochira koso, yoroshiku onegai itashimasu.	Gutai-teki ni nani o sureba ī nodesu ka.
Likewise, I look forward to working with you.	What exactly do you want me to do?

Conversation example person A	Conversation example person B
この件について、ご検討よろしくお願いいたします。	承知いたしました。できる限り早急に対応させていただきます。
このけんについて、ごけんとうよろしくおねがいいたします。	しょうちいたしました。できるかぎりそうきゅうにたいおうさせていただきます。
Kono-ken ni tsuite, go kentō yoroshiku onegai itashimasu.	Shōchi itashimashita. Dekiru kagiri sakkyū ni taiō sa sete itadakimasu.
Please consider this matter.	Understood. I'll respond as soon as possible.

Cultural Context

Very context-dependent. Can seem vague if not preceded by a specific request.

ご検討をお願いいたします。

ごけんとうをおねがいいたします。

Go kentō o onegai itashimasu.

Please consider this matter.

Variation 1	Variation 2
ご審議いただけますと幸甚です。	Kyō mo shōjin shima shou.
ごしんぎいただけますとこうじんです。	ごしんぎいただけますとこうじんです。
Go shingi itadakemasuto kōjindesu.	O kangae itadakereba saiwaidesu.
We kindly request your consideration.	We would appreciate your consideration.

Positive Response	Negative Response
承知いたしました。丁寧に検討させていただきます。	検討する余地はありません。
しょうちいたしました。ていねいにけんとうさせていただきます。	けんとうするよちはありません。
Shōchi itashimashita. Teinei ni kentō sa sete itadakimasu.	Kentō suru yochi wa arimasen.
Understood. We will carefully consider it.	There's no room for consideration.

Conversation example person A	Conversation example person B
新しい提案書を送付いたしました。ご検討をお願いいたします。	ありがとうございます。早速目を通させていただきます。
あたらしいていあんしょをそうふいたしました。ごけんとうをおねがいいたします。	ありがとうございます。さっそくめをとおさせていただきます。
Atarashī teian-sho o sōfu itashimashita. Go kentō o onegai itashimasu.	Arigatōgozaimasu. Sassoku me o tsū sa sete itadakimasu.
I've sent a new proposal. Please review it.	Thank you. I'll take a look at it right away.

Cultural Context

Implies a decision is needed. Not suitable for purely informational communications.

ご了承ください。

ごりょうしょうください。

Go ryōshō kudasai.

Please understand.

Variation 1	Variation 2
ご理解いただけますと幸いです。	Kyō mo shōjin shima shou.
ごりかいいただけますとさいわいです。	ごりかいいただけますとさいわいです。
Go rikai itadakemasuto saiwaidesu.	Go rikai itadakemasu to tasukarimasu.
Please understand.	We hope for your understanding.

Positive Response	Negative Response
了解いたしました。ご配慮ありがとうございます。	了承できません。
りょうかいいたしました。ごはいりょありがとうございます。	りょうしょうできません。
Ryōkai itashimashita. Go hairyo arigatōgozaimasu.	Ryōshō dekimasen.
Understood. Thank you for your consideration.	I cannot approve this.

Conversation example person A	Conversation example person B
納期が少々遅れる可能性がございます。ご了承ください。	了解いたしました。状況の共有ありがとうございます。
のうきがしょうしょおくれるかのうせいがございます。ごりょうしょうください。	りょうかいいたしました。じょうきょうのきょうゆうありがとうございます。
Nōki ga shōshō okureru kanō-sei ga gozaimasu. Go ryōshō kudasai.	Ryōkai itashimashita. Jōkyō no kyōyū arigatōgozaimasu.
There's a possibility that the delivery date might be slightly delayed. Please understand.	Understood. Thank you for sharing the situation.

Cultural Context

Use when you're informing of a decision, not asking for permission. Can seem presumptuous.

承知いたしました。

しょうちいたしました。

Shōchi itashimashita.

Understood.

Variation 1	Variation 2
了解いたしました。	Kyō mo shōjin shima shou.
りょうかいいたしました。	りょうかいいたしました。
Ryōkai itashimashita.	Kashikomarimashita.
Understood.	Understood.

Positive Response	Negative Response
ご連絡ありがとうございます。対応させていただきます。	本当に理解していますか。
ごれんらくありがとうございます。たいおうさせていただきます。	ほんとうにりかいしていますか。
Go renraku arigatōgozaimasu. Taiō sa sete itadakimasu.	Hontōni rikai shite imasu ka.
Thank you for letting us know. We'll take care of it.	Do you really understand?

Conversation example person A	Conversation example person B
ご指示の通り進めさせていただきます。承知いたしました。	ありがとうございます。何か不明点があればご連絡ください。
ごしじのとおりすすめさせていただきます。しょうちいたしました。	ありがとうございます。なにかふめいてんがあればごれんらくください。
Go shiji no tōri susume sasete itadakimasu. Shōchi itashimashita.	Arigatōgozaimasu. Nani ka fumei-ten ga areba go renraku kudasai.
I will proceed as instructed. Understood.	Thank you. Please contact me if you have any questions.

Cultural Context

Formal acknowledgment. May seem cold if used in response to personal news.

添付ファイルをご確認ください。

てんぷふぁいるをごかくにんください。

Tenpu fairu o go kakunin kudasai.

Please check the attached file.

Variation 1	Variation 2
同封の資料をご覧ください。	Kyō mo shōjin shima shou.
どうふうのしりょうをごらんください。	どうふうのしりょうをごらんください。
Dōfū no shiryō o goran kudasai.	Besshi no shiryō o o yomi kudasai.
Please check the attached file.	Please check the attached document.

Positive Response	Negative Response
承知いたしました。早速確認させていただきます。	添付ファイルが開けません。
しょうちいたしました。さっそくかくにんさせていただきます。	てんぷふぁいるがひらけません。
Shōchi itashimashita. Sassoku kakunin sa sete itadakimasu.	Tenpu fairu ga akemasen.
Understood. I'll check the attachment right away.	I can't open the attached file.

Conversation example person A	Conversation example person B
最新の報告書を添付いたしました。添付ファイルをご確認ください。	ありがとうございます。確認いたします。
さいしんのほうこくしょをてんぷいたしました。てんぷふぁいるをごかくにんください。	ありがとうございます。かくにんいたします。
Saishin no hōkoku-sho o tenpu itashimashita. Tenpu fairu o go kakunin kudasai.	Arigatōgozaimasu. Kakunin itashimasu.
I've attached the latest report. Please check the attached file.	Thank you. I'll check it.

Cultural Context

Ensure you've actually attached the file before using this phrase.

何かご不明な点がございましたら、お知らせください。

なにかごふめいなてんがございましたら、おしらせください。

Nani ka go fumeina ten ga gozaimashitara, oshirase kudasai.

If you have any questions, please let me know.

Variation 1	Variation 2
#N/A	Kyō mo shōjin shima shou.
#N/A	#N/A
#N/A	#N/A
#N/A	#N/A

Positive Response	Negative Response
ありがとうございます。丁寧な対応に感謝いたします。	全てが不明確です。
ありがとうございます。ていねいなたいおうにかんしゃいたします。	すべてがふめいかくです。
Arigatōgozaimasu. Teineina taiō ni kansha itashimasu.	Subete ga fu meikakudesu.
Thank you. We appreciate your thorough support.	Everything is unclear.

Conversation example person A	Conversation example person B
詳細な説明を記載しましたが、何かご不明な点がございましたら、お知らせください。	ありがとうございます。今のところ質問はありません。
しょうさいなせつめいをきさいしましたが、なにかごふめいなてんがございましたら、おしらせください。	ありがとうございます。いまのところしつもんはありません。
Shōsaina setsumei o kisai shima shitaga, nani ka go fumeina ten ga go zaimashita-ra, oshirase kudasai.	Arigatōgozaimasu. Ima no tokoro shitsumon wa arimasen.
I've included detailed explanations, but if you have any questions, please let me know.	Thank you. I don't have any questions at the moment.

Cultural Context

Can imply your explanation might be unclear. Use when complexity warrants it.

ご多忙のところ恐れ入ります。

ごたぼうのところおそれいります。

Gotabō no tokoro osoreirimasu.

I apologize for troubling you during your busy schedule.

Variation 1	Variation 2
お忙しい中、誠に申し訳ございません。	Kyō mo shōjin shima shou.
おいそがしいなか、まことにもうしわけございません。	おいそがしいなか、まことにもうしわけございません。
Oisogashī-chū, makotoni mōshiwake go zaimasen.	Itsumo o chikarazoe itadaki, arigatōgozaimasu.
I apologize for bothering you during your busy schedule.	Thank you for your continued support.

Positive Response	Negative Response
お気遣いありがとうございます。喜んで対応いたします。	本当に申し訳ないと思っていますか。
おきづかいありがとうございます。よろこんでたいおういたします。	ほんとうにもうしわけないとおもっていますか。
O kidzukai arigatōgozaimasu. Yorokonde taiō itashimasu.	Hontōni mōshiwakenai to omotte imasu ka.
Thank you for your consideration. I'm happy to help.	Do you really think you're sorry?

Conversation example person A	Conversation example person B
ご多忙のところ恐れ入りますが、会議の日程調整をお願いできますでしょうか。	承知いたしました。来週の予定を確認して、ご連絡いたします。
ごたぼうのところおそれいりますが、かいぎのにっていちょうせいをおねがいできますでしょうか。	しょうちいたしました。らいしゅうのよていをかくにんして、ごれんらくいたします。
Gotabō no tokoro osoreirimasuga, kaigi no nittei chōsei o onegai dekimasudeshou ka.	Shōchi itashimashita. Raishū no yotei o kakunin shite, go renraku itashimasu.
I'm sorry to bother you when you're busy, but could you help with scheduling the meeting?	Understood. I'll check next week's schedule and get back to you.

Cultural Context

Acknowledges you're imposing. Don't use for routine matters or you may seem overly apologetic.

お手数をおかけしますが、よろしくお願いいたします。

おてすうをおかけしますが、よろしくおねがいいたします。

Otesū o okake shimasuga, yoroshikuonegaītashimasu.

I'm sorry for the trouble, but I appreciate your help.

Variation 1	Variation 2
ご面倒をおかけしますが、ご協力いただけますと幸いです。	Kyō mo shōjin shima shou.
ごめんどうをおかけしますが、ごきょうりょくいただけますとさいわいです。	ごめんどうをおかけしますが、ごきょうりょくいただけますとさいわいです。
Go mendō o okake shimasuga, go kyōryoku itadakemasuto saiwaidesu.	Oshirase itadaki, kansha mōshiagemasu.
I'm sorry for the trouble, but I would appreciate your cooperation.	Thank you for getting in touch.

Positive Response	Negative Response
こちらこそ、ご丁寧にありがとうございます。	これは私の仕事ではありません。
こちらこそ、ごていねいにありがとうございます。	これはわたしのしごとではありません。
Kochira koso, go teinei ni arigatōgozaimasu.	Kore wa watashi no shigotode wa arimasen.
Not at all, thank you for your politeness.	This is not my job.

Conversation example person A	Conversation example person B
資料の修正をお願いしたいのですが、お手数をおかけしますが、よろしくお願いいたします。	承知いたしました。修正箇所を教えていただけますでしょうか。
しりょうのしゅうせいをおねがいしたいのですが、おてすうをおかけしますが、よろしくおねがいいたします。	しょうちいたしました。しゅうせいかしょをおしえていただけますでしょうか。
Shiryō no shūsei o onegai shitai nodesuga, otesū o okake shimasuga, yoroshiku onegai itashimasu.	Shōchi itashimashita. Shūsei kasho o oshiete itadakemasudeshou ka.
I'd like to ask you to revise the document. I'm sorry for the trouble, but I'd appreciate your help.	Understood. Could you please tell me which parts need revision?

Cultural Context

Implies you're asking for a favor. Don't use for tasks within the recipient's job duties.

ご意見をお聞かせください。

ごいけんをおきかせください。

Go iken o o kikase kudasai.

Please share your thoughts with us.

Variation 1	Variation 2
ご見解をお教えいただけますでしょうか。	Kyō mo shōjin shima shou.
ごけんかいをおしえていただけますでしょうか。	ごけんかいをおしえていただけますでしょうか。
Go kenkai o o oshie itadakemasudeshou ka.	Henshin ga okurete shimai, taihen shitsurei itashimashita.
Please share your thoughts with us.	I apologize for the delayed response.

Positive Response	Negative Response
ありがとうございます。喜んで意見を共有させていただきます。	意見を言っても無駄です。
ありがとうございます。よろこんでいけんをきょうゆうさせていただきます。	いけんをいってもむだです。
Arigatōgozaimasu. Yorokonde iken o kyōyū sa sete itadakimasu.	Iken o itte mo mudadesu.
Thank you. I'd be happy to share my opinion.	It's pointless to give my opinion.

Conversation example person A	Conversation example person B
新プロジェクトの方向性について、ご意見をお聞かせください。	承知しました。私見ではありますが、顧客ニーズにより焦点を当てるべきだと考えます。
しんぷろじぇくとのほうこうせいについて、ごいけんをおきかせください。	しょうちしました。しけんではありますが、こきゃくにーずによりしょうてんをあてるべきだとかんがえます。
Shin purojekuto no hōkō-sei ni tsuite, go iken o o kikase kudasai.	Shōchi shima shita. Shikende wa arimasuga, kokyaku nīzu ni yori shōten o aterubekida to kangaemasu.
Please share your thoughts on the direction of the new project.	Understood. In my personal opinion, I think we should focus more on customer needs.

Cultural Context

Signals you're open to feedback. Ensure you're prepared to act on the opinions received.

ご都合はいかがでしょうか。

ごつごうはいかがでしょうか。

Gotsugō wa ikagadeshou ka.

How does this work for you?

Variation 1	Variation 2
スケジュールをお伺いできますか。	Kyō mo shōjin shima shou.
すけじゅーるをおうかがいできますか。	すけじゅーるをおうかがいできますか。
Sukejūru o o ukagai dekimasu ka.	Otesūdesuga, go kakunin o onegai dekimasu ka.
How does your schedule look?	Could you please verify this?

Positive Response	Negative Response
ありがとうございます。スケジュールを確認して、すぐにご連絡いたします。	都合が悪いです。
ありがとうございます。すけじゅーるをかくにんして、すぐにごれんらくいたします。	つごうがわるいです。
Arigatōgozaimasu. Sukejūru o kakunin shite, sugu ni go renraku itashimasu.	Tsugō ga waruidesu.
Thank you. I'll check my schedule and get back to you soon.	It's not convenient for me.

Conversation example person A	Conversation example person B
来週の水曜日に会議を予定しておりますが、ご都合はいかがでしょうか。	水曜日の午後であれば参加可能です。時間を教えていただけますか。
らいしゅうのすいようびにかいぎをよていしておりますが、ごつごうはいかがでしょうか。	すいようびのごごであればさんかかのうです。じかんをおしえていただけますか。
Raishū no suiyōbi ni kaigi o yotei shite orimasuga, go tsugō wa ikagadeshou ka.	Suiyōbi no gogodeareba sanka kanōdesu. Jikan o oshiete itadakemasu ka.
We're planning a meeting for next Wednesday. How does that work for you?	I can attend if it's Wednesday afternoon. Could you tell me the specific time?

Cultural Context

Used for scheduling. Be prepared to offer multiple options if using this phrase.

お待ちしております。

おまちしております。
Omachi shite orimasu.
We look forward to hearing from you.

Variation 1	Variation 2
ご連絡をお待ち申し上げております。	Kyō mo shōjin shima shou.
ごれんらくをおまちもうしあげております。	ごれんらくをおまちもうしあげております。
Go renraku o omachi mōshiagete orimasu.	Nanitozo yoroshiku onegai mōshiagemasu.
We look forward to hearing from you.	Thank you in advance for your cooperation.

Positive Response	Negative Response
ありがとうございます。できるだけ早くご連絡いたします。	いつまで待てばいいのですか。
ありがとうございます。できるだけはやくごれんらくいたします。	いつまでまてばいいのですか。
Arigatōgozaimasu. Dekirudake hayaku go renraku itashimasu.	Itsu made mateba ī nodesu ka.
Thank you. I'll get back to you as soon as possible.	How long do I have to wait?

Conversation example person A	Conversation example person B
ご返答お待ちしております。	申し訳ありません。明日中にはご返答させていただきます。
ごへんとうおまちしております。	もうしわけありません。あしたちゅうにはごへんとうさせていただきます。
Go hentō omachi shite orimasu.	Mōshiwake arimasen. Ashita-chū ni hago hentō sa sete itadakimasu.
I'm looking forward to your reply.	I'm sorry. I'll respond by tomorrow.

Cultural Context
Implies eagerness. Can seem pushy if used for responses to routine emails.

ご検討の程、よろしくお願いいたします。

ごけんとうのほど、よろしくおねがいいたします。

Go kentō no hodo, yoroshikuonegaītashimasu.

We appreciate your consideration.

Variation 1	Variation 2
ご審議いただけますよう、お願い申し上げます。	Kyō mo shōjin shima shou.
ごしんぎいただけますよう、おねがいもうしあげます。	ごしんぎいただけますよう、おねがいもうしあげます。
Go shingi itadakemasu yō, onegai mōshiagemasu.	Otesūdesuga, go kentō itadakemasuto saiwaidesu.
We appreciate your kind consideration.	We would appreciate your consideration.

Positive Response	Negative Response
承知いたしました。慎重に検討させていただきます。	検討する価値がありません。
しょうちいたしました。しんちょうにけんとうさせていただきます。	けんとうするかちがありません。
Shōchi itashimashita. Shinchō ni kentō sa sete itadakimasu.	Kentō suru kachi ga arimasen.
Understood. We will carefully consider it.	It's not worth considering.

Conversation example person A	Conversation example person B
新しい提案書を送付いたしました。ご検討の程、よろしくお願いいたします。	ありがとうございます。慎重に検討させていただきます。
あたらしいていあんしょをそうふいたしました。ごけんとうのほど、よろしくおねがいいたします。	ありがとうございます。しんちょうにけんとうさせていただきます。
Atarashī teian-sho o sōfu itashimashita. Go kentō no hodo, yoroshiku onegai itashimasu.	Arigatōgozaimasu. Shinchō ni kentō sa sete itadakimasu.
I've sent a new proposal. Please consider it.	Thank you. I'll consider it carefully.

Cultural Context

More formal version of "ご検討をお願いいたします。" Use for significant requests.

ご協力ありがとうございます。

ごきょうりょくありがとうございます。
Go kyōryoku arigatōgozaimasu.
Thank you for your cooperation.

Variation 1	Variation 2
お力添えいただき、感謝申し上げます。	Kyō mo shōjin shima shou.
おちからぞえいただき、かんしゃもうしあげます。	おちからぞえいただき、かんしゃもうしあげます。
O chikarazoe itadaki, kansha mōshiagemasu.	Go rikai itadakemasuto saiwaidesu.
Thank you for your cooperation.	We hope for your understanding.

Positive Response	Negative Response
こちらこそ、お役に立てて嬉しく思います。	協力していません。
こちらこそ、おやくにたててうれしくおもいます。	きょうりょくしていません。
Kochira koso, o yakunitatete ureshiku omoimasu.	Kyōryoku shite imasen.
It's our pleasure to be of help.	I haven't cooperated.

Conversation example person A	Conversation example person B
プロジェクトへのご協力ありがとうございます。大変助かりました。	こちらこそ、良い経験になりました。今後ともよろしくお願いいたします。
ぷろじぇくとへのごきょうりょくありがとうございます。たいへんたすかりました。	こちらこそ、よいけいけんになりました。こんごともよろしくおねがいいたします。
Purojekuto e no go kyōryoku arigatōgozaimasu. Taihen tasukarimashita.	Kochira koso, yoi keiken ni narimashita. Kongo tomo yoroshiku onegai itashimasu.
Thank you for your cooperation on the project. It was very helpful.	It was a good experience for me as well. I look forward to working with you in the future.

Cultural Context

Use after cooperation has occurred, not preemptively.

早々のご返答をお待ちしております。

そうそうのごへんとうをおまちしております。
Sōsō no go hentō o omachi shite orimasu.
We look forward to your prompt reply.

Variation 1	Variation 2
迅速なご回答をいただけますと幸いです。	Kyō mo shōjin shima shou.
じんそくなごかいとうをいただけますとさいわいです。	じんそくなごかいとうをいただけますとさいわいです。
Jinsokuna go kaitō o itadakemasuto saiwaidesu.	Ryōkai itashimashita.
We look forward to your prompt response.	Understood.

Positive Response	Negative Response
承知いたしました。できるだけ早くご返答いたします。	急かさないでください。
しょうちいたしました。できるだけはやくごへんとういたします。	せかさないでください。
Shōchi itashimashita. Dekirudake hayaku go hentō itashimasu.	Kyū kasanaide kudasai.
Understood. I'll respond as soon as possible.	Please don't rush me.

Conversation example person A	Conversation example person B
緊急の案件ですので、早々のご返答をお待ちしております。	申し訳ありません。至急確認して、本日中にご返答いたします。
きんきゅうのあんけんですので、そうそうのごへんとうをおまちしております。	もうしわけありません。しきゅうかくにんして、ほんじつちゅうにごへんとういたします。
Kinkyū no ankendesunode, sōsō no go hentō o omachi shite orimasu.	Mōshiwake arimasen. Shikyū kakunin shite, honjitsu-chū ni go hentō itashimasu.
As this is an urgent matter, I look forward to your prompt reply.	I'm sorry. I'll check it urgently and respond by the end of today.

Cultural Context
Implies urgency. Use only when a quick response is genuinely necessary.

ご指摘ありがとうございます。

ごしてきありがとうございます。
Go shiteki arigatōgozaimasu.
Thank you for pointing that out.

Variation 1	Variation 2
ご助言いただき、感謝申し上げます。	Kyō mo shōjin shima shou.
ごじょげんいただき、かんしゃもうしあげます。	ごじょげんいただき、かんしゃもうしあげます。
Go jogen itadaki, kansha mōshiagemasu.	Betsu Soe no shiryō o goran kudasai.
Thank you for pointing that out.	Please check the attached file.

Positive Response	Negative Response
こちらこそ、貴重なご意見ありがとうございます。	指摘するつもりはありませんでした。
こちらこそ、きちょうなごいけんありがとうございます。	してきするつもりはありませんでした。
Kochira koso, kichōna go iken arigatōgozaimasu.	Shiteki suru tsumori wa arimasende shita.
Thank you for your valuable feedback.	I didn't mean to point that out.

Conversation example person A	Conversation example person B
レポートの誤りについてご指摘ありがとうございます。早速修正いたします。	こちらこそ、ご確認いただきありがとうございます。修正版の確認をお願いいたします。
れぽーとのあやまりについてごしてきありがとうございます。さっそくしゅうせいいたします。	こちらこそ、ごかくにんいただきありがとうございます。しゅうせいばんのかくにんをおねがいいたします。
Repōto no ayamari ni tsuite go shiteki arigatōgozaimasu. Sassoku shūsei itashimasu.	Kochira koso, go kakunin itadaki arigatōgozaimasu. Shūsei-ban no kakunin o onegai itashimasu.
Thank you for pointing out the error in the report. I'll correct it right away.	Thank you for checking. Please review the corrected version.

Cultural Context
Shows humility. Ensure you're genuinely open to criticism before using.

大変申し訳ございません。

たいへんもうしわけございません。
Taihen mōshiwakegozaimasen.
I sincerely apologize.

Variation 1	Variation 2
誠に恐縮でございます。	Kyō mo shōjin shima shou.
まことにきょうしゅくでございます。	まことにきょうしゅくでございます。
Makotoni kyōshukudegozaimasu.	Makotoni kyōshukudesu.
I sincerely apologize.	I'm truly sorry.

Positive Response	Negative Response
お詫びいただき恐縮です。問題ございません。	謝罪では解決しません。
おわびいただききょうしゅくです。もんだいございません。	しゃざいではかいけつしません。
Owabi itadaki kyōshukudesu. Mondai go zaimasen.	Shazaide wa kaiketsu shima sen.
Thank you for your apology. No problem at all.	An apology doesn't solve the problem.

Conversation example person A	Conversation example person B
納期の遅延について、大変申し訳ございません。	状況は理解いたしました。今後の対策を教えていただけますか。
のうきのちえんについて、たいへんもうしわけございません。	じょうきょうはりかいいたしました。こんごのたいさくをおしえていただけますか。
Nōki no chien ni tsuite, taihen mōshiwake go zaimasen.	Jōkyō wa rikai itashimashita. Kongo no taisaku o oshiete itadakemasu ka.
I deeply apologize for the delay in delivery.	I understand the situation. Could you tell me about future countermeasures?

Cultural Context
Stronger apology than just "申し訳ございません。" Use for serious mistakes only.

ご確認のほど、よろしくお願いいたします。

ごかくにんのほど、よろしくおねがいいたします。

Go kakunin no hodo, yoroshikuonegaītashimasu.

Please confirm at your earliest convenience.

Variation 1	Variation 2
お手数ですが、ご確認いただけますと幸いです。	Kyō mo shōjin shima shou.
おてすうですが、ごかくにんいただけますとさいわいです。	おてすうですが、ごかくにんいただけますとさいわいです。
Otesūdesuga, go kakunin itadakemasuto saiwaidesu.	Go kakunin itadakemasuto saiwaidesu.
We kindly ask for your confirmation.	I would appreciate your confirmation.

Positive Response	Negative Response
承知いたしました。すぐに確認させていただきます。	確認する必要はありません。
しょうちいたしました。すぐにかくにんさせていただきます。	かくにんするひつようはありません。
Shōchi itashimashita. Sugu ni kakunin sa sete itadakimasu.	Kakunin suru hitsuyō wa arimasen.
Understood. I'll check it right away.	There's no need to check.

Conversation example person A	Conversation example person B
修正した企画書を送付いたしました。ご確認のほど、よろしくお願いいたします。	承知いたしました。できるだけ早く確認してご連絡いたします。
しゅうせいしたきかくしょをそうふいたしました。ごかくにんのほど、よろしくおねがいいたします。	しょうちいたしました。できるだけはやくかくにんしてごれんらくいたします。
Shūsei shita kikaku-sho o sōfu itashimashita. Go kakunin no hodo, yoroshiku onegai itashimasu.	Shōchi itashimashita. Dekirudake hayaku kakunin shite go renraku itashimasu.
I've sent the revised proposal. Please check it.	Understood. I'll check it as soon as possible and get back to you.

Cultural Context

Polite way to request confirmation. Ensure you've provided all necessary information.

ご返答お待ちしております。

ごへんとうおまちしております。

Go hentō omachi shite orimasu.

I await your response.

Variation 1	Variation 2
ご回答いただけますよう、お願い申し上げます。	Kyō mo shōjin shima shou.
ごかいとういただけますよう、おねがいもうしあげます。	ごかいとういただけますよう、おねがいもうしあげます。
Go kaitō itadakemasu yō, onegai mōshiagemasu.	Kaitō o omachi shite orimasu.
We look forward to your response.	I look forward to your response.

Positive Response	Negative Response
ありがとうございます。できるだけ早くご返答いたします。	返答する内容がありません。
ありがとうございます。できるだけはやくごへんとういたします。	へんとうするないようがありません。
Arigatōgozaimasu. Dekirudake hayaku go hentō itashimasu.	Hentō suru naiyō ga arimasen.
Thank you. I'll respond as soon as possible.	I have nothing to respond to.

Conversation example person A	Conversation example person B
先日お送りした提案書について、ご返答お待ちしております。	申し訳ありません。明日中にはご返答させていただきます。
せんじつおおくりしたていあんしょについて、ごへんとうおまちしております。	もうしわけありません。あしたちゅうにはごへんとうさせていただきます。
Senjitsu ookuri shita teian-sho ni tsuite, go hentō omachi shite orimasu.	Mōshiwake arimasen. Ashita-chū ni hago hentō sa sete itadakimasu.
I'm waiting for your response regarding the proposal I sent the other day.	I'm sorry. I'll respond by tomorrow.

Cultural Context

Softer than "早々のご返答をお待ちしております。" Still implies expectation of a reply.

お手数ですが、ご対応をお願いいたします。

おてすうですが、ごたいおうをおねがいいたします。

Otesūdesuga, go taiō o onegai itashimasu.

I apologize for the inconvenience, but please take care of this matter.

Variation 1	Variation 2
ご面倒をおかけしますが、ご対処いただけますでしょうか。	Kyō mo shōjin shima shou.
ごめんどうをおかけしますが、ごたいしょいただけますでしょうか。	ごめんどうをおかけしますが、ごたいしょいただけますでしょうか。
Go mendō o okake shimasuga, go taisho itadakemasudeshou ka.	Osoreirimasuga, taiō o onegai shimasu.
Sorry for the trouble, but could you please handle this?	I apologize for the trouble, but please handle this.

Positive Response	Negative Response
承知いたしました。すぐに対応させていただきます。	自分で対応してください。
しょうちいたしました。すぐにたいおうさせていただきます。	じぶんでたいおうしてください。
Shōchi itashimashita. Sugu ni taiō sa sete itadakimasu.	Jibun de taiō shite kudasai.
Understood. I'll take care of it right away.	Please handle it yourself.

Conversation example person A	Conversation example person B
クライアントからの問い合わせがありました。お手数ですが、ご対応をお願いいたします。	承知いたしました。至急対応させていただきます。
くらいあんとからのといあわせがありました。おてすうですが、ごたいおうをおねがいいたします。	しょうちいたしました。しきゅうたいおうさせていただきます。
Kuraianto kara no toiawase ga Arima shita. Otesūdesuga, go taiō o onegai itashimasu.	Shōchi itashimashita. Shikyū taiō sa sete itadakimasu.
We received an inquiry from a client. I'm sorry for the trouble, but could you please handle it?	Understood. I'll address it immediately.

Cultural Context

Acknowledges the effort required. Use when asking for non-trivial tasks.

ご質問がございましたら、ご連絡ください。

ごしつもんがございましたら、ごれんらくください。

Go shitsumon ga gozaimashitara, go renraku kudasai.

If you have any questions, please contact us.

Variation 1	Variation 2
ご不明点等ございましたら、お問い合わせください。	Kyō mo shōjin shima shou.
ごふめいてんとうございましたら、おといあわせください。	ごふめいてんとうございましたら、おといあわせください。
Go fumei-ten-tō go zaimashita-ra, o toiawase kudasai.	Fumei-ten ga areba, oshirase kudasai.
If you have any questions, please contact us.	Please let me know if you have any questions.

Positive Response	Negative Response
ありがとうございます。丁寧な対応に感謝いたします。	質問する価値もありません。
ありがとうございます。ていねいなたいおうにかんしゃいたします。	しつもんするかちもありません。
Arigatōgozaimasu. Teineina taiō ni kansha itashimasu.	Shitsumon suru kachi mo arimasen.
Thank you. We appreciate your thorough support.	It's not even worth asking questions.

Conversation example person A	Conversation example person B
新しいシステムの導入について説明しました。ご質問がございましたら、ご連絡ください。	ありがとうございます。使用方法について詳しく教えていただけますか？
あたらしいしすてむのどうにゅうについてせつめいしました。ごしつもんがございましたら、ごれんらくください。	ありがとうございます。しようほうほうについてくわしくおしえていただけますか？
Atarashī shisutemu no dōnyū ni tsuite setsumei shima shita. Go shitsumon ga go zaimashita-ra, go renraku kudasai.	Arigatōgozaimasu. Shiyō hōhō ni tsuite kuwashiku oshiete itadakemasu ka?
I've explained about the new system implementation. If you have any questions, please contact me.	Thank you. Could you explain the usage method in more detail?

Cultural Context

Offers openness to questions. Ensure you're available to respond if used.

ご検討いただき、ありがとうございます。

ごけんとういただき、ありがとうございます。

Go kentō itadaki, arigatōgozaimasu.

Thank you for your consideration.

Variation 1	Variation 2
ご審議いただき、感謝申し上げます。	Kyō mo shōjin shima shou.
ごしんぎいただき、かんしゃもうしあげます。	ごしんぎいただき、かんしゃもうしあげます。
Go shingi itadaki, kansha mōshiagemasu.	Kentō shite kudasari, kansha itashimasu.
Thank you for your consideration.	Thank you for your consideration.

Positive Response	Negative Response
こちらこそ、ご提案ありがとうございます。	検討していません。
こちらこそ、ごていあんありがとうございます。	けんとうしていません。
Kochira koso, go teian arigatōgozaimasu.	Kentō shite imasen.
Thank you for your proposal. We appreciate it.	I haven't considered it.

Conversation example person A	Conversation example person B
先日の提案をご検討いただき、ありがとうございます。	こちらこそ、素晴らしい提案をありがとうございました。一部修正をお願いできますか？
せんじつのていあんをごけんとういただき、ありがとうございます。	こちらこそ、すばらしいていあんをありがとうございました。いちぶしゅうせいをおねがいできますか？
Senjitsu no teian o go kentō itadaki, arigatōgozaimasu.	Kochira koso, subarashī teian o arigatō go zaimashita. Ichi-bu shūsei o onegai dekimasu ka?
Thank you for considering our recent proposal.	Thank you for the excellent proposal. Could we request some partial revisions?

Cultural Context

Use after someone has already considered your request, not preemptively.

至急ご連絡ください。

しきゅうごれんらくください。

Shikyū go renraku kudasai.

Please contact us urgently.

Variation 1	Variation 2
緊急のご連絡をお願い申し上げます。	Kyō mo shōjin shima shou.
きんきゅうのごれんらくをおねがいもうしあげます。	きんきゅうのごれんらくをおねがいもうしあげます。
Kinkyū no go renraku o onegai mōshiagemasu.	Isogi de go renraku o onegai shimasu.
Please contact us urgently.	Please contact me urgently.

Positive Response	Negative Response
承知いたしました。すぐにご連絡いたします。	そんなに急ぐ必要はありません。
しょうちいたしました。すぐにごれんらくいたします。	そんなにいそぐひつようはありません。
Shōchi itashimashita. Sugu ni go renraku itashimasu.	Son'nani isogu hitsuyō wa arimasen.
Understood. I'll contact you immediately.	There's no need to rush.

Conversation example person A	Conversation example person B
緊急の事態が発生しました。至急ご連絡ください。	承知いたしました。すぐに電話いたします。
きんきゅうのじたいがはっせいしました。しきゅうごれんらくください。	しょうちいたしました。すぐにでんわいたします。
Kinkyū no jitai ga hassei shima shita. Shikyū go renraku kudasai.	Shōchi itashimashita. Sugu ni denwa itashimasu.
An emergency situation has occurred. Please contact me urgently.	Understood. I'll call you right away.

Cultural Context

Very urgent. Use sparingly to maintain its impact.

重ねてお詫び申し上げます。

かさねておわびもうしあげます。

Kasanete owabi mōshiagemasu.

I apologize once again.

Variation 1	Variation 2
改めて深くお詫び申し上げます。	Kyō mo shōjin shima shou.
あらためてふかくおわびもうしあげます。	あらためてふかくおわびもうしあげます。
Aratamete fukaku owabi mōshiagemasu.	Aratamete owabi itashimasu.
I apologize once again.	I apologize once again.

Positive Response	Negative Response
お気遣いありがとうございます。問題ございません。	二度と同じ過ちを繰り返さないでください。
おきづかいありがとうございます。もんだいございません。	にどとおなじあやまちをくりかえさないでください。
O kidzukai arigatōgozaimasu. Mondai go zaimasen.	Nidoto onaji ayamachi o kurikaesanaide kudasai.
Thank you for your concern. No problem at all.	Don't make the same mistake again.

Conversation example person A	Conversation example person B
度重なる遅延について、重ねてお詫び申し上げます。	ご迷惑をおかけして申し訳ございません。今後の改善策を提示させていただきます。
たびかさなるちえんについて、かさねておわびもうしあげます。	ごめいわくをおかけしてもうしわけございません。こんごのかいぜんさくをていじさせていただきます。
-Do kasanaru chien ni tsuite, kasanete owabi mōshiagemasu.	Go meiwaku o okake shite mōshiwake go zaimasen. Kongo no kaizen-saku o teiji sa sete itadakimasu.
I apologize again for the repeated delays.	I'm very sorry for the inconvenience. I'll present improvement measures for the future.

Cultural Context

Use for repeated apologies. Ensure the situation warrants multiple apologies.

ご理解いただき、感謝申し上げます。

ごりかいいただき、かんしゃもうしあげます。

Gorikai itadaki, kansha mōshiagemasu.

Thank you for your understanding.

Variation 1	Variation 2
ご了承いただき、ありがとうございます。	Kyō mo shōjin shima shou.
ごりょうしょういただき、ありがとうございます。	ごりょうしょういただき、ありがとうございます。
Go ryōshō itadaki, arigatōgozaimasu.	Rikai shite itadaki, arigatōgozaimasu.
Thank you for your understanding.	Thank you for your understanding.

Positive Response	Negative Response
こちらこそ、ご協力ありがとうございます。	理解していません。
こちらこそ、ごきょうりょくありがとうございます。	りかいしていません。
Kochira koso, go kyōryoku arigatōgozaimasu.	Rikai shite imasen.
Thank you for your cooperation. We appreciate it.	I don't understand.

Conversation example person A	Conversation example person B
難しい状況にもかかわらず、ご理解いただき、感謝申し上げます。	こちらこそ、柔軟に対応していただき、ありがとうございます。
むずかしいじょうきょうにもかかわらず、ごりかいいただき、かんしゃもうしあげます。	こちらこそ、じゅうなんにたいおうしていただき、ありがとうございます。
Muzukashī jōkyō ni mo kakawarazu, go rikai itadaki, kansha mōshiagemasu.	Kochira koso, jūnan ni taiō shite itadaki, arigatōgozaimasu.
Despite the difficult circumstances, thank you for your understanding.	Thank you for your flexible response as well.

Cultural Context

Use after someone has shown understanding, not as a request for understanding.

ご確認をお願いいたします。

ごかくにんをおねがいいたします。

Go kakunin o onegai itashimasu.

Please confirm this.

Variation 1	Variation 2
ご査収いただけますようお願い申し上げます。	Kyō mo shōjin shima shou.
ごさしゅういただけますようおねがいもうしあげます。	ごさしゅういただけますようおねがいもうしあげます。
Go sashū itadakemasu yō onegai mōshiagemasu.	Kakunin o onegai shimasu.
Please confirm this.	Please confirm.

Positive Response	Negative Response
承知いたしました。すぐに確認させていただきます。	確認する時間がありません。
しょうちいたしました。すぐにかくにんさせていただきます。	かくにんするじかんがありません。
Shōchi itashimashita. Sugu ni kakunin sa sete itadakimasu.	Kakunin suru jikan ga arimasen.
Understood. I'll check it right away.	I don't have time to check.

Conversation example person A	Conversation example person B
最終版の資料を送付いたしました。ご確認をお願いいたします。	承知いたしました。本日中に確認し、結果をご報告いたします。
さいしゅうばんのしりょうをそうふいたしました。ごかくにんをおねがいいたします。	しょうちいたしました。ほんじつちゅうにかくにんし、けっかをごほうこくいたします。
Saishū-ban no shiryō o sōfu itashimashita. Go kakunin o onegai itashimasu.	Shōchi itashimashita. Honjitsu-chū ni kakunin shi, kekka o go hōkoku itashimasu.
I've sent the final version of the document. Please check it.	Understood. I'll check it today and report back to you with the results.

Cultural Context

Direct request for confirmation. Ensure you've provided what needs to be confirmed.

ご多忙中恐縮ですが、ご対応をお願いいたします。

ごたぼうちゅうきょうしゅくですが、ごたいおうをおねがいいたします。

Gotabō chū kyōshukudesuga, go taiō o onegai itashimasu.

I'm sorry to trouble you during your busy time, but please address this matter.

Variation 1	Variation 2
お忙しい中申し訳ございませんが、ご対処いただけますでしょうか。	Kyō mo shōjin shima shou.
おいそがしいなかもうしわけございませんが、ごたいしょいただけますでしょうか。	おいそがしいなかもうしわけございませんが、ごたいしょいただけますでしょうか。
Oisogashī-chū mōshiwake go zaimasen ga, go taisho itadakemasudeshou ka.	O isogashī tokoro mōshiwake arimasenga, taiō o onegai shimasu.
I apologize for bothering you during your busy time, but could you please handle this?	I apologize for bothering you while you're busy, but please handle this.

Positive Response	Negative Response
承知いたしました。できる限り早く対応させていただきます。	これ以上の仕事は引き受けられません。
しょうちいたしました。できるかぎりはやくたいおうさせていただきます。	これいじょうのしごとはひきうけられません。
Shōchi itashimashita. Dekiru kagiri hayaku taiō sa sete itadakimasu.	Kore ijō no shigoto wa hikiuke raremasen.
Understood. I'll respond as soon as possible.	I can't take on any more work.

Conversation example person A	Conversation example person B
ご多忙中恐縮ですが、この件のご対応をお願いいたします。	承知いたしました。優先して対応させていただきます。
ごたぼうちゅうきょうしゅくですが、このけんのごたいおうをおねがいいたします。	しょうちいたしました。ゆうせんしてたいおうさせていただきます。
Gotabō chū kyōshukudesuga, kono-ken no go taiō o onegai itashimasu.	Shōchi itashimashita. Yūsen shite taiō sa sete itadakimasu.
I'm sorry to bother you when you're busy, but please address this matter.	Understood. I'll prioritize and handle this matter.

Cultural Context

Acknowledges the recipient's busy schedule. Use for non-urgent but important requests.

ご連絡ありがとうございました。

ごれんらくありがとうございました。

Go renraku arigatōgozaimashita.

Thank you for contacting us.

Variation 1	Variation 2
お知らせいただき、感謝申し上げます。	Kyō mo shōjin shima shou.
おしらせいただき、かんしゃもうしあげます。	おしらせいただき、かんしゃもうしあげます。
Oshirase itadaki, kansha mōshiagemasu.	Renraku itadaki, kansha itashimasu.
Thank you for your message.	Thank you for contacting me.

Positive Response	Negative Response
こちらこそ、ご連絡ありがとうございます。	連絡が遅すぎます。
こちらこそ、ごれんらくありがとうございます。	れんらくがおそすぎます。
Kochira koso, go renraku arigatōgozaimasu.	Renraku ga oso sugimasu.
Thank you for contacting us. We appreciate it.	Your contact is too late.

Conversation example person A	Conversation example person B
先ほどのご連絡ありがとうございました。早速確認いたします。	こちらこそ、迅速なご対応感謝いたします。
さきほどのごれんらくありがとうございました。さっそくかくにんいたします。	こちらこそ、じんそくなごたいおうかんしゃいたします。
Saki hodo no go renraku arigatō go zaimashita. Sassoku kakunin itashimasu.	Kochira koso, jinsokuna go taiō kansha itashimasu.
Thank you for your recent contact. I'll check it right away.	Thank you for your prompt response as well.

Cultural Context

Use in response to someone's contact, not preemptively.

ご返信お待ちしております。

ごへんしんおまちしております。

Go henshin omachi shite orimasu.

We look forward to your reply.

Variation 1	Variation 2
ご回答をお待ち申し上げております。	Kyō mo shōjin shima shou.
ごかいとうをおまちもうしあげております。	ごかいとうをおまちもうしあげております。
Go kaitō o omachi mōshiagete orimasu.	Henshin o omachi shite orimasu.
We look forward to your reply.	I'm looking forward to your reply.

Positive Response	Negative Response
承知いたしました。できるだけ早くご返信いたします。	返信する内容がありません。
しょうちいたしました。できるだけはやくごへんしんいたします。	へんしんするないようがありません。
Shōchi itashimashita. Dekirudake hayaku go henshin itashimasu.	Henshin suru naiyō ga arimasen.
Understood. I'll reply as soon as possible.	I have nothing to reply to.

Conversation example person A	Conversation example person B
提案書についてのご意見、ご返信お待ちしております。	申し訳ありません。明日までに詳細なフィードバックをお送りいたします。
ていあんしょについてのごいけん、ごへんしんおまちしております。	もうしわけありません。あしたまでにしょうさいなふぃーどばっくをおおくりいたします。
Teian-sho ni tsuite no go iken, go henshin omachi shite orimasu.	Mōshiwake arimasen. Ashita made ni shōsaina fīdobakku o ookuri itashimasu.
I'm looking forward to your reply with your opinions on the proposal.	I apologize. I'll send you detailed feedback by tomorrow.

Cultural Context

Polite way to request a reply. Implies less urgency than "早々のご返答をお待ちしております。"

お手数おかけして申し訳ございません。

おてすうおかけしてもうしわけございません。

Otesū okake shite mōshiwakegozaimasen.

I apologize for the inconvenience.

Variation 1	Variation 2
ご迷惑をおかけし、大変恐縮です。	Kyō mo shōjin shima shou.
ごめいわくをおかけし、たいへんきょうしゅくです。	ごめいわくをおかけし、たいへんきょうしゅくです。
Go meiwaku o okake shi, taihen kyōshukudesu.	Go meiwaku o okake shite mōshiwake arimasen.
I apologize for the inconvenience.	I apologize for the inconvenience.

Positive Response	Negative Response
お気遣いありがとうございます。問題ございません。	二度と迷惑をかけないでください。
おきづかいありがとうございます。もんだいございません。	にどとめいわくをかけないでください。
O kidzukai arigatōgozaimasu. Mondai go zaimasen.	Nidoto meiwaku o kakenaide kudasai.
Thank you for your concern. No problem at all.	Please don't trouble me again.

Conversation example person A	Conversation example person B
度々の修正依頼で、お手数おかけして申し訳ございません。	いえいえ、より良い成果物のためですので、問題ありません。
たびたびのしゅうせいいらいで、おてすうおかけしてもうしわけございません。	いえいえ、よりよいせいかぶつのためですので、もんだいありません。
Tabitabi no shūsei irai de, otesū okake shite mōshiwake go zaimasen.	Ieie, yori yoi seika-mono no tamedesunode, mondai arimasen.
I'm sorry for the trouble with repeated revision requests.	No problem at all, it's for a better end product.

Cultural Context
Use when asking for something that's clearly troublesome. Don't overuse.

ご査収ください。

ごさしゅうください。

Go sashū kudasai.

Please find attached.

Variation 1	Variation 2
ご確認いただけますようお願い申し上げます。	Kyō mo shōjin shima shou.
ごかくにんいただけますようおねがいもうしあげます。	ごかくにんいただけますようおねがいもうしあげます。
Go kakunin itadakemasu yō onegai mōshiagemasu.	Go kakunin kudasai.
Please acknowledge receipt.	Please check and confirm.

Positive Response	Negative Response
ありがとうございます。確認させていただきます。	査収する時間がありません。
ありがとうございます。かくにんさせていただきます。	さしゅうするじかんがありません。
Arigatōgozaimasu. Kakunin sa sete itadakimasu.	Sashū suru jikan ga arimasen.
Thank you. I'll review it.	I don't have time to review this.

Conversation example person A	Conversation example person B
今月の報告書をお送りしました。ご査収ください。	確かに受け取りました。ありがとうございます。
こんげつのほうこくしょをおおくりしました。ごさしゅうください。	たしかにうけとりました。ありがとうございます。
Kongetsu no hōkoku-sho o ookuri shima shita. Go sashū kudasai.	Tashika ni uketorimashita. Arigatōgozaimasu.
I've sent this month's report. Please acknowledge receipt.	I've received it. Thank you.

Cultural Context

Formal way to request review of a document. Ensure the document is actually attached.

ご指示いただきありがとうございます。

ごしじいただきありがとうございます。
Go shiji itadaki arigatōgozaimasu.
Thank you for your instructions.

Variation 1	Variation 2
ご指導いただき、感謝申し上げます。	Kyō mo shōjin shima shou.
ごしどういただき、かんしゃもうしあげます。	ごしどういただき、かんしゃもうしあげます。
Go shidō itadaki, kansha mōshiagemasu.	Shiji o itadaki, kansha itashimasu.
Thank you for your instructions.	Thank you for your instructions.

Positive Response	Negative Response
こちらこそ、ご指導ありがとうございます。	指示が不明確です。
こちらこそ、ごしどうありがとうございます。	しじがふめいかくです。
Kochira koso, go shidō arigatōgozaimasu.	Shiji ga fu meikakudesu.
Thank you for your guidance. We appreciate it.	The instructions are unclear.

Conversation example person A	Conversation example person B
先ほどのミーティングでのご指示いただきありがとうございます。	こちらこそ、積極的なご参加感謝いたします。
さきほどのみーてぃんぐでのごしじいただきありがとうございます。	こちらこそ、せっきょくてきなごさんかかんしゃいたします。
Saki hodo no mītingu de no go shiji itadaki arigatōgozaimasu.	Kochira koso, sekkyoku-tekina go sanka kansha itashimasu.
Thank you for your instructions in the recent meeting.	Thank you for your active participation as well.

Cultural Context

Use in response to receiving instructions, not preemptively.

引き続きよろしくお願いいたします。

ひきつづきよろしくおねがいいたします。

Hikitsudzuki yoroshikuonegaītashimasu.

I look forward to our continued cooperation.

Variation 1	Variation 2
今後ともお力添えいただけますと幸いです。	Kyō mo shōjin shima shou.
こんごともおちからぞえいただけますとさいわいです。	こんごともおちからぞえいただけますとさいわいです。
Kongo tomo o chikarazoe itadakemasuto saiwaidesu.	Kongo tomo yoroshiku onegai shimasu.
We look forward to your continued support.	Thank you for your continued support.

Positive Response	Negative Response
こちらこそ、今後ともよろしくお願いいたします。	これ以上の協力は難しいです。
こちらこそ、こんごともよろしくおねがいいたします。	これいじょうのきょうりょくはむずかしいです。
Kochira koso, kongo tomo yoroshiku onegai itashimasu.	Kore ijō no kyōryoku wa muzukashīdesu.
Likewise, we look forward to our continued cooperation.	Further cooperation will be difficult.

Conversation example person A	Conversation example person B
第一段階が完了しました。引き続きよろしくお願いいたします。	お疲れ様でした。次の段階も協力させていただきます。
だいいちだんかいがかんりょうしました。ひきつづきよろしくおねがいいたします。	おつかれさまでした。つぎのだんかいもきょうりょくさせていただきます。
Dai ichi dankai ga kanryō shima shita. Hikitsudzuki yoroshiku onegai itashimasu.	Otsukaresama de shita. Tsugi no dankai mo kyōryoku sa sete itadakimasu.
The first phase is complete. Please continue to support us.	Good job. I'll continue to cooperate in the next phase.

Cultural Context

Use for ongoing relationships or projects. Not suitable for one-time interactions.

ご検討いただけますと幸いです。

ごけんとういただけますとさいわいです。

Go kentō itadakemasuto saiwaidesu.

We would appreciate your consideration.

Variation 1	Variation 2
ご審議いただけますよう、お願い申し上げます。	Kyō mo shōjin shima shou.
ごしんぎいただけますよう、おねがいもうしあげます。	ごしんぎいただけますよう、おねがいもうしあげます。
Go shingi itadakemasu yō, onegai mōshiagemasu.	Kentō shite itadakereba ureshīdesu.
We would appreciate your consideration.	I would appreciate your consideration.

Positive Response	Negative Response
承知いたしました。丁寧に検討させていただきます。	検討する価値がありません。
しょうちいたしました。ていねいにけんとうさせていただきます。	けんとうするかちがありません。
Shōchi itashimashita. Teinei ni kentō sa sete itadakimasu.	Kentō suru kachi ga arimasen.
Understood. We will carefully consider it.	It's not worth considering.

Conversation example person A	Conversation example person B
新しいアイデアを提案しました。ご検討いただけますと幸いです。	興味深い提案ですね。詳細を教えていただけますか？
あたらしいあいであをていあんしました。ごけんとういただけますとさいわいです。	きょうみぶかいていあんですね。しょうさいをおしえていただけますか？
Atarashī aidea o teian shima shita. Go kentō itadakemasuto saiwaidesu.	Kyōmibukai teiandesu ne. Shōsai o oshiete itadakemasu ka?
I've proposed a new idea. I'd appreciate it if you could consider it.	That's an interesting proposal. Could you provide more details?

Cultural Context

Softer than "ご検討をお願いいたします。" Use for polite requests.

恐れ入りますが、ご確認をお願いいたします。

おそれいりますが、ごかくにんをおねがいいたします。

Osoreirimasuga, go kakunin o onegai itashimasu.

I'm sorry to trouble you, but could you please confirm this?

Variation 1	Variation 2
大変恐縮ですが、ご査収いただけますでしょうか。	Kyō mo shōjin shima shou.
たいへんきょうしゅくですが、ごさしゅういただけますでしょうか。	たいへんきょうしゅくですが、ごさしゅういただけますでしょうか。
Taihen kyōshukudesuga, go sashū itadakemasudeshou ka.	Mōshiwake arimasenga, kakunin o onegai shimasu.
I'm sorry to trouble you, but could you please confirm this?	I'm sorry to trouble you, but please confirm.

Positive Response	Negative Response
承知いたしました。すぐに確認させていただきます。	確認する必要はありません。
しょうちいたしました。すぐにかくにんさせていただきます。	かくにんするひつようはありません。
Shōchi itashimashita. Sugu ni kakunin sa sete itadakimasu.	Kakunin suru hitsuyō wa arimasen.
Understood. I'll check it right away.	There's no need to check.

Conversation example person A	Conversation example person B
恐れ入りますが、添付資料のご確認をお願いいたします。	承知いたしました。確認次第、ご連絡いたします。
おそれいりますが、てんぷしりょうのごかくにんをおねがいいたします。	しょうちいたしました。かくにんしだい、ごれんらくいたします。
Osoreirimasuga, tenpu shiryō no go kakunin o onegai itashimasu.	Shōchi itashimashita. Kakunin shidai, go renraku itashimasu.
I'm sorry to trouble you, but please check the attached document.	Understood. I'll contact you as soon as I've checked it.

Cultural Context

Very polite way to request confirmation. Use for important matters.

ご不便をおかけして申し訳ございません。

ごふべんをおかけしてもうしわけございません。
Go fuben o okake shite mōshiwakegozaimasen.
We apologize for any inconvenience caused.

Variation 1	Variation 2
ご迷惑をおかけし、誠に申し訳ございません。	Kyō mo shōjin shima shou.
ごめいわくをおかけし、まことにもうしわけございません。	ごめいわくをおかけし、まことにもうしわけございません。
Go meiwaku o okake shi, makotoni mōshiwake go zaimasen.	Go meiwaku o okake shite mōshiwake arimasen.
We apologize for any inconvenience caused.	I apologize for any inconvenience caused.

Positive Response	Negative Response
お気遣いありがとうございます。問題ございません。	不便を解消してください。
おきづかいありがとうございます。もんだいございません。	ふべんをかいしょうしてください。
O kidzukai arigatōgozaimasu. Mondai go zaimasen.	Fuben o kaishō shite kudasai.
Thank you for your concern. No problem at all.	Please resolve the inconvenience.

Conversation example person A	Conversation example person B
システムの一時停止により、ご不便をおかけして申し訳ございません。	状況は理解いたしました。復旧の見込みを教えていただけますか？
しすてむのいちじていしにより、ごふべんをおかけしてもうしわけございません。	じょうきょうはりかいいたしました。ふっきゅうのみこみをおしえていただけますか？
Shisutemu no ichiji teishi ni yori, go fuben o okake shite mōshiwake go zaimasen.	Jōkyō wa rikai itashimashita. Fukkyū no mikomi o oshiete itadakemasu ka?
We apologize for the inconvenience caused by the temporary system shutdown.	I understand the situation. Could you tell me when it's expected to be back up?

Cultural Context
Use when your actions have genuinely inconvenienced someone.

お手すきの際にご返信ください。

おてすきのさいにごへんしんください。

O tesuki no sai ni go henshin kudasai.

Please reply at your convenience.

Variation 1	Variation 2
ご都合のよろしい時にご回答ください。	Kyō mo shōjin shima shou.
ごつごうのよろしいときにごかいとうください。	ごつごうのよろしいときにごかいとうください。
Go tsugō no yoroshī toki ni go kaitō kudasai.	Jikan ga aru toki ni henshin shite kudasai.
Please reply at your convenience.	Please reply when you have a moment.

Positive Response	Negative Response
ありがとうございます。できるだけ早くご返信いたします。	手すきになる予定はありません。
ありがとうございます。できるだけはやくごへんしんいたします。	てすきになるよていはありません。
Arigatōgozaimasu. Dekirudake hayaku go henshin itashimasu.	Tesuki ni naru yotei wa arimasen.
Thank you. I'll reply as soon as possible.	I don't expect to have free time.

Conversation example person A	Conversation example person B
急ぎの案件ではありませんので、お手すきの際にご返信ください。	ありがとうございます。明日中にはご返信させていただきます。
いそぎのあんけんではありませんので、おてすきのさいにごへんしんください。	ありがとうございます。あしたちゅうにはごへんしんさせていただきます。
Isogi no ankende wa arimasen'node, o tesuki no sai ni go henshin kudasai.	Arigatōgozaimasu. Ashita-chū ni hago henshin sa sete itadakimasu.
This isn't urgent, so please reply when you have time.	Thank you. I'll reply by tomorrow.

Cultural Context

Implies no rush for reply. Use when the matter is not urgent.

ご協力のほど、よろしくお願いいたします。

ごきょうりょくのほど、よろしくおねがいいたします。

Go kyōryoku no hodo, yoroshikuonegaītashimasu.

We appreciate your cooperation.

Variation 1	Variation 2
お力添えいただけますよう、お願い申し上げます。	Kyō mo shōjin shima shou.
おちからぞえいただけますよう、おねがいもうしあげます。	おちからぞえいただけますよう、おねがいもうしあげます。
O chikarazoe itadakemasu yō, onegai mōshiagemasu.	Kyōryoku o onegai itashimasu.
We appreciate your cooperation.	We appreciate your cooperation.

Positive Response	Negative Response
承知いたしました。喜んで協力させていただきます。	協力できる余裕がありません。
しょうちいたしました。よろこんできょうりょくさせていただきます。	きょうりょくできるよゆうがありません。
Shōchi itashimashita. Yorokonde kyōryoku sa sete itadakimasu.	Kyōryoku dekiru yoyū ga arimasen.
Understood. We're happy to cooperate.	I don't have the capacity to cooperate.

Conversation example person A	Conversation example person B
新プロジェクトの立ち上げにあたり、ご協力のほど、よろしくお願いいたします。	承知いたしました。全力でサポートさせていただきます。
しんぷろじぇくとのたちあげにあたり、ごきょうりょくのほど、よろしくおねがいいたします。	しょうちいたしました。ぜんりょくでさぽーとさせていただきます。
Shin purojekuto no tachi age ni atari, go kyōryoku no hodo, yoroshiku onegai itashimasu.	Shōchi itashimashita. Zenryoku de sapōto sa sete itadakimasu.
As we launch the new project, we appreciate your cooperation.	Understood. I'll support you with all my effort.

Cultural Context

Use when asking for cooperation on a specific matter.

ご助言いただきありがとうございます。

ごじょげんいただきありがとうございます。

Go jogen itadaki arigatōgozaimasu.

Thank you for your advice.

Variation 1	Variation 2
ご指導いただき、感謝申し上げます。	Kyō mo shōjin shima shou.
ごしどういただき、かんしゃもうしあげます。	ごしどういただき、かんしゃもうしあげます。
Go shidō itadaki, kansha mōshiagemasu.	Adobaisu o itadaki, kansha itashimasu.
Thank you for your advice.	Thank you for your advice.

Positive Response	Negative Response
こちらこそ、貴重なご意見ありがとうございます。	助言したつもりはありません。
こちらこそ、きちょうなごいけんありがとうございます。	じょげんしたつもりはありません。
Kochira koso, kichōna go iken arigatōgozaimasu.	Jogen shita tsumori wa arimasen.
Thank you for your valuable advice. We appreciate it.	I didn't intend to give advice.

Conversation example person A	Conversation example person B
問題解決へのご助言いただきありがとうございます。早速試してみます。	お役に立てて嬉しいです。結果をお聞かせください。
もんだいかいけつへのごじょげんいただきありがとうございます。さっそくためしてみます。	おやくにたててうれしいです。けっかをおきかせください。
Mondai kaiketsu e no go jogen itadaki arigatōgozaimasu. Sassoku tameshite mimasu.	O yakunitatete ureshīdesu. Kekka o o kikase kudasai.
Thank you for your advice on solving the problem. I'll try it right away.	I'm glad I could help. Please let me know the results.

Cultural Context

Use in response to receiving advice, not preemptively.

ご確認いただけましたでしょうか。

ごかくにんいただけましたでしょうか。
Go kakunin itadakemashitadeshou ka.
Have you had a chance to confirm this?

Variation 1	Variation 2
お手数ですが、ご査収いただけましたか。	Kyō mo shōjin shima shou.
おてすうですが、ごさしゅういただけましたか。	おてすうですが、ごさしゅういただけましたか。
Otesūdesuga, go sashū itadakemashita ka.	Kakunin shite itadakemashita ka.
Have you had a chance to check this?	Have you had a chance to confirm?

Positive Response	Negative Response
はい、確認いたしました。ありがとうございます。	まだ確認していません。
はい、かくにんいたしました。ありがとうございます。	まだかくにんしていません。
Hai, kakunin itashimashita. Arigatōgozaimasu.	Mada kakunin shite imasen.
Yes, I've confirmed it. Thank you.	I haven't checked yet.

Conversation example person A	Conversation example person B
先日送付した書類のご確認いただけましたでしょうか。	申し訳ありません。明日中に確認してご連絡いたします。
せんじつそうふしたしょるいのごかくにんいただけましたでしょうか。	もうしわけありません。あしたちゅうにかくにんしてごれんらくいたします。
Senjitsu sōfu shita shorui no go kakunin itadakemashitadeshou ka.	Mōshiwake arimasen. Ashita-chū ni kakunin shite go renraku itashimasu.
Have you had a chance to check the documents I sent the other day?	I'm sorry. I'll check it by tomorrow and get back to you.

Cultural Context

Polite follow-up. Use when you need to check if something has been confirmed.

お手数ですが、ご返答いただけますでしょうか。

おてすうですが、ごへんとういただけますでしょうか。

Otesūdesuga, go hentō itadakemasudeshou ka.

I'm sorry to trouble you, but could you please respond?

Variation 1	Variation 2
ご面倒をおかけしますが、ご回答いただけますか。	Kyō mo shōjin shima shou.
ごめんどうをおかけしますが、ごかいとういただけますか。	ごめんどうをおかけしますが、ごかいとういただけますか。
Go mendō o okake shimasuga, go kaitō itadakemasu ka.	Mōshiwake arimasenga, hentō o itadakemasu ka.
I'm sorry to trouble you, but could you please respond?	I'm sorry to trouble you, but could you please respond?

Positive Response	Negative Response
承知いたしました。すぐにご返答させていただきます。	返答する内容がありません。
しょうちいたしました。すぐにごへんとうさせていただきます。へんとうするないようがありません。	
Shōchi itashimashita. Sugu ni go hentō sa sete itadakimasu.	Hentō suru naiyō ga arimasen.
Understood. I'll respond right away.	I have nothing to respond to.

Conversation example person A	Conversation example person B
先週の提案についてお手数ですが、ご返答いただけますでしょうか。	失礼いたしました。本日中にご返答させていただきます。
せんしゅうのていあんについておてすうですが、ごへんとういただけますでしょうか。	しつれいいたしました。ほんじつちゅうにごへんとうさせていただきます。
Senshū no teian ni tsuite otesūdesuga, go hentō itadakemasudeshou ka.	Shitsurei itashimashita. Honjitsu-chū ni go hentō sa sete itadakimasu.
I'm sorry to trouble you, but could you respond to last week's proposal?	I apologize for the delay. I'll respond by the end of today.

Cultural Context

Very polite way to request a response. Use when a reply is necessary but not urgent.

ご多用中恐縮ですが、ご検討ください。

ごたようちゅうきょうしゅくですが、ごけんとうください。

Gotayōchū kyōshukudesuga, go kentō kudasai.

I apologize for bothering you during your busy time, but please consider this.

Variation 1	Variation 2
お忙しい中申し訳ございませんが、ご審議ください。	Kyō mo shōjin shima shou.
おいそがしいなかもうしわけございませんが、ごしんぎください。	おいそがしいなかもうしわけございませんが、ごしんぎください。
Oisogashī-chū mōshiwake go zaimasen ga, go shingi kudasai.	O isogashī tokoro mōshiwake arimasenga, kentō o onegai shimasu.
I apologize for bothering you during your busy time, but please consider this.	I apologize for bothering you while you're busy, but please consider this.

Positive Response	Negative Response
承知いたしました。丁寧に検討させていただきます。	検討する時間がありません。
しょうちいたしました。ていねいにけんとうさせていただきます。	けんとうするじかんがありません。
Shōchi itashimashita. Teinei ni kentō sa sete itadakimasu.	Kentō suru jikan ga arimasen.
Understood. We will carefully consider it.	I don't have time to consider this.

Conversation example person A	Conversation example person B
ご多用中恐縮ですが、新たな提案をご検討ください。	承知いたしました。できるだけ早くお返事いたします。
ごたようちゅうきょうしゅくですが、あらたなていあんをごけんとうください。	しょうちいたしました。できるだけはやくおへんじいたします。
Go tayō-chū kyōshukudesuga, aratana teian o go kentō kudasai.	Shōchi itashimashita. Dekirudake hayaku o henji itashimasu.
I'm sorry to bother you when you're busy, but please consider this new proposal.	Understood. I'll reply as soon as possible.

Cultural Context
Acknowledges the recipient's busy schedule. Use for non-urgent consideration requests.

ご連絡お待ちしております。

ごれんらくおまちしております。

Go renraku omachi shite orimasu.

We await your contact.

Variation 1	Variation 2
ご返信をお待ち申し上げております。	Kyō mo shōjin shima shou.
ごへんしんをおまちもうしあげております。	ごへんしんをおまちもうしあげております。
Go henshin o omachi mōshiagete orimasu.	Renraku o omachi shite orimasu.
We look forward to hearing from you.	I'm looking forward to hearing from you.

Positive Response	Negative Response
ありがとうございます。できるだけ早くご連絡いたします。	連絡する内容がありません。
ありがとうございます。できるだけはやくごれんらくいたします。	れんらくするないようがありません。
Arigatōgozaimasu. Dekirudake hayaku go renraku itashimasu.	Renraku suru naiyō ga arimasen.
Thank you. I'll contact you as soon as possible.	I have nothing to contact you about.

Conversation example person A	Conversation example person B
会議の日程調整について、ご連絡お待ちしております。	申し訳ありません。明日午前中にはご連絡いたします。
かいぎのにっていちょうせいについて、ごれんらくおまちしております。	もうしわけありません。あしたごぜんちゅうにはごれんらくいたします。
Kaigi no nittei chōsei ni tsuite, go renraku omachi shite orimasu.	Mōshiwake arimasen. Ashita gozen-chū ni hago renraku itashimasu.
I'm waiting for your contact regarding the meeting schedule adjustment.	I apologize. I'll contact you by tomorrow morning.

Cultural Context

Implies expectation of contact. Use when you need the recipient to initiate the next interaction.

ご意見ありがとうございます。

ごいけんありがとうございます。

Go iken arigatōgozaimasu.

Thank you for your opinion.

Variation 1	Variation 2
ご見解をいただき、感謝申し上げます。	Kyō mo shōjin shima shou.
ごけんかいをいただき、かんしゃもうしあげます。	ごけんかいをいただき、かんしゃもうしあげます。
Go kenkai o itadaki, kansha mōshiagemasu.	Iken o itadaki, kansha itashimasu.
Thank you for your opinion.	Thank you for your opinion.

Positive Response	Negative Response
こちらこそ、貴重なご意見ありがとうございます。	意見を求めていません。
こちらこそ、きちょうなごいけんありがとうございます。	いけんをもとめていません。
Kochira koso, kichōna go iken arigatōgozaimasu.	Iken o motomete imasen.
Thank you for your valuable opinion. We appreciate it.	I didn't ask for your opinion.

Conversation example person A	Conversation example person B
プロジェクトに関するご意見ありがとうございます。検討させていただきます。	こちらこそ、意見を聞いていただきありがとうございます。
ぷろじぇくとにかんするごいけんありがとうございます。けんとうさせていただきます。	こちらこそ、いけんをきいていただきありがとうございます。
Purojekuto ni kansuru go iken arigatōgozaimasu. Kentō sa sete itadakimasu.	Kochira koso, iken o kiite itadaki arigatōgozaimasu.
Thank you for your opinion on the project. We will consider it.	Thank you for listening to my opinion as well.

Cultural Context

Use in response to receiving opinions, not preemptively.

何卒よろしくお願いいたします。

なにとぞよろしくおねがいいたします。
Nanitozo yoroshikuonegaītashimasu.
We sincerely ask for your cooperation.

Variation 1	Variation 2
何とぞご配慮いただけますようお願い申し上げます。	Kyō mo shōjin shima shou.
なにとぞごはいりょいただけますようおねがいもうしあげます。	なにとぞごはいりょいただけますようおねがいもうしあげます。
Nanitozo go hairyo itadakemasu yō onegai mōshiagemasu.	Dōzo yoroshiku onegai shimasu.
We humbly request your kind consideration.	I humbly request your kind consideration.

Positive Response	Negative Response
承知いたしました。誠心誠意対応させていただきます。	具体的に何をすればいいのですか。
しょうちいたしました。せいしんせいいたいおうさせていただきます。	ぐたいてきになにをすればいいのですか。
Shōchi itashimashita. Seishin seii taiō sa sete itadakimasu.	Gutai-teki ni nani o sureba ī nodesu ka.
Understood. We'll respond with our utmost sincerity.	What exactly do you want me to do?

Conversation example person A	Conversation example person B
初めての取り組みとなりますが、何卒よろしくお願いいたします。	承知いたしました。全力でサポートさせていただきます。
はじめてのとりくみとなりますが、なにとぞよろしくおねがいいたします。	しょうちいたしました。ぜんりょくでさぽーとさせていただきます。
Hajimete no torikumi to narimasuga, nanitozo yoroshiku onegai itashimasu.	Shōchi itashimashita. Zenryoku de sapōto sa sete itadakimasu.
This is our first attempt, so we kindly ask for your support.	Understood. I'll support you with all my effort.

Cultural Context
Very formal and strong request. Use for significant favors or important matters.

ご承知おきください。

ごしょうちおきください。

Go shōchi oki kudasai.

Please take note of this.

Variation 1	Variation 2
ご了解いただけますようお願い申し上げます。	Kyō mo shōjin shima shou.
ごりょうかいいただけますようおねがいもうしあげます。	ごりょうかいいただけますようおねがいもうしあげます。
Go ryōkai itadakemasu yō onegai mōshiagemasu.	Ryōkai shite kudasai.
Please take note of this.	Please take note of this.

Positive Response	Negative Response
承知いたしました。ありがとうございます。	承知できません。
しょうちいたしました。ありがとうございます。	しょうちできません。
Shōchi itashimashita. Arigatōgozaimasu.	Shōchi dekimasen.
Understood. Thank you.	I can't accept this.

Conversation example person A	Conversation example person B
スケジュールの変更がございましたので、ご承知おきください。	承知いたしました。変更後のスケジュールを教えていただけますか？
すけじゅーるのへんこうがございましたので、ごしょうちおきください。	しょうちいたしました。へんこうごのすけじゅーるをおしえていただけますか？
Sukejūru no henkō ga go zaimashitanode, go shōchi oki kudasai.	Shōchi itashimashita. Henkō-go no sukejūru o oshiete itadakemasu ka?
Please be informed that there has been a change in the schedule.	Understood. Could you tell me the updated schedule?

Cultural Context

Use when providing important information that needs to be remembered.

ご確認よろしくお願いいたします。

ごかくにんよろしくおねがいいたします。

Go kakunin yoroshikuonegaītashimasu.

We kindly ask for your confirmation.

Variation 1	Variation 2
ご査収のほど、よろしくお願い申し上げます。	Kyō mo shōjin shima shou.
ごさしゅうのほど、よろしくおねがいもうしあげます。	ごさしゅうのほど、よろしくおねがいもうしあげます。
Go sashū no hodo, yoroshiku onegai mōshiagemasu.	Kakunin o onegai shimasu.
We kindly ask for your confirmation.	Please confirm.

Positive Response	Negative Response
はい、確認いたします。ご連絡ありがとうございます。	確認する必要はありません。
はい、かくにんいたします。ごれんらくありがとうございます。	かくにんするひつようはありません。
Hai, kakunin itashimasu. Go renraku arigatōgozaimasu.	Kakunin suru hitsuyō wa arimasen.
Yes, I'll confirm it. Thank you for letting me know.	There's no need to check.

Conversation example person A	Conversation example person B
書類を送付いたしました。ご確認よろしくお願いいたします。	承知いたしました。確認させていただきます。
しょるいをそうふいたしました。ごかくにんよろしくおねがいいたします。	しょうちいたしました。かくにんさせていただきます。
Shorui o sōfu itashimashita. Go kakunin yoroshiku onegai itashimasu.	Shōchi itashimashita. Kakunin sa sete itadakimasu.
I have sent the documents. Please kindly confirm.	Understood. I will check them.

Cultural Context

Polite way to request confirmation. Ensure you've provided what needs to be confirmed.

恐縮ですが、ご返答いただけますでしょうか。

きょうしゅくですが、ごへんとういただけますでしょうか。

Kyōshukudesuga, go hentō itadakemasudeshou ka.

I'm sorry to trouble you, but could you please respond?

Variation 1	Variation 2
大変申し訳ございませんが、ご回答いただけますか。	Kyō mo shōjin shima shou.
たいへんもうしわけございませんが、ごかいとういただけますか。	たいへんもうしわけございませんが、ごかいとういただけますか。
Taihen mōshiwake go zaimasen ga, go kaitō itadakemasu ka.	Mōshiwake arimasenga, hentō o itadakemasu ka.
I'm sorry to trouble you, but could you please respond?	I'm sorry to trouble you, but could you please respond?

Positive Response	Negative Response
もちろんです。すぐに返答させていただきます。	返答する内容がありません。
もちろんです。すぐにへんとうさせていただきます。	へんとうするないようがありません。
Mochirondesu. Sugu ni hentō sa sete itadakimasu.	Hentō suru naiyō ga arimasen.
Of course. I'll respond right away.	I have nothing to respond to.

Conversation example person A	Conversation example person B
先日の提案について、恐縮ですが、ご返答いただけますでしょうか。	はい、明日中にご返答させていただきます。
せんじつのていあんについて、きょうしゅくですが、ごへんとういただけますでしょうか。	はい、あしたちゅうにごへんとうさせていただきます。
Senjitsu no teian ni tsuite, kyōshukudesuga, go hentō itadakemasudeshou ka.	Hai, ashita-chū ni go hentō sa sete itadakimasu.
Regarding the recent proposal, I apologize for the inconvenience, but could you please provide a response?	Yes, I will respond by tomorrow.

Cultural Context

Very polite way to request a response. Use when you need a reply but want to be extra courteous.

ご不明な点がございましたら、お問い合わせください。

ごふめいなてんがございましたら、おといあわせください。

Go fumeina ten ga gozaimashitara, o toiawase kudasai.

If you have any questions, please feel free to ask.

Variation 1	Variation 2
ご質問等ございましたら、ご連絡ください。	Kyō mo shōjin shima shou.
ごしつもんとうございましたら、ごれんらくください。	ごしつもんとうございましたら、ごれんらくください。
Go shitsumon-tō go zaimashita-ra, go renraku kudasai.	Fumei-ten ga areba, renraku shite kudasai.
If you have any questions, please contact us.	If you have any questions, please contact us.

Positive Response	Negative Response
ありがとうございます。丁寧な対応に感謝いたします。	全てが不明確です。
ありがとうございます。ていねいなたいおうにかんしゃいたします。	すべてがふめいかくです。
Arigatōgozaimasu. Teineina taiō ni kansha itashimasu.	Subete ga fu meikakudesu.
Thank you. I appreciate your thorough support.	Everything is unclear.

Conversation example person A	Conversation example person B
説明書を添付しております。ご不明な点がございましたら、お問い合わせください。	ありがとうございます。確認の上、必要があればお問い合わせいたします。
せつめいしょをてんぷしております。ごふめいなてんがございましたら、おといあわせください。	ありがとうございます。かくにんのうえ、ひつようがあればおといあわせいたします。
Setsumei-sho o tenpu shite orimasu. Go fumeina ten ga go zaimashita-ra, o toiawase kudasai.	Arigatōgozaimasu. Kakunin no ue, hitsuyō ga areba o toiawase itashimasu.
I have attached the instructions. If you have any questions, please feel free to ask.	Thank you. I'll check and contact you if needed.

Cultural Context

Offers openness to questions. Ensure you're available to respond if used.

ご対応ありがとうございます。

ごたいおうありがとうございます。

Go taiō arigatōgozaimasu.

Thank you for your response.

Variation 1	Variation 2
ご対処いただき、感謝申し上げます。	Kyō mo shōjin shima shou.
ごたいしょいただき、かんしゃもうしあげます。	ごたいしょいただき、かんしゃもうしあげます。
Go taisho itadaki, kansha mōshiagemasu.	Taiō shite itadaki, kansha itashimasu.
Thank you for your response.	Thank you for your response.

Positive Response	Negative Response
こちらこそ、ありがとうございます。今後ともよろしくお願いいたします。	対応していません。
こちらこそ、ありがとうございます。こんごともよろしくおねがいいたします。	たいおうしていません。
Kochira koso, arigatōgozaimasu. Kongo tomo yoroshiku onegai itashimasu.	Taiō shite imasen.
Thank you as well. I look forward to our continued cooperation.	I haven't dealt with it.

Conversation example person A	Conversation example person B
迅速なご対応ありがとうございます。	こちらこそ、ご対応ありがとうございます。
じんそくなごたいおうありがとうございます。	こちらこそ、ごたいおうありがとうございます。
Jinsokuna go taiō arigatōgozaimasu.	Kochira koso, go taiō arigatōgozaimasu.
Thank you for your prompt response.	Thank you for your cooperation as well.

Cultural Context

Use in response to someone's action, not preemptively.

ご検討のほどよろしくお願い申し上げます。

ごけんとうのほどよろしくおねがいもうしあげます。

Go kentō no hodo yoroshiku onegai mōshiagemasu.

We sincerely appreciate your consideration.

Variation 1	Variation 2
ご審議いただけますよう、心よりお願い申し上げます。	Kyō mo shōjin shima shou.
ごしんぎいただけますよう、こころよりおねがいもうしあげます。	ごしんぎいただけますよう、こころよりおねがいもうしあげます。
Go shingi itadakemasu yō, kokoro yori onegai mōshiagemasu.	Kentō o yoroshiku onegai itashimasu.
We sincerely request your kind consideration.	We kindly request your consideration.

Positive Response	Negative Response
承知いたしました。速やかに検討させていただきます。	検討する余地はありません。
しょうちいたしました。すみやかにけんとうさせていただきます。	けんとうするよちはありません。
Shōchi itashimashita. Sumiyaka ni kentō sa sete itadakimasu.	Kentō suru yochi wa arimasen.
Understood. I'll consider it promptly.	There's no room for consideration.

Conversation example person A	Conversation example person B
新しい提案書を送付いたしました。ご検討のほどよろしくお願い申し上げます。	拝受いたしました。慎重に検討させていただきます。
あたらしいていあんしょをそうふいたしました。ごけんとうのほどよろしくおねがいもうしあげます。	はいじゅいたしました。しんちょうにけんとうさせていただきます。
Atarashī teian-sho o sōfu itashimashita. Go kentō no hodo yoroshiku onegai mōshiagemasu.	Haiju itashimashita. Shinchō ni kentō sa sete itadakimasu.
I have sent a new proposal. We kindly request your consideration.	Received. We will carefully consider it.

Cultural Context

Very formal version of "ご検討をお願いいたします。" Use for significant requests to superiors.

お手数をおかけして恐縮です。

おてすうをおかけしてきょうしゅくです。
Otesū o okake shite kyōshukudesu.
I apologize for the trouble.

Variation 1	Variation 2
ご迷惑をおかけし、大変申し訳ございません。	Kyō mo shōjin shima shou.
ごめいわくをおかけし、たいへんもうしわけございません。	ごめいわくをおかけし、たいへんもうしわけございません。
Go meiwaku o okake shi, taihen mōshiwake go zaimasen.	Go meiwaku o okake shite mōshiwake arimasen.
I apologize for the trouble I'm causing you.	I apologize for the inconvenience.

Positive Response	Negative Response
いいえ、とんでもございません。お役に立てて光栄です。	これ以上の負担はかけないでください。
いいえ、とんでもございません。おやくにたててこうえいです。	これいじょうのふたんはかけないでください。
Īe, tondemo go zaimasen. O yakunitatete kōeidesu.	Kore ijō no futan wa kakenaide kudasai.
Not at all. It's my pleasure to be of assistance.	Please don't burden me any further.

Conversation example person A	Conversation example person B
資料の修正をお願いしてしまい、お手数をおかけして恐縮です。	お手数ではございません。お役に立てて嬉しいです。
しりょうのしゅうせいをおねがいしてしまい、おてすうをおかけしてきょうしゅくです。	おてすうではございません。おやくにたててうれしいです。
Shiryō no shūsei o onegai shite shimai, otesū o okake shite kyōshukudesu.	Otesūde wa go zaimasen. O yakunitatete ureshīdesu.
I apologize for the trouble of asking you to revise the documents.	It's no trouble at all. I'm glad to be of help.

Cultural Context

Use when asking for something that's clearly troublesome. More formal than "お手数おかけして申し訳ございません。"

ご返信ありがとうございました。

ごへんしんありがとうございました。
Go henshin arigatōgozaimashita.
Thank you for your reply.

Variation 1	Variation 2
ご回答いただき、感謝申し上げます。	Kyō mo shōjin shima shou.
ごかいとういただき、かんしゃもうしあげます。	ごかいとういただき、かんしゃもうしあげます。
Go kaitō itadaki, kansha mōshiagemasu.	Henshin itadaki, kansha itashimasu.
Thank you for your reply.	Thank you for your reply.

Positive Response	Negative Response
こちらこそ、迅速なご対応に感謝いたします。	返信が遅すぎます。
こちらこそ、じんそくなごたいおうにかんしゃいたします。	へんしんがおそすぎます。
Kochira koso, jinsokuna go taiō ni kansha itashimasu.	Henshin ga oso sugimasu.
Thank you as well. I appreciate your prompt response.	Your reply is too late.

Conversation example person A	Conversation example person B
ご多忙の中、ご返信ありがとうございました。	こちらこそ、ご連絡ありがとうございます。
ごたぼうのなか、ごへんしんありがとうございました。	こちらこそ、ごれんらくありがとうございます。
Gotabō no naka, go henshin arigatō go zaimashita.	Kochira koso, go renraku arigatōgozaimasu.
Thank you for your reply despite your busy schedule.	Thank you for your message as well.

Cultural Context
Use in response to receiving a reply, not preemptively.

ご指摘の点について、確認いたしました。

ごしてきのてんについて、かくにんいたしました。

Go shiteki no ten ni tsuite, kakunin itashimashita.

I have confirmed the point you mentioned.

Variation 1	Variation 2
ご指導いただいた事項を精査いたしました。	Kyō mo shōjin shima shou.
ごしどういただいたじこうをせいさいたしました。	ごしどういただいたじこうをせいさいたしました。
Go shidō itadaita jikō o seisa itashimashita.	Shiteki sa reta ten o kakunin shima shita.
I have confirmed the point you mentioned.	I have confirmed the point you mentioned.

Positive Response	Negative Response
ご確認ありがとうございます。丁寧な対応に感謝いたします。	指摘が不適切です。
ごかくにんありがとうございます。ていねいなたいおうにかんしゃいたします。	してきがふてきせつです。
Go kakunin arigatōgozaimasu. Teineina taiō ni kansha itashimasu.	Shiteki ga fu tekisetsudesu.
Thank you for confirming. I appreciate your thorough response.	Your point is inappropriate.

Conversation example person A	Conversation example person B
ご指摘の点について、確認いたしました。修正版を送付いたします。	ご対応ありがとうございます。修正版を拝見いたします。
ごしてきのてんについて、かくにんいたしました。しゅうせいばんをそうふいたします。	ごたいおうありがとうございます。しゅうせいばんをはいけんいたします。
Go shiteki no ten ni tsuite, kakunin itashimashita. Shūsei-ban o sōfu itashimasu.	Go taiō arigatōgozaimasu. Shūsei-ban o haiken itashimasu.
I have confirmed the point you mentioned. I will send a revised version.	Thank you for your response. I will review the revised version.

Cultural Context

Use when you've actually checked the point that was raised. Don't use preemptively.

ご連絡いただき、感謝申し上げます。

ごれんらくいただき、かんしゃもうしあげます。
Go renraku itadaki, kansha mōshiagemasu.
Thank you for contacting us.

Variation 1	Variation 2
お知らせいただき、心より御礼申し上げます。	Kyō mo shōjin shima shou.
おしらせいただき、こころよりおれいもうしあげます。	おしらせいただき、こころよりおれいもうしあげます。
Oshirase itadaki, kokoro yori orei mōshiagemasu.	Renraku o itadaki, arigatōgozaimasu.
We are grateful for your communication.	Thank you for contacting us.

Positive Response	Negative Response
こちらこそ、ありがとうございます。今後ともよろしくお願いいたします。	連絡が遅すぎます。
こちらこそ、ありがとうございます。こんごともよろしくおねがいいたします。	れんらくがおそすぎます。
Kochira koso, arigatōgozaimasu. Kongo tomo yoroshiku onegai itashimasu.	Renraku ga oso sugimasu.
Thank you as well. I look forward to our continued cooperation.	Your contact is too late.

Conversation example person A	Conversation example person B
お忙しい中、ご連絡いただき、感謝申し上げます。	こちらこそ、ご丁寧な対応に感謝いたします。
おいそがしいなか、ごれんらくいただき、かんしゃもうしあげます。	こちらこそ、ごていねいなたいおうにかんしゃいたします。
Oisogashī-chū, go renraku itadaki, kansha mōshiagemasu.	Kochira koso, go teineina taiō ni kansha itashimasu.
Thank you for contacting us despite your busy schedule.	We appreciate your kind attention as well.

Cultural Context

More formal than "ご連絡いただき、ありがとうございます。" Use for more formal situations.

ご検討いただきまして、ありがとうございます。

ごけんとういただきまして、ありがとうございます。

Go kentō itadakimashite, arigatōgozaimasu.

Thank you for your consideration.

Variation 1	Variation 2
ご審議いただき、誠にありがとうございます。	Kyō mo shōjin shima shou.
ごしんぎいただき、まことにありがとうございます。	ごしんぎいただき、まことにありがとうございます。
Go shingi itadaki, makotoni arigatōgozaimasu.	Kentō shite itadaki, kansha itashimasu.
Thank you for your consideration.	Thank you for your consideration.

Positive Response	Negative Response
こちらこそ、貴重なご意見をありがとうございます。	検討していません。
こちらこそ、きちょうなごいけんをありがとうございます。	けんとうしていません。
Kochira koso, kichōna go iken o arigatōgozaimasu.	Kentō shite imasen.
Thank you for your valuable input.	I haven't considered it.

Conversation example person A	Conversation example person B
弊社の提案をご検討いただきまして、ありがとうございます。	ご提案ありがとうございます。検討させていただきます。
へいしゃのていあんをごけんとういただきまして、ありがとうございます。	ごていあんありがとうございます。けんとうさせていただきます。
Heisha no teian o go kentō itadakimashite, arigatōgozaimasu.	Go teian arigatōgozaimasu. Kentō sa sete itadakimasu.
Thank you for considering our proposal.	Thank you for your proposal. We will consider it.

Cultural Context

Use after someone has considered your request, not preemptively. More formal than "ご検討いただき、ありがとうございます。"

お手数ですが、ご確認をお願いいたします。

おてすうですが、ごかくにんをおねがいいたします。
Otesūdesuga, go kakunin o onegai itashimasu.
I'm sorry to trouble you, but please confirm this.

Variation 1	Variation 2
ご面倒をおかけしますが、ご査収ください。	Kyō mo shōjin shima shou.
ごめんどうをおかけしますが、ごさしゅうください。	ごめんどうをおかけしますが、ごさしゅうください。
Go mendō o okake shimasuga, go sashū kudasai.	Mōshiwake arimasenga, kakunin o onegai shimasu.
I apologize for the inconvenience, but please confirm this.	I'm sorry to trouble you, but please confirm.

Positive Response	Negative Response
承知いたしました。すぐに確認させていただきます。	確認する時間がありません。
しょうちいたしました。すぐにかくにんさせていただきます。	かくにんするじかんがありません。
Shōchi itashimashita. Sugu ni kakunin sa sete itadakimasu.	Kakunin suru jikan ga arimasen.
Understood. I'll check it right away.	I don't have time to check.

Conversation example person A	Conversation example person B
修正箇所を赤字にしております。お手数ですが、ご確認をお願いいたします。	承知いたしました。確認の上、ご連絡いたします。
しゅうせいかしょをあかじにしております。おてすうですが、ごかくにんをおねがいいたします。	しょうちいたしました。かくにんのうえ、ごれんらくいたします。
Shūsei kasho o akaji ni shite orimasu. Otesūdesuga, go kakunin o onegai itashimasu.	Shōchi itashimashita. Kakunin no ue, go renraku itashimasu.
The corrections are in red. I apologize for the trouble, but please confirm.	Understood. I will check and get back to you.

Cultural Context
Polite way to request confirmation. Use when the confirmation might require some effort.

ご多忙中、誠に申し訳ございません。

ごたぼうちゅう、まことにもうしわけございません。

Gotabō-chū, makotoni mōshiwakegozaimasen.

I sincerely apologize for troubling you during your busy time.

Variation 1	Variation 2
お忙しい中、大変恐縮でございます。	Kyō mo shōjin shima shou.
おいそがしいなか、たいへんきょうしゅくでございます。	おいそがしいなか、たいへんきょうしゅくでございます。
Oisogashī-chū, taihen kyōshukudegozaimasu.	O isogashī tokoro, hontōni mōshiwake arimasen.
I'm very sorry to bother you during your busy schedule.	I'm truly sorry to bother you while you're busy.

Positive Response	Negative Response
いいえ、お気遣いありがとうございます。喜んで対応させていただきます。	忙しさを理由にしないでください。
いいえ、おきづかいありがとうございます。よろこんでたいおうさせていただきます。	いそがしさをりゆうにしないでください。
Īe, o kidzukai arigatōgozaimasu. Yorokonde taiō sa sete itadakimasu.	Isogashi-sa o riyū ni shinaide kudasai.
Not at all. Thank you for your consideration. I'm happy to help.	Don't use busyness as an excuse.

Conversation example person A	Conversation example person B
ご多忙中、誠に申し訳ございません。緊急の件でご相談があります。	承知いたしました。どのようなご相談でしょうか。
ごたぼうちゅう、まことにもうしわけございません。きんきゅうのけんでごそうだんがあります。	しょうちいたしました。どのようなごそうだんでしょうか。
Gotabō-chū, makotoni mōshiwake go zaimasen. Kinkyū no kudan de go sōdan ga arimasu.	Shōchi itashimashita. Do no yōna go sōdandeshou ka.
I'm very sorry to bother you while you're busy. I have an urgent matter to discuss.	Understood. What would you like to discuss?

Cultural Context

Use when you're significantly imposing on someone's time. Don't use for minor requests.

ご協力いただき、ありがとうございます。

ごきょうりょくいただき、ありがとうございます。

Go kyōryoku itadaki, arigatōgozaimasu.

Thank you for your cooperation.

Variation 1	Variation 2
お力添えいただき、心より感謝申し上げます。	Kyō mo shōjin shima shou.
おちからぞえいただき、こころよりかんしゃもうしあげます。	おちからぞえいただき、こころよりかんしゃもうしあげます。
O chikarazoe itadaki, kokoro yori kansha mōshiagemasu.	Kyōryoku shite itadaki, kansha itashimasu.
Thank you for your cooperation.	Thank you for your cooperation.

Positive Response	Negative Response
こちらこそ、一緒に仕事ができて光栄です。	協力していません。
こちらこそ、いっしょにしごとができてこうえいです。	きょうりょくしていません。
Kochira koso, issho ni shigoto ga dekite kōeidesu.	Kyōryoku shite imasen.
It's my pleasure to work together with you.	I haven't cooperated.

Conversation example person A	Conversation example person B
プロジェクトへのご協力いただき、ありがとうございます。	こちらこそ、ご協力させていただき光栄です。
ぷろじぇくとへのごきょうりょくいただき、ありがとうございます。	こちらこそ、ごきょうりょくさせていただきこうえいです。
Purojekuto e no go kyōryoku itadaki, arigatōgozaimasu.	Kochira koso, go kyōryoku sa sete itadaki kōeidesu.
Thank you for your cooperation on the project.	It's our pleasure to cooperate.

Cultural Context

Use after receiving cooperation, not preemptively.

ご返答いただき、感謝申し上げます。

ごへんとういただき、かんしゃもうしあげます。

Go hentō itadaki, kansha mōshiagemasu.

Thank you for your response.

Variation 1	Variation 2
ご回答いただき、誠にありがとうございます。	Kyō mo shōjin shima shou.
ごかいとういただき、まことにありがとうございます。	ごかいとういただき、まことにありがとうございます。
Go kaitō itadaki, makotoni arigatōgozaimasu.	Hentō o itadaki, arigatōgozaimasu.
We appreciate your response.	Thank you for your response.

Positive Response	Negative Response
こちらこそ、迅速なご対応に感謝いたします。	返答が不十分です。
こちらこそ、じんそくなごたいおうにかんしゃいたします。	へんとうがふじゅうぶんです。
Kochira koso, jinsokuna go taiō ni kansha itashimasu.	Hentō ga fu jūbundesu.
Thank you as well. I appreciate your prompt response.	Your response is insufficient.

Conversation example person A	Conversation example person B
お忙しい中、迅速にご返答いただき、感謝申し上げます。	こちらこそ、ご連絡ありがとうございます。
おいそがしいなか、じんそくにごへんとういただき、かんしゃもうしあげます。	こちらこそ、ごれんらくありがとうございます。
Oisogashī-naka, jinsoku ni go hentō itadaki, kansha mōshiagemasu.	Kochira koso, go renraku arigatōgozaimasu.
Thank you for your prompt reply despite your busy schedule.	Thank you for your message as well.

Cultural Context

More formal than "ご返答ありがとうございます。" Use in more formal situations.

ご確認いただけますようお願いいたします。

ごかくにんいただけますようおねがいいたします。

Go kakunin itadakemasu yō onegai itashimasu.

We kindly ask for your confirmation.

Variation 1	Variation 2
ご査収いただけますよう、お願い申し上げます。	Kyō mo shōjin shima shou.
ごさしゅういただけますよう、おねがいもうしあげます。	ごさしゅういただけますよう、おねがいもうしあげます。
Go sashū itadakemasu yō, onegai mōshiagemasu.	Kakunin shite itadakemasu yō onegai shimasu.
We kindly request your confirmation.	We kindly request your confirmation.

Positive Response	Negative Response
はい、すぐに確認させていただきます。ご連絡ありがとうございます。	確認する必要はありません。
はい、すぐにかくにんさせていただきます。ごれんらくありがとうございます。	かくにんするひつようはありません。
Hai, sugu ni kakunin sa sete itadakimasu. Go renraku arigatōgozaimasu.	Kakunin suru hitsuyō wa arimasen.
Yes, I'll check it right away. Thank you for letting me know.	There's no need to check.

Conversation example person A	Conversation example person B
添付資料をご確認いただけますようお願いいたします。	承知いたしました。確認の上、ご連絡いたします。
てんぷしりょうをごかくにんいただけますようおねがいいたします。	しょうちいたしました。かくにんのうえ、ごれんらくいたします。
Tenpu shiryō o go kakunin itadakemasu yō onegai itashimasu.	Shōchi itashimashita. Kakunin no ue, go renraku itashimasu.
Please kindly check the attached documents.	Understood. I will check and get back to you.

Cultural Context

Polite way to request confirmation. Use when confirmation is important but not urgent.

ご意見を拝聴し、検討させていただきます。

ごいけんをはいちょうし、けんとうさせていただきます。

Go iken o haichō shi, kentō sa sete itadakimasu.

We will consider your opinion.

Variation 1	Variation 2
ご見解を承り、精査いたします。	Kyō mo shōjin shima shou.
ごけんかいをうけたまわり、せいさいたします。	ごけんかいをうけたまわり、せいさいたします。
Go kenkai o uketamawari, seisa itashimasu.	Iken o kiki, kentō shimasu.
We will consider your opinion carefully.	We will consider your opinion.

Positive Response	Negative Response
ありがとうございます。貴重なご意見として参考にさせていただきます。	意見を聞く気はありません。
ありがとうございます。きちょうなごいけんとしてさんこうにさせていただきます。	いけんをきくきはありません。
Arigatōgozaimasu. Kichōna go iken to shite sankō ni sa sete itadakimasu.	Iken o kiku ki wa arimasen.
Thank you. I'll take your valuable opinion into consideration.	I'm not interested in hearing your opinion.

Conversation example person A	Conversation example person B
貴重なご意見を拝聴し、検討させていただきます。	ご検討ありがとうございます。結果をお待ちしております。
きちょうなごいけんをはいちょうし、けんとうさせていただきます。	ごけんとうありがとうございます。けっかをおまちしております。
Kichōna go iken o haichō shi, kentō sa sete itadakimasu.	Go kentō arigatōgozaimasu. Kekka o omachi shite orimasu.
We appreciate your valuable opinion and will consider it.	Thank you for your consideration. We look forward to the results.

Cultural Context

Use when you've actually listened to opinions and will consider them. Don't use preemptively.

お待たせして申し訳ございません。

おまたせしてもうしわけございません。

O mata se shite mōshiwakegozaimasen.

I apologize for keeping you waiting.

Variation 1	Variation 2
ご待機いただき、誠に恐縮でございます。	Kyō mo shōjin shima shou.
ごたいきいただき、まことにきょうしゅくでございます。	ごたいきいただき、まことにきょうしゅくでございます。
Go taiki itadaki, makotoni kyōshukudegozaimasu.	Mata sete shimai, mōshiwake arimasen.
I apologize for keeping you waiting.	I apologize for keeping you waiting.

Positive Response	Negative Response
いいえ、こちらこそお待たせして申し訳ありません。	待たせないでください。
いいえ、こちらこそおまたせしてもうしわけありません。	またせないでください。
Īe, kochira koso o mata se shite mōshiwake arimasen.	Mata senaide kudasai.
No, I should apologize for keeping you waiting.	Don't keep me waiting.

Conversation example person A	Conversation example person B
回答が遅くなり、お待たせして申し訳ございません。	いいえ、お気になさらないでください。
かいとうがおそくなり、おまたせしてもうしわけございません。	いいえ、おきになさらないでください。
Kaitō ga osoku nari, o mata se shite mōshiwake go zaimasen.	Īe, oki ni nasaranaide kudasai.
I apologize for the delay in responding.	No worries, please don't be concerned.

Cultural Context

Use when you've kept someone waiting. Don't use preemptively.

ご査収のほど、よろしくお願いいたします。

ごさしゅうのほど、よろしくおねがいいたします。
Go sashū no hodo, yoroshikuonegaītashimasu.
Please find the attached document.

Variation 1	Variation 2
ご確認いただけますよう、お願い申し上げます。	Kyō mo shōjin shima shou.
ごかくにんいただけますよう、おねがいもうしあげます。	ごかくにんいただけますよう、おねがいもうしあげます。
Go kakunin itadakemasu yō, onegai mōshiagemasu.	Kakunin o yoroshiku onegai shimasu.
We kindly request your acknowledgment.	Please check and confirm.

Positive Response	Negative Response
承知いたしました。早速確認させていただきます。	査収する時間がありません。
しょうちいたしました。さっそくかくにんさせていただきます。	さしゅうするじかんがありません。
Shōchi itashimashita. Sassoku kakunin sa sete itadakimasu.	Sashū suru jikan ga arimasen.
Understood. I'll check it immediately.	I don't have time to review this.

Conversation example person A	Conversation example person B
請求書を送付いたしました。ご査収のほど、よろしくお願いいたします。	承知いたしました。確認の上、処理させていただきます。
せいきゅうしょをそうふいたしました。ごさしゅうのほど、よろしくおねがいいたします。	しょうちいたしました。かくにんのうえ、しょりさせていただきます。
Seikyū-sho o sōfu itashimashita. Go sashū no hodo, yoroshiku onegai itashimasu.	Shōchi itashimashita. Kakunin no ue, shori sa sete itadakimasu.
I have sent the invoice. Please kindly check and process it.	Understood. I will check and process it.

Cultural Context

Formal way to request review of a document. More polite than "ご査収ください。"

ご不便をおかけし、申し訳ございません。

ごふべんをおかけし、もうしわけございません。
Go fuben o okake shi, mōshiwakegozaimasen.
We apologize for any inconvenience caused.

Variation 1	Variation 2
ご迷惑をおかけし、心よりお詫び申し上げます。	Kyō mo shōjin shima shou.
ごめいわくをおかけし、こころよりおわびもうしあげます。	ごめいわくをおかけし、こころよりおわびもうしあげます。
Go meiwaku o okake shi, kokoro yori owabi mōshiagemasu.	Fuben o okake shite, mōshiwake arimasen.
We apologize for any inconvenience caused.	I apologize for any inconvenience caused.

Positive Response	Negative Response
いいえ、こちらこそご迷惑をおかけして申し訳ありません。	不便を解消してください。
いいえ、こちらこそごめいわくをおかけしてもうしわけありません。	ふべんをかいしょうしてください。
Īe, kochira koso go meiwaku o okake shite mōshiwake arimasen.	Fuben o kaishō shite kudasai.
No, I should apologize for any inconvenience caused.	Please resolve the inconvenience.

Conversation example person A	Conversation example person B
システムの不具合でご不便をおかけし、申し訳ございません。	対応ありがとうございます。問題ありません。
しすてむのふぐあいでごふべんをおかけし、もうしわけございません。	たいおうありがとうございます。もんだいありません。
Shisutemu no fuguaide go fuben o okake shi, mōshiwake go zaimasen.	Taiō arigatōgozaimasu. Mondai arimasen.
We apologize for the inconvenience caused by the system malfunction.	Thank you for addressing it. It's not a problem.

Cultural Context

Use when your actions have genuinely inconvenienced someone. More formal than "ご不便をおかけして申し訳ございません。"

ご指示ください。

ごしじください。

Go shiji kudasai.

Please give us your instructions.

Variation 1	Variation 2
ご指導いただけますようお願い申し上げます。	Kyō mo shōjin shima shou.
ごしどういただけますようおねがいもうしあげます。	ごしどういただけますようおねがいもうしあげます。
Go shidō itadakemasu yō onegai mōshiagemasu.	Shiji o onegai shimasu.
Please give us your instructions.	Please give us instructions.

Positive Response	Negative Response
ありがとうございます。最善を尽くして対応させていただきます。	自分で判断してください。
ありがとうございます。さいぜんをつくしてたいおうさせていただきます。	じぶんではんだんしてください。
Arigatōgozaimasu. Saizen o tsukushite taiō sa sete itadakimasu.	Jibun de handan shite kudasai.
Thank you. I'll do my best to follow your instructions.	Please make your own decision.

Conversation example person A	Conversation example person B
次の段階に進むためのご指示ください。	承知しました。詳細な指示を送付いたします。
つぎのだんかいにすすむためのごしじください。	しょうちしました。しょうさいなしじをそうふいたします。
Tsugi no dankai ni susumu tame no go shiji kudasai.	Shōchi shima shita. Shōsaina shiji o sōfu itashimasu.
Please provide instructions for the next step.	Understood. I will send detailed instructions.

Cultural Context

Use when you're ready to receive instructions. Implies you're waiting for direction.

ご連絡いただけますと幸いです。

ごれんらくいただけますとさいわいです。

Go renraku itadakemasuto saiwaidesu.

We would appreciate it if you could contact us.

Variation 1	Variation 2
ご一報いただけますよう、お願い申し上げます。	Kyō mo shōjin shima shou.
ごいっぽういただけますよう、おねがいもうしあげます。	ごいっぽういただけますよう、おねがいもうしあげます。
Go ippō itadakemasu yō, onegai mōshiagemasu.	Renraku shite itadakereba ureshīdesu.
We would appreciate it if you could contact us.	I would appreciate it if you could contact me.

Positive Response	Negative Response
はい、必ずご連絡させていただきます。	連絡する内容がありません。
はい、かならずごれんらくさせていただきます。	れんらくするないようがありません。
Hai, kanarazu go renraku sa sete itadakimasu.	Renraku suru naiyō ga arimasen.
Yes, I'll make sure to contact you.	I have nothing to contact you about.

Conversation example person A	Conversation example person B
ミーティングの日程について、ご連絡いただけますと幸いです。	承知いたしました。本日中にご連絡いたします。
みーてぃんぐのにっていについて、ごれんらくいただけますとさいわいです。	しょうちいたしました。ほんじつちゅうにごれんらくいたします。
Mītingu no nittei ni tsuite, go renraku itadakemasuto saiwaidesu.	Shōchi itashimashita. Honjitsu-chū ni go renraku itashimasu.
We would appreciate it if you could contact us regarding the meeting schedule.	Understood. I will contact you by the end of today.

Cultural Context

Polite way to request contact. Use when you need the recipient to initiate contact.

ご検討をお願い申し上げます。

ごけんとうをおねがいもうしあげます。

Go kentō o onegai mōshiagemasu.

We kindly ask for your consideration.

Variation 1	Variation 2
ご審議いただけますよう、心よりお願いいたします。	Kyō mo shōjin shima shou.
ごしんぎいただけますよう、こころよりおねがいいたします。	ごしんぎいただけますよう、こころよりおねがいいたします。
Go shingi itadakemasu yō, kokoro yori onegai itashimasu.	Kentō o onegai itashimasu.
We sincerely request your consideration.	We kindly request your consideration.

Positive Response	Negative Response
承知いたしました。慎重に検討させていただきます。	検討する余地はありません。
しょうちいたしました。しんちょうにけんとうさせていただきます。	けんとうするよちはありません。
Shōchi itashimashita. Shinchō ni kentō sa sete itadakimasu.	Kentō suru yochi wa arimasen.
Understood. I'll carefully consider it.	There's no room for consideration.

Conversation example person A	Conversation example person B
新しい提案書を送付いたしました。ご検討をお願い申し上げます。	承知いたしました。慎重に検討させていただきます。
あたらしいていあんしょをそうふいたしました。ごけんとうをおねがいもうしあげます。	しょうちいたしました。しんちょうにけんとうさせていただきます。
Atarashī teian-sho o sōfu itashimashita. Go kentō o onegai mōshiagemasu.	Shōchi itashimashita. Shinchō ni kentō sa sete itadakimasu.
I have sent a new proposal. We kindly request your consideration.	Understood. We will carefully consider it.

Cultural Context

Very formal version of "ご検討をお願いいたします。" Use for significant requests to superiors.

何かございましたら、お知らせください。

なにかございましたら、おしらせください。

Nani kagozaimashitara, oshirase kudasai.

If there's anything, please let us know.

Variation 1	Variation 2
ご不明点等ございましたら、ご連絡ください。	Kyō mo shōjin shima shou.
ごふめいてんとうございましたら、ごれんらくください。	ごふめいてんとうございましたら、ごれんらくください。
Go fumei-ten-tō go zaimashita-ra, go renraku kudasai.	Nani ka mondai ga areba, renraku shite kudasai.
Please let us know if you have any concerns.	Please let us know if there's anything.

Positive Response	Negative Response
ありがとうございます。必要があればすぐにご連絡いたします。	特に何もありません。
ありがとうございます。ひつようがあればすぐにごれんらくいたします。	とくになにもありません。
Arigatōgozaimasu. Hitsuyō ga areba sugu ni go renraku itashimasu.	Tokuni nani mo arimasen.
Thank you. I'll contact you immediately if anything comes up.	There's nothing in particular.

Conversation example person A	Conversation example person B
準備は整いました。何かございましたら、お知らせください。	ありがとうございます。確認の上、ご連絡いたします。
じゅんびはととのいました。なにかございましたら、おしらせください。	ありがとうございます。かくにんのうえ、ごれんらくいたします。
Junbi wa Sei ima shita. Nani ka go zaimashita-ra, oshirase kudasai.	Arigatōgozaimasu. Kakunin no ue, go renraku itashimasu.
Preparations are complete. Please let us know if you need anything.	Thank you. I will check and get back to you.

Cultural Context

Offers openness to communication. Use when you want to be informed of any issues or changes.

ご対応いただき、ありがとうございます。

ごたいおういただき、ありがとうございます。

Go taiō itadaki, arigatōgozaimasu.

Thank you for your attention to this matter.

Variation 1	Variation 2
ご尽力いただき、感謝申し上げます。	Kyō mo shōjin shima shou.
ごじんりょくいただき、かんしゃもうしあげます。	ごじんりょくいただき、かんしゃもうしあげます。
Go jinryoku itadaki, kansha mōshiagemasu.	Taiō shite itadaki, kansha itashimasu.
Thank you for your attention to this matter.	Thank you for your response.

Positive Response	Negative Response
こちらこそ、お役に立てて光栄です。	対応していません。
こちらこそ、おやくにたててこうえいです。	たいおうしていません。
Kochira koso, o yakunitatete kōeidesu.	Taiō shite imasen.
It's my pleasure to be of assistance.	I haven't dealt with it.

Conversation example person A	Conversation example person B
迅速なご対応いただき、ありがとうございます。	こちらこそ、ご協力ありがとうございます。
じんそくなごたいおういただき、ありがとうございます。	こちらこそ、ごきょうりょくありがとうございます。
Jinsokuna go taiō itadaki, arigatōgozaimasu.	Kochira koso, go kyōryoku arigatōgozaimasu.
Thank you for your prompt response.	Thank you for your cooperation as well.

Cultural Context

Use in response to someone's action, not preemptively. More formal than "ご対応ありがとうございます。"

ご意見をお聞かせいただき、ありがとうございます。

ごいけんをおきかせいただき、ありがとうございます。

Go iken o o kikase itadaki, arigatōgozaimasu.

Thank you for sharing your opinion.

Variation 1	Variation 2
ご見解をお教えいただき、感謝申し上げます。	Kyō mo shōjin shima shou.
ごけんかいをおしえていただき、かんしゃもうしあげます。	ごけんかいをおしえていただき、かんしゃもうしあげます。
Go kenkai o o oshie itadaki, kansha mōshiagemasu.	Iken o kika sete itadaki, kansha itashimasu.
Thank you for sharing your opinion.	Thank you for sharing your opinion.

Positive Response	Negative Response
こちらこそ、貴重なご意見をありがとうございます。	意見を言っても無駄です。
こちらこそ、きちょうなごいけんをありがとうございます。	いけんをいってもむだです。
Kochira koso, kichōna go iken o arigatōgozaimasu.	Iken o itte mo mudadesu.
Thank you for sharing your valuable opinion.	It's pointless to give my opinion.

Conversation example person A	Conversation example person B
貴重なご意見をお聞かせいただき、ありがとうございます。	こちらこそ、ご検討いただきありがとうございます。
きちょうなごいけんをおきかせいただき、ありがとうございます。	こちらこそ、ごけんとういただきありがとうございます。
Kichōna go iken o o kikase itadaki, arigatōgozaimasu.	Kochira koso, go kentō itadaki arigatōgozaimasu.
Thank you for sharing your valuable opinion.	Thank you for your consideration as well.

Cultural Context

Use after receiving opinions, not preemptively. More formal than "ご意見ありがとうございます。"

ご確認のうえ、ご返答ください。

ごかくにんのうえ、ごへんとうください。

Go kakunin no ue, go hentō kudasai.

Please confirm and respond.

Variation 1	Variation 2
ご査収いただき、ご回答をお願いいたします。	Kyō mo shōjin shima shou.
ごさしゅういただき、ごかいとうをおねがいいたします。	ごさしゅういただき、ごかいとうをおねがいいたします。
Go sashū itadaki, go kaitō o onegai itashimasu.	Kakunin-go, hentō o onegai shimasu.
Please confirm and respond.	Please confirm and respond.

Positive Response	Negative Response
承知いたしました。確認後、速やかにご返答いたします。	確認する時間がありません。
しょうちいたしました。かくにんご、すみやかにごへんとうい たします。	かくにんするじかんがありません。
Shōchi itashimashita. Kakunin-go, sumiyaka ni go hentō itashimasu.	Kakunin suru jikan ga arimasen.
Understood. I'll respond promptly after confirming.	I don't have time to check.

Conversation example person A	Conversation example person B
契約書をお送りしました。ご確認のうえ、ご返答ください。	承知いたしました。確認次第、ご連絡いたしま す。
けいやくしょをおおくりしました。ごかくにんのうえ、ごへんとうくださ い。	しょうちいたしました。かくにんしだい、ごれ んらくいたします。
Keiyaku-sho o ookuri shima shita. Go kakunin no ue, go hentō kudasai.	Shōchi itashimashita. Kakunin shidai, go renraku itashimasu.
I have sent the contract. Please confirm and respond.	Understood. I will contact you after reviewing it.

Cultural Context

Use when you need both confirmation and a response. Ensure you've provided all necessary information.

お手数をおかけしますが、よろしくお願いします。

おてすうをおかけしますが、よろしくおねがいします。

Otesū o okake shimasuga, yoroshikuonegaishimasu.

I apologize for the trouble, but I appreciate your help.

Variation 1	Variation 2
ご面倒をおかけしますが、ご協力お願い申し上げます。	Kyō mo shōjin shima shou.
ごめんどうをおかけしますが、ごきょうりょくおねがいもうしあげます。	ごめんどうをおかけしますが、ごきょうりょくおねがいもうしあげます。
Go mendō o okake shimasuga, go kyōryoku onegai mōshiagemasu.	Go meiwaku o okake shimasuga, yoroshiku onegai shimasu.
I'm sorry for the trouble, but I appreciate your cooperation.	I apologize for the inconvenience, but please help us.

Positive Response	Negative Response
いいえ、喜んでお手伝いさせていただきます。	これは私の仕事ではありません。
いいえ、よろこんでおてつだいさせていただきます。	これはわたしのしごとではありません。
Ie, yorokonde otetsudai sa sete itadakimasu.	Kore wa watashi no shigotode wa arimasen.
Not at all, I'm happy to help.	This is not my job.

Conversation example person A	Conversation example person B
資料の修正をお願いしています。お手数をおかけしますが、よろしくお願いします。	承知いたしました。できるだけ早く対応いたします。
しりょうのしゅうせいをおねがいしています。おてすうをおかけしますが、よろしくおねがいします。	しょうちいたしました。できるだけはやくたいおういたします。
Shiryō no shūsei o onegai shite imasu. Otesū o okake shimasuga, yoroshiku onegai shimasu.	Shōchi itashimashita. Dekirudake hayaku taiō itashimasu.
I'm asking for document revisions. I apologize for the trouble, but thank you in advance.	Understood. I will respond as soon as possible.

Cultural Context

Use when asking for something that requires effort. Less formal than "お手数をおかけしますが、よろしくお願いいたします。"

ご理解とご協力をお願いいたします。

ごりかいとごきょうりょくをおねがいいたします。

Gorikai to go kyōryoku o onegai itashimasu.

We ask for your understanding and cooperation.

Variation 1	Variation 2
ご了承とお力添えを賜りますようお願い申し上げます。	Kyō mo shōjin shima shou.
ごりょうしょうとおちからぞえをたまわりますようおねがいもうしあげます。	ごりょうしょうとおちからぞえをたまわりますようおねがいもうしあげます。
Go ryōshō to o chikarazoe o tamawarimasu yō onegai mōshiagemasu.	Rikai to kyōryoku o onegai itashimasu.
We request your understanding and cooperation.	We ask for your understanding and cooperation.

Positive Response	Negative Response
はい、全力でサポートさせていただきます。	理解も協力もできません。
はい、ぜんりょくでさぽーとさせていただきます。	りかいもきょうりょくもできません。
Hai, zenryoku de sapōto sa sete itadakimasu.	Rikai mo kyōryoku mo dekimasen.
Yes, I'll support you with all my effort.	I can neither understand nor cooperate.

Conversation example person A	Conversation example person B
新しい方針について、ご理解とご協力をお願いいたします。	了解いたしました。全力でサポートさせていただきます。
あたらしいほうしんについて、ごりかいとごきょうりょくをおねがいいたします。	りょうかいいたしました。ぜんりょくでさぽーとさせていただきます。
Atarashī hōshin ni tsuite, go rikai to go kyōryoku o onegai itashimasu.	Ryōkai itashimashita. Zenryoku de sapōto sa sete itadakimasu.
Regarding the new policy, we ask for your understanding and cooperation.	Understood. We will support it with all our efforts.

Cultural Context

Use when you need both understanding and cooperation. Ensure the situation warrants this request.

ご返答お待ちしております。

ごへんとうおまちしております。

Go hentō omachi shite orimasu.

We look forward to your reply.

Variation 1	Variation 2
ご回答いただけますよう、お願い申し上げます。	Kyō mo shōjin shima shou.
ごかいとういただけますよう、おねがいもうしあげます。	ごかいとういただけますよう、おねがいもうしあげます。
Go kaitō itadakemasu yō, onegai mōshiagemasu.	Kaitō o omachi shite orimasu.
We look forward to your response.	I look forward to your response.

Positive Response	Negative Response
ありがとうございます。できるだけ早くご返答いたします。	返答する内容がありません。
ありがとうございます。できるだけはやくごへんとういたします。	へんとうするないようがありません。
Arigatōgozaimasu. Dekirudake hayaku go hentō itashimasu.	Hentō suru naiyō ga arimasen.
Thank you. I'll respond as soon as possible.	I have nothing to respond to.

Conversation example person A	Conversation example person B
先日お送りした提案書について、ご返答お待ちしております。	申し訳ありません。明日中にはご返答させていただきます。
せんじつおおくりしたていあんしょについて、ごへんとうおまちしております。	もうしわけありません。あしたちゅうにはごへんとうさせていただきます。
Senjitsu ookuri shita teian-sho ni tsuite, go hentō omachi shite orimasu.	Mōshiwake arimasen. Ashita-chū ni hago hentō sa sete itadakimasu.
I'm waiting for your response regarding the proposal I sent the other day.	I'm sorry. I'll respond by tomorrow.

Cultural Context

Softer than "早々のご返答をお待ちしております。" Still implies expectation of a reply.

ご多忙のところ恐縮ですが、ご確認ください。

ごたぼうのところきょうしゅくですが、ごかくにんください。

Gotabō no tokoro kyōshukudesuga, go kakunin kudasai.

I apologize for troubling you during your busy time, but please confirm this.

Variation 1	Variation 2
お忙しい中申し訳ございませんが、ご査収ください。	Kyō mo shōjin shima shou.
おいそがしいなかもうしわけございませんが、ごさしゅうください。	おいそがしいなかもうしわけございませんが、ごさしゅうください。
Oisogashī-chū mōshiwake go zaimasen ga, go sashū kudasai.	O isogashī tokoro mōshiwake arimasenga, kakunin o onegai shimasu.
I apologize for bothering you, but please confirm this.	I apologize for bothering you while you're busy, but please confirm.

Positive Response	Negative Response
はい、喜んで確認させていただきます。	確認する時間がありません。
はい、よろこんでかくにんさせていただきます。	かくにんするじかんがありません。
Hai, yorokonde kakunin sa sete itadakimasu.	Kakunin suru jikan ga arimasen.
Yes, I'm happy to check it.	I don't have time to check.

Conversation example person A	Conversation example person B
ご多忙のところ恐縮ですが、添付資料をご確認ください。	承知いたしました。確認次第、ご連絡いたします。
ごたぼうのところきょうしゅくですが、てんぷしりょうをごかくにんください。	しょうちいたしました。かくにんしだい、ごれんらくいたします。
Gotabō no tokoro kyōshukudesuga, tenpu shiryō o go kakunin kudasai.	Shōchi itashimashita. Kakunin shidai, go renraku itashimasu.
I apologize for bothering you while you're busy, but please check the attached documents.	Understood. I will contact you after reviewing it.

Cultural Context

Use when asking for confirmation from someone who is busy. Acknowledge their time constraints.

ご質問がございましたら、お知らせください。

ごしつもんがございましたら、おしらせください。

Go shitsumon ga gozaimashitara, oshirase kudasai.

If you have any questions, please let us know.

Variation 1	Variation 2
ご不明点等ございましたら、ご連絡ください。	Kyō mo shōjin shima shou.
ごふめいてんとうございましたら、ごれんらくください。	ごふめいてんとうございましたら、ごれんらくください。
Go fumei-ten-tō go zaimashita-ra, go renraku kudasai.	Shitsumon ga areba, renraku shite kudasai.
If you have any questions, please let us know.	If you have any questions, please let us know.

Positive Response	Negative Response
ありがとうございます。不明点があればすぐにお尋ねします。	質問する価値もありません。
ありがとうございます。ふめいてんがあればすぐにおたずねします。	しつもんするかちもありません。
Arigatōgozaimasu. Fumei-ten ga areba sugu ni otazune shimasu.	Shitsumon suru kachi mo arimasen.
Thank you. I'll ask immediately if I have any questions.	It's not even worth asking questions.

Conversation example person A	Conversation example person B
説明資料を送付しました。ご質問がございましたら、お知らせください。	ありがとうございます。確認の上、必要があればお問い合わせいたします。
せつめいしりょうをそうふしました。ごしつもんがございましたら、おしらせください。	ありがとうございます。かくにんのうえ、ひつようがあればおといあわせいたします。
Setsumei shiryō o sōfu shima shita. Go shitsumon ga go zaimashita-ra, oshirase kudasai.	Arigatōgozaimasu. Kakunin no ue, hitsuyō ga areba o toiawase itashimasu.
I have sent the explanatory materials. If you have any questions, please let me know.	Thank you. I will check and contact you if needed.

Cultural Context

Offers openness to questions. Slightly less formal than "ご質問がございましたら、ご連絡ください。"

ご指摘ありがとうございます。確認いたします。

ごしてきありがとうございます。かくにんいたします。

Go shiteki arigatōgozaimasu. Kakunin itashimasu.

Thank you for pointing that out. I will check on it.

Variation 1	Variation 2
ご指導いただき、感謝申し上げます。精査いたします。	Kyō mo shōjin shima shou.
ごしどういただき、かんしゃもうしあげます。せいさいいたします。	ごしどういただき、かんしゃもうしあげます。せいさいいたします。
Go shidō itadaki, kansha mōshiagemasu. Seisa itashimasu.	Shiteki itadaki, arigatōgozaimasu. Kakunin shimasu.
Thank you for pointing that out. We will verify it.	Thank you for pointing that out. I will check.

Positive Response	Negative Response
こちらこそ、貴重なご指摘をありがとうございます。	指摘するつもりはありませんでした。
こちらこそ、きちょうなごしてきをありがとうございます。	してきするつもりはありませんでした。
Kochira koso, kichōna go shiteki o arigatōgozaimasu.	Shiteki suru tsumori wa arimasende shita.
Thank you for your valuable feedback.	I didn't mean to point that out.

Conversation example person A	Conversation example person B
ご指摘ありがとうございます。確認いたします。修正版を後ほど送付いたします。	お手数おかけして申し訳ありません。修正版を待っています。
ごしてきありがとうございます。かくにんいたします。しゅうせいばんをのちほどそうふいたします。	おてすうおかけしてもうしわけありません。しゅうせいばんをまっています。
Go shiteki arigatōgozaimasu. Kakunin itashimasu. Shūsei-ban o nochihodo sōfu itashimasu.	Otesū okake shite mōshiwake arimasen. Shūsei-ban o matte imasu.
Thank you for pointing that out. I will check and send a revised version later.	I'm sorry for the trouble. I'm looking forward to the revised version.

Cultural Context

Use when you've received a correction and will check it. Don't use preemptively.

ご検討いただけますと幸いです。

ごけんとういただけますとさいわいです。

Go kentō itadakemasuto saiwaidesu.

We would appreciate your consideration.

Variation 1	Variation 2
ご審議いただけますよう、お願い申し上げます。	Kyō mo shōjin shima shou.
ごしんぎいただけますよう、おねがいもうしあげます。	ごしんぎいただけますよう、おねがいもうしあげます。
Go shingi itadakemasu yō, onegai mōshiagemasu.	Kentō shite itadakereba ureshīdesu.
We would appreciate your consideration.	I would appreciate your consideration.

Positive Response	Negative Response
承知いたしました。丁寧に検討させていただきます。	検討する価値がありません。
しょうちいたしました。ていねいにけんとうさせていただきます。	けんとうするかちがありません。
Shōchi itashimashita. Teinei ni kentō sa sete itadakimasu.	Kentō suru kachi ga arimasen.
Understood. We will carefully consider it.	It's not worth considering.

Conversation example person A	Conversation example person B
新しいアイデアを提案しました。ご検討いただけますと幸いです。	興味深い提案ですね。詳細を教えていただけますか？
あたらしいあいであをていあんしました。ごけんとういただけますとさいわいです。	きょうみぶかいていあんですね。しょうさいをおしえていただけますか？
Atarashī aidea o teian shima shita. Go kentō itadakemasuto saiwaidesu.	Kyōmibukai teiandesu ne. Shōsai o oshiete itadakemasu ka?
I've proposed a new idea. I'd appreciate it if you could consider it.	That's an interesting proposal. Could you provide more details?

Cultural Context

Softer than "ご検討をお願いいたします。" Use for polite requests.

お忙しいところ恐れ入りますが、ご返信ください。

おいそがしいところおそれいりますが、ごへんしんください。

O isogashī tokoro osoreirimasuga, go henshin kudasai.

I'm sorry to trouble you during your busy time, but please reply.

Variation 1	Variation 2
ご多忙中誠に申し訳ございませんが、ご回答ください。	Kyō mo shōjin shima shou.
ごたぼうちゅうまことにもうしわけございませんが、ごかいとうください。	ごたぼうちゅうまことにもうしわけございませんが、ごかいとうください。
Gotabō-chū makotoni mōshiwake go zaimasen ga, go kaitō kudasai.	O isogashī tokoro mōshiwake arimasenga, henshin o onegai shimasu.
I'm sorry to bother you, but please reply when you can.	I apologize for bothering you while you're busy, but please reply.

Positive Response	Negative Response
承知いたしました。できるだけ早くご返信いたします。	返信する時間がありません。
しょうちいたしました。できるだけはやくごへんしんいたします。	へんしんするじかんがありません。
Shōchi itashimashita. Dekirudake hayaku go henshin itashimasu.	Henshin suru jikan ga arimasen.
Understood. I'll reply as soon as possible.	I don't have time to reply.

Conversation example person A	Conversation example person B
お忙しいところ恐れ入りますが、ご返信ください。	承知しました。できるだけ早く返信いたします。
おいそがしいところおそれいりますが、ごへんしんください。	しょうちしました。できるだけはやくへんしんいたします。
O isogashī tokoro osoreirimasuga, go henshin kudasai.	Shōchi shima shita. Dekirudake hayaku henshin itashimasu.
I apologize for bothering you, but could you please reply?	Understood. I'll reply as soon as possible.

Cultural Context

Use when requesting a reply from someone who is busy. Acknowledge their time constraints.

ご確認いただけましたでしょうか。

ごかくにんいただけましたでしょうか。
Go kakunin itadakemashitadeshou ka.
Have you had a chance to confirm this?

Variation 1	Variation 2
お手数ですが、ご査収いただけましたか。	Kyō mo shōjin shima shou.
おてすうですが、ごさしゅういただけましたか。	おてすうですが、ごさしゅういただけましたか。
Otesūdesuga, go sashū itadakemashita ka.	Kakunin shite itadakemashita ka.
Have you had a chance to check this?	Have you had a chance to confirm?

Positive Response	Negative Response
はい、確認いたしました。ありがとうございます。	まだ確認していません。
はい、かくにんいたしました。ありがとうございます。	まだかくにんしていません。
Hai, kakunin itashimashita. Arigatōgozaimasu.	Mada kakunin shite imasen.
Yes, I've confirmed it. Thank you.	I haven't checked yet.

Conversation example person A	Conversation example person B
先日送付した書類のご確認いただけましたでしょうか。	申し訳ありません。明日中に確認してご連絡いたします。
せんじつそうふしたしょるいのごかくにんいただけましたでしょうか。	もうしわけありません。あしたちゅうにかくにんしてごれんらくいたします。
Senjitsu sōfu shita shorui no go kakunin itadakemashitadeshou ka.	Mōshiwake arimasen. Ashita-chū ni kakunin shite go renraku itashimasu.
Have you had a chance to check the documents I sent the other day?	I'm sorry. I'll check it by tomorrow and get back to you.

Cultural Context
Polite follow-up. Use when you need to check if something has been confirmed.

ご助言ありがとうございます。

ごじょげんありがとうございます。

Go jogen arigatōgozaimasu.

Thank you for your advice.

Variation 1	Variation 2
ご指導いただき、感謝申し上げます。	Kyō mo shōjin shima shou.
ごしどういただき、かんしゃもうしあげます。	ごしどういただき、かんしゃもうしあげます。
Go shidō itadaki, kansha mōshiagemasu.	Adobaisu o itadaki, kansha itashimasu.
Thank you for your advice.	Thank you for your advice.

Positive Response	Negative Response
こちらこそ、貴重なご助言をありがとうございます。	助言したつもりはありません。
こちらこそ、きちょうなごじょげんをありがとうございます。	じょげんしたつもりはありません。
Kochira koso, kichōna go jogen o arigatōgozaimasu.	Jogen shita tsumori wa arimasen.
Thank you for your valuable advice.	I didn't intend to give advice.

Conversation example person A	Conversation example person B
この件について、アドバイスをいただけますか？	ご助言ありがとうございます。
このけんについて、あどばいすをいただけますか？	ごじょげんありがとうございます。
Kono-ken ni tsuite, adobaisu o itadakemasu ka?	Go jogen arigatōgozaimasu.
Could you give me some advice on this matter?	Thank you for your advice.

Cultural Context

Use in response to receiving advice, not preemptively.

ご不明な点がございましたら、ご連絡ください。

ごふめいなてんがございましたら、ごれんらくください。

Go fumeina ten ga gozaimashitara, go renraku kudasai.

If you have any questions, please contact us.

Variation 1	Variation 2
ご質問等ございましたら、お問い合わせください。	Kyō mo shōjin shima shou.
ごしつもんとうございましたら、おといあわせください。	ごしつもんとうございましたら、おといあわせください。
Go shitsumon-tō go zaimashita-ra, o toiawase kudasai.	Fumei-ten ga areba, renraku shite kudasai.
If you have any questions, please contact us.	If you have any questions, please contact us.

Positive Response	Negative Response
ありがとうございます。必要があればすぐにご連絡いたします。	全てが不明確です。
ありがとうございます。ひつようがあればすぐにごれんらくいたします。	すべてがふめいかくです。
Arigatōgozaimasu. Hitsuyō ga areba sugu ni go renraku itashimasu.	Subete ga fu meikakudesu.
Thank you. I'll contact you immediately if I have any questions.	Everything is unclear.

Conversation example person A	Conversation example person B
新しいプロジェクトの詳細をお送りしました。ご不明な点がございましたら、ご連絡ください。	はい、確認させていただきます。質問があれば連絡します。
あたらしいぷろじぇくとのしょうさいをおおくりしました。ごふめいなてんがございましたら、ごれんらくください。	はい、かくにんさせていただきます。しつもんがあればれんらくします。
Atarashī purojekuto no shōsai o ookuri shima shita. Go fumeina ten ga go zaimashita-ra, go renraku kudasai.	Hai, kakunin sa sete itadakimasu. Shitsumon ga areba renraku shimasu.
I've sent you the details of the new project. If you have any questions, please contact me.	Yes, I'll review it. I'll contact you if I have any questions.

Cultural Context

Offers openness to questions. Ensure you're available to respond if used.

ご検討の程、よろしくお願い申し上げます。

ごけんとうのほど、よろしくおねがいもうしあげます。

Go kentō no hodo, yoroshiku onegai mōshiagemasu.

We sincerely appreciate your consideration.

Variation 1	Variation 2
ご審議いただけますよう、心よりお願いいたします。	Kyō mo shōjin shima shou.
ごしんぎいただけますよう、こころよりおねがいいたします。	ごしんぎいただけますよう、こころよりおねがいいたします。
Go shingi itadakemasu yō, kokoro yori onegai itashimasu.	Kentō o yoroshiku onegai itashimasu.
We sincerely request your kind consideration.	We kindly request your consideration.

Positive Response	Negative Response
承知いたしました。慎重に検討させていただきます。	検討する余地はありません。
しょうちいたしました。しんちょうにけんとうさせていただきます。	けんとうするよちはありません。
Shōchi itashimashita. Shinchō ni kentō sa sete itadakimasu.	Kentō suru yochi wa arimasen.
Understood. I'll carefully consider it.	There's no room for consideration.

Conversation example person A	Conversation example person B
新しい提案書を作成しました。ご検討の程、よろしくお願い申し上げます。	承知しました。慎重に検討させていただきます。
あたらしいていあんしょをさくせいしました。ごけんとうのほど、よろしくおねがいもうしあげます。	しょうちしました。しんちょうにけんとうさせていただきます。
Atarashī teian-sho o sakusei shima shita. Go kentō no hodo, yoroshiku onegai mōshiagemasu.	Shōchi shima shita. Shinchō ni kentō sa sete itadakimasu.
I've prepared a new proposal. Thank you for your consideration.	Understood. I'll carefully consider it.

Cultural Context

Very formal way to request consideration. Use for significant requests to superiors.

恐れ入りますが、ご確認をお願いできますでしょうか。

おそれいりますが、ごかくにんをおねがいできますでしょうか。
Osoreirimasuga, go kakunin o onegai dekimasudeshou ka.
I'm sorry to trouble you, but could you please confirm this?

Variation 1	Variation 2
大変恐縮ですが、ご査収いただけますでしょうか。	Kyō mo shōjin shima shou.
たいへんきょうしゅくですが、ごさしゅういただけますでしょうか。	たいへんきょうしゅくですが、ごさしゅういただけますでしょうか。
Taihen kyōshukudesuga, go sashū itadakemasudeshou ka.	Mōshiwake arimasenga, kakunin o onegai dekimasu ka.
I'm sorry to trouble you, but could you please confirm this?	I'm sorry to trouble you, but could you please confirm?

Positive Response	Negative Response
はい、喜んで確認させていただきます。	確認する必要はありません。
はい、よろこんでかくにんさせていただきます。	かくにんするひつようはありません。
Hai, yorokonde kakunin sa sete itadakimasu.	Kakunin suru hitsuyō wa arimasen.
Yes, I'd be happy to confirm it.	There's no need to check.

Conversation example person A	Conversation example person B
恐れ入りますが、添付ファイルのご確認をお願いできますでしょうか。	承知いたしました。確認次第、ご連絡いたします。
おそれいりますが、てんぷふぁいるのごかくにんをおねがいできますでしょうか。	しょうちいたしました。かくにんしだい、ごれんらくいたします。
Osoreirimasuga, tenpu fairu no go kakunin o onegai dekimasudeshou ka.	Shōchi itashimashita. Kakunin shidai, go renraku itashimasu.
I'm sorry to bother you, but could you please check the attached file?	Understood. I will contact you after reviewing it.

Cultural Context
Very polite way to request confirmation. Use for important matters when you want to be extra courteous.

ご多忙中、誠に恐縮ですが、ご対応をお願いいたします。

ごたぼうちゅう、まことにきょうしゅくですが、ごたいおうをおねがいいたします。

Gotabō-chū, makotoni kyōshukudesuga, go taiō o onegai itashimasu.

I sincerely apologize for bothering you during your busy time, but please address this matter.

Variation 1	Variation 2
お忙しい中、大変申し訳ございませんが、ご対処ください。	Kyō mo shōjin shima shou.
おいそがしいなか、たいへんもうしわけございませんが、ごたいしょください。	おいそがしいなか、たいへんもうしわけございませんが、ごたいしょください。
Oisogashī-chū, taihen mōshiwake go zaimasen ga, go taisho kudasai.	O isogashī tokoro, hontōni mōshiwake arimasenga, taiō o onegai shimasu.
I'm very sorry to bother you during your busy time, but please address this.	I'm truly sorry to bother you while you're busy, but please handle this.

Positive Response	Negative Response
承知いたしました。できる限り迅速に対応させていただきます。	これ以上の仕事は引き受けられません。
しょうちいたしました。できるかぎりじんそくにたいおうさせていただきます。	これいじょうのしごとはひきうけられません。
Shōchi itashimashita. Dekiru kagiri jinsoku ni taiō sa sete itadakimasu.	Kore ijō no shigoto wa hikiuke raremasen.
Understood. I'll respond as quickly as possible.	I can't take on any more work.

Conversation example person A	Conversation example person B
ご多忙中、誠に恐縮ですが、緊急の件についてご対応をお願いいたします。	承知いたしました。優先的に対応させていただきます。
ごたぼうちゅう、まことにきょうしゅくですが、きんきゅうのけんについてごたいおうをおねがいいたします。	しょうちいたしました。ゆうせんてきにたいおうさせていただきます。
Go tabō-chū, makotoni kyōshukudesuga, kinkyū no kudan ni tsuite go taiō o onegai itashimasu.	Shōchi itashimashita. Yūsen-teki ni taiō sa sete itadakimasu.
I sincerely apologize for bothering you while you're busy, but please address this urgent matter.	Understood. I will prioritize this matter.

Cultural Context

Use when asking for action from someone who is very busy. Acknowledge their time constraints.

ご連絡いただき、誠にありがとうございます。

ごれんらくいただき、まことにありがとうございます。

Go renraku itadaki, makotoni arigatōgozaimasu.

Thank you very much for contacting us.

Variation 1	Variation 2
お知らせいただき、心より感謝申し上げます。	Kyō mo shōjin shima shou.
おしらせいただき、こころよりかんしゃもうしあげます。	おしらせいただき、こころよりかんしゃもうしあげます。
Oshirase itadaki, kokoro yori kansha mōshiagemasu.	Renraku o itadaki, hontōni arigatōgozaimasu.
Thank you very much for contacting us.	Thank you very much for contacting us.

Positive Response	Negative Response
こちらこそ、ご連絡ありがとうございます。	連絡が遅すぎます。
こちらこそ、ごれんらくありがとうございます。	れんらくがおそすぎます。
Kochira koso, go renraku arigatōgozaimasu.	Renraku ga oso sugimasu.
Thank you for contacting me as well.	Your contact is too late.

Conversation example person A	Conversation example person B
お忙しい中、ご連絡いただき、誠にありがとうございます。	こちらこそ、迅速なご対応感謝いたします。
おいそがしいなか、ごれんらくいただき、まことにありがとうございます。	こちらこそ、じんそくなごたいおうかんしゃいたします。
Oisogashī-chū, go renraku itadaki, makotoni arigatōgozaimasu.	Kochira koso, jinsokuna go taiō kansha itashimasu.
Thank you very much for contacting us despite your busy schedule.	Thank you for your prompt response as well.

Cultural Context

Very formal thanks for contact. Use in highly formal situations or with very important clients/superiors.

何卒ご理解いただけますようお願い申し上げます。

なにとぞごりかいいただけますようおねがいもうしあげます。
Nanitozo gorikai itadakemasu yō onegai mōshiagemasu.
We sincerely ask for your understanding.

Variation 1	Variation 2
何とぞご了承いただけますよう、お願い申し上げます。	Kyō mo shōjin shima shou.
なにとぞごりょうしょういただけますよう、おねがいもうしあげます。	なにとぞごりょうしょういただけますよう、おねがいもうしあげます。
Nanitozo go ryōshō itadakemasu yō, onegai mōshiagemasu.	Dōzo go rikai itadakemasu yō onegai itashimasu.
We sincerely hope for your understanding.	We humbly request your understanding.

Positive Response	Negative Response
はい、十分に理解いたしました。ご説明ありがとうございます。	理解できません。
はい、じゅうぶんにりかいいたしました。ごせつめいありがとうございます。	りかいできません。
Hai, jūbun ni rikai itashimashita. Go setsumei arigatōgozaimasu.	Rikai dekimasen.
Yes, I fully understand. Thank you for the explanation.	I can't understand.

Conversation example person A	Conversation example person B
事情をご説明いたしました。何卒ご理解いただけますようお願い申し上げます。	ご説明ありがとうございます。検討させていただきます。
じじょうをごせつめいいたしました。なにとぞごりかいいただけますようおねがいもうしあげます。	ごせつめいありがとうございます。けんとうさせていただきます。
Jijō o go setsumei itashimashita. Nanitozo go rikai itadakemasu yō onegai mōshiagemasu.	Go setsumei arigatōgozaimasu. Kentō sa sete itadakimasu.
I have explained the situation. We sincerely ask for your understanding.	Thank you for the explanation. We will consider it.

Cultural Context

Very formal request for understanding. Use in difficult situations where understanding is crucial.

ご査収のほど、よろしくお願い申し上げます。

ごさしゅうのほど、よろしくおねがいもうしあげます。
Go sashū no hodo, yoroshiku onegai mōshiagemasu.
Please kindly acknowledge receipt.

Variation 1	Variation 2
ご確認いただけますよう、心よりお願いいたします。	Kyō mo shōjin shima shou.
ごかくにんいただけますよう、こころよりおねがいいたします。	ごかくにんいただけますよう、こころよりおねがいいたします。
Go kakunin itadakemasu yō, kokoro yori onegai itashimasu.	Kakunin o yoroshiku onegai itashimasu.
We kindly request your acknowledgment.	We kindly request your confirmation.

Positive Response	Negative Response
承知いたしました。早速確認させていただきます。	査収する時間がありません。
しょうちいたしました。さっそくかくにんさせていただきます。	さしゅうするじかんがありません。
Shōchi itashimashita. Sassoku kakunin sa sete itadakimasu.	Sashū suru jikan ga arimasen.
Understood. I'll check it immediately.	I don't have time to review this.

Conversation example person A	Conversation example person B
最終報告書を送付いたしました。ご査収のほど、よろしくお願い申し上げます。	承知いたしました。確認の上、ご連絡いたします。
さいしゅうほうこくしょをそうふいたしました。ごさしゅうのほど、よろしくおねがいもうしあげます。	しょうちいたしました。かくにんのうえ、ごれんらくいたします。
Saishū hōkoku-sho o sōfu itashimashita. Go sashū no hodo, yoroshiku onegai mōshiagemasu.	Shōchi itashimashita. Kakunin no ue, go renraku itashimasu.
I have sent the final report. We would appreciate your review and acceptance.	Understood. I will check and get back to you.

Cultural Context
Very formal way to request review of a document. Use for important documents sent to superiors.

ご多用中大変恐縮ですが、ご検討ください。

ごたようちゅうたいへんきょうしゅくですが、ごけんとうください。

Gotayōchū taihen kyōshukudesuga, go kentō kudasai.

I'm very sorry to trouble you during your busy time, but please consider this.

Variation 1	Variation 2
お忙しい中誠に申し訳ございませんが、ご審議ください。	Kyō mo shōjin shima shou.
おいそがしいなかまことにもうしわけございませんが、ごしんぎください。	おいそがしいなかまことにもうしわけございませんが、ごしんぎください。
Oisogashī-chū makotoni mōshiwake go zaimasen ga, go shingi kudasai.	O isogashī tokoro taihen mōshiwake arimasenga, kentō o onegai shimasu.
I'm very sorry to trouble you during your busy time, but please consider this.	I'm very sorry to trouble you while you're busy, but please consider this.

Positive Response	Negative Response
はい、喜んで検討させていただきます。	検討する時間がありません。
はい、よろこんでけんとうさせていただきます。	けんとうするじかんがありません。
Hai, yorokonde kentō sa sete itadakimasu.	Kentō suru jikan ga arimasen.
Yes, I'd be happy to consider it.	I don't have time to consider this.

Conversation example person A	Conversation example person B
ご多用中大変恐縮ですが、新しい提案のご検討ください。	承知いたしました。できるだけ早く検討いたします。
ごたようuちゅうたいへんきょうしゅくですが、あたらしいていあんのごけんとうください。	しょうちいたしました。できるだけはやくけんとういたします。
Go tayō-chū taihen kyōshukudesuga, atarashī teian no go kentō kudasai.	Shōchi itashimashita. Dekirudake hayaku kentō itashimasu.
I'm very sorry to bother you while you're busy, but please consider our new proposal.	Understood. I will consider it as soon as possible.

Cultural Context

Use when asking for consideration from someone who is extremely busy. Acknowledge their time constraints.

今後ともよろしくお願い申し上げます。

こんごともよろしくおねがいもうしあげます。
Kongotomoyoroshiku onegai mōshiagemasu.
We look forward to our continued relationship.

Variation 1	Variation 2
引き続きお力添えいただけますよう、お願い申し上げます。	Kyō mo shōjin shima shou.
ひきつづきおちからぞえいただけますよう、おねがいもうしあげます。	ひきつづきおちからぞえいただけますよう、おねがいもうしあげます。
Hikitsudzuki o chikarazoe itadakemasu yō, onegai mōshiagemasu.	Kongo tomo yoroshiku onegai itashimasu.
We look forward to your continued support.	We look forward to your continued support.

Positive Response	Negative Response
こちらこそ、今後ともよろしくお願いいたします。	これ以上の協力は難しいです。
こちらこそ、こんごともよろしくおねがいいたします。	これいじょうのきょうりょくはむずかしいです。
Kochira koso, kongo tomo yoroshiku onegai itashimasu.	Kore ijō no kyōryoku wa muzukashīdesu.
Likewise, I look forward to our continued cooperation.	Further cooperation will be difficult.

Conversation example person A	Conversation example person B
お取引ありがとうございました。今後ともよろしくお願い申し上げます。	こちらこそ、今後ともよろしくお願いいたします。
おとりひきありがとうございました。こんごともよろしくおねがいもうしあげます。	こちらこそ、こんごともよろしくおねがいいたします。
O torihiki arigatō go zaimashita. Kongo tomo yoroshiku onegai mōshiagemasu.	Kochira koso, kongo tomo yoroshiku onegai itashimasu.
Thank you for your business. We look forward to our continued relationship.	Likewise, we look forward to working with you in the future.

Cultural Context
Use at the end of communications to express hope for continued good relations. Not for one-time interactions.

ご指示いただけますと幸いです。

ごしじいただけますとさいわいです。
Go shiji itadakemasuto saiwaidesu.
We would appreciate your instructions.

Variation 1	Variation 2
ご指導いただけますよう、お願い申し上げます。	Kyō mo shōjin shima shou.
ごしどういただけますよう、おねがいもうしあげます。	ごしどういただけますよう、おねがいもうしあげます。
Go shidō itadakemasu yō, onegai mōshiagemasu.	Shiji o itadakereba ureshīdesu.
We would appreciate your instructions.	I would appreciate your instructions.

Positive Response	Negative Response
はい、喜んでご指示に従わせていただきます。	自分で判断してください。
はい、よろこんでごしじにしたがわせていただきます。	じぶんではんだんしてください。
Hai, yorokon de go shiji ni shitagawa sete itadakimasu.	Jibun de handan shite kudasai.
Yes, I'd be happy to follow your instructions.	Please make your own decision.

Conversation example person A	Conversation example person B
次のステップについて、ご指示いただけますと幸いです。	承知しました。詳細な指示を送付いたします。
つぎのすてっぷについて、ごしじいただけますとさいわいです。	しょうちしました。しょうさいなしじをそうふいたします。
Tsugi no suteppu ni tsuite, go shiji itadakemasuto saiwaidesu.	Shōchi shima shita. Shōsaina shiji o sōfu itashimasu.
We would appreciate your instructions regarding the next step.	Understood. I will send detailed instructions.

Cultural Context
Polite way to request instructions. Implies you're waiting for direction but not demanding it.

ご返答いただき、誠にありがとうございます。

ごへんとういただき、まことにありがとうございます。

Go hentō itadaki, makotoni arigatōgozaimasu.

Thank you very much for your response.

Variation 1	Variation 2
ご回答いただき、心より感謝申し上げます。	Kyō mo shōjin shima shou.
ごかいとういただき、こころよりかんしゃもうしあげます。	ごかいとういただき、こころよりかんしゃもうしあげます。
Go kaitō itadaki, kokoro yori kansha mōshiagemasu.	Hentō o itadaki, hontōni arigatōgozaimasu.
Thank you very much for your response.	Thank you very much for your response.

Positive Response	Negative Response
こちらこそ、迅速なご返答に感謝いたします。	返答が不十分です。
こちらこそ、じんそくなごへんとうにかんしゃいたします。	へんとうがふじゅうぶんです。
Kochira koso, jinsokuna go hentō ni kansha itashimasu.	Hentō ga fu jūbundesu.
Thank you for your prompt response as well.	Your response is insufficient.

Conversation example person A	Conversation example person B
お忙しい中、迅速にご返答いただき、誠にありがとうございます。	こちらこそ、ご連絡ありがとうございます。
おいそがしいなか、じんそくにごへんとういただき、まことにありがとうございます。	こちらこそ、ごれんらくありがとうございます。
Oisogashī-chū, jinsoku ni go hentō itadaki, makotoni arigatōgozaimasu.	Kochira koso, go renraku arigatōgozaimasu.
Thank you very much for your prompt reply despite your busy schedule.	Thank you for your message as well.

Cultural Context

Very formal thanks for a reply. Use in highly formal situations or with very important clients/superiors.

お手数ではございますが、ご対応いただけますでしょうか。

おてすうではございますが、ごたいおういただけますでしょうか。

Otesūde wagozaimasuga, go taiō itadakemasudeshou ka.

I apologize for the trouble, but could you please address this?

Variation 1	Variation 2
ご面倒をおかけして恐縮ですが、ご対処いただけますか。	Kyō mo shōjin shima shou.
ごめんどうをおかけしてきょうしゅくですが、ごたいしょいただけますか。	ごめんどうをおかけしてきょうしゅくですが、ごたいしょいただけますか。
Go mendō o okake shite kyōshukudesuga, go taisho itadakemasu ka.	Mōshiwake arimasenga, taiō shite itadakemasu ka.
I apologize for the trouble, but could you please handle this?	I'm sorry to trouble you, but could you please handle this?

Positive Response	Negative Response
はい、喜んで対応させていただきます。	これは私の仕事ではありません。
はい、よろこんでたいおうさせていただきます。	これはわたしのしごとではありません。
Hai, yorokonde taiō sa sete itadakimasu.	Kore wa watashi no shigotode wa arimasen.
Yes, I'd be happy to handle it.	This is not my job.

Conversation example person A	Conversation example person B
お手数ではございますが、添付資料のご確認とご対応いただけますでしょうか。	承知いたしました。確認の上、対応させていただきます。
おてすうではございませんが、てんぷしりょうのごかくにんとごたいおういただけますでしょうか。	しょうちいたしました。かくにんのうえ、たいおうさせていただきます。
Otesūde wagozaimasuga, tenpu shiryō no go kakunin to go taiō itadakemasudeshou ka.	Shōchi itashimashita. Kakunin no ue, taiō sa sete itadakimasu.
I apologize for the inconvenience, but could you please check and respond to the attached documents?	Understood. I will check and respond accordingly.

Cultural Context

Very polite way to request action. Use when the action might require significant effort.

ご意見を拝聴し、早急に検討させていただきます。

ごいけんをはいちょうし、そうきゅうにけんとうさせていただきます。

Go iken o haichō shi, sakkyū ni kentō sa sete itadakimasu.

We will carefully consider your opinion and respond promptly.

Variation 1	Variation 2
ご見解を承り、速やかに精査いたします。	Kyō mo shōjin shima shou.
ごけんかいをうけたまわり、すみやかにせいさいたします。	ごけんかいをうけたまわり、すみやかにせいさいたします。
Go kenkai o uketamawari, sumiyaka ni seisa itashimasu.	Iken o kiki, sumiyaka ni kentō shimasu.
We will carefully consider your opinion and respond promptly.	We'll listen to your opinion and consider it promptly.

Positive Response	Negative Response
ありがとうございます。迅速な対応、期待しております。	意見を聞く気はありません。
ありがとうございます。じんそくなたいおう、きたいしております。	いけんをきくきはありません。
Arigatōgozaimasu. Jinsokuna taiō, kitai shite orimasu.	Iken o kiku ki wa arimasen.
Thank you. I look forward to your prompt consideration.	I'm not interested in hearing your opinion.

Conversation example person A	Conversation example person B
貴重なご意見を拝聴し、早急に検討させていただきます。	ご検討ありがとうございます。結果をお待ちしております。
きちょうなごいけんをはいちょうし、そうきゅうにけんとうさせていただきます。	ごけんとうありがとうございます。けっかをおまちしております。
Kichōna go iken o haichō shi, sakkyū ni kentō sa sete itadakimasu.	Go kentō arigatōgozaimasu. Kekka o omachi shite orimasu.
We have heard your valuable opinion and will consider it promptly.	Thank you for your consideration. We look forward to the results.

Cultural Context

Use when you've received opinions and will consider them quickly. Implies urgency in your consideration.

ご多忙中、大変恐縮ではございますが、ご確認ください。

ごたぼうちゅう、たいへんきょうしゅくではございますが、ごかくにんください。

Gotabō-chū, taihen kyōshukude wagozaimasuga, go kakunin kudasai.

I'm very sorry to trouble you during your busy time, but please confirm this.

Variation 1	Variation 2
お忙しい中、誠に申し訳ありませんが、確認をお願いいたします。	Kyō mo shōjin shima shou.
おいそがしいなか、まことにもうしわけありませんが、かくにんをおねがいいたします。	おいそがしいなか、まことにもうしわけありませんが、かくにんをおねがいいたします。
Oisogashī-chū, makotoni mōshiwake arimasenga, kakunin o onegai itashimasu.	O isogashī tokoro mōshiwake arimasenga, kakunin o onegai shimasu.
I apologize for bothering you during your busy schedule, but please confirm this.	I apologize for bothering you while you're busy, but please check this.

Positive Response	Negative Response
承知いたしました。できる限り早く確認させていただきます。	確認する時間がありません。
しょうちいたしました。できるかぎりはやくかくにんさせていただきます。	かくにんするじかんがありません。
Shōchi itashimashita. Dekiru kagiri hayaku kakunin sa sete itadakimasu.	Kakunin suru jikan ga arimasen.
Understood. I'll check it as soon as possible.	I don't have time to check.

Conversation example person A	Conversation example person B
ご多忙中、大変恐縮ではございますが、添付書類をご確認ください。	承知いたしました。できるだけ早く確認いたします。
ごたぼうちゅう、たいへんきょうしゅくではございますが、てんぷしょるいをごかくにんください。	しょうちいたしました。できるだけはやくかくにんいたします。
Gotabō-chū, taihen kyōshukude wagozaimasuga, tenpu shorui o go kakunin kudasai.	Shōchi itashimashita. Dekirudake hayaku kakunin itashimasu.
I'm very sorry to bother you while you're busy, but please check the attached documents.	Understood. I will check them as soon as possible.

Cultural Context

Very formal way to request confirmation from someone who is extremely busy. Use for crucial matters only.

何かご不明な点がございましたら、遠慮なくお問い合わせください。

なにかごふめいなてんがございましたら、えんりょなくおといあわせください。

Nani ka go fumeina ten ga gozaimashitara, enryonaku o toiawase kudasai.

If you have any questions, please do not hesitate to contact us.

Variation 1	Variation 2
分からないことがありましたら、お気軽にご連絡ください。	Kyō mo shōjin shima shou.
わからないことがありましたら、おきがるにごれんらくください。	わからないことがありましたら、おきがるにごれんらくください。
Wakaranai koto ga Arima shitara, o kigaru ni go renraku kudasai.	Fumei-ten ga areba, kigaru ni renraku shite kudasai.
If you have any questions, please don't hesitate to contact us.	If you have any questions, please feel free to contact us.

Positive Response	Negative Response
ありがとうございます。不明点があれば、ぜひ相談させていただきます。	問い合わせる前に自分で調べてください。
ありがとうございます。ふめいてんがあれば、ぜひそうだんさせていただきます。	といあわせるまえにじぶんでしらべてください。
Arigatōgozaimasu. Fumei-ten ga areba, zehi sōdan sa sete itadakimasu.	Toiawaseru mae ni jibun de shirabete kudasai.
Thank you. If I have any questions, I'll definitely consult with you.	Please research on your own before inquiring.

Conversation example person A	Conversation example person B
新しい手順書を配布しましたが、何かご不明な点がございましたら、遠慮なくお問い合わせください。	承知しました。確認して分からない点があれば連絡します。
あたらしいてじゅんしょをはいふしましたが、なにかごふめいなてんがございましたら、えんりょなくおといあわせください。	しょうちしました。かくにんしてわからないてんがあればれんらくします。
Atarashī tejun-sho o haifu shima shitaga, nani ka go fumeina ten ga go zaimashita-ra, enryonaku o toiawase kudasai.	Shōchi shima shita. Kakunin shite wakaranai ten ga areba renraku shimasu.
I've distributed the new procedure manual. If you have any questions, please don't hesitate to ask.	Understood. I'll check it and contact you if I have any questions.

Cultural Context

This phrase encourages questions but may not always result in actual inquiries due to cultural hesitation.

お疲れ様です。

おつかれさまです。
Otsukaresamadesu.
Good work today.

Variation 1	Variation 2
ご苦労様です。	Kyō mo shōjin shima shou.
ごくろうさまです。	ごくろうさまです。
Gokurō-samadesu.	Taihen otsukaresamadesu.
Good work.	Thank you so much for your hard work.

Positive Response	Negative Response
ありがとうございます。今日も頑張りましょう。	まだ仕事中です。
ありがとうございます。きょうもがんばりましょう。	まだしごとちゅうです。
Arigatōgozaimasu. Kyō mo ganbari ma shou.	Mada shigoto-chūdesu.
Thank you. Let's do our best today as well.	I'm still working.

Conversation example person A	Conversation example person B
お疲れ様です。今日の会議の議事録を送ります。	ありがとうございます。確認します。
おつかれさまです。きょうのかいぎのぎじろくをおくります。	ありがとうございます。かくにんします。
Otsukaresamadesu. Kyō no kaigi no giji-roku o okurimasu.	Arigatōgozaimasu. Kakunin shimasu.
Good work today. I'm sending the minutes of today's meeting.	Thank you. I'll review it.

Cultural Context
While expressing appreciation, it's not always appropriate in formal situations or with superiors.

承知しました。

しょうちしました。
Shōchi shimashita.
Understood.

Variation 1	Variation 2
了解しました。	Kyō mo shōjin shima shou.
りょうかいしました。	りょうかいしました。
Ryōkai shima shita.	Shōchi itashimashita.
Understood.	Understood.

Positive Response	Negative Response
ありがとうございます。適切に対応いたします。	本当に理解していますか？
ありがとうございます。てきせつにたいおういたします。	ほんとうにりかいしていますか？
Arigatōgozaimasu. Tekisetsu ni taiō itashimasu.	Hontōni rikai shite imasu ka?
Thank you. I'll respond appropriately.	Do you really understand?

Conversation example person A	Conversation example person B
来週の出張の件ですが、承知しました。準備を進めます。	了解です。何か必要なものがあれば教えてください。
らいしゅうのしゅっちょうのけんですが、しょうちしました。じゅんびをすすめます。	りょうかいです。なにかひつようなものがあればおしえてください。
Raishū no shutchō no kudandesuga, shōchi shima shita. Junbi o susumemasu.	Ryōkaidesu. Nani ka hitsuyōna mono ga areba oshiete kudasai.
Regarding next week's business trip, I've understood. I'll start the preparations.	Understood. Please let me know if you need anything.

Cultural Context
This acknowledgment doesn't necessarily mean the task will be completed or fully understood.

了解です。

りょうかいです。
Ryōkaidesu.
Got it.

Variation 1	Variation 2
承知しました。	Kyō mo shōjin shima shou.
しょうちしました。	しょうちしました。
Shōchi shima shita.	Ryōkai itashimashita.
Got it.	Acknowledged.

Positive Response	Negative Response
承知いたしました。すぐに取り掛かります。	了解したなら早く対応してください。
しょうちいたしました。すぐにとりかかります。	りょうかいしたならはやくたいおうしてください。
Shōchi itashimashita. Sugu ni torikakarimasu.	Ryōkai shitanara hayaku taiō shite kudasai.
Understood. I'll start on it right away.	If you understand, please respond quickly.

Conversation example person A	Conversation example person B
新しいプロジェクトの開始日を来月に変更する件、了解です。	承知しました。スケジュールを調整します。
あたらしいぷろじぇくとのかいしびをらいげつにへんこうするけん、りょうかいです。	しょうちしました。すけじゅーるをちょうせいします。
Atarashī purojekuto no kaishi-bi o rai tsuki ni henkō suru kudan, ryōkaidesu.	Shōchi shima shita. Sukejūru o chōsei shimasu.
I understand about changing the start date of the new project to next month.	Understood. I'll adjust the schedule.

Cultural Context
Can be seen as too casual in formal settings; doesn't guarantee action.

確認しました。

かくにんしました。
Kakunin shimashita.
Confirmed.

Variation 1	Variation 2
把握しました。	Kyō mo shōjin shima shou.
はあくしました。	はあくしました。
Haaku shima shita.	Rikai shima shita.
Confirmed.	Comprehended.

Positive Response	Negative Response
ありがとうございます。必要な対応を進めます。	確認だけでなく、行動してください。
ありがとうございます。ひつようなたいおうをすすめます。	かくにんだけでなく、こうどうしてください。
Arigatōgozaimasu. Hitsuyōna taiō o susumemasu.	Kakunin dakedenaku, kōdō shite kudasai.
Thank you. I'll proceed with the necessary actions.	Don't just confirm, take action.

Conversation example person A	Conversation example person B
送付いただいた報告書、確認しました。内容に問題ありません。	ありがとうございます。安心しました。
そうふいただいたほうこくしょ、かくにんしました。ないようにもんだいありません。	ありがとうございます。あんしんしました。
Sōfu itadaita hōkoku-sho, kakunin shima shita. Naiyō ni mondai arimasen.	Arigatōgozaimasu. Anshin shima shita.
I've checked the report you sent. There are no issues with the content.	Thank you. I'm relieved to hear that.

Cultural Context
Doesn't always mean thorough verification has been done.

よろしくお願いします。

よろしくおねがいします。
Yoroshikuonegaishimasu.
Please take care of this.

Variation 1	Variation 2
お願い申し上げます。	Kyō mo shōjin shima shou.
おねがいもうしあげます。	おねがいもうしあげます。
Onegai mōshiagemasu.	Yoroshiku onegai itashimasu.
Best regards.	I humbly request.

Positive Response	Negative Response
こちらこそ、よろしくお願いいたします。	具体的に何をすればいいですか？
こちらこそ、よろしくおねがいいたします。	ぐたいてきになにをすればいいですか？
Kochira koso, yoroshiku onegai itashimasu.	Gutai-teki ni nani o sureba īdesu ka?
Likewise, please take care of me as well.	What specifically should I do?

Conversation example person A	Conversation example person B
新入社員の研修を担当することになりました。よろしくお願いします。	了解です。サポートが必要な際は言ってください。
しんにゅうしゃいんのけんしゅうをたんとうすることになりました。よろしくおねがいします。	りょうかいです。さぽーとがひつようなさいはいってください。
Shin'nyū shain no kenshū o tantō suru koto ni narimashita. Yoroshiku onegai shimasu.	Ryōkaidesu. Sapōto ga hitsuyōna sai wa itte kudasai.
I've been assigned to handle the training for new employees. I look forward to your cooperation.	Understood. Let me know if you need any support.

Cultural Context
A versatile phrase that can mean different things based on context; may be overused.

進捗を教えてください。

しんちょくをおしえてください。
Shinchoku o oshietekudasai.
Please update me on the progress.

Variation 1	Variation 2
現状を知らせてください。	Kyō mo shōjin shima shou.
げんじょうをしらせてください。	げんじょうをしらせてください。
Genjō o shira sete kudasai.	Jōkyō o oshirase kudasai.
Please provide an update.	Please inform me of the current situation.

Positive Response	Negative Response
はい、現在の状況を詳しくご報告いたします。	進捗がないのでお伝えすることはありません。
はい、げんざいのじょうきょうをくわしくごほうこくいたします。	しんちょくがないのでおつたえすることはありません。
Hai, genzai no jōkyō o kuwashiku go hōkoku itashimasu.	Shinchoku ga nainode otsutae suru koto wa arimasen.
Yes, I'll give you a detailed report on the current situation.	There's no progress, so I have nothing to report.

Conversation example person A	Conversation example person B
プロジェクトAの進捗を教えてください。	現在、計画の70%まで完了しています。来週中に終わる見込みです。
ぷろじぇくとえーのしんちょくをおしえてください。	げんざい、けいかくの70%までかんりょうしています。らいしゅうちゅうにおわるみこみです。
Purojekuto A no shinchoku o oshiete kudasai.	Genzai, keikaku no nana juppāsento made kanryō shite imasu. Raishū-chū ni owaru mikomidesu.
Please update me on the progress of Project A.	Currently, we've completed 70% of the plan. We expect to finish by next week.

Cultural Context

May be perceived as pressure or micromanagement if used too frequently.

至急対応お願いします。

しきゅうたいおうおねがいします。

Shikyū taiō onegaishimasu.

Please handle this urgently.

Variation 1	Variation 2
早急にご対応ください。	Kyō mo shōjin shima shou.
さっきゅうにごたいおうください。	さっきゅうにごたいおうください。
Sakkyū ni go taiō kudasai.	Shikyū go taiō negaimasu.
Please respond urgently.	Please respond promptly.

Positive Response	Negative Response
承知いたしました。最優先で取り組みます。	他の優先事項があります。
しょうちいたしました。さいゆうせんでとりくみます。	ほかのゆうせんじこうがあります。
Shōchi itashimashita. Sai yūsen de torikumimasu.	Hoka no yūsen jikō ga arimasu.
Understood. I'll work on it with top priority.	I have other priorities.

Conversation example person A	Conversation example person B
サーバーがダウンしているようです。至急対応お願いします。	承知しました。直ちに確認して対応します。
さーばーがだうんしているようです。しきゅうたいおうおねがいします。	しょうちしました。ただちにかくにんしてたいおうします。
Sābā ga daun shite iru yōdesu. Shikyū taiō onegai shimasu.	Shōchi shima shita. Tadachini kakunin shite taiō shimasu.
It seems the server is down. Please address this urgently.	Understood. I'll check and address it immediately.

Cultural Context

Could create unnecessary stress if overused; urgency may be subjective.

検討します。

けんとうします。
Kentō shimasu.
I'll look into it.

Variation 1	Variation 2
考えます。	Kyō mo shōjin shima shou.
かんがえます。	かんがえます。
Kangaemasu.	Kōryo shimasu.
I will consider it.	I will consider it.

Positive Response	Negative Response
ありがとうございます。慎重に検討し、ご報告いたします。	いつまでに結果を出せますか？
ありがとうございます。しんちょうにけんとうし、ごほうこくいたします。	いつまでにけっかをだせますか？
Arigatōgozaimasu. Shinchō ni kentō shi, go hōkoku itashimasu.	Itsu made ni kekka o dasemasu ka?
Thank you. I'll consider it carefully and report back to you.	By when can you provide results?

Conversation example person A	Conversation example person B
新しい提案ありがとうございます。検討します。	はい、よろしくお願いします。結果をお待ちしています。
あたらしいていあんありがとうございます。けんとうします。	はい、よろしくおねがいします。けっかをおまちしています。
Atarashī teian arigatōgozaimasu. Kentō shimasu.	Hai, yoroshiku onegai shimasu. Kekka o omachi shite imasu.
Thank you for the new proposal. I'll consider it.	Yes, thank you. I look forward to hearing the results.

Cultural Context
Often used as a polite way to delay or avoid decisions.

報告ありがとうございます。

ほうこくありがとうございます。
Hōkoku arigatōgozaimasu.
Thank you for the report.

Variation 1	Variation 2
ご報告感謝いたします。	Kyō mo shōjin shima shou.
ごほうこくかんしゃいたします。	ごほうこくかんしゃいたします。
Go hōkoku kansha itashimasu.	Go renraku arigatōgozaimasu.
Thank you for the report.	Thank you for your report.

Positive Response	Negative Response
こちらこそ、ありがとうございます。今後の方針に活かします。	報告が遅すぎます。
こちらこそ、ありがとうございます。こんごのほうしんにいかします。	ほうこくがおそすぎます。
Kochira koso, arigatōgozaimasu. Kongo no hōshin ni ikashimasu.	Hōkoku ga oso sugimasu.
Thank you as well. We'll use this for our future policy.	Your report is too late.

Conversation example person A	Conversation example person B
月次レポートの報告ありがとうございます。内容を確認します。	お手数おかけしました。何か質問があればお知らせください。
げつじれぽーとのほうこくありがとうございます。ないようをかくにんします。	おてすうおかけしました。なにかしつもんがあればおしらせください。
Tsuki-ji repōto no hōkoku arigatōgozaimasu. Naiyō o kakunin shimasu.	Otesū okake shima shita. Nani ka shitsumon ga areba oshirase kudasai.
Thank you for the monthly report. I'll review the content.	Sorry for the trouble. Please let me know if you have any questions.

Cultural Context
Doesn't necessarily mean the report was satisfactory or will be acted upon.

明日の会議の件です。

あすのかいぎのけんです。

Ashita no kaigi no kudandesu.

Regarding tomorrow's meeting.

Variation 1	Variation 2
明日のミーティングについてです。	Kyō mo shōjin shima shou.
あしたのみーてぃんぐについてです。	あしたのみーてぃんぐについてです。
Ashita no mītingu ni tsuitedesu.	Ashita no kaigi ni kanshitedesu.
Regarding tomorrow's meeting.	Regarding tomorrow's meeting.

Positive Response	Negative Response
承知いたしました。準備を整えて臨みます。	明日は予定が入っています。
しょうちいたしました。じゅんびをととのえてのぞみます。	あしたはよていがはいっています。
Shōchi itashimashita. Junbi o totonoete nozomimasu.	Ashita wa yotei ga haitte imasu.
Understood. I'll be fully prepared for the meeting.	I have plans for tomorrow.

Conversation example person A	Conversation example person B
明日の会議の件です。資料は準備できましたか？	はい、準備完了です。今からメールで送ります。
あすのかいぎのけんです。しりょうはじゅんびできましたか？	はい、じゅんびかんりょうです。いまからめーるでおくります。
Ashita no kaigi no kudandesu. Shiryō wa junbi dekimashita ka?	Hai, junbi kanryōdesu. Ima kara mēru de okurimasu.
Regarding tomorrow's meeting, have you prepared the materials?	Yes, they're ready. I'll send them by email now.

Cultural Context

Vague; requires context and may not convey urgency.

資料を添付しました。

しりょうをてんぷしました。
Shiryō o tenpu shimashita.
I've attached the documents.

Variation 1	Variation 2
書類を付けました。	Kyō mo shōjin shima shou.
しょるいをつけました。	しょるいをつけました。
Shorui o tsukemashita.	Shiryō o dōfū shima shita.
I have attached the documents.	I have attached the documents.

Positive Response	Negative Response
ありがとうございます。すぐに確認いたします。	添付ファイルが開けません。
ありがとうございます。すぐにかくにんいたします。	てんぷふぁいるがひらけません。
Arigatōgozaimasu. Sugu ni kakunin itashimasu.	Tenpu fairu ga akemasen.
Thank you. I'll check it right away.	I can't open the attachment.

Conversation example person A	Conversation example person B
プレゼン用の資料を添付しました。ご確認ください。	ありがとうございます。確認します。
ぷれぜんようのしりょうをてんぷしました。ごかくにんください。	ありがとうございます。かくにんします。
Purezen-yō no shiryō o tenpu shima shita. Go kakunin kudasai.	Arigatōgozaimasu. Kakunin shimasu.
I've attached the presentation materials. Please check them.	Thank you. I'll review them.

Cultural Context
Doesn't ensure the recipient will open or read the attachment.

ご確認ください。

ごかくにんください。

Go kakunin kudasai.

Please check this.

Variation 1	Variation 2
ご確認お願いします。	Kyō mo shōjin shima shou.
ごかくにんおねがいします。	ごかくにんおねがいします。
Go kakunin onegai shimasu.	Go kakunin yoroshiku onegai shimasu.
Please confirm.	Please kindly confirm.

Positive Response	Negative Response
承知いたしました。丁寧に確認させていただきます。	確認する時間がありません。
しょうちいたしました。ていねいにかくにんさせていただきます。	かくにんするじかんがありません。
Shōchi itashimashita. Teinei ni kakunin sa sete itadakimasu.	Kakunin suru jikan ga arimasen.
Understood. I'll check it carefully.	I don't have time to check.

Conversation example person A	Conversation example person B
新しい契約書の草案ができました。ご確認ください。	承知しました。確認の上、フィードバックいたします。
あたらしいけいやくしょのそうあんができました。ごかくにんください。	しょうちしました。かくにんのうえ、ふぃーどばっくいたします。
Atarashī keiyaku-sho no sōan ga dekimashita. Go kakunin kudasai.	Shōchi shima shita. Kakunin no ue, fīdobakku itashimasu.
The draft of the new contract is ready. Please review it.	Understood. I'll review it and provide feedback.

Cultural Context

May be seen as passing responsibility; doesn't specify what needs confirmation.

修正版をアップしました。

しゅうせいばんをあっぷしました。
Shūsei-ban o appushimashita.
I've uploaded the revised version.

Variation 1	Variation 2
修正したものをアップロードしました。	Kyō mo shōjin shima shou.
しゅうせいしたものをあっぷろーどしました。	しゅうせいしたものをあっぷろーどしました。
Shūsei shita mono o appurōdo shima shita.	Shūsei-ban o kōshin shima shita.
I have uploaded the revised version.	I have uploaded the revised version.

Positive Response	Negative Response
ありがとうございます。早速確認させていただきます。	また修正が必要です。
ありがとうございます。さっそくかくにんさせていただきます。	またしゅうせいがひつようです。
Arigatōgozaimasu. Sassoku kakunin sa sete itadakimasu.	Mata shūsei ga hitsuyōdesu.
Thank you. I'll check it immediately.	It needs further revisions.

Conversation example person A	Conversation example person B
ご指摘いただいた点を反映し、修正版をアップしました。	ありがとうございます。早速確認します。
ごしてきいただいたてんをはんえいし、しゅうせいばんをあっぷしました。	ありがとうございます。さっそくかくにんします。
Go shiteki itadaita ten o han'ei shi, shūsei-ban o appu shima shita.	Arigatōgozaimasu. Sassoku kakunin shimasu.
I've uploaded the revised version reflecting your comments.	Thank you. I'll check it right away.

Cultural Context
Doesn't guarantee the changes meet expectations or will be reviewed promptly.

共有ありがとうございます。

きょうゆうありがとうございます。

Kyōyū arigatōgozaimasu.

Thank you for sharing.

Variation 1	Variation 2
共有していただきありがとうございます。	Kyō mo shōjin shima shou.
きょうゆうしていただきありがとうございます。	きょうゆうしていただきありがとうございます。
Kyōyū shite itadaki arigatōgozaimasu.	Kyōyū itadaki kansha shimasu.
Thank you for sharing.	Thank you for sharing.

Positive Response	Negative Response
こちらこそ、ありがとうございます。有効に活用させていただきます。	この情報は既に知っています。
こちらこそ、ありがとうございます。ゆうこうにかつようさせていただきます。	このじょうほうはすでにしっています。
Kochira koso, arigatōgozaimasu. Yūkō ni katsuyō sa sete itadakimasu.	Kono jōhō wa sudeni shitte imasu.
Thank you as well. I'll make good use of it.	I already know this information.

Conversation example person A	Conversation example person B
市場調査の結果の共有ありがとうございます。とても参考になりました。	お役に立てて嬉しいです。さらに詳しい分析が必要であればお知らせください。
しじょうちょうさのけっかのきょうゆうありがとうございます。とてもさんこうになりました。	おやくにたててうれしいです。さらにくわしいぶんせきがひつようであればおしらせください。
Ichiba chōsa no kekka no kyōyū arigatōgozaimasu. Totemo sankō ni narimashita.	O yakunitatete ureshīdesu. Sara ni kuwashī bunseki ga hitsuyōdeareba oshirase kudasai.
Thank you for sharing the market research results. They were very helpful.	I'm glad it was useful. Please let me know if you need more detailed analysis.

Cultural Context

Politeness doesn't always indicate the shared information was useful or will be used.

フォローお願いします。

ふぉろーおねがいします。

Forō onegaishimasu.

Please follow up on this.

Variation 1	Variation 2
引き続きよろしくお願いします。	Kyō mo shōjin shima shou.
ひきつづきよろしくおねがいします。	ひきつづきよろしくおねがいします。
Hikitsudzuki yoroshiku onegai shimasu.	Kongo tomo dōzo yoroshiku onegai shimasu.
Please follow up.	I look forward to your continued support.

Positive Response	Negative Response
承知いたしました。責任を持って対応いたします。	自分でフォローしてください。
しょうちいたしました。せきにんをもってたいおういたします。	じぶんでふぉろーしてください。
Shōchi itashimashita. Sekinin o motte taiō itashimasu.	Jibun de forō shite kudasai.
Understood. I'll handle it responsibly.	Please follow up on your own.

Conversation example person A	Conversation example person B
クライアントからの問い合わせがありました。フォローお願いします。	承知しました。すぐに対応いたします。
くらいあんとからのといあわせがありました。ふぉろーおねがいします。	しょうちしました。すぐにたいおういたします。
Kuraianto kara no toiawase ga Arima shita. Forō onegai shimasu.	Shōchi shima shita. Sugu ni taiō itashimasu.
We received an inquiry from the client. Please follow up on this.	Understood. I'll handle it right away.

Cultural Context

Can be vague; may not specify what kind of follow-up is needed.

スケジュールを調整します。

すけじゅーるをちょうせいします。

Sukejūru o chōsei shimasu.

I'll adjust the schedule.

Variation 1	Variation 2
日程を調整します。	Kyō mo shōjin shima shou.
にっていをちょうせいします。	にっていをちょうせいします。
Nittei o chōsei shimasu.	Sukejūru chōsei shimasu.
I will adjust the schedule.	I will arrange the schedule.

Positive Response	Negative Response
ありがとうございます。ご都合の良い日程でお願いいたします。	スケジュールの変更は困ります。
ありがとうございます。ごつごうのよいにっていでおねがいいたします。	すけじゅーるのへんこうはこまります。
Arigatōgozaimasu. Go tsugō no yoi nittei de onegai itashimasu.	Sukejūru no henkō wa komarimasu.
Thank you. Please let me know your preferred dates.	Schedule changes are inconvenient.

Conversation example person A	Conversation example person B
来週の会議、スケジュールを調整します。ご都合はいかがですか？	水曜日の午後であれば参加可能です。
らいしゅうのかいぎ、すけじゅーるをちょうせいします。ごつごうはいかがですか？	すいようびのごごであればさんかかのうです。
Raishū no kaigi, sukejūru o chōsei shimasu. Go tsugō wa ikagadesu ka?	Suiyōbi no gogodeareba sanka kanōdesu.
I'll adjust the schedule for next week's meeting. How does your schedule look?	I can attend if it's Wednesday afternoon.

Cultural Context

Doesn't guarantee successful rescheduling or everyone's availability.

締め切りはいつですか？

しめきりはいつですか？
Shimekiri wa itsudesu ka?
When is the deadline?

Variation 1	Variation 2
期限はいつですか？	Kyō mo shōjin shima shou.
きげんはいつですか？	きげんはいつですか？
Kigen wa itsudesu ka?	Teishutsu kigen wa itsudesu ka?
When is the deadline?	When is the deadline?

Positive Response	Negative Response
締め切りを確認し、必ず間に合わせます。	締め切りは既に過ぎています。
しめきりをかくにんし、かならずまにあわせます。	しめきりはすでにすぎています。
Shimekiri o kakunin shi, kanarazu maniawa semasu.	Shimekiri wa sudeni sugite imasu.
I'll check the deadline and make sure to meet it.	The deadline has already passed.

Conversation example person A	Conversation example person B
新しいプロジェクトの企画書の締め切りはいつですか？	来週の金曜日までにお願いします。
あたらしいぷろじぇくとのきかくしょのしめきりはいつですか？	らいしゅうのきんようびまでにおねがいします。
Atarashī purojekuto no kikaku-sho no shimekiri wa itsudesu ka?	Raishū no kin'yōbi made ni onegai shimasu.
When is the deadline for the new project proposal?	Please submit it by next Friday.

Cultural Context
May be perceived as unprepared if this information should be known.

遅れそうです。

おくれそうです。

Okure-sōdesu.

I might be late.

Variation 1	Variation 2
遅延する可能性があります。	Kyō mo shōjin shima shou.
ちえんするかのうせいがあります。	ちえんするかのうせいがあります。
Chien suru kanō-sei ga arimasu.	Okureru osore ga arimasu.
It might be delayed.	There is a possibility of delay.

Positive Response	Negative Response
状況を理解しました。できる限りサポートいたします。	遅れは許容できません。
じょうきょうをりかいしました。できるかぎりさぽーといたします。	おくれはきょようできません。
Jōkyō o rikai shima shita. Dekiru kagiri sapōto itashimasu.	Okure wa kyoyō dekimasen.
I understand the situation. I'll support you as much as possible.	Delays are not acceptable.

Conversation example person A	Conversation example person B
申し訳ありません。交通渋滞で遅れそうです。	了解です。気をつけてお越しください。
もうしわけありません。こうつうじゅうたいでおくれそうです。	りょうかいです。きをつけておこしください。
Mōshiwake arimasen. Kōtsū jūtai de okure-sōdesu.	Ryōkaidesu. Ki o tsukete okoshi kudasai.
I'm sorry. I might be late due to traffic congestion.	Understood. Please come safely.

Cultural Context

Vague; doesn't specify the extent of the delay or propose solutions.

今日中に完了します。

きょうじゅうにかんりょうします。

Kon'nichijūni kanryō shimasu.

I'll complete it by today.

Variation 1	Variation 2
本日中に終了します。	Kyō mo shōjin shima shou.
ほんじつちゅうにしゅうりょうします。	ほんじつちゅうにしゅうりょうします。
Honjitsu-chū ni shūryō shimasu.	Honjitsu-chū ni kanryō shimasu.
I will finish it today.	It will be completed by the end of today.

Positive Response	Negative Response
素晴らしいです。お疲れ様です。	本当に間に合いますか？
すばらしいです。おつかれさまです。	ほんとうにまにあいますか？
Subarashīdesu. Otsukaresamadesu.	Hontōni maniaimasu ka?
That's great. Thank you for your hard work.	Can you really finish it in time?

Conversation example person A	Conversation example person B
レポートの修正、今日中に完了します。	ありがとうございます。お待ちしています。
れぽーとのしゅうせい、きょうじゅうにかんりょうします。	ありがとうございます。おまちしています。
Repōto no shūsei, kyō-chū ni kanryō shimasu.	Arigatōgozaimasu. Omachi shite imasu.
I'll complete the report corrections by the end of today.	Thank you. I'll be waiting for it.

Cultural Context

Might create unrealistic expectations if the task is complex.

明日の朝一で対応します。

あすのあさいちでたいおうします。

Asunoasa ichi de taiō shimasu.

I'll handle it first thing tomorrow morning.

Variation 1	Variation 2
明日の始業時間に対応します。	Kyō mo shōjin shima shou.
あしたのしぎょうじかんにたいおうします。	あしたのしぎょうじかんにたいおうします。
Ashita no shigyō jikan ni taiō shimasu.	Ashita no kinmu kaishi jikoku ni taisho shimasu.
I will handle it first thing tomorrow morning.	I will address it at the start of business hours tomorrow.

Positive Response	Negative Response
承知いたしました。迅速な対応、ありがとうございます。	今すぐ対応してください。
しょうちいたしました。じんそくなたいおう、ありがとうございます。	いまぐたいおうしてください。
Shōchi itashimashita. Jinsokuna taiō, arigatōgozaimasu.	Ima sugu taiō shite kudasai.
Understood. Thank you for your prompt response.	Please respond immediately.

Conversation example person A	Conversation example person B
クライアントからの緊急の要請、明日の朝一で対応します。	助かります。よろしくお願いします。
くらいあんとからのきんきゅうのようせい、あしたのあさいちでたいおうします。	たすかります。よろしくおねがいします。
Kuraianto kara no kinkyū no yōsei, ashita no asa ichi de taiō shimasu.	Tasukarimasu. Yoroshiku onegai shimasu.
I'll address the urgent request from the client first thing tomorrow morning.	That's helpful. Thank you in advance.

Cultural Context

"First thing in the morning" can be subjective and may not meet urgent needs.

お手数ですが、よろしくお願いします。

おてすうですが、よろしくおねがいします。
Otesūdesuga, yoroshikuonegaishimasu.
Sorry for the trouble, but please take care of this.

Variation 1	Variation 2
ご面倒をおかけしますが、よろしくお願いします。	Kyō mo shōjin shima shou.
ごめんどうをおかけしますが、よろしくおねがいします。	ごめんどうをおかけしますが、よろしくおねがいします。
Go mendō o okake shimasuga, yoroshiku onegai shimasu.	Otesūdesuga, yoroshiku onegai itashimasu.
Sorry for the trouble, but please take care of it.	I apologize for the inconvenience, but please take care of it.

Positive Response	Negative Response
こちらこそ、お手数をおかけして申し訳ありません。喜んで対応いたします。	これは本来あなたの仕事です。
こちらこそ、おてすうをおかけしてもうしわけありません。よろこんでたいおういたします。	これはほんらいあなたのしごとです。
Kochira koso, otesū o okake shite mōshiwake arimasen. Yorokonde taiō itashimasu.	Kore wa honrai anata no shigotodesu.
I'm sorry for the trouble. I'm happy to help.	This is actually your job.

Conversation example person A	Conversation example person B
お手数ですが、この書類に捺印をお願いします。	承知しました。すぐに対応します。
おてすうですが、このしょるいになついんをおねがいします。	しょうちしました。すぐにたいおうします。
Otesūdesuga, kono shorui ni natsuin o onegai shimasu.	Shōchi shima shita. Sugu ni taiō shimasu.
I apologize for the trouble, but could you please stamp this document?	Understood. I'll take care of it right away.

Cultural Context
The politeness might obscure the importance or urgency of the request.

連絡ありがとうございます。

れんらくありがとうございます。

Renraku arigatōgozaimasu.

Thank you for contacting me.

Variation 1	Variation 2
ご連絡ありがとうございます。	Kyō mo shōjin shima shou.
ごれんらくありがとうございます。	ごれんらくありがとうございます。
Go renraku arigatōgozaimasu.	Go ippō arigatōgozaimasu.
Thank you for contacting me.	Thank you for contacting me.

Positive Response	Negative Response
こちらこそ、ありがとうございます。今後とも宜しくお願いいたします。	もっと早く連絡すべきでした。
こちらこそ、ありがとうございます。こんごともよろしくおねがいいたします。	もっとはやくれんらくすべきでした。
Kochira koso, arigatōgozaimasu. Kongo tomo yoroshiku onegai itashimasu.	Motto hayaku renraku subekide shita.
Thank you as well. I look forward to our continued cooperation.	You should have contacted me earlier.

Conversation example person A	Conversation example person B
進捗の連絡ありがとうございます。引き続きよろしくお願いします。	はい、引き続き頑張ります。
しんちょくのれんらくありがとうございます。ひきつづきよろしくおねがいします。	はい、ひきつづきがんばります。
Shinchoku no renraku arigatōgozaimasu. Hikitsudzuki yoroshiku onegai shimasu.	Hai, hikitsudzuki ganbarimasu.
Thank you for the progress update. Please continue your good work.	Yes, I'll continue to do my best.

Cultural Context

A generic response that doesn't indicate if the communication was helpful.

詳細を教えてください。

しょうさいをおしえてください。

Shōsai o oshietekudasai.

Please provide more details.

Variation 1	Variation 2
詳しい情報を教えてください。	Kyō mo shōjin shima shou.
くわしいじょうほうをおしえてください。	くわしいじょうほうをおしえてください。
Kuwashī jōhō o oshiete kudasai.	Shōsai o oshirase kudasai.
Please provide more details.	Please provide detailed information.

Positive Response	Negative Response
承知いたしました。できる限り詳しくご説明いたします。	詳細は既に共有済みです。
しょうちいたしました。できるかぎりくわしくごせつめいいたします。	しょうさいはすでにきょうゆうずみです。
Shōchi itashimashita. Dekiru kagiri kuwashiku go setsumei itashimasu.	Shōsai wa sudeni kyōyū-zumidesu.
Understood. I'll explain in as much detail as possible.	Details have already been shared.

Conversation example person A	Conversation example person B
新規プロジェクトの詳細を教えてください。	はい、プロジェクトの目的、スコープ、スケジュールについて説明します。
しんきぷろじぇくとのしょうさいをおしえてください。	はい、ぷろじぇくとのもくてき、すこーぷ、すけじゅーるについてせつめいします。
Shinki purojekuto no shōsai o oshiete kudasai.	Hai, purojekuto no mokuteki, sukōpu, sukejūru ni tsuite setsumei shimasu.
Could you provide more details about the new project?	Yes, I'll explain the project's purpose, scope, and schedule.

Cultural Context

May be seen as lack of initiative if information is readily available.

確認中です。

かくにんちゅうです。

Kakunin-chūdesu.

I'm checking on it.

Variation 1	Variation 2
確認しています。	Kyō mo shōjin shima shou.
かくにんしています。	かくにんしています。
Kakunin shite imasu.	Chōsa-chūdesu.
I am checking.	I am checking.

Positive Response	Negative Response
ありがとうございます。確認でき次第、ご連絡いたします。	確認に時間がかかりすぎています。
ありがとうございます。かくにんできしだい、ごれんらくいたします。	かくにんにじかんがかかりすぎています。
Arigatōgozaimasu. Kakunin deki shidai, go renraku itashimasu.	Kakunin ni jikan ga kakari sugite imasu.
Thank you. I'll contact you as soon as I've confirmed.	It's taking too long to confirm.

Conversation example person A	Conversation example person B
ご質問いただいた件について確認中です。もう少々お待ちください。	分かりました。結果をお待ちしています。
ごしつもんいただいたけんについてかくにんちゅうです。もうしょうしょうおまちください。	わかりました。けっかをおまちしています。
Go shitsumon itadaita kudan ni tsuite kakunin-chūdesu. Mō shōshō omachi kudasai.	Wakarimashita. Kekka o omachi shite imasu.
I'm currently checking on the matter you inquired about. Please wait a little longer.	I understand. I'll wait for the results.

Cultural Context

Doesn't provide a timeline for when confirmation will be completed.

承諾しました。

しょうだくしました。
Shōdaku shimashita.
I've approved it.

Variation 1	Variation 2
同意しました。	Kyō mo shōjin shima shou.
どういしました。	どういしました。
Dōi shima shita.	Sanseidesu.
I have agreed.	I agree.

Positive Response	Negative Response
ありがとうございます。責任を持って進めてまいります。	承諾する前にもっと検討すべきでした。
ありがとうございます。せきにんをもってすすめてまいります。	しょうだくするまえにもっとけんとうすべきでした。
Arigatōgozaimasu. Sekinin o motte susumete mairimasu.	Shōdaku suru mae ni motto kentō subekide shita.
Thank you. I'll proceed responsibly.	You should have considered more before accepting.

Conversation example person A	Conversation example person B
提案いただいた新しいアプローチ、承諾しました。進めてください。	ありがとうございます。早速取り掛かります。
ていあんいただいたあたらしいあぷろーち、しょうだくしました。すすめてください。	ありがとうございます。さっそくとりかかります。
Teian itadaita atarashī apurōchi, shōdaku shima shita. Susumete kudasai.	Arigatōgozaimasu. Sassoku torikakarimasu.
I've approved the new approach you proposed. Please proceed.	Thank you. I'll start working on it right away.

Cultural Context
Doesn't necessarily mean the person fully understands or agrees with the decision.

申し訳ありません。

もうしわけありません。
Mōshiwake arimasen.
I apologize.

Variation 1	Variation 2
恐れ入ります。	Kyō mo shōjin shima shou.
おそれいります。	おそれいります。
Osoreirimasu.	Mōshiwake go zaimasen.
I apologize.	I am terribly sorry.

Positive Response	Negative Response
問題ありません。一緒に解決策を見つけましょう。	謝罪だけでは不十分です。
もんだいありません。いっしょにかいけつさくをみつけましょう。	しゃざいだけではふじゅうぶんです。
Mondai arimasen. Issho ni kaiketsu-saku o mitsuke ma shou.	Shazai dakede wa fu jūbundesu.
No problem. Let's find a solution together.	An apology alone is not enough.

Conversation example person A	Conversation example person B
申し訳ありません。報告書の提出が遅れてしまいました。	了解しました。今後の対策を考えましょう。
もうしわけありません。ほうこくしょのていしゅつがおくれてしまいました。	りょうかいしました。こんごのたいさくをかんがえましょう。
Mōshiwake arimasen. Hōkoku-sho no teishutsu ga okurete shimaimashita.	Ryōkai shima shita. Kongo no taisaku o kangae ma shou.
I apologize. The submission of the report was delayed.	I understand. Let's think about preventive measures for the future.

Cultural Context

Overuse can diminish its sincerity; doesn't always solve the issue at hand.

対応中です。

たいおうちゅうです。
Taiō-chūdesu.
I'm working on it.

Variation 1	Variation 2
対応しています。	Kyō mo shōjin shima shou.
たいおうしています。	たいおうしています。
Taiō shite imasu.	Shori shite imasu.
I am working on it.	I am handling it.

Positive Response	Negative Response
ありがとうございます。進捗があり次第、ご報告いたします。	対応が遅すぎます。
ありがとうございます。しんちょくがありしだい、ごほうこくいたします。	たいおうがおそすぎます。
Arigatōgozaimasu. Shinchoku ga ari shidai, go hōkoku itashimasu.	Taiō ga oso sugimasu.
Thank you. I'll report as soon as there's progress.	Your response is too slow.

Conversation example person A	Conversation example person B
システムエラーの件、現在対応中です。もうしばらくお待ちください。	了解しました。進捗があればご連絡ください。
しすてむえらーのけん、げんざいたいおうちゅうです。もうしばらくおまちください。	りょうかいしました。しんちょくがあればごれんらくください。
Shisutemu erā no kudan, genzai taiō-chūdesu. Mō shibaraku omachi kudasai.	Ryōkai shima shita. Shinchoku ga areba go renraku kudasai.
Regarding the system error, we're currently addressing it. Please wait a little longer.	Understood. Please update me if there's any progress.

Cultural Context
Vague; doesn't provide specifics on progress or estimated completion time.

完了しました。

かんりょうしました。

Kanryō shimashita.

It's been completed.

Variation 1	Variation 2
終了しました。	Kyō mo shōjin shima shou.
しゅうりょうしました。	しゅうりょうしました。
Shūryō shima shita.	Kanryō itashimashita.
It is completed.	It has been completed.

Positive Response	Negative Response
お疲れ様です。素晴らしい仕事ぶりですね。	品質をチェックする必要があります。
おつかれさまです。すばらしいしごとぶりですね。	ひんしつをちぇっくするひつようがあります。
Otsukaresamadesu. Subarashī shigoto-buridesu ne.	Hinshitsu o chekku suru hitsuyō ga arimasu.
Good job. That's excellent work.	We need to check the quality.

Conversation example person A	Conversation example person B
データの更新作業が完了しました。ご確認をお願いします。	確認します。ありがとうございます。
でーたのこうしんさぎょうがかんりょうしました。ごかくにんをおねがいします。	かくにんします。ありがとうございます。
Dēta no kōshin sagyō ga kanryō shima shita. Go kakunin o onegai shimasu.	Kakunin shimasu. Arigatōgozaimasu.
The data update process has been completed. Please verify it.	I'll check it. Thank you.

Cultural Context

Doesn't necessarily mean the task was done to the expected standard.

協力ありがとうございます。

きょうりょくありがとうございます。

Kyōryoku arigatōgozaimasu.

Thank you for your cooperation.

Variation 1	Variation 2
ご協力感謝いたします。	Kyō mo shōjin shima shou.
ごきょうりょくかんしゃいたします。	ごきょうりょくかんしゃいたします。
Go kyōryoku kansha itashimasu.	Go kyōryoku arigatōgozaimasu.
Thank you for your cooperation.	Thank you for your cooperation.

Positive Response	Negative Response
こちらこそ、ありがとうございます。今後ともよろしくお願いいたします。	もっと積極的に協力してください。
こちらこそ、ありがとうございます。こんごともよろしくおねがいいたします。	もっとせっきょくてきにきょうりょくしてください。
Kochira koso, arigatōgozaimasu. Kongo tomo yoroshiku onegai itashimasu.	Motto sekkyoku-teki ni kyōryoku shite kudasai.
Thank you as well. I look forward to our continued cooperation.	Please cooperate more proactively.

Conversation example person A	Conversation example person B
プロジェクトの成功、皆様の協力ありがとうございます。	お役に立てて嬉しいです。今後もよろしくお願いします。
ぷろじぇくとのせいこう、みなさまのきょうりょくありがとうございます。	おやくにたててうれしいです。こんごもよろしくおねがいします。
Purojekuto no seikō, minasama no kyōryoku arigatōgozaimasu.	O yakunitatete ureshīdesu. Kongo mo yoroshiku onegai shimasu.
Thank you everyone for your cooperation in making this project a success.	I'm glad I could help. Looking forward to our continued cooperation.

Cultural Context

May be used prematurely before actual cooperation has occurred.

問題ありません。

もんだいありません。

Mondai arimasen.

No problem.

Variation 1	Variation 2
大丈夫です。	Kyō mo shōjin shima shou.
だいじょうぶです。	だいじょうぶです。
Daijōbudesu.	Ijō arimasen.
No problem.	No problem.

Positive Response	Negative Response
ありがとうございます。安心しました。	本当に問題がないか確認してください。
ありがとうございます。あんしんしました。	ほんとうにもんだいがないかかくにんしてください。
Arigatōgozaimasu. Anshin shima shita.	Hontōni mondai ga nai ka kakunin shite kudasai.
Thank you. I'm relieved to hear that.	Please make sure there really are no problems.

Conversation example person A	Conversation example person B
提出された書類を確認しました。問題ありません。	ありがとうございます。安心しました。
ていしゅつされたしょるいをかくにんしました。もんだいありません。	ありがとうございます。あんしんしました。
Teishutsu sa reta shorui o kakunin shima shita. Mondai arimasen.	Arigatōgozaimasu. Anshin shima shita.
I've checked the submitted documents. There are no issues.	Thank you. I'm relieved to hear that.

Cultural Context

Might downplay genuine concerns or issues that need addressing.

お待たせしました。

おまたせしました。
Omataseshimashita.
Sorry to keep you waiting.

Variation 1	Variation 2
お待たせして申し訳ありません。	Kyō mo shōjin shima shou.
おまたせしてもうしわけありません。	おまたせしてもうしわけありません。
O mata se shite mōshiwake arimasen.	O mata se ita shima shita.
Sorry to keep you waiting.	Sorry to keep you waiting.

Positive Response	Negative Response
いえいえ、こちらこそお待たせして申し訳ありません。	待たせすぎです。
いえいえ、こちらこそおまたせしてもうしわけありません。	またせすぎです。
Ieie, kochira koso o mata se shite mōshiwake arimasen.	Mata se sugidesu.
No, I should be the one apologizing for keeping you waiting.	You've kept me waiting too long.

Conversation example person A	Conversation example person B
お待たせしました。ご要望の資料が準備できました。	ありがとうございます。確認させていただきます。
おまたせしました。ごようぼうのしりょうがじゅんびできました。	ありがとうございます。かくにんさせていただきます。
O mata se shima shita. Go yōbō no shiryō ga junbi dekimashita.	Arigatōgozaimasu. Kakunin sa sete itadakimasu.
Sorry to keep you waiting. The requested materials are now ready.	Thank you. I'll take a look at them.

Cultural Context
Doesn't always adequately address the inconvenience caused by waiting.

返信ありがとうございます。

へんしんありがとうございます。
Henshin arigatōgozaimasu.
Thank you for your reply.

Variation 1	Variation 2
ご返信ありがとうございます。	Kyō mo shōjin shima shou.
ごへんしんありがとうございます。	ごへんしんありがとうございます。
Go henshin arigatōgozaimasu.	Go kaitō arigatōgozaimasu.
Thank you for your reply.	Thank you for your reply.

Positive Response	Negative Response
こちらこそ、迅速なご対応ありがとうございます。	返信が遅すぎます。
こちらこそ、じんそくなごたいおうありがとうございます。	へんしんがおそすぎます。
Kochira koso, jinsokuna go taiō arigatōgozaimasu.	Henshin ga oso sugimasu.
Thank you for your prompt response as well.	Your reply is too late.

Conversation example person A	Conversation example person B
迅速なご返信ありがとうございます。早速進めていきます。	こちらこそ迅速な対応感謝します。よろしくお願いします。
じんそくなごへんしんありがとうございます。さっそくすすめていきます。	こちらこそじんそくなたいおうかんしゃします。よろしくおねがいします。
Jinsokuna go henshin arigatōgozaimasu. Sassoku susumete ikimasu.	Kochira koso jinsokuna taiō kansha shimasu. Yoroshiku onegai shimasu.
Thank you for your prompt reply. I'll proceed right away.	I appreciate your quick response as well. Thank you in advance.

Cultural Context
Doesn't indicate if the reply was satisfactory or if further action is needed.

今後ともよろしくお願いします。

こんごともよろしくおねがいします。

Kongotomoyoroshiku onegaishimasu.

I look forward to our continued cooperation.

Variation 1	Variation 2
今後ともご指導ご鞭撻のほどよろしくお願い申し上げます。	Kyō mo shōjin shima shou.
こんごともごしどうごべんたつのほどよろしくおねがいもうしあげます。	こんごともごしどうごべんたつのほどよろしくおねがいもうしあげます。
Kongo to mo go shidō go bentatsu no hodo yoroshiku onegai mōshiagemasu.	Kongo to mo go shiji go shien no hodo yoroshiku onegai itashimasu.
I look forward to your continued guidance and support.	I humbly request your continued guidance and encouragement.

Positive Response	Negative Response
こちらこそ、今後とも宜しくお願いいたします。	今後の改善を期待します。
こちらこそ、こんごともよろしくおねがいいたします。	こんごのかいぜんをきたいします。
Kochira koso, kongo tomo yoroshiku onegai itashimasu.	Kongo no kaizen o kitai shimasu.
Likewise, I look forward to our continued cooperation.	I expect improvements in the future.

Conversation example person A	Conversation example person B
無事プロジェクトが完了しました。今後ともよろしくお願いします。	お疲れ様でした。今後とも頑張りましょう。
ぶじぷろじぇくとがかんりょうしました。こんごともよろしくおねがいします。	おつかれさまでした。こんごともがんばりましょう。
Buji purojekuto ga kanryō shima shita. Kongo tomo yoroshiku onegai shimasu.	Otsukaresama de shita. Kongo tomo ganbari ma shou.
The project has been successfully completed. I look forward to our continued cooperation.	Good job. Let's keep up the good work.

Cultural Context

A formulaic phrase that doesn't guarantee future cooperation or goodwill.

確認させてください。

かくにんさせてください。
Kakunin sa sete kudasai.
Let me confirm that.

Variation 1	Variation 2
確認します。	Kyō mo shōjin shima shou.
かくにんします。	かくにんします。
Kakunin shimasu.	Shirabemasu.
Let me check.	I will check.

Positive Response	Negative Response
もちろんです。どうぞご確認ください。	確認に時間をかけすぎています。
もちろんです。どうぞごかくにんください。	かくにんにじかんをかけすぎています。
Mochirondesu. Dōzo go kakunin kudasai.	Kakunin ni jikan o kake sugite imasu.
Of course. Please go ahead and confirm.	You're taking too much time to confirm.

Conversation example person A	Conversation example person B
提案内容について、もう一度確認させてください。	もちろんです。どの部分が不明確でしょうか？
ていあんないようについて、もういちどかくにんさせてください。	もちろんです。どのぶぶんがふめいかくでしょうか？
Teian naiyō ni tsuite, mōichido kakunin sa sete kudasai.	Mochirondesu. Dono bubun ga fu meikakudeshou ka?
Let me confirm the proposal details once again.	Of course. Which part is unclear?

Cultural Context
Doesn't specify what needs confirmation or how long it will take.

後ほど連絡します。

のちほどれんらくします。
Nochihodo renraku shimasu.
I'll contact you later.

Variation 1	Variation 2
追って連絡します。	Kyō mo shōjin shima shou.
おってれんらくします。	おってれんらくします。
Otte renraku shimasu.	Nochihodo go renraku shimasu.
I will contact you later.	I will contact you later.

Positive Response	Negative Response
承知いたしました。ご連絡お待ちしております。	いつ頃連絡がもらえますか？
しょうちいたしました。ごれんらくおまちしております。	いつごろれんらくがもらえますか？
Shōchi itashimashita. Go renraku omachi shite orimasu.	Itsu koro renraku ga moraemasu ka?
Understood. I'll be waiting for your contact.	When can I expect to hear from you?

Conversation example person A	Conversation example person B
件の件、確認でき次第後ほど連絡します。	承知しました。連絡お待ちしています。
くだんのけん、かくにんできしだいのちほどれんらくします。	しょうちしました。れんらくおまちしています。
-Ken no kudan, kakunin deki shidai nochihodo renraku shimasu.	Shōchi shima shita. Renraku omachi shite imasu.
Regarding that matter, I'll contact you later once I've confirmed.	Understood. I'll wait for your contact.

Cultural Context
"Later" is vague and doesn't provide a specific timeframe.

承知いたしました。

しょうちいたしました。
Shōchi itashimashita.
I understand.

Variation 1	Variation 2
了解いたしました。	Kyō mo shōjin shima shou.
りょうかいいたしました。	りょうかいいたしました。
Ryōkai itashimashita.	Kashikomarimashita.
Understood.	Understood.

Positive Response	Negative Response
ご連絡ありがとうございます。対応させていただきます。	本当に理解していますか。
ごれんらくありがとうございます。たいおうさせていただきます。	ほんとうにりかいしていますか。
Go renraku arigatōgozaimasu. Taiō sa sete itadakimasu.	Hontōni rikai shite imasu ka.
Thank you for letting us know. We'll take care of it.	Do you really understand?

Conversation example person A	Conversation example person B
ご指示の通り進めさせていただきます。承知いたしました。	ありがとうございます。何か不明点があればご連絡ください。
ごしじのとおりすすめさせていただきます。しょうちいたしました。	ありがとうございます。なにかふめいてんがあればごれんらくください。
Go shiji no tōri susume sasete itadakimasu. Shōchi itashimashita.	Arigatōgozaimasu. Nani ka fumei-ten ga areba go renraku kudasai.
I will proceed as instructed. Understood.	Thank you. Please contact me if you have any questions.

Cultural Context
Formal acknowledgment. May seem cold if used in response to personal news.

助かります。

たすかります。
Tasukarimasu.
That's helpful.

Variation 1	Variation 2
ありがたいです。	Kyō mo shōjin shima shou.
ありがたいです。	ありがたいです。
Arigataidesu.	Kansha itashimasu.
That would be helpful.	I am grateful.

Positive Response	Negative Response
こちらこそ、お役に立てて嬉しいです。	これは当然の仕事です。
こちらこそ、おやくにたててうれしいです。	これはとうぜんのしごとです。
Kochira koso, o yakunitatete ureshīdesu.	Kore wa tōzen no shigotodesu.
I'm glad I could be of help.	This is just part of your job.

Conversation example person A	Conversation example person B
迅速なご対応、助かります。	お役に立てて嬉しいです。今後もお気軽にご相談ください。
じんそくなごたいおう、たすかります。	おやくにたててうれしいです。こんごもおきがるにごそうだんください。
Jinsokuna go taiō, tasukarimasu.	O yakunitatete ureshīdesu. Kongo mo o kigaru ni go sōdan kudasai.
Your prompt response is very helpful.	I'm glad I could help. Please feel free to consult me anytime.

Cultural Context
Expresses gratitude but doesn't always convey the full extent of appreciation.

相談があります。

そうだんがあります。

Sōdan ga arimasu.

I have something to consult about.

Variation 1	Variation 2
相談したいことがあります。	Kyō mo shōjin shima shou.
そうだんしたいことがあります。	そうだんしたいことがあります。
Sōdan shitai koto ga arimasu.	Sōdan koto ga arimasu.
I need to discuss something.	I have something I would like to discuss.

Positive Response	Negative Response
承知いたしました。どのようなことでしょうか？	今は忙しいので後にしてください。
しょうちいたしました。どのようなことでしょうか？	いまはいそがしいのであとにしてください。
Shōchi itashimashita. Do no yōna kotodeshou ka?	Ima wa isogashīnode nochi ni shite kudasai.
Understood. What would you like to consult about?	I'm busy now, please ask later.

Conversation example person A	Conversation example person B
新規プロジェクトについて相談があります。お時間いただけますか？	もちろんです。今お話しできます。
しんきぷろじぇくとについてそうだんがあります。おじかんいただけますか？	もちろんです。いまおはなしできます。
Shinki purojekuto ni tsuite sōdan ga arimasu. O jikan itadakemasu ka?	Mochirondesu. Ima ohanashi dekimasu.
I have something to discuss about the new project. Do you have a moment?	Of course. I can talk now.

Cultural Context

May create unnecessary concern if the topic isn't specified.

お忙しいところ申し訳ありません。

おいそがしいところもうしわけありません。
O isogashī tokoro mōshiwake arimasen.
Sorry to bother you when you're busy.

Variation 1	Variation 2
お時間をいただき恐縮です。	Kyō mo shōjin shima shou.
おじかんをいただききょうしゅくです。	おじかんをいただききょうしゅくです。
O jikan o itadaki kyōshukudesu.	O jikan o itadaki arigatōgozaimasu.
Sorry for taking up your time.	I apologize for taking up your time.

Positive Response	Negative Response
いえいえ、こちらこそ遠慮なくお声かけください。	簡潔にお願いします。
いえいえ、こちらこそえんりょなくおこえかけください。	かんけつにおねがいします。
Ieie, kochira koso enryonaku o koe kake kudasai.	Kanketsu ni onegai shimasu.
No, please don't hesitate to contact me anytime.	Please be brief.

Conversation example person A	Conversation example person B
お忙しいところ申し訳ありません。緊急の承認をお願いできますか？	大丈夫です。内容を確認して対応します。
おいそがしいところもうしわけありません。きんきゅうのしょうにんをおねがいできますか？	だいじょうぶです。ないようをかくにんしてたいおうします。
O isogashī tokoro mōshiwake arimasen. Kinkyū no shōnin o onegai dekimasu ka?	Daijōbudesu. Naiyō o kakunin shite taiō shimasu.
I'm sorry to bother you when you're busy. Could I ask for an urgent approval?	No problem. I'll check the content and take care of it.

Cultural Context
Acknowledgment of busyness doesn't justify interruption or lessen the work impact.

対応ありがとうございます。

たいおうありがとうございます。

Taiō arigatōgozaimasu.

Thank you for your response.

Variation 1	Variation 2
ご対応ありがとうございます。	Kyō mo shōjin shima shou.
ごたいおうありがとうございます。	ごたいおうありがとうございます。
Go taiō arigatōgozaimasu.	Go kyōryoku arigatōgozaimasu.
Thank you for your support.	Thank you for your assistance.

Positive Response	Negative Response
こちらこそ、お役に立てて嬉しいです。	対応が不十分です。
こちらこそ、おやくにたててうれしいです。	たいおうがふじゅうぶんです。
Kochira koso, o yakunitatete ureshīdesu.	Taiō ga fu jūbundesu.
I'm glad I could be of help.	Your response is insufficient.

Conversation example person A	Conversation example person B
迅速なご対応ありがとうございます。大変助かりました。	こちらこそ、お役に立てて嬉しいです。
じんそくなごたいおうありがとうございます。たいへんたすかりました。	こちらこそ、おやくにたててうれしいです。
Jinsokuna go taiō arigatōgozaimasu. Taihen tasukarimashita.	Kochira koso, o yakunitatete ureshīdesu.
Thank you for your prompt action. It was very helpful.	I'm glad I could be of help.

Cultural Context

Doesn't specify if the response was satisfactory or sufficient.

確認お願いします。

かくにんおねがいします。
Kakunin onegaishimasu.
Please confirm this.

Variation 1	Variation 2
ご確認お願いします。	Kyō mo shōjin shima shou.
ごかくにんおねがいします。	ごかくにんおねがいします。
Go kakunin onegai shimasu.	Go kakunin itadakemasudeshou ka.
Please check.	Please confirm.

Positive Response	Negative Response
承知いたしました。すぐに確認いたします。	確認する時間がありません。
しょうちいたしました。すぐにかくにんいたします。	かくにんするじかんがありません。
Shōchi itashimashita. Sugu ni kakunin itashimasu.	Kakunin suru jikan ga arimasen.
Understood. I'll check it right away.	I don't have time to check.

Conversation example person A	Conversation example person B
最新版の資料をアップロードしました。確認お願いします。	承知しました。すぐに確認します。
さいしんばんのしりょうをあっぷろーどしました。かくにんおねがいします。	しょうちしました。すぐにかくにんします。
Saishin-ban no shiryō o appurōdo shima shita. Kakunin onegai shimasu.	Shōchi shima shita. Sugu ni kakunin shimasu.
I've uploaded the latest version of the document. Please check it.	Understood. I'll check it right away.

Cultural Context
Doesn't clarify what needs to be confirmed or by when.

了解いたしました。

りょうかいいたしました。

Ryōkai itashimashita.

I understand.

Variation 1	Variation 2
承知いたしました。	Kyō mo shōjin shima shou.
しょうちいたしました。	しょうちいたしました。
Shōchi itashimashita.	Ryōkai shima shita.
Understood.	Understood.

Positive Response	Negative Response
ありがとうございます。適切に対応いたします。	本当に理解していますか？
ありがとうございます。てきせつにたいおういたします。	ほんとうにりかいしていますか？
Arigatōgozaimasu. Tekisetsu ni taiō itashimasu.	Hontōni rikai shite imasu ka?
Thank you. I'll respond appropriately.	Do you really understand?

Conversation example person A	Conversation example person B
スケジュール変更の件、了解いたしました。対応します。	ご協力感謝します。よろしくお願いします。
すけじゅーるへんこうのけん、りょうかいいたしました。たいおうします。	ごきょうりょくかんしゃします。よろしくおねがいします。
Sukejūru henkō no kudan, ryōkai itashimashita. Taiō shimasu.	Go kyōryoku kansha shimasu. Yoroshiku onegai shimasu.
I've understood about the schedule change. I'll adjust accordingly.	Thank you for your cooperation. I appreciate it.

Cultural Context

Formal acknowledgment that doesn't guarantee understanding or agreement.

お手数おかけします。

おてすうおかけします。
Otesū okake shimasu.
Sorry for the inconvenience.

Variation 1	Variation 2
ご迷惑をおかけします。	Kyō mo shōjin shima shou.
ごめいわくをおかけします。	ごめいわくをおかけします。
Go meiwaku o okake shimasu.	Go fuben o okake shimasu.
Sorry for the inconvenience.	I apologize for the inconvenience.

Positive Response	Negative Response
いえいえ、お気遣いありがとうございます。喜んでお手伝いいたします。	これは本来あなたの仕事です。
いえいえ、おきづかいありがとうございます。よろこんでおてつだいいたします。	これはほんらいあなたのしごとです。
Ieie, o kidzukai arigatōgozaimasu. Yorokonde otetsudai itashimasu.	Kore wa honrai anata no shigotodesu.
Not at all, thank you for your consideration. I'm happy to help.	This is actually your job.

Conversation example person A	Conversation example person B
度々の修正依頼で、お手数おかけします。	問題ありません。良いものを作り上げるために必要なプロセスです。
たびたびのしゅうせいいらいで、おてすうおかけします。	もんだいありません。よいものをつくりあげるためにひつようなぷろせすです。
Tabitabi no shūsei irai de, otesū okake shimasu.	Mondai arimasen. Yoi mono o tsukuriageru tame ni hitsuyōna purosesudesu.
I'm sorry for the trouble with these repeated revision requests.	No problem. It's a necessary process to create a good final product.

Cultural Context
Politeness doesn't reduce the actual burden of the request.

宜しくお願い致します。

よろしくおねがいいたします。
Yoroshikuonegaiitashimasu.
Thank you in advance.

Variation 1	Variation 2
よろしくお願いいたします。	Kyō mo shōjin shima shou.
よろしくおねがいいたします。	よろしくおねがいいたします。
Yoroshiku onegai itashimasu.	Dōzo yoroshiku onegai mōshiagemasu.
Best regards.	Best regards.

Positive Response	Negative Response
こちらこそ、よろしくお願いいたします。	具体的に何をすればいいですか？
こちらこそ、よろしくおねがいいたします。	ぐたいてきになにをすればいいですか？
Kochira koso, yoroshiku onegai itashimasu.	Gutai-teki ni nani o sureba īdesu ka?
Likewise, I look forward to working with you.	What specifically should I do?

Conversation example person A	Conversation example person B
新しいチームメンバーです。宜しくお願い致します。	こちらこそよろしくお願いします。何か質問があればいつでも聞いてください。
あたらしいちーむめんばーです。よろしくおねがいいたします。	こちらこそよろしくおねがいします。なにかしつもんがあればいつでもきいてください。
Atarashī chīmu menbādesu. Yoroshiku onegai itashimasu.	Kochira koso yoroshiku onegai shimasu. Nani ka shitsumon ga areba itsu demo kiite kudasai.
I'm a new team member. Nice to meet you and I look forward to working with you.	Nice to meet you too. Please feel free to ask if you have any questions.

Cultural Context
Very formal version that can be too deferential in some contexts.

質問があります。

しつもんがあります。

Shitsumon ga arimasu.

I have a question.

Variation 1	Variation 2
質問したいことがあります。	Kyō mo shōjin shima shou.
しつもんしたいことがあります。	しつもんしたいことがあります。
Shitsumon shitai koto ga arimasu.	Shitsumon jikō ga arimasu.
I have a question.	I have a question.

Positive Response	Negative Response
はい、どのような質問でしょうか？お聞かせください。	今は質問を受け付ける時間がありません。
はい、どのようなしつもんでしょうか？おきかせください。	いまはしつもんをうけつけるじかんがありません。
Hai, do no yōna shitsumondeshou ka? O kika se kudasai.	Ima wa shitsumon o uketsukeru jikan ga arimasen.
Yes, what kind of question do you have? Please let me know.	I don't have time for questions now.

Conversation example person A	Conversation example person B
プロジェクトの進め方について質問があります。	どうぞ、質問してください。できる限り詳しく回答します。
ぷろじぇくとのすすめかたについてしつもんがあります。	どうぞ、しつもんしてください。できるかぎりくわしくかいとうします。
Purojekuto no susumekata ni tsuite shitsumon ga arimasu.	Dōzo, shitsumon shite kudasai. Dekiru kagiri kuwashiku kaitō shimasu.
I have a question about how to proceed with the project.	Please go ahead and ask. I'll answer as thoroughly as possible.

Cultural Context

May create anticipation or concern without specifying the nature of the question.

回答ありがとうございます。

かいとうありがとうございます。

Kaitō arigatōgozaimasu.

Thank you for your answer.

Variation 1	Variation 2
ご回答ありがとうございます。	Kyō mo shōjin shima shou.
ごかいとうありがとうございます。	ごかいとうありがとうございます。
Go kaitō arigatōgozaimasu.	Go henji arigatōgozaimasu.
Thank you for your response.	Thank you for your response.

Positive Response	Negative Response
こちらこそ、お役に立てて嬉しいです。	回答が不十分です。
こちらこそ、おやくにたててうれしいです。	かいとうがふじゅうぶんです。
Kochira koso, o yakunitatete ureshīdesu.	Kaitō ga fu jūbundesu.
I'm glad I could be of help.	Your answer is insufficient.

Conversation example person A	Conversation example person B
丁寧な回答ありがとうございます。非常に参考になりました。	お役に立てて嬉しいです。他に不明点があればいつでも聞いてください。
ていねいなかいとうありがとうございます。ひじょうにさんこうになりました。	おやくにたててうれしいです。ほかにふめいてんがあればいつでもきいてください。
Teineina kaitō arigatōgozaimasu. Hijō ni sankō ni narimashita.	O yakunitatete ureshīdesu. Hoka ni fumei-ten ga areba itsu demo kiite kudasai.
Thank you for your detailed answer. It was very helpful.	I'm glad I could help. Feel free to ask if you have any other questions.

Cultural Context

Doesn't indicate if the answer was helpful or sufficient.

検討します。

けんとうします。
Kentō shimasu.
I'll consider it.

Variation 1	Variation 2
考えます。	Kyō mo shōjin shima shou.
かんがえます。	かんがえます。
Kangaemasu.	Kōryo shimasu.
I will consider it.	I will consider it.

Positive Response	Negative Response
ありがとうございます。慎重に検討し、ご報告いたします。	いつまでに結果を出せますか？
ありがとうございます。しんちょうにけんとうし、ごほうこくいたします。	いつまでにけっかをだせますか？
Arigatōgozaimasu. Shinchō ni kentō shi, go hōkoku itashimasu.	Itsu made ni kekka o dasemasu ka?
Thank you. I'll consider it carefully and report back to you.	By when can you provide results?

Conversation example person A	Conversation example person B
新しい提案ありがとうございます。検討します。	はい、よろしくお願いします。結果をお待ちしています。
あたらしいていあんありがとうございます。けんとうします。	はい、よろしくおねがいします。けっかをおまちしています。
Atarashī teian arigatōgozaimasu. Kentō shimasu.	Hai, yoroshiku onegai shimasu. Kekka o omachi shite imasu.
Thank you for the new proposal. I'll consider it.	Yes, thank you. I look forward to hearing the results.

Cultural Context
Often used as a polite way to delay or avoid decisions.

フィードバックをお願いします。

ふぃーどばっくをおねがいします。

Fīdobakku o onegaishimasu.

Please provide feedback.

Variation 1	Variation 2
意見や感想をお聞かせください。	Kyō mo shōjin shima shou.
いけんやかんそうをおきかせください。	いけんやかんそうをおきかせください。
Iken ya kansō o o kikase kudasai.	Go iken o o kikase kudasai.
Please provide your feedback.	Please provide your feedback.

Positive Response	Negative Response
はい、建設的な意見を出すよう心がけます。	建設的なフィードバックがありません。
はい、けんせつてきないけんをだすようこころがけます。	けんせつてきなふぃーどばっくがありません。
Hai, kensetsu-tekina iken o dasu yō kokorogakemasu.	Kensetsu-tekina fīdobakku ga arimasen.
Yes, I'll try to provide constructive feedback.	I don't have any constructive feedback.

Conversation example person A	Conversation example person B
新製品のプロトタイプについて、フィードバックをお願いします。	デザインは良いですが、使いやすさに改善の余地があります。
しんせいひんのぷろとたいぷについて、ふぃーどばっくをおねがいします。	でざいんはよいですが、つかいやすさにかいぜんのよちがあります。
Shin seihin no purototaipu ni tsuite, fīdobakku o onegai shimasu.	Dezain wa yoidesuga, tsukai yasu-sa ni kaizen no yochi ga arimasu.
Please provide feedback on the new product prototype.	The design is good, but there's room for improvement in usability.

Cultural Context
Create a safe environment for constructive feedback.

ミーティングの日程調整をお願いします。

みーてぃんぐのにっていちょうせいをおねがいします。

Mītingu no nittei chōsei o onegaishimasu.

Please arrange the meeting schedule.

Variation 1	Variation 2
会議の日程調整をお願いします。	Kyō mo shōjin shima shou.
かいぎのにっていちょうせいをおねがいします。	かいぎのにっていちょうせいをおねがいします。
Kaigi no nittei chōsei o onegai shimasu.	Kaigi no sukejūru chōsei o onegai itashimasu.
Please arrange a meeting schedule.	Please arrange the meeting schedule.

Positive Response	Negative Response
承知いたしました。皆様のご都合の良い日程を探します。	スケジュールが詰まっています。
しょうちいたしました。みなさまのごつごうのよいにっていをさがします。	すけじゅーるがつまっています。
Shōchi itashimashita. Minasama no go tsugō no yoi nittei o sagashimasu.	Sukejūru ga tsumatte imasu.
Understood. I'll find a date that works for everyone.	My schedule is full.

Conversation example person A	Conversation example person B
来週のミーティングの日程調整をお願いします。	承知しました。参加者全員の予定を確認して、最適な日時を提案します。
らいしゅうのみーてぃんぐのにっていちょうせいをおねがいします。	しょうちしました。さんかしゃぜんいんのよていをかくにんして、さいてきなにちじをていあんします。
Raishū no mītingu no nittei chōsei o onegai shimasu.	Shōchi shima shita. Sanka-sha zen'in no yotei o kakunin shite, saitekina nichiji o teian shimasu.
Please arrange the schedule for next week's meeting.	Understood. I'll check everyone's availability and suggest the best time.

Cultural Context

Doesn't provide preferred dates or times, potentially prolonging the process.

修正しました。

しゅうせいしました。

Shūsei shimashita.

I've made the corrections.

Variation 1	Variation 2
変更しました。	Kyō mo shōjin shima shou.
へんこうしました。	へんこうしました。
Henkō shima shita.	Shūsei itashimashita.
I have made the changes.	I have made the changes.

Positive Response	Negative Response
ありがとうございます。迅速な対応に感謝します。	まだ修正が必要です。
ありがとうございます。じんそくなたいおうにかんしゃします。	まだしゅうせいがひつようです。
Arigatōgozaimasu. Jinsokuna taiō ni kansha shimasu.	Mada shūsei ga hitsuyōdesu.
Thank you. I appreciate your quick response.	It still needs more revisions.

Conversation example person A	Conversation example person B
修正しました。確認をお願いします。	承知いたしました。確認します。
しゅうせいしました。かくにんをおねがいします。	しょうちいたしました。かくにんします。
Shūsei shima shita. Kakunin o onegai shimasu.	Shōchi itashimashita. Kakunin shimasu.
I've made the corrections. Please check.	Understood. I'll check it.

Cultural Context

Doesn't specify what was changed or if all requested modifications were made.

確認をお願いします。

かくにんをおねがいします。
Kakunin o onegaishimasu.
Please check this.

Variation 1	Variation 2
ご確認お願いします。	Kyō mo shōjin shima shou.
ごかくにんおねがいします。	ごかくにんおねがいします。
Go kakunin onegai shimasu.	Go kakunin itadakereba saiwaidesu.
Please review.	Please kindly check.

Positive Response	Negative Response
承知しました。すぐに確認いたします。	確認する時間がありません。
しょうちしました。すぐにかくにんいたします。	かくにんするじかんがありません。
Shōchi shima shita. Sugu ni kakunin itashimasu.	Kakunin suru jikan ga arimasen.
Understood. I'll check it right away.	I don't have time to check.

Conversation example person A	Conversation example person B
この書類の内容について、確認をお願いします。	了解しました。確認後、ご連絡いたします。
このしょるいのないようについて、かくにんをおねがいします。	りょうかいしました。かくにんご、ごれんらくいたします。
Kono shorui no naiyō ni tsuite, kakunin o onegai shimasu.	Ryōkai shima shita. Kakunin-go, go renraku itashimasu.
Please check the contents of this document.	Understood. I'll contact you after checking.

Cultural Context
Doesn't clarify what needs confirmation or the urgency level.

今週中に完了予定です。

こんしゅうちゅうにかんりょうよていです。

Konshū-chū ni kanryō yoteidesu.

It's scheduled to be completed this week.

Variation 1	Variation 2
今週中に終了予定です。	Kyō mo shōjin shima shou.
こんしゅうちゅうにしゅうりょうよていです。	こんしゅうちゅうにしゅうりょうよていです。
Konshū-chū ni shūryō yoteidesu.	Konshū-chū ni kanryō suru yoteidesu.
It is scheduled to be completed this week.	It is scheduled to be completed within this week.

Positive Response	Negative Response
素晴らしいです。順調に進んでいますね。	もっと早く完了させてください。
すばらしいです。じゅんちょうにすすんでいますね。	もっとはやくかんりょうさせてください。
Subarashīdesu. Junchō ni susunde ima su ne.	Motto hayaku kanryō sa sete kudasai.
Great. It's progressing smoothly.	Please complete it sooner.

Conversation example person A	Conversation example person B
今週中に完了予定です。	了解です。期限までに間に合いますね。
こんしゅうちゅうにかんりょうよていです。	りょうかいです。きげんまでにまにあいますね。
Konshū-chū ni kanryō yoteidesu.	Ryōkaidesu. Kigen made ni maniaimasu ne.
It's scheduled to be completed this week.	Got it. It will be in time for the deadline.

Cultural Context

"Within this week" is vague and doesn't provide a specific completion date.

アップデートありがとうございます。

あっぷでーとありがとうございます。

Appudēto arigatōgozaimasu.

Thank you for the update.

Variation 1	Variation 2
最新情報をお知らせいただきありがとうございます。	Kyō mo shōjin shima shou.
さいしんじょうほうをおしらせいただきありがとうございます。	さいしんじょうほうをおしらせいただきありがとうございます。
Saishin jōhō o oshirase itadaki arigatōgozaimasu.	Saishin no jōhō teikyō arigatōgozaimasu.
Thank you for the update.	Thank you for providing the latest information.

Positive Response	Negative Response
こちらこそ、常に情報共有してくださり感謝です。	アップデートが遅すぎます。
こちらこそ、つねにじょうほうきょうゆうしてくださりかんしゃです。	あっぷでーとがおそすぎます。
Kochira koso, tsuneni jōhō kyōyū shite kudasari kanshadesu.	Appudēto ga oso sugimasu.
Thank you for always sharing information.	Your update is too late.

Conversation example person A	Conversation example person B
アップデートありがとうございます。	こちらこそ。今後の方針を確認したいです。
あっぷでーとありがとうございます。	こちらこそ。こんごのほうしんをかくにんしたいです。
Appudēto arigatōgozaimasu.	Kochira koso. Kongo no hōshin o kakunin shitaidesu.
Thank you for the update.	You're welcome. I'd like to confirm our future direction.

Cultural Context

Doesn't indicate if the update was sufficient or if more information is needed.

遅くなり申し訳ありません。

おそくなりもうしわけありません。
Osoku nari mōshiwake arimasen.
I apologize for the delay.

Variation 1	Variation 2
遅れて申し訳ありません。	Kyō mo shōjin shima shou.
おくれてもうしわけありません。	おくれてもうしわけありません。
Okurete mōshiwake arimasen.	Chien shite mōshiwake go zaimasen.
Sorry for the delay.	I apologize for the delay.

Positive Response	Negative Response
問題ありません。丁寧な仕事に感謝します。	遅れは許容できません。
もんだいありません。ていねいなしごとにかんしゃします。	おくれはきょようできません。
Mondai arimasen. Teineina shigoto ni kansha shimasu.	Okure wa kyoyō dekimasen.
No problem. Thank you for your thorough work.	Delays are not acceptable.

Conversation example person A	Conversation example person B
遅くなり申し訳ありません。	お気になさらないでください。お手数をおかけして申し訳ありません。
おそくなりもうしわけありません。	おきになさらないでください。おてすうをおかけしてもうしわけありません。
Osoku nari mōshiwake arimasen.	Oki ni nasaranaide kudasai. Otesū o okake shite mōshiwake arimasen.
I'm sorry for the delay.	Don't worry about it. I'm sorry for the trouble.

Cultural Context
Apology doesn't always mitigate the impact of the delay.

ご協力お願いします。

ごきょうりょくおねがいします。

Go kyōryoku onegaishimasu.

Please cooperate with us.

Variation 1	Variation 2
ご協力をお願いいたします。	Kyō mo shōjin shima shou.
ごきょうりょくをおねがいいたします。	ごきょうりょくをおねがいいたします。
Go kyōryoku o onegai itashimasu.	Go shien o onegai mōshiagemasu.
Please cooperate.	I kindly request your cooperation.

Positive Response	Negative Response
もちろんです。喜んでお手伝いさせていただきます。	協力できる余裕がありません。
もちろんです。よろこんでおてつだいさせていただきます。	きょうりょくできるよゆうがありません。
Mochirondesu. Yorokonde otetsudai sa sete itadakimasu.	Kyōryoku dekiru yoyū ga arimasen.
Of course. I'd be happy to help.	I don't have capacity to cooperate.

Conversation example person A	Conversation example person B
ご協力お願いします。	承知いたしました。全力で協力します。
ごきょうりょくおねがいします。	しょうちいたしました。ぜんりょくできょうりょくします。
Go kyōryoku onegai shimasu.	Shōchi itashimashita. Zenryoku de kyōryoku shimasu.
Please cooperate with us.	Understood. I'll cooperate fully.

Cultural Context

Doesn't specify what kind of cooperation is needed or to what extent.

承知いたしました。

しょうちいたしました。
Shōchi itashimashita.
Understood.

Variation 1	Variation 2
了解いたしました。	Kyō mo shōjin shima shou.
りょうかいいたしました。	りょうかいいたしました。
Ryōkai itashimashita.	Kashikomarimashita.
Understood.	Understood.

Positive Response	Negative Response
ご連絡ありがとうございます。対応させていただきます。	本当に理解していますか。
ごれんらくありがとうございます。たいおうさせていただきます。	ほんとうにりかいしていますか。
Go renraku arigatōgozaimasu. Taiō sa sete itadakimasu.	Hontōni rikai shite imasu ka.
Thank you for letting us know. We'll take care of it.	Do you really understand?

Conversation example person A	Conversation example person B
ご指示の通り進めさせていただきます。承知いたしました。	ありがとうございます。何か不明点があればご連絡ください。
ごしじのとおりすすめさせていただきます。しょうちいたしました。	ありがとうございます。なにかふめいてんがあればごれんらくください。
Go shiji no tōri susume sasete itadakimasu. Shōchi itashimashita.	Arigatōgozaimasu. Nani ka fumei-ten ga areba go renraku kudasai.
I will proceed as instructed. Understood.	Thank you. Please contact me if you have any questions.

Cultural Context
Formal acknowledgment. May seem cold if used in response to personal news.

対応可能です。

たいおうかのうです。

Taiō kanōdesu.

I can handle it.

Variation 1	Variation 2
対応できます。	Kyō mo shōjin shima shou.
たいおうできます。	たいおうできます。
Taiō dekimasu.	Shori kanōdesu.
I can handle it.	I can handle it.

Positive Response	Negative Response
素晴らしいです。迅速な対応に感謝します。	いつまでに対応できますか？
すばらしいです。じんそくなたいおうにかんしゃします。	いつまでにたいおうできますか？
Subarashīdesu. Jinsokuna taiō ni kansha shimasu.	Itsu made ni taiō dekimasu ka?
Great. Thank you for your quick response.	By when can you respond?

Conversation example person A	Conversation example person B
来週の会議に参加できますか？	対応可能です。
らいしゅうのかいぎにさんかできますか？	たいおうかのうです。
Raishū no kaigi ni sanka dekimasu ka?	Taiō kanōdesu.
Can you attend next week's meeting?	I can manage that.

Cultural Context

Doesn't specify when or how the matter will be addressed.

期限までに間に合います。

きげんまでにまにあいます。
Kigen made ni maniaimasu.
I can make it by the deadline.

Variation 1	Variation 2
締め切りまでに完了します。	Kyō mo shōjin shima shou.
しめきりまでにかんりょうします。	しめきりまでにかんりょうします。
Shimekiri made ni kanryō shimasu.	Kigen made ni shūryō shimasu.
It will be done by the deadline.	It will be completed by the deadline.

Positive Response	Negative Response
安心しました。計画通りに進んでいますね。	本当に間に合いますか？
あんしんしました。けいかくどおりにすすんでいますね。	ほんとうにまにあいますか？
Anshin shima shita. Keikaku-dōri ni susunde ima su ne.	Hontōni maniaimasu ka?
I'm relieved. It's progressing as planned.	Can you really meet the deadline?

Conversation example person A	Conversation example person B
レポートの提出期限は明日までですが、期限までに間に合いますか？	はい、期限までに間に合います。
れぽーとのていしゅつきげんはあしたまでですが、きげんまでにまにあいますか？	はい、きげんまでにまにあいます。
Repōto no teishutsu kigen wa ashita made desuga, kigen made ni mani aimasu ka?	Hai, kigen made ni maniaimasu.
The deadline for the report is tomorrow. Can you make it in time?	Yes, I'll make it in time for the deadline.

Cultural Context
Doesn't provide a buffer for unexpected issues or quality checks.

今確認中です。

いまかくにんちゅうです。
Ima kakunin-chūdesu.
I'm checking on it now.

Variation 1	Variation 2
現在確認しています。	Kyō mo shōjin shima shou.
げんざいかくにんしています。	げんざいかくにんしています。
Genzai kakunin shite imasu.	Tadaima chōsa-chūdesu.
I am checking now.	I am currently checking.

Positive Response	Negative Response
ありがとうございます。丁寧な対応に感謝します。	確認に時間がかかりすぎています。
ありがとうございます。ていねいなたいおうにかんしゃします。	かくにんにじかんがかかりすぎています。
Arigatōgozaimasu. Teineina taiō ni kansha shimasu.	Kakunin ni jikan ga kakari sugite imasu.
Thank you. I appreciate your careful attention.	It's taking too long to confirm.

Conversation example person A	Conversation example person B
クライアントからの問い合わせについて、状況を教えてください。	今確認中です。もう少しお時間をいただけますか？
くらいあんとからのといあわせについて、じょうきょうをおしえてください。	いまかくにんちゅうです。もうすこしおじかんをいただけますか？
Kuraianto kara no toiawase ni tsuite, jōkyō o oshiete kudasai.	Ima kakunin-chūdesu. Mōsukoshi o jikan o itadakemasu ka?
Please update me on the status of the client's inquiry.	I'm checking on it now. Could you give me a little more time?

Cultural Context
Doesn't provide an estimated time for completion of the confirmation.

追って連絡します。

おってれんらくします。
Otte renraku shimasu.
I'll follow up later.

Variation 1	Variation 2
後ほど連絡します。	Kyō mo shōjin shima shou.
のちほどれんらくします。	のちほどれんらくします。
Nochihodo renraku shimasu.	Otte go renraku itashimasu.
I will get back to you later.	I will contact you later.

Positive Response	Negative Response
承知しました。詳細な情報をお待ちしております。	いつ頃連絡がもらえますか？
しょうちしました。しょうさいなじょうほうをおまちしております。	いつごろれんらくがもらえますか？
Shōchi shima shita. Shōsaina jōhō o omachi shite orimasu.	Itsu koro renraku ga moraemasu ka?
Understood. I look forward to the detailed information.	When can I expect to hear from you?

Conversation example person A	Conversation example person B
プロジェクトの進捗状況を教えてください。	追って連絡します。情報をまとめてからご報告いたします。
ぷろじぇくとのしんちょくじょうきょうをおしえてください。	おってれんらくします。じょうほうをまとめてからごほうこくいたします。
Purojekuto no shinchoku jōkyō o oshiete kudasai.	Otte renraku shimasu. Jōhō o matomete kara go hōkoku itashimasu.
Please inform me about the project's progress.	I'll contact you later. I'll report after compiling the information.

Cultural Context

"Later" is vague and doesn't provide a specific timeframe for follow-up.

お手数をおかけして申し訳ありません。

おてすうをおかけしてもうしわけありません。
Otesū o okake shite mōshiwake arimasen.
I'm sorry for the trouble.

Variation 1	Variation 2
ご面倒をおかけして恐縮です。	Kyō mo shōjin shima shou.
ごめんどうをおかけしてきょうしゅくです。	ごめんどうをおかけしてきょうしゅくです。
Go mendō o okake shite kyōshukudesu.	Go meiwaku o okake shite mōshiwake go zaimasen.
Sorry for the trouble.	I apologize for the trouble.

Positive Response	Negative Response
気にしないでください。お互いの協力が大切です。	これは本来あなたの仕事です。
きにしないでください。おたがいのきょうりょくがたいせつです。	これはほんらいあなたのしごとです。
Ki ni shinaide kudasai. Otagai no kyōryoku ga taisetsudesu.	Kore wa honrai anata no shigotodesu.
Don't worry about it. Our cooperation is important.	This is actually your job.

Conversation example person A	Conversation example person B
お手数をおかけして申し訳ありません。この資料の修正をお願いできますか？	問題ありません。喜んで対応いたします。
おてすうをおかけしてもうしわけありません。このしりょうのしゅうせいをおねがいできますか？	もんだいありません。よろこんでたいおういたします。
Ote-sū o okake shite mōshiwake arimasen. Kono shiryō no shūsei o onegai dekimasu ka?	Mondai arimasen. Yorokonde taiō itashimasu.
I'm sorry for the trouble, but could you please revise this document?	No problem. I'd be happy to help.

Cultural Context
Politeness doesn't reduce the actual inconvenience caused.

至急確認お願いします。

しきゅうかくにんおねがいします。
Shikyū kakunin onegaishimasu.
Please check this urgently.

Variation 1	Variation 2
至急ご確認お願いします。	Kyō mo shōjin shima shou.
しきゅうごかくにんおねがいします。	しきゅうごかくにんおねがいします。
Shikyū go kakunin onegai shimasu.	Dai shikyū go kakunin kudasai.
Please check urgently.	Please confirm as soon as possible.

Positive Response	Negative Response
承知しました。最優先で確認いたします。	他の優先事項があります。
しょうちしました。さいゆうせんでかくにんいたします。	ほかのゆうせんじこうがあります。
Shōchi shima shita. Sai yūsen de kakunin itashimasu.	Hoka no yūsen jikō ga arimasu.
Understood. I'll check it with top priority.	I have other priorities.

Conversation example person A	Conversation example person B
至急確認お願いします。クライアントから重要な連絡が入りました。	承知しました。すぐに確認いたします。
しきゅうかくにんおねがいします。くらいあんとからじゅうようなれんらくがはいりました。	しょうちしました。すぐにかくにんいたします。
Shikyū kakunin onegai shimasu. Kuraianto kara jūyōna renraku ga hairimashita.	Shōchi shima shita. Sugu ni kakunin itashimasu.
Please check urgently. We've received an important message from the client.	Understood. I'll check it right away.

Cultural Context
"Urgent" is subjective and may create unnecessary stress.

対応完了しました。

たいおうかんりょうしました。

Taiō kanryō shimashita.

The task has been completed.

Variation 1	Variation 2
対応が終了しました。	Kyō mo shōjin shima shou.
たいおうがしゅうりょうしました。	たいおうがしゅうりょうしました。
Taiō ga shūryō shima shita.	Shori ga kanryō shima shita.
The response is completed.	The handling has been completed.

Positive Response	Negative Response
素晴らしいです。迅速な対応に感謝します。	品質をチェックする必要があります。
すばらしいです。じんそくなたいおうにかんしゃします。	ひんしつをちぇっくするひつようがあります。
Subarashīdesu. Jinsokuna taiō ni kansha shimasu.	Hinshitsu o chekku suru hitsuyō ga arimasu.
Great. Thank you for your quick action.	We need to check the quality.

Conversation example person A	Conversation example person B
対応完了しました。	ありがとうございます。スケジュール確認をお願いします。
たいおうかんりょうしました。	ありがとうございます。すけじゅーるかくにんをおねがいします。
Taiō kanryō shima shita.	Arigatōgozaimasu. Sukejūru kakunin o onegai shimasu.
The response has been completed.	Thank you. Please confirm the schedule.

Cultural Context

Doesn't necessarily mean the task was done to the expected standard.

スケジュール確認をお願いします。

すけじゅーるかくにんをおねがいします。
Sukejūru kakunin o onegaishimasu.
Please confirm the schedule.

Variation 1	**Variation 2**
日程確認をお願いします。	Kyō mo shōjin shima shou.
にっていかくにんをおねがいします。	にっていかくにんをおねがいします。
Nittei kakunin o onegai shimasu.	Sukejūru kakunin o onegai itashimasu.
Please confirm the schedule.	Please confirm the schedule.

Positive Response	**Negative Response**
承知しました。すぐに確認して返信します。	スケジュールの変更は困ります。
しょうちしました。すぐにかくにんしてへんしんします。	すけじゅーるのへんこうはこまります。
Shōchi shima shita. Sugu ni kakunin shite henshin shimasu.	Sukejūru no henkō wa komarimasu.
Understood. I'll check and reply promptly.	Schedule changes are inconvenient.

Conversation example person A	**Conversation example person B**
来月のイベントについて、スケジュール確認をお願いします。	はい、確認して明日中にお知らせします。
らいげつのいべんとについて、すけじゅーるかくにんをおねがいします。	はい、かくにんしてあしたちゅうにおしらせします。
Raigetsu no ibento ni tsuite, sukejūru kakunin o onegai shimasu.	Hai, kakunin shite ashita-chū ni oshirase shimasu.
Please confirm the schedule for next month's event.	Yes, I'll check and let you know by tomorrow.

Cultural Context
Doesn't specify which dates or times need to be checked.

連絡ありがとうございました。

れんらくありがとうございました。
Renraku arigatōgozaimashita.
Thank you for contacting me.

Variation 1	Variation 2
ご連絡ありがとうございました。	Kyō mo shōjin shima shou.
ごれんらくありがとうございました。	ごれんらくありがとうございました。
Go renraku arigatō go zaimashita.	Go ippō arigatō go zaimashita.
Thank you for contacting me.	Thank you for contacting me.

Positive Response	Negative Response
こちらこそ、常に情報共有してくださり感謝です。	もっと早く連絡すべきでした。
こちらこそ、つねにじょうほうきょうゆうしてくださりかんしゃです。	もっとはやくれんらくすべきでした。
Kochira koso, tsuneni jōhō kyōyū shite kudasari kanshadesu.	Motto hayaku renraku subekide shita.
Thank you for always sharing information.	You should have contacted me earlier.

Conversation example person A	Conversation example person B
連絡ありがとうございました。	こちらこそ。ミーティングの議事録を共有します。
れんらくありがとうございました。	こちらこそ。みーてぃんぐのぎじろくをきょうゆうします。
Renraku arigatō go zaimashita.	Kochira koso. Mītingu no giji-roku o kyōyū shimasu.
Thank you for contacting me.	You're welcome. I'll share the meeting minutes.

Cultural Context
Doesn't indicate if the communication was sufficient or helpful.

今後の方針を確認したいです。

こんごのほうしんをかくにんしたいです。

Kongo no hōshin o kakunin shitaidesu.

I'd like to confirm the future policy.

Variation 1	Variation 2
今後の進め方を確認したいです。	Kyō mo shōjin shima shou.
こんごのすすめかたをかくにんしたいです。	こんごのすすめかたをかくにんしたいです。
Kongo no susumekata o kakunin shitaidesu.	Kongo no hōshin o kakunin sa sete kudasai.
I would like to confirm the future plan.	I would like to confirm the future course of action.

Positive Response	Negative Response
素晴らしいです。一緒に方向性を確認しましょう。	方針はすでに決まっています。
すばらしいです。いっしょにほうこうせいをかくにんしましょう。	ほうしんはすでにきまっています。
Subarashīdesu. Issho ni hōkō-sei o kakunin shima shou.	Hōshin wa sudeni kimatte imasu.
Great. Let's confirm the direction together.	The policy has already been decided.

Conversation example person A	Conversation example person B
プロジェクトの進行状況を踏まえて、今後の方針を確認したいです。	了解しました。次回のミーティングで詳しく話し合いましょう。
ぷろじぇくとのしんこうじょうきょうをふまえて、こんごのほうしんをかくにんしたいです。	りょうかいしました。じかいのみーてぃんぐでくわしくはなしあいましょう。
Purojekuto no shinkō jōkyō o fumaete, kongo no hōshin o kakunin shitai desu.	Ryōkai shima shita. Jikai no mītingu de kuwashiku hanashiai ma shou.
Based on the project's progress, I'd like to confirm our future direction.	Understood. Let's discuss it in detail at the next meeting.

Cultural Context

Doesn't specify which aspects of future plans need clarification.

ミーティングの議事録を共有します。

みーてぃんぐのぎじろくをきょうゆうします。

Mītingu no gijiroku o kyōyū shimasu.

I'll share the meeting minutes.

Variation 1	Variation 2
会議の議事録を共有します。	Kyō mo shōjin shima shou.
かいぎのぎじろくをきょうゆうします。	かいぎのぎじろくをきょうゆうします。
Kaigi no giji-roku o kyōyū shimasu.	Kaigi no giji yōshi o kyōyū shimasu.
I will share the meeting minutes.	I will share the meeting minutes.

Positive Response	Negative Response
ありがとうございます。詳細な記録に感謝します。	議事録が不十分です。
ありがとうございます。しょうさいなきろくにかんしゃします。	ぎじろくがふじゅうぶんです。
Arigatōgozaimasu. Shōsaina kiroku ni kansha shimasu.	Giji-roku ga fu jūbundesu.
Thank you. I appreciate the detailed record.	The minutes are insufficient.

Conversation example person A	Conversation example person B
昨日のミーティングの議事録を共有します。ご確認ください。	ありがとうございます。確認させていただきます。
きのうのみーてぃんぐのぎじろくをきょうゆうします。ごかくにんください。	ありがとうございます。かくにんさせていただきます。
Kinō no mītingu no giji-roku o kyōyū shimasu. Go kakunin kudasai.	Arigatōgozaimasu. Kakunin sa sete itadakimasu.
I'm sharing the minutes from yesterday's meeting. Please review them.	Thank you. I'll review them.

Cultural Context

Doesn't ensure recipients will read or act on the information.

今週のタスクリストです。

こんしゅうのたすくりすとです。

Konshū no tasuku risutodesu.

Here's this week's task list.

Variation 1	Variation 2
今週の作業リストです。	Kyō mo shōjin shima shou.
こんしゅうのさぎょうりすとです。	こんしゅうのさぎょうりすとです。
Konshū no sagyō risutodesu.	Konshū no sagyō ichirandesu.
Here is this week's task list.	This is the task list for this week.

Positive Response	Negative Response
素晴らしいです。計画的に進められそうですね。	タスクが多すぎます。
すばらしいです。けいかくてきにすすめられそうですね。	たすくがおおすぎます。
Subarashīdesu. Keikaku-teki ni susume rare-sōdesu ne.	Tasuku ga ō sugimasu.
Great. We can proceed in a planned manner.	There are too many tasks.

Conversation example person A	Conversation example person B
今週のタスクリストです。	ありがとうございます。期限の延長は可能ですか？
こんしゅうのたすくりすとです。	ありがとうございます。きげんのえんちょうはかのうですか？
Konshū no tasuku risutodesu.	Arigatōgozaimasu. Kigen no enchō wa kanōdesu ka?
Here's this week's task list.	Thank you. Is it possible to extend the deadline?

Cultural Context

Doesn't indicate priorities or deadlines within the list.

期限の延長は可能ですか？

きげんのえんちょうはかのうですか？

Kigen no enchō wa kanōdesu ka?

Is it possible to extend the deadline?

Variation 1	Variation 2
締め切りの延長は可能ですか？	Kyō mo shōjin shima shou.
しめきりのえんちょうはかのうですか？	しめきりのえんちょうはかのうですか？
Shimekiri no enchō wa kanōdesu ka?	Kigen no enki wa kanōdeshou ka?
Is it possible to extend the deadline?	Is it possible to extend the deadline?

Positive Response	Negative Response
承知しました。状況を確認して検討いたします。	期限の延長は認められません。
しょうちしました。じょうきょうをかくにんしてけんとういたします。	きげんのえんちょうはみとめられません。
Shōchi shima shita. Jōkyō o kakunin shite kentō itashimasu.	Kigen no enchō wa mitome raremasen.
Understood. I'll check the situation and consider it.	Extension of the deadline is not allowed.

Conversation example person A	Conversation example person B
予想以上に作業に時間がかかっています。期限の延長は可能ですか？	状況を確認し、クライアントと相談してみます。
よそういじょうにさぎょうにじかんがかかっています。きげんのえんちょうはかのうですか？	じょうきょうをかくにんし、くらいあんととそうだんしてみます。
Yosō ijō ni sagyō ni jikan ga kakatte imasu. Kigen no enchō wa kanō desu ka?	Jōkyō o kakunin shi, kuraianto to sōdan shite mimasu.
The work is taking longer than expected. Is it possible to extend the deadline?	I'll check the situation and consult with the client.

Cultural Context

May be seen as poor planning if asked too close to the deadline.

資料の最新版をアップロードしました。

しりょうのさいしんばんをあっぷろーどしました。

Shiryō no saishinhan o appurōdo shimashita.

I've uploaded the latest version of the document.

Variation 1	Variation 2
資料の最新版をアップしました。	Kyō mo shōjin shima shou.
しりょうのさいしんばんをあっぷしました。	しりょうのさいしんばんをあっぷしました。
Shiryō no saishin-ban o appu shima shita.	Shiryō no saishin bājon o appurōdo shima shita.
I have uploaded the latest version of the document.	I have uploaded the latest version of the document.

Positive Response	Negative Response
ありがとうございます。最新情報の共有に感謝します。	変更点が分かりません。
ありがとうございます。さいしんじょうほうのきょうゆうにかんしゃします。	へんこうてんがわかりません。
Arigatōgozaimasu. Saishin jōhō no kyōyū ni kansha shimasu.	Henkō-ten ga wakarimasen.
Thank you. I appreciate sharing the latest information.	I can't see what's been changed.

Conversation example person A	Conversation example person B
資料の最新版をアップロードしました。	確認しました。今日の作業内容を報告します。
しりょうのさいしんばんをあっぷろーどしました。	かくにんしました。きょうのさぎょうないようをほうこくします。
Shiryō no saishin-ban o appurōdo shima shita.	Kakunin shima shita. Kyō no sagyō naiyō o hōkoku shimasu.
I've uploaded the latest version of the document.	Confirmed. I'll report today's work content.

Cultural Context

Doesn't specify what changes were made or if review is needed.

今日の作業内容を報告します。

きょうのさぎょうないようをほうこくします。

Kyō no sagyō naiyō o hōkoku shimasu.

I'm reporting today's work content.

Variation 1	Variation 2
本日の作業内容を報告します。	Kyō mo shōjin shima shou.
ほんじつのさぎょうないようをほうこくします。	ほんじつのさぎょうないようをほうこくします。
Honjitsu no sagyō naiyō o hōkoku shimasu.	Honjitsu no gyōmu naiyō o hōkoku itashimasu.
I will report today's work.	I will report today's work content.

Positive Response	Negative Response
素晴らしいです。詳細な報告に感謝します。	報告が不十分です。
すばらしいです。しょうさいなほうこくにかんしゃします。	ほうこくがふじゅうぶんです。
Subarashīdesu. Shōsaina hōkoku ni kansha shimasu.	Hōkoku ga fu jūbundesu.
Great. Thank you for the detailed report.	Your report is insufficient.

Conversation example person A	Conversation example person B
今日の作業内容を報告します。予定通り進んでいます。	ありがとうございます。引き続きよろしくお願いします。
きょうのさぎょうないようをほうこくします。よていどおりすすんでいます。	ありがとうございます。ひきつづきよろしくおねがいします。
Kyō no sagyō naiyō o hōkoku shimasu. Yotei-dōri susunde imasu.	Arigatōgozaimasu. Hikitsudzuki yoroshiku onegai shimasu.
I'm reporting today's work progress. We're on schedule.	Thank you. Please keep up the good work.

Cultural Context

Doesn't necessarily include analysis or implications of the work done.

プロジェクトの進捗状況です。

ぷろじぇくとのしんちょくじょうきょうです。

Purojekuto no shinchoku jōkyōdesu.

This is the project progress status.

Variation 1	Variation 2
プロジェクトの進行状況です。	Kyō mo shōjin shima shou.
ぷろじぇくとのしんこうじょうきょうです。	ぷろじぇくとのしんこうじょうきょうです。
Purojekuto no shinkō jōkyōdesu.	Purojekuto no genjō hōkokudesu.
Here is the project progress status.	Here is an update on the project's progress.

Positive Response	Negative Response
ありがとうございます。順調に進んでいますね。	進捗が遅れています。
ありがとうございます。じゅんちょうにすすんでいますね。	しんちょくがおくれています。
Arigatōgozaimasu. Junchō ni susunde ima su ne.	Shinchoku ga okurete imasu.
Thank you. It's progressing smoothly.	The progress is behind schedule.

Conversation example person A	Conversation example person B
プロジェクトの進捗状況です。	了解しました。フィードバックありがとうございます。
ぷろじぇくとのしんちょくじょうきょうです。	りょうかいしました。ふぃーどばっくありがとうございます。
Purojekuto no shinchoku jōkyōdesu.	Ryōkai shima shita. Fīdobakku arigatōgozaimasu.
Here's the project progress status.	Understood. Thank you for the feedback.

Cultural Context

May not include detailed analysis or potential roadblocks.

フィードバックありがとうございます。

ふぃーどばっくありがとうございます。

Fīdobakku arigatōgozaimasu.

Thank you for your feedback.

Variation 1	Variation 2
ご意見ありがとうございます。	Kyō mo shōjin shima shou.
ごいけんありがとうございます。	ごいけんありがとうございます。
Go iken arigatōgozaimasu.	Go kansō arigatōgozaimasu.
Thank you for your feedback.	Thank you for your opinion.

Positive Response	Negative Response
こちらこそ、建設的な意見に感謝します。	フィードバックが不十分です。
こちらこそ、けんせつてきないけんにかんしゃします。	ふぃーどばっくがふじゅうぶんです。
Kochira koso, kensetsu-tekina iken ni kansha shimasu.	Fīdobakku ga fu jūbundesu.
Thank you for your constructive feedback.	Your feedback is insufficient.

Conversation example person A	Conversation example person B
先日の提案書へのコメント、フィードバックありがとうございます。	どういたしまして。今後の改善に活かしてください。
せんじつのていあんしょへのこめんと、ふぃーどばっくありがとうございます。	どういたしまして。こんごのかいぜんにいかしてください。
Senjitsu no teian-sho e no komento, fīdobakku arigatō gozaimasu.	Dōitashimashite. Kongo no kaizen ni ikashite kudasai.
Thank you for your feedback on the proposal I submitted the other day.	You're welcome. Please use it for future improvements.

Cultural Context

Doesn't indicate how the feedback will be used or implemented.

明日の予定を確認させてください。

あすのよていをかくにんさせてください。
Ashita no yotei o kakunin sa sete kudasai.
Let me confirm tomorrow's schedule.

Variation 1	Variation 2
明日の予定を確認します。	Kyō mo shōjin shima shou.
あしたのよていをかくにんします。	あしたのよていをかくにんします。
Ashita no yotei o kakunin shimasu.	Ashita no sukejūru o kakunin shimasu.
Let me confirm tomorrow's schedule.	I will confirm tomorrow's schedule.

Positive Response	Negative Response
もちろんです。スケジュールを共有しましょう。	明日のスケジュールは変更できません。
もちろんです。すけじゅーるをきょうゆうしましょう。	あしたのすけじゅーるはへんこうできません。
Mochirondesu. Sukejūru o kyōyū shima shou.	Ashita no sukejūru wa henkō dekimasen.
Of course. Let's share the schedule.	Tomorrow's schedule can't be changed.

Conversation example person A	Conversation example person B
明日の予定を確認させてください。	はい、今週の目標を達成しました。
あしたのよていをかくにんさせてください。	はい、こんしゅうのもくひょうをたっせいしました。
Ashita no yotei o kakunin sa sete kudasai.	Hai, konshū no mokuhyō o tassei shima shita.
Let me confirm tomorrow's schedule.	Yes, we've achieved this week's goals.

Cultural Context
May be seen as last-minute if important meetings are involved.

今週の目標を達成しました。

こんしゅうのもくひょうをたっせいしました。
Konshū no mokuhyō o tassei shimashita.
I've achieved this week's goal.

Variation 1	Variation 2
今週設定した目標は全て達成することができました。	Kyō mo shōjin shima shou.
こんしゅうせっていしたもくひょうはすべてたっせいすることができました。	こんしゅうせっていしたもくひょうはすべてたっせいすることができました。
Konshū settei shita mokuhyō wa subete tassei suru koto ga dekimashita.	Konshū tateta mokuhyō wa subete tassei dekimashita.
I successfully completed all the goals set for this week.	I was able to achieve all the goals set for this week.

Positive Response	Negative Response
おめでとうございます！素晴らしい成果ですね。	目標が低すぎます。
おめでとうございます！すばらしいせいかですね。	もくひょうがひくすぎます。
Omedetōgozaimasu! Subarashī seikadesu ne.	Mokuhyō ga hiku sugimasu.
Congratulations! That's a great achievement.	The goal was set too low.

Conversation example person A	Conversation example person B
今週の目標を達成しました。次週の目標設定について相談したいです。	おめでとうございます。次週の目標設定を一緒に行いましょう。
こんしゅうのもくひょうをたっせいしました。じしゅうのもくひょうせっていについてそうだんしたいです。	おめでとうございます。じしゅうのもくひょうせっていをいっしょにおこないましょう。
Konshū no mokuhyō o tassei shimashita. Jishū no mokuhyō settei ni tsuite sōdan shitai desu.	Omedetōgozaimasu. Jishū no mokuhyō settei o issho ni gyō ima shou.
We've achieved this week's goal. I'd like to discuss setting goals for next week.	Congratulations. Let's set next week's goals together.

Cultural Context
Doesn't necessarily mean the quality of work met expectations.

緊急の連絡事項があります。

きんきゅうのれんらくじこうがあります。

Kinkyū no renraku jikō ga arimasu.

There's an urgent matter to communicate.

Variation 1	Variation 2
緊急の連絡があります。	Kyō mo shōjin shima shou.
きんきゅうのれんらくがあります。	きんきゅうのれんらくがあります。
Kinkyū no renraku ga arimasu.	Shikyū no go renraku ga arimasu.
I have an urgent message.	There is an urgent message.

Positive Response	Negative Response
承知しました。すぐに対応いたします。	今は対応できません。
しょうちしました。すぐにたいおういたします。	いまはたいおうできません。
Shōchi shima shita. Sugu ni taiō itashimasu.	Ima wa taiō dekimasen.
Understood. I'll respond immediately.	I can't deal with it now.

Conversation example person A	Conversation example person B
緊急の連絡事項があります。	承知しました。タスクの優先順位を確認したいです。
きんきゅうのれんらくじこうがあります。	しょうちしました。たすくのゆうせんじゅんいをかくにんしたいです。
Kinkyū no renraku jikō ga arimasu.	Shōchi shima shita. Tasuku no yūsen jun'i o kakunin shitaidesu.
There's an urgent matter to communicate.	Understood. I'd like to confirm the task priorities.

Cultural Context

"Urgent" is subjective and may cause unnecessary alarm.

タスクの優先順位を確認したいです。

たすくのゆうせんじゅんいをかくにんしたいです。
Tasuku no yūsen jun'i o kakunin shitaidesu.
I'd like to confirm the task priorities.

Variation 1	Variation 2
作業の優先順位を確認したいです。	Kyō mo shōjin shima shou.
さぎょうのゆうせんじゅんいをかくにんしたいです。	さぎょうのゆうせんじゅんいをかくにんしたいです。
Sagyō no yūsen jun'i o kakunin shitaidesu.	Tasuku no yūsen-do o kakunin sa sete kudasai.
I would like to confirm the task priority.	I would like to confirm the task priorities.

Positive Response	Negative Response
良い提案です。一緒に優先順位を決めましょう。	優先順位は既に決まっています。
よいていあんです。いっしょにゆうせんじゅんいをきめましょう。	ゆうせんじゅんいはすでにきまっています。
Yoi teiandesu. Issho ni yūsen jun'i o kime ma shou.	Yūsen jun'i wa sudeni kimatte imasu.
Good suggestion. Let's decide the priorities together.	The priorities have already been set.

Conversation example person A	Conversation example person B
複数のプロジェクトが同時進行中です。タスクの優先順位を確認したいです。	了解しました。明日のミーティングで詳しく話し合いましょう。
ふくすうのぷろじぇくとがどうじしんこうちゅうです。たすくのゆうせんじゅんいをかくにんしたいです。	りょうかいしました。あしたのみーてぃんぐでくわしくはなしあいましょう。
Fukusū no purojekuto ga dōji shinkō-chūdesu. Tasuku no yūsen jun'i o kakunin shitai desu.	Ryōkai shima shita. Ashita no mītingu de kuwashiku hanashiai ma shou.
Multiple projects are running simultaneously. I'd like to confirm the task priorities.	Understood. Let's discuss it in detail at tomorrow's meeting.

Cultural Context
Might imply lack of clarity in original task assignment.

新しいプロジェクトの概要です。

あたらしいぷろじぇくとのがいようです。

Atarashī purojekuto no gaiyōdesu.

This is an overview of the new project.

Variation 1	Variation 2
新規プロジェクトの概要です。	Kyō mo shōjin shima shou.
しんきぷろじぇくとのがいようです。	しんきぷろじぇくとのがいようです。
Shinki purojekuto no gaiyōdesu.	Shin purojekuto no gaiyōdesu.
Here is an overview of the new project.	This is an overview of the new project.

Positive Response	Negative Response
興味深いですね。詳細を教えてください。	今は新しいプロジェクトを始める余裕がありません。
きょうみぶかいですね。しょうさいをおしえてください。	いまはあたらしいぷろじぇくとをはじめるよゆうがありません。
Kyōmibukaidesu ne. Shōsai o oshiete kudasai.	Ima wa atarashī purojekuto o hajimeru yoyū ga arimasen.
That's interesting. Please tell me more details.	We don't have capacity to start a new project now.

Conversation example person A	Conversation example person B
新しいプロジェクトの概要です。	了解です。チームミーティングの日程調整をお願いします。
あたらしいぷろじぇくとのがいようです。	りょうかいです。ちーむみーてぃんぐのにっていちょうせいをおねがいします。
Atarashī purojekuto no gaiyōdesu.	Ryōkaidesu. Chīmu mītingu no nittei chōsei o onegai shimasu.
Here's an overview of the new project.	Got it. Please arrange the team meeting schedule.

Cultural Context

Doesn't guarantee all necessary details are included.

チームミーティングの日程調整をお願いします。

ちーむみーてぃんぐのにっていちょうせいをおねがいします。

Chīmumītingu no nittei chōsei o onegaishimasu.

Please arrange the team meeting schedule.

Variation 1	Variation 2
チーム会議の日程調整をお願いします。	Kyō mo shōjin shima shou.
ちーむかいぎのにっていちょうせいをおねがいします。	ちーむかいぎのにっていちょうせいをおねがいします。
Chīmu kaigi no nittei chōsei o onegai shimasu.	Chīmu mītingu no sukejūru chōsei o onegai itashimasu.
Please arrange the team meeting schedule.	Please arrange the team meeting schedule.

Positive Response	Negative Response
承知しました。皆の予定を確認して調整します。	スケジュールが合いません。
しょうちしました。みなのよていをかくにんしてちょうせいします。	すけじゅーるがあいません。
Shōchi shima shita. Mina no yotei o kakunin shite chōsei shimasu.	Sukejūru ga aimasen.
Understood. I'll check everyone's schedule and coordinate.	Our schedules don't match.

Conversation example person A	Conversation example person B
来月のチームミーティングの日程調整をお願いします。	承知しました。皆さんの予定を確認して、最適な日程を提案します。
らいげつのちーむみーてぃんぐのにっていちょうせいをおねがいします。	しょうちしました。みなさんのよていをかくにんして、さいてきなにっていをていあんします。
Raigetsu no chīmu mītingu no nittei chōsei o onegai shimasu.	Shōchi shima shita. Minasan no yotei o kakunin shite, saitekina nittei o teian shimasu.
Please coordinate the schedule for next month's team meeting.	Understood. I'll check everyone's schedule and propose the best date.

Cultural Context

Doesn't provide preferred dates or times, potentially prolonging the process.

今月の目標達成状況です。

こんげつのもくひょうたっせいじょうきょうです。

Kongetsu no mokuhyō tassei jōkyōdesu.

This is the status of this month's goal achievement.

Variation 1	Variation 2
今月の目標に対する進捗状況をご報告いたします。	Kyō mo shōjin shima shou.
こんげつのもくひょうにたいするしんちょくじょうきょうをごほうこくいたします。	こんげつのもくひょうにたいするしんちょくじょうきょうをごほうこくいたします。
Kongetsu no mokuhyō ni taisuru shinchoku jōkyō o go hōkoku itashimasu.	Kongetsu no mokuhyō ni taisuru shinchoku jōkyō o hōkoku shimasu.
I would like to report on the progress made towards this month's goals.	I will report on the progress against this month's goals.

Positive Response	Negative Response
ありがとうございます。順調に進んでいますね。	目標達成率が低すぎます。
ありがとうございます。じゅんちょうにすすんでいますね。	もくひょうたっせいりつがひくすぎます。
Arigatōgozaimasu. Junchō ni susunde ima su ne.	Mokuhyō tassei-ritsu ga hiku sugimasu.
Thank you. It's progressing well.	The goal achievement rate is too low.

Conversation example person A	Conversation example person B
今月の目標達成状況です。	確認しました。クライアントからのフィードバックです。
こんげつのもくひょうたっせいじょうきょうです。	かくにんしました。くらいあんとからのふぃーどばっくです。
Kongetsu no mokuhyō tassei jōkyōdesu.	Kakunin shima shita. Kuraianto kara no fīdobakkudesu.
Here's this month's goal achievement status.	Confirmed. Here's feedback from the client.

Cultural Context

May not include analysis of why goals were or weren't met.

クライアントからのフィードバックです。

くらいあんとからのふぃーどばっくです。

Kuraianto kara no fīdobakkudesu.

This is feedback from the client.

Variation 1	Variation 2
顧客からのご意見です。	Kyō mo shōjin shima shou.
こきゃくからのごいけんです。	こきゃくからのごいけんです。
Kokyaku kara no go ikendesu.	Okyakusama kara no go kansōdesu.
Here is the feedback from the client.	This is feedback from the customer.

Positive Response	Negative Response
貴重な情報をありがとうございます。改善に活かしましょう。	ネガティブなフィードバックばかりですね。
きちょうなじょうほうをありがとうございます。かいぜんにいかしましょう。	ねがてぃぶなふぃーどばっくばかりですね。
Kichōna jōhō o arigatōgozaimasu. Kaizen ni ikashi ma shou.	Negatibuna fīdobakku bakaridesu ne.
Thank you for the valuable information. Let's use it for improvement.	It's all negative feedback.

Conversation example person A	Conversation example person B
先日のプレゼンテーションについて、クライアントからのフィードバックです。	ありがとうございます。チーム全体で共有し、改善点を検討します。
せんじつのぷれぜんてーしょんについて、くらいあんとからのふぃーどばっくです。	ありがとうございます。ちーむぜんたいできょうゆうし、かいぜんてんをけんとうします。
Senjitsu no purezentēshon ni tsuite, kuraianto kara no fīdobakku desu.	Arigatōgozaimasu. Chīmu zentai de kyōyū shi, kaizen-ten o kentō shimasu.
Here's the client's feedback on our recent presentation.	Thank you. We'll share it with the entire team and consider areas for improvement.

Cultural Context

Doesn't specify if the feedback is positive or negative.

リソース配分の提案があります。

りそーすはいぶんのていあんがあります。

Risōsu haibun no teian ga arimasu.

I have a proposal for resource allocation.

Variation 1	Variation 2
人員配置の案があります。	Kyō mo shōjin shima shou.
じんいんはいちのあんがあります。	じんいんはいちのあんがあります。
Jin'in haichi no an ga arimasu.	Yōin haichi no teian ga arimasu.
I have a proposal for resource allocation.	I have a proposal for personnel allocation.

Positive Response	Negative Response
素晴らしいです。効率的な運用につながりそうですね。	現在のリソース配分を変更する余裕はありません。
すばらしいです。こうりつてきなうんようにつながりそうですね。	げんざいのりそーすはいぶんをへんこうするよゆうはありません。
Subarashīdesu. Kōritsu-tekina un'yō ni tsunagari-sōdesu ne.	Genzai no risōsu haibun o henkō suru yoyū wa arimasen.
Great. It seems it will lead to efficient operation.	We can't afford to change the current resource allocation.

Conversation example person A	Conversation example person B
リソース配分の提案があります。	興味深いです。今週のハイライトをまとめました。
りそーすはいぶんのていあんがあります。	きょうみぶかいです。こんしゅうのはいらいとをまとめました。
Risōsu haibun no teian ga arimasu.	Kyōmibukaidesu. Konshū no hai raito o matomemashita.
I have a proposal for resource allocation.	Interesting. I've summarized this week's highlights.

Cultural Context

Doesn't indicate the urgency or impact of the proposed changes.

今週のハイライトをまとめました。

こんしゅうのはいらいとをまとめました。
Konshū no hairaito o matomemashita.
I've summarized this week's highlights.

Variation 1	Variation 2
今週の注目点を要約しました。	Kyō mo shōjin shima shou.
こんしゅうのちゅうもくてんをようやくしました。	こんしゅうのちゅうもくてんをようやくしました。
Konshū no chūmoku-ten o yōyaku shima shita.	Konshū no chūmoku pointo o yōyaku shima shita.
I have summarized this week's highlights.	I have summarized this week's highlights.

Positive Response	Negative Response
ありがとうございます。重要ポイントが明確ですね。	重要な点が抜けています。
ありがとうございます。じゅうようぽいんとがめいかくですね。	じゅうようなてんがぬけています。
Arigatōgozaimasu. Jūyō pointo ga meikakudesu ne.	Jūyōna ten ga nukete imasu.
Thank you. The key points are clear.	You've missed important points.

Conversation example person A	Conversation example person B
今週のハイライトをまとめました。ご確認ください。	ありがとうございます。早速確認させていただきます。
こんしゅうのはいらいとをまとめました。ごかくにんください。	ありがとうございます。さっそくかくにんさせていただきます。
Konshū no hairaito o matomemashita. Go kakunin kudasai.	Arigatōgozaimasu. Sassoku kakunin sa sete itadakimasu.
I've summarized this week's highlights. Please review.	Thank you. I'll review it right away.

Cultural Context
May not include critical issues or challenges faced.

プレゼン資料のレビューをお願いします。

ぷれぜんしりょうのれびゅーをおねがいします。

Purezen shiryō no rebyū o onegaishimasu.

Please review the presentation materials.

Variation 1	Variation 2
発表資料の確認をお願いします。	Kyō mo shōjin shima shou.
はっぴょうしりょうのかくにんをおねがいします。	はっぴょうしりょうのかくにんをおねがいします。
Happyō shiryō no kakunin o onegai shimasu.	Purezen shiryō no kakunin o onegai itashimasu.
Please review the presentation materials.	Please review the presentation materials.

Positive Response	Negative Response
承知しました。丁寧にレビューさせていただきます。	レビューする時間がありません。
しょうちしました。ていねいにれびゅーさせていただきます。	れびゅーするじかんがありません。
Shōchi shima shita. Teinei ni rebyū sa sete itadakimasu.	Rebyū suru jikan ga arimasen.
Understood. I'll review it carefully.	I don't have time to review.

Conversation example person A	Conversation example person B
プレゼン資料のレビューをお願いします。	承知しました。新しいツールの導入について相談があります。
ぷれぜんしりょうのれびゅーをおねがいします。	しょうちしました。あたらしいつーるのどうにゅうについてそうだんがあります。
Purezen shiryō no rebyū o onegai shimasu.	Shōchi shima shita. Atarashī tsūru no dōnyū ni tsuite sōdan ga arimasu.
Please review the presentation materials.	Understood. I have a question about introducing a new tool.

Cultural Context

Doesn't specify what aspects need review or by when.

新しいツールの導入について相談があります。

あたらしいつールのどうにゅうについてそうだんがあります。

Atarashī tsūru no dōnyū ni tsuite sōdan ga arimasu.

I'd like to consult about introducing a new tool.

Variation 1	Variation 2
新規ソフトウェアの採用について相談があります。	Kyō mo shōjin shima shou.
しんきそふとうぇあのさいようについてそうだんがあります。	しんきそふとうぇあのさいようについてそうだんがあります。
Shinki sofutō~ea no saiyō ni tsuite sōdan ga arimasu.	Atarashī sofutō~ea no dōnyū ni tsuite go sōdan ga arimasu.
I need to discuss the introduction of a new tool.	I have a question regarding the adoption of new software.

Positive Response	Negative Response
興味深いですね。詳しく聞かせてください。	今は新しいツールを検討する余裕がありません。
きょうみぶかいですね。くわしくきかせてください。	いまはあたらしいつールをけんとうするよゆうがありません。
Kyōmibukaidesu ne. Kuwashiku kika sete kudasai.	Ima wa atarashī tsūru o kentō suru yoyū ga arimasen.
That's interesting. Please tell me more about it.	We can't consider new tools right now.

Conversation example person A	Conversation example person B
業務効率化のため、新しいツールの導入について相談があります。	興味深いですね。詳細を教えていただけますか？
ぎょうむこうりつかのため、あたらしいつールのどうにゅうについてそうだんがあります。	きょうみぶかいですね。しょうさいをおしえていただけますか？
Gyōmu kōritsu-ka no tame, atarashī tsūru no dōnyū ni tsuite sōdan ga arimasu.	Kyōmibukaidesu ne. Shōsai o oshiete itadakemasu ka?
I'd like to discuss introducing a new tool to improve work efficiency.	That sounds interesting. Could you provide more details?

Cultural Context

Doesn't indicate the potential impact or urgency of the tool adoption.

今月の予算使用状況です。

こんげつのよさんしようじょうきょうです。

Kongetsu no yosan shiyō jōkyōdesu.

This is the status of this month's budget usage.

Variation 1	Variation 2
今月の経費使用状況です。	Kyō mo shōjin shima shou.
こんげつのけいひしようじょうきょうです。	こんげつのけいひしようじょうきょうです。
Kongetsu no keihi shiyō jōkyōdesu.	Kongetsu no keihi shiyō jissekidesu.
Here is the budget usage status for this month.	This is the expense usage status for this month.

Positive Response	Negative Response
ありがとうございます。適切に管理されていますね。	予算オーバーしています。
ありがとうございます。てきせつにかんりされていますね。	よさんおーばーしています。
Arigatōgozaimasu. Tekisetsu ni kanri sa rete imasu ne.	Yosan ōbā shite imasu.
Thank you. It seems to be managed appropriately.	We're over budget.

Conversation example person A	Conversation example person B
今月の予算使用状況です。	了解です。チーム全体での情報共有をお願いします。
こんげつのよさんしようじょうきょうです。	りょうかいです。ちーむぜんたいでのじょうほうきょうゆうをおねがいします。
Kongetsu no yosan shiyō jōkyōdesu.	Ryōkaidesu. Chīmu zentai de no jōhō kyōyū o onegai shimasu.
Here's this month's budget usage status.	Got it. Please share the information with the entire team.

Cultural Context

May not include analysis or recommendations for budget management.

チーム全体での情報共有をお願いします。

ちーむぜんたいでのじょうほうきょうゆうをおねがいします。

Chīmu zentai de no jōhō kyōyū o onegaishimasu.

Please share this information with the entire team.

Variation 1	Variation 2
部署全体での情報共有をお願いします。	Kyō mo shōjin shima shou.
ぶしょぜんたいでのじょうほうきょうゆうをおねがいします。	ぶしょぜんたいでのじょうほうきょうゆうをおねがいします。
Busho zentai de no jōhō kyōyū o onegai shimasu.	Bumon zentai de no jōhō kyōyū o onegai itashimasu.
Please share the information with the entire team.	Please share the information with the entire department.

Positive Response	Negative Response
承知しました。透明性の高い運営に努めます。	情報共有の方法を改善する必要があります。
しょうちしました。とうめいせいのたかいうんえいにつとめます。	じょうほうきょうゆうのほうほうをかいぜんするひつようがあります。
Shōchi shima shita. Tōmei-sei no takai un'ei ni tsutomemasu.	Jōhō kyōyū no hōhō o kaizen suru hitsuyō ga arimasu.
Understood. We'll strive for transparent operations.	We need to improve our information sharing method.

Conversation example person A	Conversation example person B
この重要な更新について、チーム全体での情報共有をお願いします。	承知しました。全員にメールで通知し、次回のミーティングでも取り上げます。
このじゅうようなこうしんについて、ちーむぜんたいでのじょうほうきょうゆうをおねがいします。	しょうちしました。ぜんいんにめーるでつうちし、じかいのみーてぃんぐでもとりあげます。
Kono jūyōna kōshin ni tsuite, chīmu zentai de no jōhō kyōyū o onegai shimasu.	Shōchi shima shita. Zen'in ni mēru de tsūchi shi, jikai no mītingu demo toriagemasu.
Please share this important update with the entire team.	Understood. I'll notify everyone by email and address it in the next meeting.

Cultural Context

Doesn't specify what information needs to be shared or how.

顧客からの問い合わせ対応をお願いします。

こきゃくからのといあわせたいおうをおねがいします。
Kokyaku kara no toiawase taiō o onegaishimasu.
Please handle the customer inquiry.

Variation 1	Variation 2
クライアントからの質問対応をお願いします。	Kyō mo shōjin shima shou.
くらいあんとからのしつもんたいおうをおねがいします。	くらいあんとからのしつもんたいおうをおねがいします。
Kuraianto kara no shitsumon taiō o onegai shimasu.	Torihiki-saki kara no toiawase taiō o onegai itashimasu.
Please handle the customer inquiries.	Please handle the inquiries from the client.

Positive Response	Negative Response
承知しました。迅速かつ丁寧に対応いたします。	それは本来あなたの担当です。
しょうちしました。じんそくかつていねいにたいおういたします。	それはほんらいあなたのたんとうです。
Shōchi shima shita. Jinsoku katsu teinei ni taiō itashimasu.	Sore wa honrai anata no tantōdesu.
Understood. I'll respond promptly and courteously.	That's originally your responsibility.

Conversation example person A	Conversation example person B
顧客からの問い合わせ対応をお願いします。	承知しました。新入社員の研修スケジュールです。
こきゃくからのといあわせたいおうをおねがいします。	しょうちしました。しんにゅうしゃいんのけんしゅうすけじゅーるです。
Kokyaku kara no toiawase taiō o onegai shimasu.	Shōchi shima shita. Shin'nyū shain no kenshū sukejūrudesu.
Please handle the customer inquiry.	Understood. Here's the training schedule for new employees.

Cultural Context
Doesn't provide context or urgency of the customer inquiry.

新入社員の研修スケジュールです。

しんにゅうしゃいんのけんしゅうすけじゅーるです。

Shin'nyū shain no kenshū sukejūrudesu.

This is the training schedule for new employees.

Variation 1	Variation 2
新人社員の教育スケジュールです。	Kyō mo shōjin shima shou.
しんじんしゃいんのきょういくすけじゅーるです。	しんじんしゃいんのきょういくすけじゅーるです。
Shinjin shain no kyōiku sukejūrudesu.	Shin'nyū shain no kenshū yotei-hyōdesu.
Here is the training schedule for new employees.	This is the training schedule for new employees.

Positive Response	Negative Response
ありがとうございます。充実したプログラムですね。	研修内容が不十分です。
ありがとうございます。じゅうじつしたぷろぐらむですね。	けんしゅうないようがふじゅうぶんです。
Arigatōgozaimasu. Jūjitsu shita puroguramudesu ne.	Kenshū naiyō ga fu jūbundesu.
Thank you. It's a comprehensive program.	The training content is insufficient.

Conversation example person A	Conversation example person B
来月からの新入社員の研修スケジュールです。ご確認ください。	ありがとうございます。確認して、必要があれば調整します。
らいげつからのしんにゅうしゃいんのけんしゅうすけじゅーるです。ごかくにんください。	ありがとうございます。かくにんして、ひつようがあればちょうせいします。
Raigetsu kara no shin'nyū shain no kenshū sukejūru desu. Go kakunin kudasai.	Arigatōgozaimasu. Kakunin shite, hitsuyō ga areba chōsei shimasu.
Here's the training schedule for new employees starting next month. Please review.	Thank you. I'll review it and make adjustments if necessary.

Cultural Context

Doesn't indicate if input or changes are needed.

今週の KPI レポートです。

こんしゅうのけーぴーあいれぽーとです。
Konshū no KPI repōtodesu.
This is this week's KPI report.

Variation 1	Variation 2
今週の業績指標報告です。	Kyō mo shōjin shima shou.
こんしゅうのぎょうせきしひょうほうこくです。	こんしゅうのぎょうせきしひょうほうこくです。
Konshū no gyōseki shihyō hōkokudesu.	Konshū no gyōseki shisū hōkokudesu.
Here is this week's KPI report.	This is the performance index report for this week.

Positive Response	Negative Response
ありがとうございます。目標に向けて順調ですね。	KPI が目標に達していません。
ありがとうございます。もくひょうにむけてじゅんちょうですね。	けーぴーあいがもくひょうにたっしていません。
Arigatōgozaimasu. Mokuhyō ni mukete junchōdesu ne.	KPI ga mokuhyō ni tasshite imasen.
Thank you. We're progressing well towards our goals.	The KPIs are not meeting the targets.

Conversation example person A	Conversation example person B
今週の KPI レポートです。	確認しました。プロジェクトのリスク分析をしました。
こんしゅうのけーぴーあいれぽーとです。	かくにんしました。ぷろじぇくとのりすくぶんせきをしました。
Konshū no kē pīai repōtodesu.	Kakunin shima shita. Purojekuto no risuku bunseki o shima shita.
Here's this week's KPI report.	Confirmed. I've conducted a risk analysis for the project.

Cultural Context
May not include analysis or action items based on the KPIs.

プロジェクトのリスク分析をしました。

ぷろじぇくとのりすくぶんせきをしました。
Purojekuto no risuku bunseki o shimashita.
I've done a risk analysis for the project.

Variation 1	Variation 2
案件のリスク評価をしました。	Kyō mo shōjin shima shou.
あんけんのりすくひょうかをしました。	あんけんのりすくひょうかをしました。
Anken no risuku hyōka o shima shita.	Anken no risuku bunseki o shima shita.
I have conducted a risk analysis for the project.	I have conducted a risk assessment for the case.

Positive Response	Negative Response
素晴らしいです。事前対策に活かしましょう。	リスク対策が不十分です。
すばらしいです。じぜんたいさくにいかしましょう。	りすくたいさくがふじゅうぶんです。
Subarashīdesu. Jizen taisaku ni ikashi ma shou.	Risuku taisaku ga fu jūbundesu.
Great. Let's use it for preventive measures.	The risk countermeasures are insufficient.

Conversation example person A	Conversation example person B
プロジェクトのリスク分析をしました。結果をご確認ください。	ありがとうございます。早急に確認し、対策を検討します。
ぷろじぇくとのりすくぶんせきをしました。けっかをごかくにんください。	ありがとうございます。そうきゅうにかくにんし、たいさくをけんとうします。
Purojekuto no risuku bunseki o shimashita. Kekka o go kakunin kudasai.	Arigatōgozaimasu. Sakkyū ni kakunin shi, taisaku o kentō shimasu.
I've completed the project risk analysis. Please review the results.	Thank you. I'll review it promptly and consider countermeasures.

Cultural Context

Doesn't specify if immediate action is needed based on the analysis.

新規提案のブレインストーミングをしましょう。

しんきていあんのぶれいんすとーみんぐをしましょう。

Shinki teian no bureinsutōmingu o shimashou.

Let's brainstorm for new proposals.

Variation 1	Variation 2
新企画のアイデア出しをしましょう。	Kyō mo shōjin shima shou.
しんきかくのあいでぃあだしをしましょう。	しんきかくのあいでぃあだしをしましょう。
Shin kikaku no aidea-dashi o shima shou.	Shin kikaku no hassō o dashiai ma shou.
Let's brainstorm for new proposals.	Let's brainstorm ideas for the new project.

Positive Response	Negative Response
良いアイデアです。創造的な議論を楽しみにしています。	今はブレインストーミングをする時間がありません。
よいあいであです。そうぞうてきなぎろんをたのしみにしています。	いまはぶれいんすとーみんぐをするじかんがありません。
Yoi aideadesu. Sōzō-tekina giron o tanoshimi ni shite imasu.	Ima wa burein sutōmingu o suru jikan ga arimasen.
Good idea. I'm looking forward to creative discussions.	We don't have time for brainstorming now.

Conversation example person A	Conversation example person B
新規提案のブレインストーミングをしましょう。	良いアイデアです。今月の売上レポートです。
しんきていあんのぶれいんすとーみんぐをしましょう。	よいあいであです。こんげつのうりあげれぽーとです。
Shinki teian no burein sutōmingu o shima shou.	Yoi aideadesu. Kongetsu no uriage repōtodesu.
Let's brainstorm for new proposals.	Good idea. Here's this month's sales report.

Cultural Context

Doesn't provide context or preparation materials for the session.

今月の売上レポートです。

こんげつのうりあげれぽーとです。
Kongetsu no uriage repōtodesu.
This is this month's sales report.

Variation 1	Variation 2
今月の売上高報告です。	Kyō mo shōjin shima shou.
こんげつのうりあげだかほうこくです。	こんげつのうりあげだかほうこくです。
Kongetsu no uriage-kō hōkokudesu.	Kongetsu no uriage jisseki hōkokudesu.
Here is this month's sales report.	This is the sales report for this month.

Positive Response	Negative Response
ありがとうございます。好調な結果ですね。	売上が目標に達していません。
ありがとうございます。こうちょうなけっかですね。	うりあげがもくひょうにたっしていません。
Arigatōgozaimasu. Kōchōna kekkadesu ne.	Uriage ga mokuhyō ni tasshite imasen.
Thank you. It's a favorable result.	Sales are not meeting the target.

Conversation example person A	Conversation example person B
今月の売上レポートです。前月比 10%増となっています。	素晴らしい結果ですね。詳細を確認させていただきます。
こんげつのうりあげれぽーとです。ぜんげつひ 10%ぞうとなっています。	すばらしいけっかですね。しょうさいをかくにんさせていただきます。
Kongetsu no uriage repōtodesu. Zengetsu-hi juppāsento-zō to natte imasu.	Subarashī kekkadesu ne. Shōsai o kakunin sa sete itadakimasu.
Here's this month's sales report. We're up 10% compared to last month.	That's great news. I'll review the details.

Cultural Context

May not include analysis or comparison to targets/previous periods.

チーム内での役割分担を確認します。

ちーむないでのやくわりぶんたんをかくにんします。
Chīmu-nai de no yakuwari buntan o kakunin shimasu.
I'll confirm the role distribution within the team.

Variation 1	Variation 2
グループ内での担当割り振りを確認します。	Kyō mo shōjin shima shou.
ぐるーぷないでのたんとうわりふりをかくにんします。	ぐるーぷないでのたんとうわりふりをかくにんします。
Gurūpu-nai de no tantō warifuri o kakunin shimasu.	Chīmu-nai de no tantō wariate o kakunin shimasu.
I will confirm the role assignments within the team.	I will confirm the task assignments within the group.

Positive Response	Negative Response
承知しました。効率的な運営につながりますね。	役割分担の見直しが必要です。
しょうちしました。こうりつてきなうんえいにつながりますね。	やくわりぶんたんのみなおしがひつようです。
Shōchi shima shita. Kōritsu-tekina un'ei ni tsunagarimasu ne.	Yakuwari buntan no minaoshi ga hitsuyōdesu.
Understood. It will lead to efficient operations.	We need to review the role distribution.

Conversation example person A	Conversation example person B
チーム内での役割分担を確認します。	了解です。新しいマーケティング戦略の提案です。
ちーむないでのやくわりぶんたんをかくにんします。	りょうかいです。あたらしいまーけてぃんぐせんりゃくのていあんです。
Chīmu-nai de no yakuwari buntan o kakunin shimasu.	Ryōkaidesu. Atarashī māketingu senryaku no teiandesu.
I'll confirm the role distribution within the team.	Understood. Here's a proposal for a new marketing strategy.

Cultural Context
Doesn't indicate if changes to roles are being considered.

新しいマーケティング戦略の提案です。

あたらしいまーけてぃんぐせんりゃくのていあんです。

Atarashī māketingu senryaku no teiandesu.

This is a proposal for a new marketing strategy.

Variation 1	Variation 2
新規営業戦略の提案です。	Kyō mo shōjin shima shou.
しんきえいぎょうせんりゃくのていあんです。	しんきえいぎょうせんりゃくのていあんです。
Shinki eigyō senryaku no teiandesu.	Atarashī eigyō senjutsu no teiandesu.
Here is a proposal for a new marketing strategy.	This is a proposal for a new sales strategy.

Positive Response	Negative Response
興味深いですね。詳しく聞かせてください。	現在の戦略を変更する余裕はありません。
きょうみぶかいですね。くわしくきかせてください。	げんざいのせんりゃくをへんこうするよゆうはありません。
Kyōmibukaidesu ne. Kuwashiku kika sete kudasai.	Genzai no senryaku o henkō suru yoyū wa arimasen.
That's interesting. Please tell me more about it.	We can't afford to change our current strategy.

Conversation example person A	Conversation example person B
新しいマーケティング戦略の提案です。ご検討いただけますでしょうか。	興味深い提案ですね。次回の戦略会議で議題にあげましょう。
あたらしいまーけてぃんぐせんりゃくのていあんです。ごけんとういただけますでしょうか。	きょうみぶかいていあんですね。じかいのせんりゃくかいぎでぎだいにあげましょう。
Atarashī māketingu senryaku no teian desu. Go kentō itadakemasu deshō ka?	Kyōmibukai teiandesu ne. Jikai no senryaku kaigi de gidai ni age ma shou.
Here's a proposal for a new marketing strategy. Could you please review it?	That's an interesting proposal. Let's put it on the agenda for the next strategy meeting.

Cultural Context

Doesn't specify the urgency or expected timeline for review.

今週の振り返りミーティングの議題です。

こんしゅうのふりかえりみーてぃんぐのぎだいです。

Konshū no furikaeri mītingu no gidaidesu.

These are the agenda items for this week's review meeting.

Variation 1	Variation 2
今週の反省会の議題です。	Kyō mo shōjin shima shou.
こんしゅうのはんせいかいのぎだいです。	こんしゅうのはんせいかいのぎだいです。
Konshū no hansei-kai no gidaidesu.	Konshū no furikaeri-kai no gidaidesu.
Here are the topics for this week's retrospective meeting.	These are the topics for this week's reflection meeting.

Positive Response	Negative Response
ありがとうございます。建設的な議論ができそうですね。	議題が多すぎます。
ありがとうございます。けんせつてきなぎろんができそうですね。	ぎだいがおおすぎます。
Arigatōgozaimasu. Kensetsu-tekina giron ga deki-sōdesu ne.	Gidai ga ō sugimasu.
Thank you. It seems we can have constructive discussions.	There are too many agenda items.

Conversation example person A	Conversation example person B
今週の振り返りミーティングの議題です。	確認しました。週次レポートを提出しました。
こんしゅうのふりかえりみーてぃんぐのぎだいです。	かくにんしました。しゅうじれぽーとをていしゅつしました。
Konshū no furikaeri mītingu no gidaidesu.	Kakunin shima shita. Shū-ji repōto o teishutsu shima shita.
Here are the agenda items for this week's review meeting.	Confirmed. I've submitted the weekly report.

Cultural Context

Doesn't indicate if additional topics can be added.

週次レポートを提出しました。

しゅうじれぽーとをていしゅつしました。
Shū-ji repōto o teishutsu shimashita.
I've submitted the weekly report.

Variation 1	Variation 2
週報を提出しました。	Kyō mo shōjin shima shou.
しゅうほうをていしゅつしました。	しゅうほうをていしゅつしました。
Shūhō o teishutsu shima shita.	Shū-ji hōkoku-sho o teishutsu shima shita.
I have submitted the weekly report.	I have submitted the weekly report.

Positive Response	Negative Response
ありがとうございます。迅速な報告に感謝します。	レポートの内容が不十分です。
ありがとうございます。じんそくなほうこくにかんしゃします。	れぽーとのないようがふじゅうぶんです。
Arigatōgozaimasu. Jinsokuna hōkoku ni kansha shimasu.	Repōto no naiyō ga fu jūbundesu.
Thank you. I appreciate your prompt report.	The content of the report is insufficient.

Conversation example person A	Conversation example person B
週次レポートを提出しました。ご確認をお願いいたします。	ありがとうございます。内容を確認し、フィードバックいたします。
しゅうじれぽーとをていしゅつしました。ごかくにんをおねがいいたします。	ありがとうございます。ないようをかくにんし、ふぃーどばっくいたします。
Shūji repōto o teishutsu shimashita. Go kakunin o onegai itashimasu.	Arigatōgozaimasu. Naiyō o kakunin shi, fīdobakku itashimasu.
I've submitted the weekly report. Please review it.	Thank you. I'll review the content and provide feedback.

Cultural Context
Doesn't ensure the report will be read or acted upon promptly.

オンラインミーティングの URL を送ります。

おんらいんみーてぃんぐのゆーあーるえるをおくります。
Onrainmītingu no URL o okurimasu.
I'll send the URL for the online meeting.

Variation 1	Variation 2
ウェブ会議のリンクを送ります。	Kyō mo shōjin shima shou.
うぇぶかいぎのりんくをおくります。	うぇぶかいぎのりんくをおくります。
U~ebu kaigi no rinku o okurimasu.	Onrain kaigi no rinku o ookuri shimasu.
I will send the online meeting URL.	I will send the link for the web meeting.

Positive Response	Negative Response
ありがとうございます。参加を楽しみにしています。	オンラインミーティングは避けたいです。
ありがとうございます。さんかをたのしみにしています。	おんらいんみーてぃんぐはさけたいです。
Arigatōgozaimasu. Sanka o tanoshimi ni shite imasu.	Onrain mītingu wa saketaidesu.
Thank you. I'm looking forward to participating.	I'd prefer to avoid online meetings.

Conversation example person A	Conversation example person B
オンラインミーティングの URL を送ります。	ありがとうございます。参加いたします。
おんらいんみーてぃんぐのゆーあーるえるをおくります。	ありがとうございます。さんかいたします。
Onrain mītingu no URL o okurimasu.	Arigatōgozaimasu. Sanka itashimasu.
I'll send the URL for the online meeting.	Thank you. I'll participate.

Cultural Context
Doesn't specify if any preparation is needed before the meeting.

業務改善の提案があります。

ぎょうむかいぜんのていあんがあります。

Gyōmu kaizen no teian ga arimasu.

I have a suggestion for business improvement.

Variation 1	Variation 2
仕事の効率化の提案があります。	Kyō mo shōjin shima shou.
しごとのこうりつかのていあんがあります。	しごとのこうりつかのていあんがあります。
Shigoto no kōritsu-ka no teian ga arimasu.	Gyōmu no kōritsu-ka ni tsuite no teian ga arimasu.
I have a proposal for work improvement.	I have a proposal for improving work efficiency.

Positive Response	Negative Response
素晴らしいです。前向きに検討しましょう。	今は業務を変更する余裕がありません。
すばらしいです。まえむきにけんとうしましょう。	いまはぎょうむをへんこうするよゆうがありません。
Subarashīdesu. Maemuki ni kentō shima shou.	Ima wa gyōmu o henkō suru yoyū ga arimasen.
Great. Let's consider it positively.	We can't afford to change our operations now.

Conversation example person A	Conversation example person B
業務改善の提案があります。効率化について検討しましょう。	興味深いですね。具体的な内容を教えてください。
ぎょうむかいぜんのていあんがあります。こうりつかについてけんとうしましょう。	きょうみぶかいですね。ぐたいてきないようをおしえてください。
Gyōmu kaizen no teian ga arimasu. Kōritsu-ka ni tsuite kentō shima shou.	Kyōmibukaidesu ne. Gutai-tekina naiyō o oshiete kudasai.
I have a proposal for business improvement. Let's consider ways to increase efficiency.	That's interesting. Could you tell me more about the specific details?

Cultural Context

Doesn't indicate the scope or potential impact of the improvements.

今日の業務終了です。お疲れ様でした。

きょうのぎょうむしゅうりょうです。おつかれさまでした。

Kyō no gyōmu shūryōdesu. Otsukaresamadeshita.

That's the end of today's work. Good job everyone.

Variation 1	Variation 2
#N/A	Kyō mo shōjin shima shou.
#N/A	#N/A
#N/A	#N/A
#N/A	#N/A

Positive Response	Negative Response
お疲れ様でした。素晴らしい一日の成果でしたね。	まだ仕事が残っています。
おつかれさまでした。すばらしいいちにちのせいかでしたね。	まだしごとがのこっています。
Otsukaresamadeshita. Subarashī ichinichi no seikadeshita ne.	Mada shigoto ga nokotte imasu.
Thank you for your hard work. It was a great day's achievement.	There's still work left to do.

Conversation example person A	Conversation example person B
皆さん、本日の作業お疲れ様でした。良い一日でしたね。	今日の業務終了です。お疲れ様でした。明日も頑張りましょう。
みなさん、ほんじつのさぎょうおつかれさまでした。よいいちにちでしたね。	きょうのぎょうむしゅうりょうです。おつかれさまでした。あしたもがんばりましょう。
Minasan, honjitsu no sagyō otsukaresama de shita. Yoi ichi-nichi de shita ne.	Kyō no gyōmu shūryōdesu. Otsukaresama de shita. Ashita mo ganbari ma shou.
Everyone, thank you for your hard work today. It was a good day, wasn't it?	That's the end of today's work. Good job everyone. Let's do our best again tomorrow.

Cultural Context

This phrase is typically used by managers to subordinates. Using it to superiors may be inappropriate.

以下の通りご報告いたします。

いかのとおりごほうこくいたします。

Ika no tōri go hōkoku itashimasu.

I would like to report as follows.

Variation 1	Variation 2
下記の通りご報告いたします。	Kyō mo shōjin shima shou.
かきのとおりごほうこくいたします。	かきのとおりごほうこくいたします。
Kaki no tōri go hōkoku itashimasu.	Kaki no tōri go renraku itashimasu.
I would like to report as follows.	I will report as follows.

Positive Response	Negative Response
情報提供ありがとうございます。	報告が長すぎて、要点が分かりません。
じょうほうていきょうありがとうございます。	ほうこくがながすぎて、ようてんがわかりません。
Jōhō teikyō arigatōgozaimasu.	Hōkoku ga naga sugite, yōten ga wakarimasen.
Thank you for the information.	The report is too long, and I can't grasp the main points.

Conversation example person A	Conversation example person B
先週の会議の結果について、以下の通りご報告いたします。	承知しました。報告内容を確認させていただきます。
せんしゅうのかいぎのけっかについて、いかのとおりごほうこくいたします。	しょうちしました。ほうこくないようをかくにんさせていただきます。
Senshū no kaigi no kekka ni tsuite, ika no tōri go hōkoku itashimasu.	Shōchi shima shita. Hōkoku naiyō o kakunin sa sete itadakimasu.
I would like to report the results of last week's meeting as follows.	Understood. I will review the contents of the report.

Cultural Context

Ensure the report is concise yet comprehensive. Being too verbose can be seen as inefficient in Japanese business culture.

本件につきまして、ご検討をお願いいたします。

ほんけんにつきまして、ごけんとうをおねがいいたします。

Honken ni tsukimashite, go kentō o onegai itashimasu.

Please consider this matter.

Variation 1	Variation 2
本件に関しまして、ご審議をお願いいたします。	Kyō mo shōjin shima shou.
ほんけんにかんしまして、ごしんぎをおねがいいたします。	ほんけんにかんしまして、ごしんぎをおねがいいたします。
Honken ni kanshimashite, go shingi o onegai itashimasu.	Hon anken ni kanshite, go kentō o onegai mōshiagemasu.
Regarding this matter, please consider it.	Regarding this matter, I kindly request your deliberation.

Positive Response	Negative Response
早速検討に入ります。	検討する時間的余裕がありません。
さっそくけんとうにはいります。	けんとうするじかんてきよゆうがありません。
Sassoku kentō ni hairimasu.	Kentō suru jikan-teki yoyū ga arimasen.
We'll start considering it right away.	We don't have time to consider this.

Conversation example person A	Conversation example person B
新規プロジェクトの提案書を送付しました。本件につきまして、ご検討をお願いいたします。	了解いたしました。慎重に検討し、後ほど意見をお伝えします。
しんきぷろじぇくとのていあんしょをそうふしました。ほんけんにつきまして、ごけんとうをおねがいいたします。	りょうかいいたしました。しんちょうにけんとうし、のちほどいけんをおつたえします。
Shinki purojekuto no teian-sho o sōfu shima shita. Honken ni tsukimashite, go kentō o onegai itashimasu.	Ryōkai itashimashita. Shinchō ni kentō shi, nochihodo iken o otsutae shimasu.
I have sent the proposal for the new project. Please review this matter.	Understood. I will carefully consider it and give you my opinion later.

Cultural Context

This implies you're leaving the decision to the recipient. Be prepared to provide additional information if asked.

今回の提案は、以下の点に基づいています。

こんかいのていあんは、いかのてんにもとづいています。

Konkai no teian wa, ika no ten ni motodzuite imasu.

This proposal is based on the following points.

Variation 1	Variation 2
今回の提案は、下記の点に基づいています。	Kyō mo shōjin shima shou.
こんかいのていあんは、かきのてんにもとづいています。	こんかいのていあんは、かきのてんにもとづいています。
Konkai no teian wa, kaki no ten ni motodzuite imasu.	Hon teian wa,-ji no ten o konkyo to shite imasu.
This proposal is based on the following points.	This proposal is based on the following points.

Positive Response	Negative Response
提案の背景がよく分かりました。	提案の根拠が薄弱に感じます。
ていあんのはいけいがよくわかりました。	ていあんのこんきょがはくじゃくにかんじます。
Teian no haikei ga yoku wakarimashita.	Teian no konkyo ga hakujaku ni kanjimasu.
I now understand the context of the proposal.	The basis for this proposal seems weak.

Conversation example person A	Conversation example person B
今回の提案は、以下の点に基づいています。市場調査と顧客フィードバックを重視しました。	なるほど。それぞれの点について詳しく説明していただけますか。
こんかいのていあんは、いかのてんにもとづいています。しじょうちょうさとこきゃくふぃーどばっくをじゅうしました。	なるほど。それぞれのてんについてくわしくせつめいしていただけますか。
Konkai no teian wa, ika no ten ni motodzuite imasu. Shijō chōsa to kokyaku fīdobakku o jūshi shima shita.	Naruhodo. Sorezore no ten ni tsuite kuwashiku setsumei shite itadakemasu ka.
This proposal is based on the following points. We focused on market research and customer feedback.	I see. Could you explain each point in more detail?

Cultural Context

The points should be well-researched and aligned with company goals. Trivial points may diminish credibility.

本プロジェクトの目的は次の通りです。

ほんぷろじぇくとのもくてきはつぎのとおりです。
Hon purojekuto no mokuteki wa tsugi no tōridesu.
The objectives of this project are as follows.

Variation 1	Variation 2
本企画の目的は次の通りです。	Kyō mo shōjin shima shou.
ほんきかくのもくてきはつぎのとおりです。	ほんきかくのもくてきはつぎのとおりです。
Hon kikaku no mokuteki wa tsugi no tōridesu.	Hon purojekuto no mokuteki wa ika no tōridesu.
The purpose of this project is as follows.	The purpose of this project is as follows.

Positive Response	Negative Response
目的が明確で素晴らしいですね。	目的が曖昧で具体性に欠けています。
もくてきがめいかくですばらしいですね。	もくてきがあいまいでぐたいせいにかけています。
Mokuteki ga meikaku de subarashīdesu ne.	Mokuteki ga aimaide gutai-sei ni kakete imasu.
The purpose is clear and excellent.	The purpose is vague and lacks specificity.

Conversation example person A	Conversation example person B
本プロジェクトの目的は次の通りです。顧客満足度の向上と業務効率化を目指します。	理解しました。目的達成のための具体的な戦略も教えてください。
ほんぷろじぇくとのもくてきはつぎのとおりです。こきゃくまんぞくどのこうじょうとぎょうむこうりつかをめざします。	りかいしました。もくてきたっせいのためのぐたいてきなせんりゃくもおしえてください。
Hon purojekuto no mokuteki wa tsugi no tōridesu. Kokyaku manzoku-do no kōjō to gyōmu kōritsu-ka o mezashimasu.	Rikai shima shita. Mokuteki tassei no tame no gutai-tekina senryaku mo oshiete kudasai.
The objectives of this project are as follows. We aim to improve customer satisfaction and operational efficiency.	I understand. Please also tell me about the specific strategies to achieve these objectives.

Cultural Context
Objectives should be clear and aligned with the company's overall strategy. Vague goals may be seen as poor planning.

現状の課題として以下が挙げられます。

げんじょうのかだいとしていかがあげられます。

Genjō no kadai to shite ika ga age raremasu.

The following issues are identified as current challenges.

Variation 1	Variation 2
現状の問題点として以下が挙げられます。	Kyō mo shōjin shima shou.
げんじょうのもんだいてんとしていかがあげられます。	げんじょうのもんだいてんとしていかがあげられます。
Genjō no mondai-ten to shite ika ga age raremasu.	Genzai no kadai to shite ika no ten ga arimasu.
The following can be mentioned as current issues.	The following can be mentioned as current issues.

Positive Response	Negative Response
課題を共有できて良かったです。	課題の優先順位が不明確です。
かだいをきょうゆうできてよかったです。	かだいのゆうせんじゅんいがふめいかくです。
Kadai o kyōyū dekite yokattadesu.	Kadai no yūsen jun'i ga fu meikakudesu.
I'm glad we could share these issues.	The priority of these issues is unclear.

Conversation example person A	Conversation example person B
現状の課題として以下が挙げられます。特に人材不足と技術の陳腐化が深刻です。	課題を認識しました。これらの解決に向けた対策案はありますか？
げんじょうのかだいとしていかがあげられます。とくにじんざいぶそくとぎじゅつのちんぷかがしんこくです。	かだいをにんしきしました。これらのかいけつにむけたたいさくあんはありますか？
Genjō no kadai to shite ika ga age raremasu. Tokuni jinzai fusoku to gijutsu no chinpu-ka ga shinkokudesu.	Kadai o ninshiki shima shita. Korera no kaiketsu ni muketa taisaku-an wa arimasu ka?
The following are identified as current issues. In particular, the shortage of human resources and outdated technology are serious concerns.	I acknowledge these issues. Do you have any proposed measures to address them?

Cultural Context

Avoid assigning blame when listing challenges. Focus on objective facts rather than subjective opinions.

実施にあたっての留意点は以下の通りです。

じっしにあたってのりゅういてんはいかのとおりです。

Jisshi ni atatte no ryūi-ten wa ika no tōridesu.

Points to note for implementation are as follows.

Variation 1	Variation 2
実行にあたっての注意点は以下の通りです。	Kyō mo shōjin shima shou.
じっこうにあたってのちゅういてんはいかのとおりです。	じっこうにあたってのちゅういてんはいかのとおりです。
Jikkō ni atatte no chūi-ten wa ika no tōridesu.	Jisshi ni atatte no ryūi-ten wa tsugi no tōridesu.
The points to keep in mind during implementation are as follows.	The points to note when implementing are as follows.

Positive Response	Negative Response
重要なポイントですね。注意します。	留意点が多すぎて実行が困難に思えます。
じゅうようなぽいんとですね。ちゅういします。	りゅういてんがおおすぎてじっこうがこんなんにおもえます。
Jūyōna pointodesu ne. Chūi shimasu.	Ryūi-ten ga ō sugite jikkō ga kon'nan ni omoemasu.
These are important points. We'll be careful.	There are too many points to consider, making implementation seem difficult.

Conversation example person A	Conversation example person B
実施にあたっての留意点は以下の通りです。特にコンプライアンスの遵守に注意が必要です。	承知しました。これらの点を踏まえて慎重に進めていきます。
じっしにあたってのりゅういてんはいかのとおりです。とくにこんぷらいあんすのじゅんしゅにちゅういがひつようです。	しょうちしました。これらのてんをふまえてしんちょうにすすめていきます。
Jisshi ni atatte no ryūi-ten wa ika no tōridesu. Tokuni konpuraiansu no junshu ni chūi ga hitsuyōdesu.	Shōchi shima shita. Korera no ten o fumaete shinchō ni susumete ikimasu.
The points to keep in mind during implementation are as follows. Particular attention needs to be paid to compliance.	Understood. We will proceed carefully, taking these points into account.

Cultural Context

Points should be specific and actionable. Avoid stating obvious information as it may be seen as underestimating your audience.

本施策により、以下の効果が期待されます。

ほんしさくにより、いかのこうかがきたいされます。

Hon shisaku ni yori, ika no kōka ga kitai sa remasu.

The following effects are expected from this measure.

Variation 1	Variation 2
本取り組みにより、以下の効果が期待されます。	Kyō mo shōjin shima shou.
ほんとりくみにより、いかのこうかがきたいされます。	ほんとりくみにより、いかのこうかがきたいされます。
Hon torikumi ni yori, ika no kōka ga kitai sa remasu.	Hon shisaku ni yori,-ji no kōka ga mikoma remasu.
The following effects are expected from this measure.	The following effects are expected from this initiative.

Positive Response	Negative Response
期待できる効果ですね。楽しみです。	期待される効果が楽観的すぎます。
きたいできるこうかですね。たのしみです。	きたいされるこうかがらっかんてきすぎます。
Kitai dekiru kōkadesu ne. Tanoshimidesu.	Kitai sa re ru kōka ga rakkan-teki sugimasu.
These are promising effects. Looking forward to it.	The expected effects seem too optimistic.

Conversation example person A	Conversation example person B
本施策により、以下の効果が期待されます。主に生産性向上とコスト削減が見込まれます。	期待される効果は魅力的ですね。具体的な数値目標はありますか？
ほんしさくにより、いかのこうかがきたいされます。おもにせいさんせいこうじょうとこすとさくげんがみこまれます。	きたいされるこうかはみりょくてきですね。ぐたいてきなすうちもくひょうはありますか？
Hon shisaku ni yori, ika no kōka ga kitai sa remasu. Omo ni seisan-sei kōjō to kosuto sakugen ga mikoma remasu.	Kitai sa re ru kōka wa miryoku-tekidesu ne. Gutai-tekina sūchi mokuhyō wa arimasu ka?
The following effects are expected from this measure. Mainly, we anticipate improved productivity and cost reduction.	The expected effects are attractive. Do you have any specific numerical targets?

Cultural Context

Be conservative in your estimates. Overpromising is particularly frowned upon in Japanese business culture.

今後のスケジュールは下記の通りです。

こんごのすけじゅーるはかきのとおりです。

Kongo no sukejūru wa kaki no tōridesu.

The future schedule is as follows.

Variation 1	Variation 2
今後の予定は下記の通りです。	Kyō mo shōjin shima shou.
こんごのよていはかきのとおりです。	こんごのよていはかきのとおりです。
Kongo no yotei wa kaki no tōridesu.	Kongo no sukejūru wa ika no tōridesu.
The future schedule is as follows.	The future schedule is as follows.

Positive Response	Negative Response
タイトなスケジュールですが頑張りましょう。	スケジュールが非現実的に思えます。
たいとなすけじゅーるですががんばりましょう。	すけじゅーるがひげんじつてきにおもえます。
Taitona sukejūrudesu ga ganbarimashō.	Sukejūru ga hi genjitsu-teki ni omoemasu.
It's a tight schedule, but let's do our best.	The schedule seems unrealistic.

Conversation example person A	Conversation example person B
今後のスケジュールは下記の通りです。来月から順次実施していく予定です。	スケジュールを確認しました。各段階での進捗報告をお願いします。
こんごのすけじゅーるはかきのとおりです。らいげつからじゅんじじっしていくよていです。	すけじゅーるをかくにんしました。かくだんかいでのしんちょくほうこくをおねがいします。
Kongo no sukejūru wa kaki no tōridesu. Rai tsuki kara junji jisshi shite iku yoteidesu.	Sukejūru o kakunin shima shita. Kaku dankai de no shinchoku hōkoku o onegai shimasu.
The future schedule is as follows. We plan to implement it gradually starting next month.	I have confirmed the schedule. Please provide progress reports at each stage.

Cultural Context

Ensure the schedule is realistic. In Japan, meeting deadlines is crucial for maintaining trust.

本件に関するご質問がございましたら、ご連絡ください。

ほんけんにかんするごしつもんがございましたら、ごれんらくください。

Honken ni kansuru go shitsumon ga go zaimashita-ra, go renraku kudasai.

If you have any questions regarding this matter, please contact us.

Variation 1	Variation 2
本件に関するご不明点がございましたら、ご連絡ください。	Kyō mo shōjin shima shou.
ほんけんにかんするごふめいてんががございましたら、ごれんらくください。	ほんけんにかんするごふめいてんががございましたら、ごれんらくください。
Honken ni kansuru go fumei-ten ga go zaimashita-ra, go renraku kudasai.	Hon anken ni tsuite go shitsumon ga Arima shitara, o toiawase kudasai.
If you have any questions regarding this matter, please contact us.	If you have any questions regarding this matter, please contact us.

Positive Response	Negative Response
丁寧な対応に感謝します。	質問の回答に時間がかかりすぎます。
ていねいなたいおうにかんしゃします。	しつもんのかいとうにじかんがかかりすぎます。
Teineina taiō ni kansha shimasu.	Shitsumon no kaitō ni jikan ga kakari sugimasu.
I appreciate your careful attention.	It takes too long to get answers to questions.

Conversation example person A	Conversation example person B
本件に関するご質問がございましたら、ご連絡ください。随時対応いたします。	ありがとうございます。不明点があれば連絡させていただきます。
ほんけんにかんするごしつもんがございましたら、ごれんらくください。ずいじたいおういたします。	ありがとうございます。ふめいてんがあればれんらくさせていただきます。
Honken ni kansuru go shitsumon ga go zaimashita-ra, go renraku kudasai. Zuiji taiō itashimasu.	Arigatōgozaimasu. Fumei-ten ga areba renraku sa sete itadakimasu.
If you have any questions regarding this matter, please contact us. We will respond as needed.	Thank you. I will contact you if I have any questions.

Cultural Context

Be prepared to respond promptly. Slow responses may be interpreted as lack of preparation or commitment.

添付資料をご参照ください。

てんぷしりょうをごさんしょうください。

Tenpu shiryō o go sanshō kudasai.

Please refer to the attached documents.

Variation 1	Variation 2
添付ファイルをご確認ください。	Kyō mo shōjin shima shou.
てんぷふぁいるをごかくにんください。	てんぷふぁいるをごかくにんください。
Tenpu fairu o go kakunin kudasai.	Tenpu shiryō o go kakunin kudasai.
Please refer to the attached documents.	Please check the attached file.

Positive Response	Negative Response
早速目を通してみます。	添付資料が多すぎて全て確認する時間がありません。
さっそくめをとおしてみます。	てんぷしりょうがおおすぎてすべてかくにんするじかんがありません。
Sassoku me o tooshite mimasu.	Tenpu shiryō ga ō sugite subete kakunin suru jikan ga arimasen.
I'll take a look at it right away.	There are too many attachments to check everything.

Conversation example person A	Conversation example person B
詳細な分析結果は添付資料をご参照ください。グラフや表で視覚化しています。	了解しました。添付資料を確認いたします。
しょうさいなぶんせきけっかはてんぷしりょうをごさんしょうください。ぐらふやひょうでしかくかしています。	りょうかいしました。てんぷしりょうをかくにんいたします。
Shōsaina bunseki kekka wa tenpu shiryō o go sanshō kudasai. Gurafu ya hyō de shikaku-ka shite imasu.	Ryōkai shima shita. Tenpu shiryō o kakunin itashimasu.
Please refer to the attached documents for detailed analysis results. They are visualized in graphs and tables.	Understood. I will check the attached documents.

Cultural Context

Ensure all attachments are properly labeled. Disorganized attachments may be seen as unprofessional.

本提案のポイントは以下の三点です。

ほんていあんのぽいんとはいかのさんてんです。

Hon teian no pointo wa ika no san-tendesu.

The key points of this proposal are the following three.

Variation 1	Variation 2
本提案の要点は以下の三点です。	Kyō mo shōjin shima shou.
ほんていあんのようてんはいかのさんてんです。	ほんていあんのようてんはいかのさんてんです。
Hon teian no yōten wa ika no san-tendesu.	Hon teian no pointo wa tsugi no 3-tendesu.
The key points of this proposal are the following three points.	The key points of this proposal are the following three.

Positive Response	Negative Response
要点を押さえていて分かりやすいです。	ポイントが三点では不十分に思えます。
ようてんをおさえていてわかりやすいです。	ぽいんとがさんてんではふじゅうぶんんにおもえます。
Yōten o osaete ite wakariyasuidesu.	Pointo ga san-tende wa fu jūbun ni omoemasu.
It's easy to understand as it covers the key points.	Three points seem insufficient for this proposal.

Conversation example person A	Conversation example person B
本提案のポイントは以下の三点です。効率化、コスト削減、顧客満足度向上に焦点を当てています。	重要なポイントですね。各点についてもう少し詳しく説明していただけますか？
ほんていあんのぽいんとはいかのさんてんです。こうりつか、こすとさくげん、こきゃくまんぞくどこうじょうにしょうてんをあてています。	じゅうようなぽいんとですね。かくてんについてもうすこしくわしくせつめいしていただけますか？
Hon teian no pointo wa ika no san-tendesu. Kōritsu-ka, kosuto sakugen, kokyaku manzoku-do kōjō ni shōten o atete imasu.	Jūyōna pointodesu ne. Kaku-ten ni tsuite mōsukoshi kuwashiku setsumei shite itadakemasu ka?
The main points of this proposal are the following three. We focus on efficiency, cost reduction, and improving customer satisfaction.	These are important points. Could you explain each point in a bit more detail?

Cultural Context

These should be the most crucial aspects. More than three points may be seen as lack of focus.

実施に際しては、関係部署との連携が不可欠です。

じっしにさいしては、かんけいぶしょとのれんけいがふかけつです。

Jisshi ni saishite wa, kankei busho to no renkei ga fukaketsudesu.

Cooperation with relevant departments is essential for implementation.

Variation 1	Variation 2
実行に際しては、関連部署との協力が不可欠です。	Kyō mo shōjin shima shou.
じっこうにさいしては、かんれんぶしょとのきょうりょくがふかけつです。	じっこうにさいしては、かんれんぶしょとのきょうりょくがふかけつです。
Jikkō ni saishite wa, kanren busho to no kyōryoku ga fukaketsudesu.	Jisshi ni atatte wa, kankei bumon to no renkei ga hitsuyō fukaketsudesu.
When implementing, cooperation with related departments is essential.	When implementing, cooperation with related departments is essential.

Positive Response	Negative Response
部署間の協力を促進します。	部署間の連携が難しいと思います。
ぶしょかんのきょうりょくをそくしんします。	ぶしょかんのれんけいがむずかしいとおもいます。
Bushokan no kyōryoku o sokushin shimasu.	Busho-kan no renkei ga muzukashī to omoimasu.
We'll promote cooperation between departments.	Interdepartmental cooperation seems difficult.

Conversation example person A	Conversation example person B
実施に際しては、関係部署との連携が不可欠です。特に営業部門との協力が重要になります。	承知しました。関係部署との調整は私が担当いたします。
じっしにさいしては、かんけいぶしょとのれんけいがふかけつです。とくにえいぎょうぶもんとのきょうりょくがじゅうようになります。	しょうちしました。かんけいぶしょとのちょうせいはわたしがたんとういたします。
Jisshi ni saishite wa, kankei busho to no renkei ga fukaketsudesu. Tokuni eigyō bumon to no kyōryoku ga jūyō ni narimasu.	Shōchi shima shita. Kankei busho to no chōsei wa watashi ga tantō itashimasu.
Cooperation with related departments is essential for implementation. Collaboration with the sales department will be particularly important.	Understood. I will be in charge of coordinating with the related departments.

Cultural Context

This implies you've considered cross-departmental collaboration. Be prepared to explain how you'll facilitate this.

本計画の成功には、全社的な取り組みが必要です。

ほんけいかくのせいこうには、ぜんしゃてきなとりくみがひつようです。

Hon keikaku no seikō ni wa, zensha-tekina torikumi ga hitsuyōdesu.

Company-wide efforts are necessary for the success of this plan.

Variation 1	Variation 2
本企画の成功には、全社的な協力が必要です。	Kyō mo shōjin shima shou.
ほんきかくのせいこうには、ぜんしゃてきなきょうりょくがひつようです。	ほんきかくのせいこうには、ぜんしゃてきなきょうりょくがひつようです。
Hon kikaku no seikō ni wa, zensha-tekina kyōryoku ga hitsuyōdesu.	Hon purojekuto no seikō ni wa, zensha-tekina kyōryoku ga hitsuyō fukaketsudesu.
The success of this plan requires company-wide efforts.	The success of this project requires company-wide cooperation.

Positive Response	Negative Response
全員で力を合わせて取り組みましょう。	全社的な取り組みは現実的ではありません。
ぜんいんでちからをあわせてとりくみましょう。	ぜんしゃてきなとりくみはげんじつてきではありません。
Zen'in de chikara o awasete torikumimashō.	Zensha-tekina torikumi wa genjitsu-tekide wa arimasen.
Let's all work together on this.	A company-wide effort is not realistic.

Conversation example person A	Conversation example person B
本計画の成功には、全社的な取り組みが必要です。部門の垣根を越えた協力をお願いします。	理解しました。全社一丸となって取り組みましょう。
ほんけいかくのせいこうには、ぜんしゃてきなとりくみがひつようです。ぶもんのかきねをこえたきょうりょくをおねがいします。	りかいしました。ぜんしゃいちがんとなってとりくみましょう。
Hon keikaku no seikō ni wa, zensha-tekina torikumi ga hitsuyōdesu. Bumon no kakine o koeta kyōryoku o onegai shimasu.	Rikai shima shita. Zensha ichigan to natte torikumi ma shou.
The success of this plan requires a company-wide effort. Please cooperate across departmental boundaries.	I understand. Let's work together as a whole company.

Cultural Context

This suggests a major initiative. Ensure you have support from higher management before making such a statement.

詳細につきましては、別途ご説明いたします。

しょうさいにつきましては、べっとごせつめいいたします。

Shōsai ni tsukimashite wa, betto go setsumei itashimasu.

Details will be explained separately.

Variation 1	Variation 2
詳細につきましては、追ってご説明いたします。	Kyō mo shōjin shima shou.
しょうさいにつきましては、おってごせつめいいたします。	しょうさいにつきましては、おってごせつめいいたします。
Shōsai ni tsukimashite wa, otte go setsumei itashimasu.	Kuwashiku wa, nochihodo go setsumei shimasu.
I will explain the details separately.	Details will be explained later.

Positive Response	Negative Response
詳細な説明を楽しみにしています。	詳細の説明が遅すぎます。
しょうさいなせつめいをたのしみにしています。	しょうさいのせつめいがおそすぎます。
Shōsaina setsumei o tanoshimi ni shite imasu.	Shōsai no setsumei ga oso sugimasu.
I'm looking forward to the detailed explanation.	The detailed explanation is coming too late.

Conversation example person A	Conversation example person B
本提案の詳細につきましては、別途ご説明いたします。来週のミーティングで詳しくお話しします。	承知しました。ミーティングを楽しみにしています。
ほんていあんのしょうさいにつきましては、べっとごせつめいいたします。らいしゅうのみーてぃんぐでくわしくおはなしします。	しょうちしました。みーてぃんぐをたのしみにしています。
Hon teian no shōsai ni tsukimashite wa, betto go setsumei itashimasu. Raishū no mītingu de kuwashiku ohanashi shimasu.	Shōchi shima shita. Mītingu o tanoshimi ni shite imasu.
I will explain the details of this proposal separately. We will discuss it in detail at next week's meeting.	Understood. I'm looking forward to the meeting.

Cultural Context

Be prepared to provide a comprehensive explanation when asked. Lack of immediate follow-up may be seen as unprepared.

本案件の進捗状況は以下の通りです。

ほんあんけんのしんちょくじょうきょうはいかのとおりです。

Hon anken no shinchoku jōkyō wa ika no tōridesu.

The progress status of this matter is as follows.

Variation 1	Variation 2
本件の進行状況は以下の通りです。	Kyō mo shōjin shima shou.
ほんけんのしんこうじょうきょうはいかのとおりです。	ほんけんのしんこうじょうきょうはいかのとおりです。
Honken no shinkō jōkyō wa ika no tōridesu.	Hon anken no shinchoku jōkyō wa tsugi no tōridesu.
The progress status of this matter is as follows.	The progress status of this matter is as follows.

Positive Response	Negative Response
順調に進んでいるようで安心しました。	進捗が予定より遅れているように見えます。
じゅんちょうにすすんでいるようであんしんしました。	しんちょくがよていよりおくれているようにみえます。
Junchō ni susunde iru yōde anshin shimashita.	Shinchoku ga yotei yori okurete iru yō ni miemasu.
I'm relieved to see it's progressing well.	The progress seems to be behind schedule.

Conversation example person A	Conversation example person B
本案件の進捗状況は以下の通りです。現在、予定通りに進んでいます。	進捗状況を確認しました。引き続き順調な進行をお願いします。
ほんあんけんのしんちょくじょうきょうはいかのとおりです。げんざい、よていどおりにすすんでいます。	しんちょくじょうきょうをかくにんしました。ひきつづきじゅんちょうなしんこうをおねがいします。
Hon anken no shinchoku jōkyō wa ika no tōridesu. Genzai, yotei-dōri ni susunde imasu.	Shinchoku jōkyō o kakunin shima shita. Hikitsudzuki junchōna shinkō o onegai shimasu.
The progress status of this project is as follows. Currently, it is proceeding as scheduled.	I have confirmed the progress status. Please continue to proceed smoothly.

Cultural Context

Ensure the progress report is up-to-date. Outdated information may be seen as poor project management.

今回の分析結果から、次のことが明らかになりました。

こんかいのぶんせきけっかから、つぎのことがあきらかになりました。

Konkai no bunseki kekka kara,-ji no koto ga akiraka ni narimashita.

The following has become clear from this analysis.

Variation 1	Variation 2
今回の調査結果から、次のことが判明しました。	Kyō mo shōjin shima shou.
こんかいのちょうさけっかから、つぎのことがはんめいしました。	こんかいのちょうさけっかから、つぎのことがはんめいしました。
Konkai no chōsa kekka kara,-ji no koto ga hanmei shima shita.	Konkai no chōsa kara, ika no koto ga akiraka ni narimashita.
From the results of this analysis, the following became clear.	From this survey, the following things became clear.

Positive Response	Negative Response
興味深い結果ですね。活用していきましょう。	分析結果の信頼性に疑問があります。
きょうみぶかいけっかですね。かつようしていきましょう。	ぶんせきけっかのしんらいせいにぎもんがあります。
Kyōmibukai kekkadesu ne. Katsuyō shite ikimashō.	Bunseki kekka no shinrai-sei ni gimon ga arimasu.
Interesting results. Let's make use of them.	I have doubts about the reliability of these analysis results.

Conversation example person A	Conversation example person B
今回の分析結果から、次のことが明らかになりました。主に顧客ニーズの変化が顕著です。	興味深い結果ですね。この変化にどう対応していくべきでしょうか？
こんかいのぶんせきけっかから、つぎのことがあきらかになりました。おもにこきゃくにーずのへんかがけんちょです。	きょうみぶかいけっかですね。このへんかにどうたいおうしていくべきでしょうか？
Konkai no bunseki kekka kara,-ji no koto ga akiraka ni narimashita. Omo ni kokyaku nīzu no henka ga kenchodesu.	Kyōmibukai kekkadesu ne. Kono henka ni dō taiō shite ikubekideshou ka?
From the results of this analysis, the following has become clear. Mainly, the change in customer needs is notable.	That's an interesting result. How should we respond to this change?

Cultural Context

Be prepared to explain the methodology behind your analysis. Conclusions without clear reasoning may be questioned.

本提案の実現可能性について検討いたしました。

ほんていあんのじつげんかのうせいについてけんとういたしました。

Hon teian no jitsugen kanō-sei ni tsuite kentō itashimashita.

We have examined the feasibility of this proposal.

Variation 1	Variation 2
本提案の実行可能性について検討いたしました。	Kyō mo shōjin shima shou.
ほんていあんのじっこうかのうせいについてけんとういたしました。	ほんていあんのじっこうかのうせいについてけんとういたしました。
Hon teian no jikkō kanō-sei ni tsuite kentō itashimashita.	Hon teian no jitsugen kanō-sei ni tsuite kentō shima shita.
We have examined the feasibility of this proposal.	I have examined the feasibility of this proposal.

Positive Response	Negative Response
綿密な検討をありがとうございます。	実現可能性の検討が不十分に思えます。
めんみつなけんとうをありがとうございます。	じつげんかのうせいのけんとうがふじゅうぶんにおもえます。
Menmitsuna kentō o arigatōgozaimasu.	Jitsugen kanō-sei no kentō ga fu jūbun ni omoemasu.
Thank you for the thorough consideration.	The feasibility study seems insufficient.

Conversation example person A	Conversation example person B
本提案の実現可能性について検討いたしました。技術的には十分可能だと判断しています。	実現可能性が高いのは良いニュースです。コスト面での検討結果も教えてください。
ほんていあんのじつげんかのうせいについてけんとういたしました。ぎじゅつてきにはじゅうぶんかのうだとはんだんしています。	じつげんかのうせいがたかいのはよいにゅーすです。こすとめんでのけんとうけっかもおしえてください。
Hon teian no jitsugen kanō-sei ni tsuite kentō itashimashita. Gijutsu-teki ni wa jūbun kanōda to handan shite imasu.	Jitsugen kanō-sei ga takai no wa yoi nyūsudesu. Kosuto-men de no kentō kekka mo oshiete kudasai.
We have examined the feasibility of this proposal. We judge it to be technically quite possible.	It's good news that the feasibility is high. Please also tell me about the cost considerations.

Cultural Context

This implies a thorough feasibility study. Be ready to present detailed analysis if asked.

今後の改善点として、以下が挙げられます。

こんごのかいぜんてんとして、いかがあげられます。

Kongo no kaizen-ten to shite, ika ga age raremasu.

The following are identified as future improvement points.

Variation 1	Variation 2
今後の課題として、以下が挙げられます。	Kyō mo shōjin shima shou.
こんごのかだいとして、いかがあげられます。	こんごのかだいとして、いかがあげられます。
Kongo no kadai to shite, ika ga age raremasu.	Kongo no kadai to shite,-ji no ten ga arimasu.
The following can be mentioned as future improvement points.	The following can be mentioned as future issues.

Positive Response	Negative Response
建設的な提案ですね。取り組んでいきます。	改善点が具体性に欠けています。
けんせつてきなていあんですね。とりくんでいきます。	かいぜんてんがぐたいせいにかけています。
Kensetsu-tekina teiandesu ne. Torikunde ikimasu.	Kaizen-ten ga gutai-sei ni kakete imasu.
These are constructive suggestions. We'll work on them.	The improvement points lack specificity.

Conversation example person A	Conversation example person B
今後の改善点として、以下が挙げられます。特に社内コミュニケーションの強化が必要です。	承知しました。具体的な改善策を検討しましょう。
こんごのかいぜんてんとして、いかがあげられます。とくにしゃないこみゅにけーしょんのきょうかがひつようです。	しょうちしました。ぐたいてきなかいぜんさくをけんとうしましょう。
Kongo no kaizen-ten to shite, ika ga age raremasu. Tokuni shanai komyunikēshon no kyōka ga hitsuyōdesu.	Shōchi shima shita. Gutai-tekina kaizen-saku o kentō shima shou.
The following points are identified for future improvement. In particular, strengthening internal communication is necessary.	Understood. Let's consider specific improvement measures.

Cultural Context

Focus on constructive improvements. Avoid criticizing current processes or individuals.

本施策の導入により、業務効率の向上が見込まれます。

ほんしさくのどうにゅうにより、ぎょうむこうりつのこうじょうがみこまれます。

Hon shisaku no dōnyū ni yori, gyōmu kōritsu no kōjō ga mikoma remasu.

Improvement in operational efficiency is expected by introducing this measure.

Variation 1	Variation 2
本取り組みの導入により、業務効率の改善が見込まれます。	Kyō mo shōjin shima shou.
ほんとりくみのどうにゅうにより、ぎょうむこうりつのかいぜんがみこまれます。	ほんとりくみのどうにゅうにより、ぎょうむこうりつのかいぜんがみこまれます。
Hon torikumi no dōnyū ni yori, gyōmu kōritsu no kaizen ga mikoma remasu.	Hon shisaku no dōnyū ni yori, gyōmu kōritsu no kōjō ga kitai sa remasu.
The introduction of this measure is expected to improve work efficiency.	The introduction of this initiative is expected to improve work efficiency.

Positive Response	Negative Response
効率化は重要ですね。期待しています。	効率向上の根拠が不明確です。
こうりつかはじゅうようですね。きたいしています。	こうりつこうじょうのこんきょがふめいかくです。
Kōritsu-ka wa jūyōdesu ne. Kitai shite imasu.	Kōritsu kōjō no konkyo ga fu meikakudesu.
Efficiency is crucial. We're looking forward to it.	The basis for efficiency improvement is unclear.

Conversation example person A	Conversation example person B
本施策の導入により、業務効率の向上が見込まれます。約20%の生産性向上を予測しています。	それは素晴らしい予測ですね。具体的にどの業務で効率が上がるのでしょうか？
ほんしさくのどうにゅうにより、ぎょうむこうりつのこうじょうがみこまれます。やく20%のせいさんせいこうじょうをよそくしています。	それはすばらしいよそくですね。ぐたいてきにどのぎょうむでこうりつがあがるのでしょうか？
Hon shisaku no dōnyū ni yori, gyōmu kōritsu no kōjō ga mikoma remasu. Yaku ni jū-pāsento no seisan-sei kōjō o yosoku shite imasu.	Sore wa subarashī yosokudesu ne. Gutai-teki ni dono gyōmu de kōritsu ga agaru nodeshou ka?
With the implementation of this measure, we expect an improvement in operational efficiency. We predict a 20% increase in productivity.	That's an impressive prediction. In which specific operations do you expect efficiency to improve?

Cultural Context

Be prepared to quantify the expected efficiency gains. Vague promises of improvement may be seen as unreliable.

本件に関する決定事項は下記の通りです。

ほんけんにかんするけっていじこうはかきのとおりです。

Honken ni kansuru kettei jikō wa kaki no tōridesu.

Decisions regarding this matter are as follows.

Variation 1	Variation 2
本件に関する決定事項は以下の通りです。	Kyō mo shōjin shima shou.
ほんけんにかんするけっていじこうはいかのとおりです。	ほんけんにかんするけっていじこうはいかのとおりです。
Honken ni kansuru kettei jikō wa ika no tōridesu.	Hon anken ni kansuru kettei naiyō wa tsugi no tōridesu.
The decision items regarding this matter are as follows.	The decisions made regarding this matter are as follows.

Positive Response	Negative Response
明確な決定で助かります。進めていきましょう。	決定事項に異議があります。
めいかくなけっていでたすかります。すすめていきましょう。	けっていじこうにいぎがあります。
Meikakuna kettei de tasukarimasu. Susumete iki ma shou.	Kettei jikō ni igi ga arimasu.
Clear decisions are helpful. Let's move forward.	I have objections to these decisions.

Conversation example person A	Conversation example person B
本件に関する決定事項は下記の通りです。来月から新システムの導入を開始します。	了解しました。新システム導入に向けて準備を進めます。
ほんけんにかんするけっていじこうはかきのとおりです。らいげつからしんしすてむのどうにゅうをかいしします。	りょうかいしました。しんしすてむどうにゅうにむけてじゅんびをすすめます。
Honken ni kansuru kettei jikō wa kaki no tōridesu. Rai tsuki kara shin shisutemu no dōnyū o kaishi shimasu.	Ryōkai shima shita. Shin shisutemu dōnyū ni mukete junbi o susumemasu.
The decisions regarding this matter are as follows. We will start implementing the new system from next month.	Understood. We will proceed with preparations for the new system implementation.

Cultural Context

Ensure all stakeholders are aware of these decisions. Surprising people with new information can be seen as poor communication.

今回の結果を踏まえ、次のステップに進みたいと思います。

こんかいのけっかをふまえ、つぎのすてっぷにすすみたいとおもいます。

Konkai no kekka o fumae,-ji no suteppu ni Suzumu mitai to omoimasu.

Based on these results, we would like to proceed to the next step.

Variation 1	Variation 2
今回の結果を受け、次の段階に進みたいと思います。	Kyō mo shōjin shima shou.
こんかいのけっかをうけ、つぎのだんかいにすすみたいとおもいます。	こんかいのけっかをうけ、つぎのだんかいにすすみたいとおもいます。
Konkai no kekka o uke, tsugi no dankai ni Suzumu mitai to omoimasu.	Konkai no kekka o fumae,-ji no suteppu ni Suzumu mitai to kangaete imasu.
Based on the results this time, I would like to proceed to the next step.	Based on the results this time, I would like to move to the next stage.

Positive Response	Negative Response
次のステップに向けて準備します。	次のステップに進むのは時期尚早だと思います。
つぎのすてっぷにむけてじゅんびします。	つぎのすてっぷにすすむのはじきしょうそうだとおもいます。
Tsugi no suteppu ni mukete junbi shimasu.	Tsugi no suteppu ni susumu no wa jiki shōsōda to omoimasu.
We'll prepare for the next step.	I think it's premature to move to the next step.

Conversation example person A	Conversation example person B
今回の結果を踏まえ、次のステップに進みたいと思います。具体的な実施計画を策定します。	賛成です。実施計画の策定に協力させていただきます。
こんかいのけっかをふまえ、つぎのすてっぷにすすみたいとおもいます。ぐたいてきなじっしけいかくをさくていします。	さんせいです。じっしけいかくのさくていにきょうりょくさせていただきます。
Konkai no kekka o fumae, tsugi no suteppu ni Suzumu mitai to omoimasu. Gutai-tekina jisshi keikaku o sakutei shimasu.	Sanseidesu. Jisshi keikaku no sakutei ni kyōryoku sa sete itadakimasu.
Based on these results, I'd like to move on to the next step. We will formulate a specific implementation plan.	I agree. I'll cooperate in formulating the implementation plan.

Cultural Context

This implies you're seeking approval. Be prepared to justify why moving forward is the best course of action.

本提案のメリットは以下の通りです。

ほんていあんのめりっとはいかのとおりです。

Hon teian no meritto wa ika no tōridesu.

The benefits of this proposal are as follows.

Variation 1	Variation 2
本提案の利点は以下の通りです。	Kyō mo shōjin shima shou.
ほんていあんのりてんはいかのとおりです。	ほんていあんのりてんはいかのとおりです。
Hon teian no riten wa ika no tōridesu.	Hon teian no meritto wa tsugi no tōridesu.
The advantages of this proposal are as follows.	The advantages of this proposal are as follows.

Positive Response	Negative Response
メリットが魅力的ですね。実現が楽しみです。	メリットよりデメリットの方が大きいように思えます。
めりっとがみりょくてきですね。じつげんがたのしみです。	めりっとよりでめりっとのほうがおおきいようにおもえます。
Meritto ga miryoku-tekidesu ne. Jitsugen ga tanoshimidesu.	Meritto yori demeritto no kata ga ōkī yō ni omoemasu.
The benefits are attractive. Looking forward to realizing them.	The disadvantages seem to outweigh the advantages.

Conversation example person A	Conversation example person B
本提案のメリットは以下の通りです。コスト削減と顧客満足度向上が主な利点です。	メリットは理解しました。デメリットや潜在的なリスクはありますか？
ほんていあんのめりっとはいかのとおりです。こすとさくげんとこきゃくまんぞくどこうじょうがおもなりてんです。	めりっとはりかいしました。でめりっとやせんざいてきなりすくはありますか？
Hon teian no meritto wa ika no tōridesu. Kosuto sakugen to kokyaku manzoku-do kōjō ga omona ritendesu.	Meritto wa rikai shima shita. Demeritto ya senzai-tekina risuku wa arimasu ka?
The benefits of this proposal are as follows. Cost reduction and improved customer satisfaction are the main advantages.	I understand the benefits. Are there any disadvantages or potential risks?

Cultural Context

Be prepared to address potential drawbacks as well. Presenting only positives may be seen as one-sided.

実施にあたってのリスクとして、以下が考えられます。

じっしにあたってのりすくとして、いかがかんがえられます。

Jisshi ni atatte no risuku to shite, ika ga kangae raremasu.

The following risks are anticipated for implementation.

Variation 1	Variation 2
実行にあたってのリスクとして、以下が想定されます。	Kyō mo shōjin shima shou.
じっこうにあたってのりすくとして、いかがそうていされます。	じっこうにあたってのりすくとして、いかがそうていされます。
Jikkō ni atatte no risuku to shite, ika ga sōtei sa remasu.	Jisshi ni atatte no risuku to shite,-ji no ten ga kangae raremasu.
The following can be considered as risks when implementing.	The following can be considered as risks when implementing.

Positive Response	Negative Response
リスク管理は重要ですね。対策を考えましょう。	リスクが過小評価されているように思えます。
りすくかんりはじゅうようですね。たいさくをかんがえましょう。	りすくがかしょうひょうかされているようにおもえます。
Risuku kanri wa jūyōdesu ne. Taisaku o kangae ma shou.	Risuku ga kashō hyōka sa rete iru yō ni omoemasu.
Risk management is important. Let's consider countermeasures.	The risks seem to be underestimated.

Conversation example person A	Conversation example person B
実施にあたってのリスクとして、以下が考えられます。初期投資の負担と従業員の抵抗が予想されます。	リスクを認識しました。それぞれのリスクに対する対策案はありますか？
じっしにあたってのりすくとして、いかがかんがえられます。しょきとうしのふたんとじゅうぎょういんのていこうがよそうされます。	りすくをにんしきしました。それぞれのりすくにたいするたいさくあんはありますか？
Jisshi ni atatte no risuku to shite, ika ga kangae raremasu. Shoki tōshi no futan to jūgyō-in no teikō ga yosō sa remasu.	Risuku o ninshiki shima shita. Sorezore no risuku ni taisuru taisaku-an wa arimasu ka?
The following risks are anticipated in implementation. Initial investment burden and employee resistance are expected.	I acknowledge the risks. Do you have countermeasures for each of these risks?

Cultural Context

Demonstrating risk awareness is important, but also be prepared to discuss mitigation strategies.

本計画の推進体制は下記の通りです。

ほんけいかくのすいしんたいせいはかきのとおりです。

Hon keikaku no suishin taisei wa kaki no tōridesu.

The promotion structure for this plan is as follows.

Variation 1	Variation 2
本企画の推進体制は以下の通りです。	Kyō mo shōjin shima shou.
ほんきかくのすいしんたいせいはいかのとおりです。	ほんきかくのすいしんたいせいはいかのとおりです。
Hon kikaku no suishin taisei wa ika no tōridesu.	Hon purojekuto no suishin taisei wa tsugi no tōridesu.
The promotion system for this plan is as follows.	The promotion system for this project is as follows.

Positive Response	Negative Response
体制が整っていて心強いです。	推進体制が不十分に思えます。
たいせいがととのっていてこころづよいです。	すいしんたいせいがふじゅうぶんにおもえます。
Taisei ga totonotte ite kokorodzuyoidesu.	Suishin taisei ga fu jūbun ni omoemasu.
It's reassuring to see the structure in place.	The promotion system seems inadequate.

Conversation example person A	Conversation example person B
本計画の推進体制は下記の通りです。プロジェクトリーダーを中心に各部門から代表者を選出します。	体制案を承知しました。各部門の協力を得られるよう調整いたします。
ほんけいかくのすいしんたいせいはかきのとおりです。ぷろじぇくとりーだーをちゅうしんにかくぶもんからだいひょうしゃをせんしゅつします。	たいせいあんをしょうちしました。かくぶもんのきょうりょくをえられるようちょうせいいたします。
Hon keikaku no suishin taisei wa kaki no tōridesu. Purojekuto rīdā o chūshin ni kaku bumon kara daihyō-sha o senshutsu shimasu.	Taisei-an o shōchi shima shita. Kaku bumon no kyōryoku o e rareru yō chōsei itashimasu.
The promotion system for this plan is as follows. We will select representatives from each department, centered around the project leader.	I understand the proposed system. I will coordinate to ensure cooperation from each department.

Cultural Context

Ensure all mentioned individuals are aware of their roles. Surprising people with responsibilities can cause issues.

今回の提案に至った背景は以下の通りです。

こんかいのていあんにいたったはいけいはいかのとおりです。

Konkai no teian ni itatta haikei wa ika no tōridesu.

The background leading to this proposal is as follows.

Variation 1	Variation 2
今回の提案に至った経緯は以下の通りです。	Kyō mo shōjin shima shou.
こんかいのていあんにいたったいきさつはいかのとおりです。	こんかいのていあんにいたったいきさつはいかのとおりです。
Konkai no teian ni itatta ikisatsu wa ika no tōridesu.	Konkai no teian ni itatta haikei wa tsugi no tōridesu.
The background that led to this proposal is as follows.	The background that led to this proposal is as follows.

Positive Response	Negative Response
背景を理解できました。提案の意義が明確です。	背景の説明が不十分です。
はいけいをりかいできました。ていあんのいぎがめいかくです。	はいけいのせつめいがふじゅうぶんです。
Haikei o rikai dekimashita. Teian no igi ga meikakudesu.	Haikei no setsumei ga fu jūbundesu.
I understand the background. The proposal's significance is clear.	The explanation of the background is insufficient.

Conversation example person A	Conversation example person B
今回の提案に至った背景は以下の通りです。市場環境の変化と競合他社の動向が主な要因です。	背景について理解しました。この提案はそれらの課題にどう対応するのでしょうか？
こんかいのていあんにいたったはいけいはいかのとおりです。しじょうかんきょうのへんかときょうごうたしゃのどうこうがおもなよういんです。	はいけいについてりかいしました。このていあんはそれらのかだいにどうたいおうするのでしょうか？
Konkai no teian ni itatta haikei wa ika no tōridesu. Ichiba kankyō no henka to kyōgō tasha no dōkō ga omona yōindesu.	Haikei ni tsuite rikai shima shita. Kono teian wa sorera no kadai ni dō taiō suru nodeshou ka?
The background that led to this proposal is as follows. Changes in the market environment and trends of competitors are the main factors.	I understand the background. How does this proposal address these challenges?

Cultural Context

This provides context for your proposal. Ensure it aligns with known company issues or goals.

本件の実施により、以下の効果が期待できます。

ほんけんのじっしにより、いかのこうかがきたいできます。

Honken no jisshi ni yori, ika no kōka ga kitai dekimasu.

The following effects can be expected by implementing this matter.

Variation 1	Variation 2
本件の実行により、以下の効果が期待できます。	Kyō mo shōjin shima shou.
ほんけんのじっこうにより、いかのこうかがきたいできます。	ほんけんのじっこうにより、いかのこうかがきたいできます。
Honken no jikkō ni yori, ika no kōka ga kitai dekimasu.	Hon anken no jisshi ni yori,-ji no kōka ga mikomemasu.
The following effects can be expected by implementing this matter.	The following effects can be expected by implementing this matter.

Positive Response	Negative Response
大きな効果が期待できそうですね。	期待される効果が現実的ではありません。
おおきなこうかがきたいできそうですね。	きたいされるこうかがげんじつてきではありません。
Ōkina kōka ga kitai deki-sōdesu ne.	Kitai sa re ru kōka ga genjitsu-tekide wa arimasen.
It seems we can expect significant effects.	The expected effects are not realistic.

Conversation example person A	Conversation example person B
本件の実施により、以下の効果が期待できます。主に業務効率の向上と顧客満足度の改善です。	期待される効果は魅力的です。具体的な数値目標はありますか？
ほんけんのじっしにより、いかのこうかがきたいできます。おもにぎょうむこうりつのこうじょうとこきゃくまんぞくどのかいぜんです。	きたいされるこうかはみりょくてきです。ぐたいてきなすうちもくひょうはありますか？
Honken no jisshi ni yori, ika no kōka ga kitai dekimasu. Omo ni gyōmu kōritsu no kōjō to kokyaku manzoku-do no kaizendesu.	Kitai sa re ru kōka wa miryoku-tekidesu. Gutai-tekina sūchi mokuhyō wa arimasu ka?
The following effects can be expected from the implementation of this matter. Mainly, improvement in operational efficiency and customer satisfaction.	The expected effects are attractive. Do you have any specific numerical targets?

Cultural Context

Be conservative in your predictions. Overestimating benefits can damage credibility.

今後の課題として、以下の点が挙げられます。

こんごのかだいとして、いかのてんがあげられます。
Kongo no kadai to shite, ika no ten ga age raremasu.
The following points are raised as future issues.

Variation 1	Variation 2
今後の問題点として、以下の点が挙げられます。	Kyō mo shōjin shima shou.
こんごのもんだいてんとして、いかのてんがあげられます。	こんごのもんだいてんとして、いかのてんがあげられます。
Kongo no mondai-ten to shite, ika no ten ga age raremasu.	Kongo no kadai to shite,-ji no ten ga kangae raremasu.
The following points can be mentioned as future issues.	The following points can be considered as future issues.

Positive Response	Negative Response
課題を認識できて良かったです。対応を考えましょう。	課題の解決策が示されていません。
かだいをにんしきできてよかったです。たいおうをかんがえましょう。	かだいのかいけつさくがしめされていません。
Kadai o ninshiki dekite yokattadesu. Taiō o kangae ma shou.	Kadai no kaiketsu-saku ga shì Sa rete imasen.
It's good we've identified these issues. Let's consider how to address them.	Solutions to these challenges are not provided.

Conversation example person A	Conversation example person B
今後の課題として、以下の点が挙げられます。人材育成と技術革新への対応が急務です。	課題を理解しました。これらの課題に対する行動計画を立てましょう。
こんごのかだいとして、いかのてんがあげられます。じんざいいくせいとぎじゅつかくしんへのたいおうがきゅうむです。	かだいをりかいしました。これらのかだいにたいするこうどうけいかくをたてましょう。
Kongo no kadai to shite, ika no ten ga age raremasu. Jinzai ikusei to gijutsu kakushin e no taiō ga kyūmudesu.	Kadai o rikai shima shita. Korera no kadai ni taisuru kōdō keikaku o tate ma shou.
The following points are identified as future challenges. Human resource development and response to technological innovation are urgent tasks.	I understand the challenges. Let's create an action plan to address these issues.

Cultural Context
Acknowledging challenges shows foresight, but be prepared to discuss how you plan to address them.

本提案の実施スケジュールは以下の通りです。

ほんていあんのじっしすけじゅーるはいかのとおりです。

Hon teian no jisshi sukejūru wa ika no tōridesu.

The implementation schedule for this proposal is as follows.

Variation 1	Variation 2
本提案の実行スケジュールは以下の通りです。	Kyō mo shōjin shima shou.
ほんていあんのじっこうすけじゅーるはいかのとおりです。	ほんていあんのじっこうすけじゅーるはいかのとおりです。
Hon teian no jikkō sukejūru wa ika no tōridesu.	Hon teian no jisshi sukejūru wa tsugi no tōridesu.
The implementation schedule for this proposal is as follows.	The implementation schedule for this proposal is as follows.

Positive Response	Negative Response
具体的なスケジュールで見通しが立ちますね。	スケジュールが厳しすぎます。
ぐたいてきなすけじゅーるでみとおしがたちますね。	すけじゅーるがきびしすぎます。
Gutai-tekina sukejūru de mitōshi ga tachimasu ne.	Sukejūru ga kibishi sugimasu.
The specific schedule gives us a clear outlook.	The schedule is too tight.

Conversation example person A	Conversation example person B
本提案の実施スケジュールは以下の通りです。来月から準備を開始し、3ヶ月後の本格導入を目指します。	スケジュールを確認しました。各段階でのマイルストーンを設定しましょう。
ほんていあんのじっしすけじゅーるはいかのとおりです。らいげつからじゅんびをかいしし、3かげつごのほんかくどうにゅうをめざします。	すけじゅーるをかくにんしました。かくだんかいでのまいるすとーんをせっていしましょう。
Hon teian no jisshi sukejūru wa ika no tōridesu. Rai tsuki kara junbi o kaishi shi, san-kagetsu-go no honkaku dōnyū o mezashimasu.	Sukejūru o kakunin shima shita. Kaku dankai de no mairu sutōn o settei shima shou.
The implementation schedule for this proposal is as follows. We will start preparations next month and aim for full implementation in three months.	I have confirmed the schedule. Let's set milestones for each stage.

Cultural Context

Ensure the schedule is realistic and allows for potential delays. Missing deadlines is viewed very negatively in Japan.

実施に必要な予算は下記の通りです。

じっしにひつようなよさんはかきのとおりです。

Jisshi ni hitsuyōna yosan wa kaki no tōridesu.

The budget required for implementation is as follows.

Variation 1	Variation 2
実行に必要な予算は以下の通りです。	Kyō mo shōjin shima shou.
じっこうにひつようなよさんはいかのとおりです。	じっこうにひつようなよさんはいかのとおりです。
Jikkō ni hitsuyōna yosan wa ika no tōridesu.	Jisshi ni hitsuyōna yosan wa tsugi no tōridesu.
The budget required for implementation is as follows.	The budget required for implementation is as follows.

Positive Response	Negative Response
予算の内訳が明確で助かります。	予算が高すぎます。
よさんのうちわけがめいかくでたすかります。	よさんがたかすぎます。
Yosan no uchiwake ga meikakude tasukarimasu.	Yosan ga taka sugimasu.
The clear budget breakdown is helpful.	The budget is too high.

Conversation example person A	Conversation example person B
実施に必要な予算は下記の通りです。初期投資として 1000 万円、運用費用として月額 50 万円を見込んでいます。	予算案を理解しました。投資対効果の試算結果も共有いただけますか？
じっしにひつようなよさんはかきのとおりです。しょきとうしとして 1000 まんえん、うんようひようとしてげつがく 50 まんえんをみこんでいます。	よさんあんをりかいしました。とうしたいこうかのしさんけっかもきょうゆういただけますか？
Jisshi ni hitsuyōna yosan wa kaki no tōridesu. Shoki tōshi to shite sen man-en, un'yō hiyō to shite getsugaku go jū man-en o mikonde imasu.	Yosan-an o rikai shima shita. Tōshi tai kōka no shisan kekka mo kyōyū itadakemasu ka?
The budget required for implementation is as follows. We anticipate an initial investment of 10 million yen and monthly operating costs of 500,000 yen.	I understand the budget proposal. Can you also share the calculated return on investment?

Cultural Context

Be prepared to justify each budget item. Inflated or vague budget requests may be scrutinized.

実施後のモニタリング方法は下記の通りです。

じっしごのもにたりんぐほうほうはかきのとおりです。

Jisshi-go no monitaringu hōhō wa kaki no tōridesu.

The post-implementation monitoring method is as follows.

Variation 1	Variation 2
実行後のモニタリング方法は以下の通りです。	Kyō mo shōjin shima shou.
じっこうごのもにたりんぐほうほうはいかのとおりです。	じっこうごのもにたりんぐほうほうはいかのとおりです。
Jikkō-go no monitaringu hōhō wa ika no tōridesu.	Jisshi-go no monitaringu hōhō wa tsugi no tōridesu.
The monitoring method after implementation is as follows.	The method for monitoring after implementation is as follows.

Positive Response	Negative Response
継続的な改善につながりそうですね。	モニタリング方法が不十分に思えます。
けいぞくてきなかいぜんにつながりそうですね。	もにたりんぐほうほうがふじゅうぶんにおもえます。
Keizoku-tekina kaizen ni tsunagari-sōdesu ne.	Monitaringu hōhō ga fu jūbun ni omoemasu.
This should lead to continuous improvement.	The monitoring method seems inadequate.

Conversation example person A	Conversation example person B
実施後のモニタリング方法は下記の通りです。月次レポートと四半期ごとの詳細分析を行います。	モニタリング方法について了解しました。結果の共有方法も決めておきましょう。
じっしごのもにたりんぐほうほうはかきのとおりです。げつじれぽーととしはんきごとのしょうさいぶんせきをおこないます。	もにたりんぐほうほうについてりょうかいしました。けっかのきょうゆうほうほうもきめておきましょう。
Jisshi-go no monitaringu hōhō wa kaki no tōridesu. Tsuki-ji repōto to shihanki-goto no shōsai bunseki o okonaimasu.	Monitaringu hōhō ni tsuite ryōkai shima shita. Kekka no kyōyū hōhō mo kimete oki ma shou.
The post-implementation monitoring method is as follows. We will conduct monthly reports and detailed analyses every quarter.	I understand the monitoring method. Let's also decide on how to share the results.

Cultural Context

This shows you've thought about long-term success. Be prepared to explain how you'll act on the monitoring results.

実施にあたっての課題と対策は以下の通りです。

じっしにあたってのかだいとたいさくはいかのとおりです。

Jisshi ni atatte no kadai to taisaku wa ika no tōridesu.

The challenges and countermeasures for implementation are as follows.

Variation 1	Variation 2
実行にあたっての問題点と対策は以下の通りです。	Kyō mo shōjin shima shou.
じっこうにあたってのもんだいてんとたいさくはいかのとおりです。	じっこうにあたってのもんだいてんとたいさくはいかのとおりです。
Jikkō ni atatte no mondai-ten to taisaku wa ika no tōridesu.	Jisshi ni atatte no kadai to taiō-saku wa tsugi no tōridesu.
The issues and countermeasures when implementing are as follows.	The issues and countermeasures when implementing are as follows.

Positive Response	Negative Response
綿密な計画ですね。実行に移しましょう。	対策が具体性に欠けています。
めんみつなけいかくですね。じっこうにうつしましょう。	たいさくがぐたいせいにかけています。
Menmitsuna keikakudesu ne. Jikkō ni Utsuri shima shou.	Taisaku ga gutai-sei ni kakete imasu.
It's a thorough plan. Let's put it into action.	The countermeasures lack specificity.

Conversation example person A	Conversation example person B
実施にあたっての課題と対策は以下の通りです。主に人材不足に対して、外部リソースの活用を検討しています。	課題と対策を理解しました。外部リソース活用の具体的な計画を教えてください。
じっしにあたってのかだいとたいさくはいかのとおりです。おもにじんざいぶそくにたいして、がいぶりそーすのかつようをけんとうしています。	かだいとたいさくをりかいしました。がいぶりそーすかつようのぐたいてきなけいかくをおしえてください。
Jisshi ni atatte no kadai to taisaku wa ika no tōridesu. Omo ni jinzai fusoku ni taishite, gaibu risōsu no katsuyō o kentō shite imasu.	Kadai to taisaku o rikai shima shita. Gaibu risōsu katsuyō no gutai-tekina keikaku o oshiete kudasai.
The challenges and countermeasures for implementation are as follows. Mainly, we are considering utilizing external resources to address the shortage of human resources.	I understand the challenges and countermeasures. Please tell me about the specific plans for utilizing external resources.

Cultural Context

Demonstrating that you've considered potential issues and solutions shows thorough planning.

本提案のターゲットユーザーは以下の通りです。

ほんていあんのたーげっとゆーざーはいかのとおりです。

Hon teian no tāgetto yūzā wa ika no tōridesu.

The target users for this proposal are as follows.

Variation 1	Variation 2
本提案の対象ユーザーは以下の通りです。	Kyō mo shōjin shima shou.
ほんていあんのたいしょうゆーざーはいかのとおりです。	ほんていあんのたいしょうゆーざーはいかのとおりです。
Hon teian no taishō yūzā wa ika no tōridesu.	Hon teian no taishō-sha wa tsugi no tōridesu.
The target users of this proposal are as follows.	The target users of this proposal are as follows.

Positive Response	Negative Response
ターゲットが明確で戦略が立てやすそうです。	ターゲットユーザーの選定根拠が不明確です。
たーげっとがめいかくでせんりゃくがたてやすそうです。	たーげっとゆーざーのせんていこんきょがふめいかくです。
Tāgetto ga meikakude senryaku ga tateyasu sōdesu.	Tāgetto yūzā no sentei konkyo ga fu meikakudesu.
The clear target makes it easier to strategize.	The basis for selecting target users is unclear.

Conversation example person A	Conversation example person B
本提案のターゲットユーザーは以下の通りです。主に20代から40代の都市部在住者を想定しています。	ターゲット層は理解しました。このターゲット選定の根拠を教えてください。
ほんていあんのたーげっとゆーざーはいかのとおりです。おもに20だいから40だいのとしぶざいじゅうしゃをそうていしています。	たーげっとそうはりかいしました。このたーげっとせんていのこんきょをおしえてください。
Hon teian no tāgetto yūzā wa ika no tōridesu. Omo ni ni jū-dai kara yon-jū-dai no toshi-bu zaijū-sha o sōtei shite imasu.	Tāgetto-sō wa rikai shima shita. Kono tāgetto sentei no konkyo o oshiete kudasai.
The target users for this proposal are as follows. We mainly anticipate urban residents in their 20s to 40s.	I understand the target demographic. Can you explain the basis for selecting this target?

Cultural Context

Be specific about who will benefit. Vague or overly broad target groups may weaken your proposal.

今回のプロジェクトの成功基準は下記の通りです。

こんかいのぷろじぇくとのせいこうきじゅんはかきのとおりです。

Konkai no purojekuto no seikō kijun wa kaki no tōridesu.

The success criteria for this project are as follows.

Variation 1	Variation 2
今回の企画の成功基準は以下の通りです。	Kyō mo shōjin shima shou.
こんかいのきかくのせいこうきじゅんはいかのとおりです。	こんかいのきかくのせいこうきじゅんはいかのとおりです。
Konkai no kikaku no seikō kijun wa ika no tōridesu.	Konkai no purojekuto no seikō kijun wa tsugi no tōridesu.
The success criteria for this project are as follows.	The success criteria for this project are as follows.

Positive Response	Negative Response
具体的な基準があると評価しやすいですね。	成功基準が厳しすぎます。
ぐたいてきなきじゅんがあるとひょうかしやすいですね。	せいこうきじゅんがきびしすぎます。
Gutai-tekina kijun ga aru to hyōka shi yasuidesu ne.	Seikō kijun ga kibishi sugimasu.
Specific criteria make it easier to evaluate.	The success criteria are too strict.

Conversation example person A	Conversation example person B
今回のプロジェクトの成功基準は下記の通りです。売上高10%増加と顧客満足度5ポイント上昇を目指します。	成功基準を確認しました。これらの指標をどのように測定しますか？
こんかいのぷろじぇくとのせいこうきじゅんはかきのとおりです。うりあげだか10%ぞうかとこきゃくまんぞくど5ぽいんとじょうしょうをめざします。	せいこうきじゅんをかくにんしました。これらのしひょうをどのようにそくていしますか？
Konkai no purojekuto no seikō kijun wa kaki no tōridesu. Uriage-daka juppāsento zōka to kokyaku manzoku-do go pointo jōshō o mezashimasu.	Seikō kijun o kakunin shima shita. Korera no shihyō o dono yō ni sokutei shimasu ka?
The success criteria for this project are as follows. We aim for a 10% increase in sales and a 5-point rise in customer satisfaction.	I have confirmed the success criteria. How will these indicators be measured?

Cultural Context

Ensure success criteria are measurable and aligned with company goals. Subjective criteria may be questioned.

本計画の中長期的な展望は以下の通りです。

ほんけいかくのちゅうちょうきてきなてんぼうはいかのとおりです。

Hon keikaku no naka chōki-tekina tenbō wa ika no tōridesu.

The medium to long-term outlook for this plan is as follows.

Variation 1	Variation 2
本企画の中長期的な見通しは以下の通りです。	Kyō mo shōjin shima shou.
ほんきかくのちゅうちょうきてきなみとおしはいかのとおりです。	ほんきかくのちゅうちょうきてきなみとおしはいかのとおりです。
Hon kikaku no naka chōki-tekina mitōshi wa ika no tōridesu.	Hon purojekuto no naka chōki-tekina tenbō wa tsugi no tōridesu.
The medium- to long-term prospects for this plan are as follows.	The medium to long-term outlook for this project is as follows.

Positive Response	Negative Response
将来を見据えた計画ですね。素晴らしいです。	中長期的な展望が楽観的すぎます。
しょうらいをみすえたけいかくですね。すばらしいです。	ちゅうちょうきてきなてんぼうがらっかんてきすぎます。
Shōrai o misueta keikakudesu ne. Subarashīdesu.	Chū chōki-tekina tenbō ga rakkan-teki sugimasu.
It's a forward-looking plan. Excellent.	The medium to long-term outlook is too optimistic.

Conversation example person A	Conversation example person B
本計画の中長期的な展望は以下の通りです。5年後には市場シェア30%の獲得を目指しています。	野心的な目標ですね。その達成に向けた具体的な戦略を教えてください。
ほんけいかくのちゅうちょうきてきなてんぼうはいかのとおりです。5ねんごにはしじょうしぇあ30%のかくとくをめざしています。	やしんてきなもくひょうですね。そのたっせいにむけたぐたいてきなせんりゃくをおしえてください。
Hon keikaku no naka chōki-tekina tenbō wa ika no tōridesu. Go-nen-go ni wa ichiba shea san jū pāsento no kakutoku o mezashite imasu.	Yashin-tekina mokuhyōdesu ne. Sono tassei ni muketa gutai-tekina senryaku o oshiete kudasai.
The medium to long-term outlook for this plan is as follows. We aim to achieve a 30% market share in 5 years.	That's an ambitious goal. Could you tell me about the specific strategies to achieve this?

Cultural Context

This shows strategic thinking. Ensure it aligns with known company long-term goals.

実施後の評価方法は以下の通りです。

じっしごのひょうかほうほうはいかのとおりです。

Jisshi-go no hyōka hōhō wa ika no tōridesu.

The post-implementation evaluation method is as follows.

Variation 1	Variation 2
実行後の評価方法は以下の通りです。	Kyō mo shōjin shima shou.
じっこうごのひょうかほうほうはいかのとおりです。	じっこうごのひょうかほうほうはいかのとおりです。
Jikkō-go no hyōka hōhō wa ika no tōridesu.	Jisshi-go no hyōka hōhō wa tsugi no tōridesu.
The evaluation method after implementation is as follows.	The evaluation method after implementation is as follows.

Positive Response	Negative Response
客観的な評価ができそうですね。	評価方法が適切ではありません。
きゃっかんてきなひょうかができそうですね。	ひょうかほうほうがてきせつではありません。
Kyakkan-tekina hyōka ga deki-sōdesu ne.	Hyōka hōhō ga tekisetsude wa arimasen.
It seems we can make an objective evaluation.	The evaluation method is not appropriate.

Conversation example person A	Conversation example person B
実施後の評価方法は以下の通りです。KPI の達成度と従業員満足度調査を主な指標とします。	評価方法を理解しました。評価結果はどのように活用する予定ですか？
じっしごのひょうかほうほうはいかのとおりです。KPI のたっせいどとじゅうぎょういんまんぞくどちょうさをおもなしひょうとします。	ひょうかほうほうをりかいしました。ひょうかけっかはどのようにかつようするよていですか？
Jisshi-go no hyōka hōhō wa ika no tōridesu. Kēpīai no tassei-do to jūgyō-in manzoku-do chōsa o omona shihyō to shimasu.	Hyōka hōhō o rikai shima shita. Hyōka kekka wa dono yō ni katsuyō suru yoteidesu ka?
The evaluation method after implementation is as follows. We will use KPI achievement and employee satisfaction surveys as our main indicators.	I understand the evaluation method. How do you plan to utilize the evaluation results?

Cultural Context

Be prepared to explain how you'll act on evaluation results. Mere measurement without action may be seen as wasteful.

本提案の差別化要因は以下の点です。

ほんていあんのさべつかよういんはいかのてんです。

Hon teian no sabetsu-ka yōin wa ika no tendesu.

The differentiating factors of this proposal are as follows.

Variation 1	Variation 2
本提案の優位性は以下の点です。	Kyō mo shōjin shima shou.
ほんていあんのゆういせいはいかのてんです。	ほんていあんのゆういせいはいかのてんです。
Hon teian no yūi-sei wa ika no tendesu.	Hon teian no tsuyomi wa tsugi no tendesu.
The differentiation factors of this proposal are the following points.	The strengths of this proposal are the following points.

Positive Response	Negative Response
競争力のある提案ですね。期待しています。	差別化要因が不十分に思えます。
きょうそうりょくのあるていあんですね。きたいしています。	さべつかよういんがふじゅうぶんにおもえます。
Kyōsō-ryoku no aru teiandesu ne. Kitai shite imasu.	Sabetsu-ka yōin ga fu jūbun ni omoemasu.
It's a competitive proposal. We have high expectations.	The differentiating factors seem insufficient.

Conversation example person A	Conversation example person B
本提案の差別化要因は以下の点です。独自の AI 技術の活用が最大の強みとなります。	差別化要因は明確ですね。競合他社の動向も踏まえた分析結果はありますか？
ほんていあんのさべつかよういんはいかのてんです。どくじの AI ぎじゅつのかつようがさいだいのつよみとなります。	さべつかよういんはめいかくですね。きょうごうたしゃのどうこうもふまえたぶんせきけっかはありますか？
Hon teian no sabetsu-ka yōin wa ika no tendesu. Dokuji no ēai gijutsu no katsuyō ga saidai no tsuyomi to narimasu.	Sabetsu-ka yōin wa meikakudesu ne. Kyōgō tasha no dōkō mo fumaeta bunseki kekka wa arimasu ka?
The differentiation factors of this proposal are as follows. The use of our proprietary AI technology will be our greatest strength.	The differentiation factors are clear. Do you have analysis results that also take into account competitors' trends?

Cultural Context

Ensure these points are truly unique. Commonplace features presented as differentiators may damage credibility.

今回の施策によるコスト削減効果は以下の通りです。

こんかいのしさくによるこすとさくげんこうかはいかのとおりです。

Konkai no shisaku ni yoru kosuto sakugen kōka wa ika no tōridesu.

The cost reduction effects of this measure are as follows.

Variation 1	Variation 2
今回の取り組みによるコスト削減効果は以下の通りです。	Kyō mo shōjin shima shou.
こんかいのとりくみによるこすとさくげんこうかはいかのとおりです。	こんかいのとりくみによるこすとさくげんこうかはいかのとおりです。
Konkai no torikumi ni yoru kosuto sakugen kōka wa ika no tōridesu.	Konkai no shisaku ni yoru kosuto sakugen kōka wa tsugi no tōridesu.
The cost reduction effect of this measure is as follows.	The cost reduction effect of this initiative is as follows.

Positive Response	Negative Response
コスト削減の可能性が高そうですね。	コスト削減効果が過大評価されているように思えます。
こすとさくげんのかのうせいがたかそうですね。	こすとさくげんこうかがかだいひょうかされているようにおもえます。
Kosuto sakugen no kanō-sei ga taka-sōdesu ne.	Kosuto sakugen kōka ga kadai hyōka sa rete iru yō ni omoemasu.
The potential for cost reduction seems high.	The cost reduction effects seem to be overestimated.

Conversation example person A	Conversation example person B
今回の施策によるコスト削減効果は以下の通りです。年間約 5000 万円の削減を見込んでいます。	大きな削減効果ですね。その内訳と算出根拠を教えていただけますか?
こんかいのしさくによるこすとさくげんこうかはいかのとおりです。ねんかんやく 5000 まんえんのさくげんをみこんでいます。	おおきなさくげんこうかですね。そのうちわけとさんしゅつこんきょをおしえていただけますか?
Konkai no shisaku ni yoru kosuto sakugen kōka wa ika no tōridesu. Nenkan yaku go sen man-en no sakugen o mikonde imasu.	Ōkina sakugen kōkadesu ne. Sono uchiwake to sanshutsu konkyo o oshiete itadakemasu ka?
The cost reduction effect of this measure is as follows. We expect an annual reduction of about 50 million yen.	That's a significant cost reduction. Could you provide a breakdown and the basis for this calculation?

Cultural Context
Be conservative in estimates. Overestimating cost savings can lead to disappointment and loss of trust.

本計画の実施により想定されるリスクは以下の通りです。

ほんけいかくのじっしによりそうていされるりすくはいかのとおりです。

Hon keikaku no jisshi ni yori sōtei sa re ru risuku wa ika no tōridesu.

The anticipated risks from implementing this plan are as follows.

Variation 1	Variation 2
本企画の実行により想定されるリスクは以下の通りです。	Kyō mo shōjin shima shou.
ほんきかくのじっこうによりそうていされるりすくはいかのとおりです。	ほんきかくのじっこうによりそうていされるりすくはいかのとおりです。
Hon kikaku no jikkō ni yori sōtei sa re ru risuku wa ika no tōridesu.	Hon purojekuto no jisshi ni yori sōtei sa re ru risuku wa tsugi no tōridesu.
The risks assumed by the implementation of this plan are as follows.	The risks assumed by implementing this project are as follows.

Positive Response	Negative Response
リスクの洗い出しが丁寧ですね。対策を立てましょう。	リスク対策が不十分です。
りすくのあらいだしがていねいですね。たいさくをたてましょう。	りすくたいさくがふじゅうぶんです。
Risuku no araidashi ga teineidesu ne. Taisaku o tate ma shou.	Risuku taisaku ga fu jūbundesu.
The risk identification is thorough. Let's plan countermeasures.	The risk countermeasures are insufficient.

Conversation example person A	Conversation example person B
本計画の実施により想定されるリスクは以下の通りです。初期の生産性低下と顧客離れが懸念されます。	リスクを認識しました。各リスクに対する具体的な対策案はありますか？
ほんけいかくのじっしによりそうていされるりすくはいかのとおりです。しょきのせいさんせいていかとこきゃくざかれがけねんされます。	りすくをにんしきしました。かくりすくにたいするぐたいてきなたいさくあんはありますか？
Hon keikaku no jisshi ni yori sōtei sa reru risuku wa ika no tōridesu. Shoki no seisan-sei teika to kokyaku banare ga kenen sa remasu.	Risuku o ninshiki shima shita. Kaku risuku ni taisuru gutai-tekina taisaku-an wa arimasu ka?
The risks anticipated from implementing this plan are as follows. Initial productivity decline and customer churn are concerns.	I acknowledge the risks. Do you have specific countermeasures for each risk?

Cultural Context
Acknowledging risks shows foresight, but be prepared to discuss mitigation strategies.

実施にあたっての法的考慮事項は下記の通りです。

じっしにあたってのほうてきこうりょじこうはかきのとおりです。

Jisshi ni atatte no hō-teki kōryo jikō wa kaki no tōridesu.

The legal considerations for implementation are as follows.

Variation 1	Variation 2
実行にあたっての法的留意点は以下の通りです。	Kyō mo shōjin shima shou.
じっこうにあたってのほうてきりゅういてんはいかのとおりです。	じっこうにあたってのほうてきりゅういてんはいかのとおりです。
Jikkō ni atatte no hō-teki ryūi-ten wa ika no tōridesu.	Jisshi ni atatte no hō-teki chūi-ten wa tsugi no tōridesu.
The legal considerations when implementing are as follows.	The legal points to note when implementing are as follows.

Positive Response	Negative Response
法的な側面も押さえていて安心です。	法的考慮事項の検討が不十分です。
ほうてきなそくめんもおさえていてあんしんです。	ほうてきこうりょじこうのけんとうがふじゅうぶんです。
Hō-tekina sokumen mo osaete ite anshindesu.	Hō-teki kōryo jikō no kentō ga fu jūbundesu.
It's reassuring that legal aspects are covered.	The consideration of legal issues is insufficient.

Conversation example person A	Conversation example person B
実施にあたっての法的考慮事項は下記の通りです。個人情報保護法とコンプライアンスに特に注意が必要です。	法的考慮事項を理解しました。社内の法務部門と連携して進めましょう。
じっしにあたってのほうてきこうりょじこうはかきのとおりです。こじんじょうほうほごほうとこんぷらいあんすにとくにちゅういがひつようです。	ほうてきこうりょじこうをりかいしました。しゃないのほうむぶもんとれんけいしてすすめましょう。
Jisshi ni atatte no hōteki kōryo jikō wa kaki no tōridesu. Kojin jōhō hogo-hō to konpuraiansu ni tokuni chūi ga hitsuyōdesu.	Hō-teki kōryo jikō o rikai shima shita. Shanai no hōmu bumon to renkei shite susume ma shou.
The legal considerations for implementation are as follows. Particular attention needs to be paid to the Personal Information Protection Law and compliance.	I understand the legal considerations. Let's proceed in cooperation with the internal legal department.

Cultural Context

This shows due diligence. Ensure you've consulted with appropriate legal experts if necessary.

本提案の競合分析結果は以下の通りです。

ほんていあんのきょうごうぶんせきけっかはいかのとおりです。

Hon teian no kyōgō bunseki kekka wa ika no tōridesu.

The results of the competitive analysis for this proposal are as follows.

Variation 1	Variation 2
本提案の競合他社分析結果は以下の通りです。	Kyō mo shōjin shima shou.
ほんていあんのきょうごうたしゃぶんせきけっかはいかのとおりです。	ほんていあんのきょうごうたしゃぶんせきけっかはいかのとおりです。
Hon teian no kyōgō tasha bunseki kekka wa ika no tōridesu.	Hon teian no kyōgō tasha bunseki kekka wa tsugi no tōridesu.
The competitive analysis results of this proposal are as follows.	The competitor analysis results of this proposal are as follows.

Positive Response	Negative Response
市場での位置づけがよく分かりました。	競合分析が表面的です。
しじょうでのいちづけがよくわかりました。	きょうごうぶんせきがひょうめんてきです。
Ichiba de no ichidzuke ga yoku wakarimashita.	Kyōgō bunseki ga hyōmen-tekidesu.
I now understand our market positioning well.	The competitive analysis is superficial.

Conversation example person A	Conversation example person B
本提案の競合分析結果は以下の通りです。当社の技術力が最大の競争優位性となっています。	分析結果を確認しました。競合他社の弱点をどのように活用する予定ですか？
ほんていあんのきょうごうぶんせきけっかはいかのとおりです。とうしゃのぎじゅつりょくがさいだいのきょうそうゆういせいとなっています。	ぶんせきけっかをかくにんしました。きょうごうたしゃのじゃくてんをどのようにかつようするよていですか？
Hon teian no kyōgō bunseki kekka wa ika no tōridesu. Tōsha no gijutsu-ryoku ga saidai no kyōsō yūi-sei to natte imasu.	Bunseki kekka o kakunin shima shita. Kyōgō tasha no jakuten o dono yō ni katsuyō suru yoteidesu ka?
The results of the competitive analysis for this proposal are as follows. Our company's technological capability is our greatest competitive advantage.	I've confirmed the analysis results. How do you plan to utilize the weaknesses of competitors?

Cultural Context

Ensure your analysis is current and comprehensive. Outdated or superficial analysis may be criticized.

今回の計画の実施体制は以下の通りです。

こんかいのけいかくのじっしたいせいはいかのとおりです。

Konkai no keikaku no jisshi taisei wa ika no tōridesu.

The implementation structure for this plan is as follows.

Variation 1	Variation 2
今回の企画の実行体制は以下の通りです。	Kyō mo shōjin shima shou.
こんかいのきかくのじっこうたいせいはいかのとおりです。	こんかいのきかくのじっこうたいせいはいかのとおりです。
Konkai no kikaku no jikkō taisei wa ika no tōridesu.	Konkai no purojekuto no jisshi taisei wa tsugi no tōridesu.
The implementation system for this plan is as follows.	The implementation system for this project is as follows.

Positive Response	Negative Response
役割分担が明確で良いですね。	実施体制が脆弱に思えます。
やくわりぶんたんがめいかくでよいですね。	じっしたいせいがぜいじゃくにおもえます。
Yakuwari buntan ga meikakude yoidesu ne.	Jisshi taisei ga zeijaku ni omoemasu.
The clear division of roles is good.	The implementation structure seems weak.

Conversation example person A	Conversation example person B
今回の計画の実施体制は以下の通りです。プロジェクトマネージャーを中心に、各部門からメンバーを選出します。	実施体制を理解しました。各メンバーの役割と責任を明確にしておきましょう。
こんかいのけいかくのじっしたいせいはいかのとおりです。ぷろじぇくとまねージゃーをちゅうしんに、かくぶもんからめんばーをせんしゅつします。	じっしたいせいをりかいしました。かくめんばーのやくわりとせきにんをめいかくにしておきましょう。
Konkai no keikaku no jisshi taisei wa ika no tōridesu. Purojekuto manējā o chūshin ni, kaku bumon kara menbā o senshutsu shimasu.	Jisshi taisei o rikai shima shita. Kaku menbā no yakuwari to sekinin o meikaku ni shite oki ma shou.
The implementation structure for this plan is as follows. We will select members from each department, centered around the project manager.	I understand the implementation structure. Let's clarify the roles and responsibilities of each member.

Cultural Context

Ensure all mentioned parties are aware of their roles. Surprising people with responsibilities can cause issues.

本施策の導入スケジュールは下記の通りです。

ほんしさくのどうにゅうすけじゅーるはかきのとおりです。

Hon shisaku no dōnyū sukejūru wa kaki no tōridesu.

The implementation schedule for this measure is as follows.

Variation 1	Variation 2
本取り組みの導入スケジュールは以下の通りです。	Kyō mo shōjin shima shou.
ほんとりくみのどうにゅうすけじゅーるはいかのとおりです。	ほんとりくみのどうにゅうすけじゅーるはいかのとおりです。
Hon torikumi no dōnyū sukejūru wa ika no tōridesu.	Hon shisaku no dōnyū sukejūru wa tsugi no tōridesu.
The introduction schedule for this measure is as follows.	The introduction schedule for this initiative is as follows.

Positive Response	Negative Response
段階的な導入で無理なく進められそうです。	導入スケジュールが急すぎます。
だんかいてきなどうにゅうでむりなくすすめられそうです。	どうにゅうすけじゅーるがせわしすぎます。
Dankai-tekina dōnyū de muri naku susume rare-sōdesu.	Dōnyū sukejūru ga kyū sugimasu.
The phased implementation seems manageable.	The implementation schedule is too rushed.

Conversation example person A	Conversation example person B
本施策の導入スケジュールは下記の通りです。来月から準備を開始し、3ヶ月後の本格導入を目指します。	スケジュールを確認しました。各段階でのマイルストーンを設定しましょう。
ほんしさくのどうにゅうすけじゅーるはかきのとおりです。らいげつからじゅんびをかいしし、3かげつごのほんかくどうにゅうをめざします。	すけじゅーるをかくにんしました。かくだんかいでのまいるすとーんをせっていしましょう。
Hon shisaku no dōnyū sukejūru wa kaki no tōridesu. Rai tsuki kara junbi o kaishi shi, 3-kagetsu-go no honkaku dōnyū o mezashimasu.	Sukejūru o kakunin shima shita. Kaku dankai de no mairu sutōn o settei shima shou.
The implementation schedule for this measure is as follows. We will start preparations next month and aim for full implementation in three months.	I have confirmed the schedule. Let's set milestones for each stage.

Cultural Context

Be realistic about timelines. In Japanese business culture, delays are viewed very negatively.

実施後のフォローアップ計画は以下の通りです。

じっしごのふぉろーあっぷけいかくはいかのとおりです。

Jisshi-go no forō appu keikaku wa ika no tōridesu.

The follow-up plan after implementation is as follows.

Variation 1	Variation 2
実行後のフォローアップ計画は以下の通りです。	Kyō mo shōjin shima shou.
じっこうごのふぉろーあっぷけいかくはいかのとおりです。	じっこうごのふぉろーあっぷけいかくはいかのとおりです。
Jikkō-go no forō appu keikaku wa ika no tōridesu.	Jisshi-go no forō appu keikaku wa tsugi no tōridesu.
The follow-up plan after implementation is as follows.	The follow-up plan after implementation is as follows.

Positive Response	Negative Response
継続的なサポートが期待できますね。	フォローアップ計画が不十分です。
けいぞくてきなさぽーとがきたいできますね。	ふぉろーあっぷけいかくがふじゅうぶんです。
Keizoku-tekina sapōto ga kitai dekimasu ne.	Forō appu keikaku ga fu jūbundesu.
We can expect continuous support.	The follow-up plan is insufficient.

Conversation example person A	Conversation example person B
実施後のフォローアップ計画は以下の通りです。月次レビューと四半期ごとの詳細分析を行います。	フォローアップ計画を理解しました。問題が発生した場合の対応手順も決めておきましょう。
じっしごのふぉろーあっぷけいかくはいかのとおりです。げつじれびゅーとしはんきごとのしょうさいぶんせきをおこないます。	ふぉろーあっぷけいかくをりかいしました。もんだいがはっせいしたばあいのたいおうてじゅんもきめておきましょう。
Jisshi-go no forōappu keikaku wa ika no tōridesu. Tsuki-ji rebyū to shihanki-goto no shōsai bunseki o okonaimasu.	Forō appu keikaku o rikai shima shita. Mondai ga hassei shita baai no taiō tejun mo kimete oki ma shou.
The follow-up plan after implementation is as follows. We will conduct monthly reviews and detailed analyses every quarter.	I understand the follow-up plan. Let's also decide on the response procedures in case problems arise.

Cultural Context

This shows long-term commitment. Be prepared to explain how you'll ensure the plan is followed.

実施にあたっての責任分担は下記の通りです。

じっしにあたってのせきにんぶんたんはかきのとおりです。

Jisshi ni atatte no sekinin buntan wa kaki no tōridesu.

The division of responsibilities for implementation is as follows.

Variation 1	Variation 2
実行にあたっての責任分担は以下の通りです。	Kyō mo shōjin shima shou.
じっこうにあたってのせきにんぶんたんはいかのとおりです。	じっこうにあたってのせきにんぶんたんはいかのとおりです。
Jikkō ni atatte no sekinin buntan wa ika no tōridesu.	Jisshi ni atatte no sekinin buntan wa tsugi no tōridesu.
The division of responsibilities when implementing is as follows.	The division of responsibilities when implementing is as follows.

Positive Response	Negative Response
責任の所在が明確で良いですね。	責任分担が不明確です。
せきにんのしょざいがめいかくでよいですね。	せきにんぶんたんがふめいかくです。
Sekinin no shozai ga meikakude yoidesu ne.	Sekinin buntan ga fu meikakudesu.
It's good that responsibilities are clearly defined.	The division of responsibilities is unclear.

Conversation example person A	Conversation example person B
実施にあたっての責任分担は下記の通りです。各部門の責任者を明確にし、全体の統括は経営企画部が担当します。	責任分担を確認しました。部門間の連携をスムーズにする工夫も必要ですね。
じっしにあたってのせきにんぶんたんはかきのとおりです。かくぶもんのせきにんしゃをめいかくにし、ぜんたいのとうかつはけいえいきかくぶがたんとうします。	せきにんぶんたんをかくにんしました。ぶもんかんのれんけいをすむーずにするくふうもひつようですね。
Jisshi ni atatte no sekinin buntan wa kaki no tōridesu. Kaku bumon no sekinin-sha o meikaku ni shi, zentai no tōkatsu wa keiei kikaku-bu ga tantō shimasu.	Sekinin buntan o kakunin shima shita. Bumon-kan no renkei o sumūzu ni suru kufū mo hitsuyōdesu ne.
The division of responsibilities for implementation is as follows. We will clarify the person in charge of each department, and the overall coordination will be handled by the Corporate Planning Department.	I have confirmed the division of responsibilities. We also need to devise ways to smooth interdepartmental coordination, don't we?

Cultural Context

Clear responsibility allocation is crucial. Ensure all parties are aware of and agree to their responsibilities.

本提案のコスト構造は以下の通りです。

ほんていあんのこすとこうぞうはいかのとおりです。

Hon teian no kosuto kōzō wa ika no tōridesu.

The cost structure of this proposal is as follows.

Variation 1	Variation 2
本提案の費用構造は以下の通りです。	Kyō mo shōjin shima shou.
ほんていあんのひようこうぞうはいかのとおりです。	ほんていあんのひようこうぞうはいかのとおりです。
Hon teian no hiyō kōzō wa ika no tōridesu.	Hon teian no kosuto kōzō wa tsugi no tōridesu.
The cost structure of this proposal is as follows.	The cost structure of this proposal is as follows.

Positive Response	Negative Response
コストの内訳が透明で分かりやすいです。	コスト構造が複雑すぎます。
こすとのうちわけがとうめいでわかりやすいです。	こすとこうぞうがふくざつすぎます。
Kosuto no uchiwake ga tōmeide wakari yasuidesu.	Kosuto kōzō ga fukuzatsu sugimasu.
The cost breakdown is transparent and easy to understand.	The cost structure is too complicated.

Conversation example person A	Conversation example person B
本提案のコスト構造は以下の通りです。初期投資と運用コストの内訳を詳細に分析しています。	コスト構造を理解しました。コスト削減の余地はありますか?
ほんていあんのこすとこうぞうはいかのとおりです。しょきとうしとうんようこすとのうちわけをしょうさいにぶんせきしています。	こすとこうぞうをりかいしました。こすとさくげんのよちはありますか?
Hon teian no kosuto kōzō wa ika no tōridesu. Shoki tōshi to un'yō kosuto no uchiwake o shōsai ni bunseki shite imasu.	Kosuto kōzō o rikai shima shita. Kosuto sakugen no yochi wa arimasu ka?
The cost structure of this proposal is as follows. We have analyzed in detail the breakdown of initial investment and operational costs.	I understand the cost structure. Is there room for cost reduction?

Cultural Context

Be prepared to justify each cost item. Vague or inflated costs may be scrutinized.

今回の施策の対象範囲は以下の通りです。

こんかいのしさくのたいしょうはんいはいかのとおりです。
Konkai no shisaku no taishō han'i wa ika no tōridesu.
The scope of this measure is as follows.

Variation 1	Variation 2
今回の取り組みの対象範囲は以下の通りです。	Kyō mo shōjin shima shou.
こんかいのとりくみのたいしょうはんいはいかのとおりです。	こんかいのとりくみのたいしょうはんいはいかのとおりです。
Konkai no torikumi no taishō han'i wa ika no tōridesu.	Konkai no shisaku no taishō han'i wa tsugi no tōridesu.
The scope of this measure is as follows.	The scope of this initiative is as follows.

Positive Response	Negative Response
適切な範囲設定ですね。効果的だと思います。	対象範囲が広すぎます。
てきせつなはんいせっていですね。こうかてきだとおもいます。	たいしょうはんいがひろすぎます。
Tekisetsuna han'i setteidesu ne. Kōka-tekida to omoimasu.	Taishō han'i ga hiro sugimasu.
The scope setting seems appropriate and effective.	The scope is too broad.

Conversation example person A	Conversation example person B
今回の施策の対象範囲は以下の通りです。まずは国内事業部門から開始し、段階的にグローバル展開を目指します。	対象範囲を確認しました。各段階での具体的な展開計画を共有してください。
こんかいのしさくのたいしょうはんいはいかのとおりです。まずはこくないじぎょうぶもんからかいしし、だんかいてきにぐろーばるてんかいをめざします。	たいしょうはんいをかくにんしました。かくだんかいでのぐたいてきなてんかいけいかくをきょうゆうしてください。
Konkai no shisaku no taishō han'i wa ika no tōridesu. Mazu wa kokunai jigyō bumon kara kaishi shi, dankaiteki ni gurōbaru tenkai o mezashimasu.	Taishō han'i o kakunin shima shita. Kaku dankai de no gutai-tekina tenkai keikaku o kyōyū shite kudasai.
The scope of this measure is as follows. We will start with the domestic business division and aim for gradual global expansion.	I have confirmed the scope. Please share the specific expansion plans for each stage.

Cultural Context

Be specific about what is and isn't included. Vague boundaries can lead to scope creep.

本計画の実施により予想される課題は以下の通りです。

ほんけいかくのじっしによりよそうされるかだいはいかのとおりです。

Hon keikaku no jisshi ni yori yosō sa re ru kadai wa ika no tōridesu.

The anticipated issues from implementing this plan are as follows.

Variation 1	Variation 2
本企画の実行により予想される問題点は以下の通りです。	Kyō mo shōjin shima shou.
ほんきかくのじっこうによりよそうされるもんだいてんはいかのとおりです。	ほんきかくのじっこうによりよそうされるもんだいてんはいかのとおりです。
Hon kikaku no jikkō ni yori yosō sa re ru mondai-ten wa ika no tōridesu.	Hon purojekuto no jisshi ni yori yosō sa re ru kadai wa tsugi no tōridesu.
The issues expected by the implementation of this plan are as follows.	The issues that are expected to occur by implementing this project are as follows.

Positive Response	Negative Response
予想される課題を事前に把握できて良いです。	予想される課題への対策が示されていません。
よそうされるかだいをじぜんにはあくできてよいです。	よそうされるかだいへのたいさくがしめされていません。
Yosō sa re ru kadai o jizen ni haaku dekite yoidesu.	Yosō sa re ru kadai e no taisaku ga shì Sa rete imasen.
It's good to be aware of potential issues in advance.	Countermeasures for anticipated issues are not shown.

Conversation example person A	Conversation example person B
本計画の実施により予想される課題は以下の通りです。人材育成と既存システムとの統合が主な課題となります。	予想される課題を理解しました。各課題に対する対策案を検討しましょう。
ほんけいかくのじっしによりよそうされるかだいはいかのとおりです。じんざいいくせいときそんしすてむとのとうごうがおもなかだいとなります。	よそうされるかだいをりかいしました。かくかだいにたいするたいさくあんをけんとうしましょう。
Hon keikaku no jisshi ni yori yosō sareru kadai wa ika no tōridesu. Jinzai ikusei to kizon shisutemu to no tōgō ga omona kadai to narimasu.	Yosō sa re ru kadai o rikai shima shita. Kaku kadai ni taisuru taisaku-an o kentō shima shou.
The challenges expected from implementing this plan are as follows. Human resource development and integration with existing systems will be the main challenges.	I understand the anticipated challenges. Let's consider countermeasures for each challenge.

Cultural Context

Acknowledging potential issues shows foresight. Be prepared to discuss how you plan to address these challenges.

実施後の効果測定方法は下記の通りです。

じっしごのこうかそくていほうほうはかきのとおりです。

Jisshi-go no kōka sokutei hōhō wa kaki no tōridesu.

The method for measuring the effects after implementation is as follows.

Variation 1	Variation 2
実行後の効果測定方法は以下の通りです。	Kyō mo shōjin shima shou.
じっこうごのこうかそくていほうほうはいかのとおりです。	じっこうごのこうかそくていほうほうはいかのとおりです。
Jikkō-go no kōka sokutei hōhō wa ika no tōridesu.	Jisshi-go no kōka sokutei hōhō wa tsugi no tōridesu.
The effect measurement method after implementation is as follows.	The method for measuring effectiveness after implementation is as follows.

Positive Response	Negative Response
具体的な指標があり、評価しやすそうです。	効果測定方法が不適切です。
ぐたいてきなしひょうがあり、ひょうかしやすそうです。	こうかそくていほうほうがふてきせつです。
Gutai-tekina shihyō ga ari, hyōka shiyasu sōdesu.	Kōka sokutei hōhō ga fu tekisetsudesu.
The specific indicators should make evaluation easier.	The method for measuring effects is inappropriate.

Conversation example person A	Conversation example person B
実施後の効果測定方法は下記の通りです。KPI の達成度と顧客満足度調査を主な指標とします。	効果測定方法を確認しました。測定結果の分析と活用方法も決めておきましょう。
じっしごのこうかそくていほうほうはかきのとおりです。KPI のたっせいどときゃくまんぞくどちょうさをおもなしひょうとします。	こうかそくていほうほうをかくにんしました。そくていけっかのぶんせきとかつようほうほうもきめておきましょう。
Jisshi-go no kōka sokutei hōhō wa kaki no tōridesu. Kēpīai no tassei-do to kokyaku manzoku-do chōsa o omona shihyō to shimasu.	Kōka sokutei hōhō o kakunin shima shita. Sokutei kekka no bunseki to katsuyō hōhō mo kimete oki ma shou.
The method for measuring the effects after implementation is as follows. We will use KPI achievement and customer satisfaction surveys as our main indicators.	I have confirmed the effect measurement method. Let's also decide on how to analyze and utilize the measurement results.

Cultural Context

Ensure measurement methods are objective and relevant. Subjective or irrelevant metrics may be questioned.

本提案の長所と短所は以下の通りです。

ほんていあんのちょうしょとたんしょはいかのとおりです。

Hon teian no chōsho to tansho wa ika no tōridesu.

The advantages and disadvantages of this proposal are as follows.

Variation 1	Variation 2
本提案の利点と欠点は以下の通りです。	Kyō mo shōjin shima shou.
ほんていあんのりてんとけってんはいかのとおりです。	ほんていあんのりてんとけってんはいかのとおりです。
Hon teian no riten to ketten wa ika no tōridesu.	Hon teian no meritto to demeritto wa tsugi no tōridesu.
The advantages and disadvantages of this proposal are as follows.	The advantages and disadvantages of this proposal are as follows.

Positive Response	Negative Response
バランスの取れた分析ですね。参考になります。	短所への対策が示されていません。
ばらんすのとれたぶんせきですね。さんこうになります。	たんしょへのたいさくがしめされていません。
Baransu no toreta bunsekidesu ne. Sankō ni narimasu.	Tansho e no taisaku ga shì Sa rete imasen.
It's a balanced analysis. Very informative.	Countermeasures for the disadvantages are not shown.

Conversation example person A	Conversation example person B
新規事業計画について説明します。本提案の長所と短所は以下の通りです。	詳細な分析ありがとうございます。検討させていただきます。
しんきじぎょうけいかくについてせつめいします。ほんていあんのちょうしょとたんしょはいかのとおりです。	しょうさいなぶんせきありがとうございます。けんとうさせていただきます。
Shinki jigyō keikaku ni tsuite setsumei shimasu. Hon teian no chōsho to tansho wa ika no tōridesu.	Shōsaina bunseki arigatōgozaimasu. Kentō sa sete itadakimasu.
Let me explain the new business plan. The pros and cons of this proposal are as follows.	Thank you for the detailed analysis. We'll review it.

Cultural Context

Presenting both pros and cons shows balanced thinking. Be prepared to explain how you'll maximize strengths and mitigate weaknesses.

今回の分析から得られた洞察は以下の通りです。

こんかいのぶんせきからえられたどうさつはいかのとおりです。

Konkai no bunseki kara e rareta dōsatsu wa ika no tōridesu.

The insights gained from this analysis are as follows.

Variation 1	Variation 2
今回の分析から得られた知見は以下の通りです。	Kyō mo shōjin shima shou.
こんかいのぶんせきからえられたちけんはいかのとおりです。	こんかいのぶんせきからえられたちけんはいかのとおりです。
Konkai no bunseki kara e rareta chiken wa ika no tōridesu.	Konkai no bunseki kara e rareta dōsatsu wa tsugi no tōridesu.
The insights gained from this analysis are as follows.	The insights gained from this analysis are as follows.

Positive Response	Negative Response
興味深い洞察ですね。今後に活かせそうです。	洞察が表面的に思えます。
きょうみぶかいどうさつですね。こんごにいかせそうです。	どうさつがひょうめんてきにおもえます。
Kyōmibukai dōsatsudesu ne. Kongo ni ikase-sōdesu.	Dōsatsu ga hyōmen-teki ni omoemasu.
These are interesting insights. We can use them in the future.	The insights seem superficial.

Conversation example person A	Conversation example person B
市場調査の結果をまとめました。今回の分析から得られた洞察は以下の通りです。	興味深い結果ですね。これを基に戦略を立てましょう。
しじょうちょうさのけっかをまとめました。こんかいのぶんせきからえられたどうさつはいかのとおりです。	きょうみぶかいけっかですね。これをもとにせんりゃくをたてましょう。
Shijō chōsa no kekka o matsumemashita. Konkai no bunseki kara erareta dōsatsu wa ika no tōridesu.	Kyōmibukai kekkadesu ne. Kore o ki ni senryaku o tate ma shou.
We've summarized the market research results. The insights gained from this analysis are as follows.	Interesting results. Let's use this to formulate our strategy.

Cultural Context

Ensure insights are actionable and relevant. Obvious or irrelevant insights may damage your credibility.

本計画の実施に必要なリソースは下記の通りです。

ほんけいかくのじっしにひつようなりそーすはかきのとおりです。

Hon keikaku no jisshi ni hitsuyōna risōsu wa kaki no tōridesu.

The resources needed to implement this plan are as follows.

Variation 1	Variation 2
本企画の実行に必要な資源は以下の通りです。	Kyō mo shōjin shima shou.
ほんきかくのじっこうにひつようなしげんはいかのとおりです。	ほんきかくのじっこうにひつようなしげんはいかのとおりです。
Hon kikaku no jikkō ni hitsuyōna shigen wa ika no tōridesu.	Hon purojekuto no jisshi ni hitsuyōna risōsu wa tsugi no tōridesu.
The resources required for the implementation of this plan are as follows.	The resources required to implement this project are as follows.

Positive Response	Negative Response
リソースの見積もりが明確で計画が立てやすいです。	必要なリソースが過大に思えます。
りそーすのみつもりがめいかくでけいかくがたてやすいです。	ひつようなりそーすがかだいにおもえます。
Risōsu no mitsumori ga meikakude keikaku ga tate yasuidesu.	Hitsuyōna risōsu ga kadai ni omoemasu.
The clear resource estimation makes planning easier.	The required resources seem excessive.

Conversation example person A	Conversation example person B
プロジェクト開始前の最終確認です。本計画の実施に必要なリソースは下記の通りです。	リソースリストを確認しました。予算内で調整可能です。
ぷろじぇくとかいしまえのさいしゅうかくにんです。ほんけいかくのじっしにひつようなりそーすはかきのとおりです。	りそーすりすとをかくにんしました。よさんないでちょうせいかのうです。
Purojekuto kaishi-mae no saishū kakunin desu. Hon keikaku no jisshi ni hitsuyōna risōsu wa kaki no tōridesu.	Risōsu risuto o kakunin shima shita. Yosan-nai de chōsei kanōdesu.
This is the final check before starting the project. The resources needed to implement this plan are as follows.	I've checked the resource list. We can adjust within the budget.

Cultural Context

Be comprehensive in your resource list. Overlooking necessary resources may be seen as poor planning.

今回の施策の波及効果は下記の通りです。

こんかいのしさくのはきゅうこうかはかきのとおりです。
Konkai no shisaku no hakyū kōka wa kaki no tōridesu.
The ripple effects of this measure are as follows.

Variation 1	Variation 2
今回の取り組みの波及効果は以下の通りです。	Kyō mo shōjin shima shou.
こんかいのとりくみのはきゅうこうかはいかのとおりです。	こんかいのとりくみのはきゅうこうかはいかのとおりです。
Konkai no torikumi no hakyū kōka wa ika no tōridesu.	Konkai no shisaku no hakyū kōka wa tsugi no tōridesu.
The ripple effects of this measure are as follows.	The ripple effects of this initiative are as follows.

Positive Response	Negative Response
広範囲に良い影響が期待できそうですね。	波及効果が楽観的すぎます。
こうはんいによいえいきょうがきたいできそうですね。	はきゅうこうかがらっかんてきすぎます。
Kōhan'i ni yoi eikyō ga kitai deki-sōdesu ne.	Hakyū kōka ga rakkan-teki sugimasu.
It seems we can expect positive effects over a wide range.	The ripple effects are too optimistic.

Conversation example person A	Conversation example person B
マーケティング戦略の見直しを行いました。今回の施策の波及効果は下記の通りです。	波及効果の予測は非常に重要ですね。ありがとうございます。
まーけてぃんぐせんりゃくのみなおしをおこないました。こんかいのしさくのはきゅうこうかはかきのとおりです。	はきゅうこうかのよそくはひじょうにじゅうようですね。ありがとうございます。
Māketingu senryaku no minaoshi o okonaimashita. Konkai no shisaku no hakyū kōka wa kaki no tōridesu.	Hakyū kōka no yosoku wa hijō ni jūyōdesu ne. Arigatōgozaimasu.
We've revised our marketing strategy. The ripple effects of this measure are as follows.	Predicting the ripple effects is crucial. Thank you.

Cultural Context

Consider both positive and negative ripple effects. Overlooking potential negative impacts may be seen as short-sighted.

本計画の実施に伴うリスク管理方針は以下の通りです。

ほんけいかくのじっしにともなうりすくかんりほうしんはいかのとおりです。

Hon keikaku no jisshi ni tomonau risuku kanri hōshin wa ika no tōridesu.

The risk management policy for implementing this plan is as follows.

Variation 1	Variation 2
本企画の実行に伴うリスク管理方針は以下の通りです。	Kyō mo shōjin shima shou.
ほんきかくのじっこうにともなうりすくかんりほうしんはいかのとおりです。	ほんきかくのじっこうにともなうりすくかんりほうしんはいかのとおりです。
Hon kikaku no jikkō ni tomonau risuku kanri hōshin wa ika no tōridesu.	Hon purojekuto no jisshi ni tomonau risuku kanri hōshin wa tsugi no tōridesu.
The risk management policy associated with the implementation of this plan is as follows.	The risk management policy associated with the implementation of this project is as follows.

Positive Response	Negative Response
リスク管理の方針が明確で安心です。	リスク管理方針が不十分です。
りすくかんりのほうしんがめいかくであんしんです。	りすくかんりほうしんがふじゅうぶんです。
Risuku kanri no hōshin ga meikakude anshindesu.	Risuku kanri hōshin ga fu jūbundesu.
The clear risk management policy is reassuring.	The risk management policy is insufficient.

Conversation example person A	Conversation example person B
新規プロジェクトの提案書を作成しました。本計画の実施に伴うリスク管理方針は以下の通りです。	リスク管理は重要ですね。詳細を確認させていただきます。
しんきぷろじぇくとのていあんしょをさくせいしました。ほんけいかくのじっしにともなうりすくかんりほうしんはいかのとおりです。	りすくかんりはじゅうようですね。しょうさいをかくにんさせていただきます。
Shinki purojekuto no teian-sho o sakusei shimashita. Hon keikaku no jisshi ni tomonau risuku kanri hōshin wa ika no tōridesu.	Risuku kanri wa jūyōdesu ne. Shōsai o kakunin sa sete itadakimasu.
I've prepared the proposal for the new project. The risk management policy for implementing this plan is as follows.	Risk management is important. I'll review the details.

Cultural Context

This shows proactive thinking. Be prepared to explain how you'll implement these risk management strategies.

実施後の改善サイクルは下記の通りです。

じっしごのかいぜんさいくるはかきのとおりです。

Jisshi-go no kaizen saikuru wa kaki no tōridesu.

The improvement cycle after implementation is as follows.

Variation 1	Variation 2
実行後の改善サイクルは以下の通りです。	Kyō mo shōjin shima shou.
じっこうごのかいぜんさいくるはいかのとおりです。	じっこうごのかいぜんさいくるはいかのとおりです。
Jikkō-go no kaizen saikuru wa ika no tōridesu.	Jisshi-go no kaizen saikuru wa tsugi no tōridesu.
The improvement cycle after implementation is as follows.	The improvement cycle after implementation is as follows.

Positive Response	Negative Response
継続的な改善が期待できますね。	改善サイクルが長すぎます。
けいぞくてきなかいぜんがきたいできますね。	かいぜんさいくるがながすぎます。
Keizoku-tekina kaizen ga kitai dekimasu ne.	Kaizen saikuru ga naga sugimasu.
We can expect continuous improvement.	The improvement cycle is too long.

Conversation example person A	Conversation example person B
品質管理プロセスを見直しました。実施後の改善サイクルは下記の通りです。	継続的な改善は大切ですね。このサイクルを徹底しましょう。
ひんしつかんりぷろせすをみなおしました。じっしごのかいぜんさいくるはかきのとおりです。	けいぞくてきなかいぜんはたいせつですね。このさいくるをてっていしましょう。
Hinshitsu kanri purosesu o minaoshimashita. Jisshi-go no kaizen saikuru wa kaki no tōridesu.	Keizoku-tekina kaizen wa taisetsudesu ne. Kono saikuru o tettei shima shou.
We've revised the quality management process. The improvement cycle after implementation is as follows.	Continuous improvement is crucial. Let's thoroughly implement this cycle.

Cultural Context

This demonstrates commitment to continuous improvement. Be prepared to explain how you'll ensure the cycle is followed.

本提案の費用対効果分析結果は以下の通りです。

ほんていあんのひようたいこうかぶんせきけっかはいかのとおりです。

Hon teian no hiyō tai kōka bunseki kekka wa ika no tōridesu.

The results of the cost-benefit analysis for this proposal are as follows.

Variation 1	Variation 2
本提案のコストパフォーマンス分析結果は以下の通りです。	Kyō mo shōjin shima shou.
ほんていあんのこすとぱふぉーまんすぶんせきけっかはいかのとおりです。	ほんていあんのこすとぱふぉーまんすぶんせきけっかはいかのとおりです。
Hon teian no kosuto pafōmansu bunseki kekka wa ika no tōridesu.	Hon teian no hiyō tai kōka bunseki kekka wa tsugi no tōridesu.
The cost-effectiveness analysis results of this proposal are as follows.	The cost-effectiveness analysis results of this proposal are as follows.

Positive Response	Negative Response
投資の妥当性がよく分かります。	費用対効果が低いように思えます。
とうしのだとうせいがよくわかります。	ひようたいこうかがひくいようїおもえます。
Tōshi no datō-sei ga yoku wakarimasu.	Hiyō tai kōka ga hikui yō ni omoemasu.
The investment's validity is clear.	The cost-effectiveness seems low.

Conversation example person A	Conversation example person B
投資案件の評価を行いました。本提案の費用対効果分析結果は以下の通りです。	分析結果を拝見しました。投資判断の参考にさせていただきます。
とうしあんけんのひょうかをおこないました。ほんていあんのひようたいこうかぶんせきけっかはいかのとおりです。	ぶんせきけっかをはいけんしました。とうしはんだんのさんこうにさせていただきます。
Tōshi anken no hyōka o okonaimashita. Hon teian no hiyō tai kōka bunseki kekka wa ika no tōridesu.	Bunseki kekka o haiken shima shita. Tōshi handan no sankō ni sa sete itadakimasu.
We've evaluated the investment proposal. The cost-benefit analysis results for this proposal are as follows.	I've reviewed the analysis results. We'll use this as a reference for our investment decision.

Cultural Context

Be conservative in your analysis. Overly optimistic ROI projections may damage credibility.

本案の骨子は次の通りです。

ほんあんのこっしはつぎのとおりです。

Hon'an no kosshi wa tsugi no tōridesu.

The outline of this proposal is as follows.

Variation 1	Variation 2
本案の概要は次の通りです。	Kyō mo shōjin shima shou.
ほんあんのがいようはつぎのとおりです。	ほんあんのがいようはつぎのとおりです。
Hon'an no gaiyō wa tsugi no tōridesu.	Hon'an no gaiyō wa ika no tōridesu.
The outline of this proposal is as follows.	The outline of this proposal is as follows.

Positive Response	Negative Response
提案の要点が簡潔にまとまっていますね。	骨子が具体性に欠けています。
ていあんのようてんがかんけつにまとまっていますね。	こっしがぐたいせいにかけています。
Teian no yōten ga kanketsu ni matomatte imasu ne.	Kosshi ga gutai-sei ni kakete imasu.
The proposal's key points are concisely summarized.	The outline lacks specificity.

Conversation example person A	Conversation example person B
経営戦略の見直しを行いました。本案の骨子は次の通りです。	戦略の方向性が明確になりましたね。詳細を詰めていきましょう。
けいえいせんりゃくのみなおしをおこないました。ほんあんのこっしはつぎのとおりです。	せんりゃくのほうこうせいがめいかくになりましたね。しょうさいをつめていきましょう。
Keiei senryaku no minaoshi o okonaimashita. Hon'an no kosshi wa tsugi no tōridesu.	Senryaku no hōkō-sei ga meikaku ni narimashita ne. Shōsai o tsumete iki ma shou.
We've revised our management strategy. The outline of this plan is as follows.	The direction of the strategy has become clear. Let's work out the details.

Cultural Context

Ensure the outline is comprehensive yet concise. Too much detail may be seen as unfocused, too little as unprepared.

実行に移す際の懸念事項をリストアップしました。

じっこうにうつすさいのけねんじこうをりすとあっぷしました。

Jikkō ni utsusu sai no kenen jikō o risuto appu shima shita.

We have listed the concerns when putting this into action.

Variation 1	Variation 2
実施に移す際の懸念事項を列挙しました。	Kyō mo shōjin shima shou.
じっしにうつすさいのけねんじこうをれっきょしました。	じっしにうつすさいのけねんじこうをれっきょしました。
Jisshi ni utsusu sai no kenen jikō o rekkyo shima shita.	Jikkō ni utsusu sai no kenen-ten o rekkyo shima shita.
I have listed the concerns when moving to implementation.	I have listed the concerns when moving to implementation.

Positive Response	Negative Response
事前に懸念事項を把握できて助かります。	懸念事項への対策が示されていません。
じぜんにけねんじこうをはあくできてたすかります。	けねんじこうへのたいさくがしめされていません。
Jizen ni kenen jikō o haaku dekite tasukarimasu.	Kenen jikō e no taisaku ga shì Sa rete imasen.
It's helpful to be aware of concerns in advance.	Countermeasures for the concerns are not provided.

Conversation example person A	Conversation example person B
プロジェクト実施前の最終チェックです。実行に移す際の懸念事項をリストアップしました。	リストを確認しました。対策を検討しておきましょう。
ぷろじぇくとじっしまえのさいしゅうちぇっくです。じっこうにうつすさいのけねんじこうをりすとあっぷしました。	りすとをかくにんしました。たいさくをけんとうしておきましょう。
Purojekuto jisshi-mae no saishū chekku desu. Jikkō ni utsusu sai no kenen jikō o risutoappushimashita.	Risuto o kakunin shima shita. Taisaku o kentō shite oki ma shou.
This is the final check before project implementation. I've listed up the concerns when moving to execution.	I've checked the list. Let's consider countermeasures.

Cultural Context

This shows foresight. Be prepared to discuss how you plan to address each concern.

当プロジェクトの成否を左右する要因を分析しました。

とうぷろじぇくとのせいひをさゆうするよういんをぶんせきしました。

Tō purojekuto no seihi o sayū suru yōin o bunseki shima shita.

We analyzed the factors that will determine the success or failure of this project.

Variation 1	Variation 2
当企画の成否を左右する要因を分析しました。	Kyō mo shōjin shima shou.
とうきかくのせいひをさゆうするよういんをぶんせきしました。	とうきかくのせいひをさゆうするよういんをぶんせきしました。
Tō kikaku no seihi o sayū suru yōin o bunseki shima shita.	Hon purojekuto no seihi o sayū suru yōin o bunseki shima shita.
We have analyzed the factors that determine the success or failure of this project.	I have analyzed the factors that determine the success or failure of this project.

Positive Response	Negative Response
重要な分析ですね。成功に向けて活用しましょう。	分析が表面的に思えます。
じゅうようなぶんせきですね。せいこうにむけてかつようしましょう。	ぶんせきがひょうめんてきにおもえます。
Jūyōna bunsekidesu ne. Seikō ni mukete katsuyō shima shou.	Bunseki ga hyōmen-teki ni omoemasu.
Important analysis. Let's use it for success.	The analysis seems superficial.

Conversation example person A	Conversation example person B
プロジェクト成功のための分析を行いました。当プロジェクトの成否を左右する要因を分析しました。	重要な分析ですね。これらの要因に注意して進めていきましょう。
ぷろじぇくとせいこうのためのぶんせきをおこないました。とうぷろじぇくとのせいひをさゆうするよういんをぶんせきしました。	じゅうようなぶんせきですね。これらのよういんにちゅういしてすすめていきましょう。
Purojekuto seikō no tame no bunseki o okonaimashita. Tō purojekuto no seihi o sayū suru yōin o bunseki shimashita.	Jūyōna bunsekidesu ne. Korera no yōin ni chūi shite susumete iki ma shou.
We've conducted an analysis for project success. We've analyzed the factors that will determine the success or failure of this project.	This is a crucial analysis. Let's proceed while paying attention to these factors.

Cultural Context

This demonstrates strategic thinking. Ensure you've considered both internal and external factors.

本戦略の独自性について説明いたします。

ほんせんりゃくのどくじせいについてせつめいいたします。
Hon senryaku no dokuji-sei ni tsuite setsumei itashimasu.
We will explain the uniqueness of this strategy.

Variation 1	Variation 2
本戦略の独創性について説明いたします。	Kyō mo shōjin shima shou.
ほんせんりゃくのどくそうせいについてせつめいいたします。	ほんせんりゃくのどくそうせいについてせつめいいたします。
Hon senryaku no dokusō-sei ni tsuite setsumei itashimasu.	Hon senryaku no orijinariti ni tsuite setsumei shimasu.
I will explain the uniqueness of this strategy.	I will explain the originality of this strategy.

Positive Response	Negative Response
他社との差別化が明確ですね。	独自性が感じられません。
たしゃとのさべつかがめいかくですね。	どくじせいがかんじられません。
Tasha to no sabetsu-ka ga meikakudesu ne.	Dokuji-sei ga kanji raremasen.
The differentiation from competitors is clear.	I don't see any uniqueness in this strategy.

Conversation example person A	Conversation example person B
新たな市場戦略を立案しました。本戦略の独自性について説明いたします。	興味深い戦略ですね。競合との差別化が図れそうです。
あらたなしじょうせんりゃくをりつあんしました。ほんせんりゃくのどくじせいについてせつめいいたします。	きょうみぶかいせんりゃくですね。きょうごうとのさべつかがはかれそうです。
Aratana shijō senryaku o ritsuan shimashita. Hon senryaku no dokujisei ni tsuite setsumei itashimasu.	Kyōmibukai senryakudesu ne. Kyōgō to no sabetsu-ka ga hakare-sōdesu.
We've developed a new market strategy. Let me explain the uniqueness of this strategy.	It's an interesting strategy. We should be able to differentiate ourselves from competitors.

Cultural Context
Ensure the uniqueness is genuine and relevant. False claims of uniqueness can severely damage credibility.

想定される副次的効果は以下の通りです。

そうていされるふくじてきこうかはいかのとおりです。
Sōtei sa reru fuku ji-teki kōka wa ika no tōridesu.
The expected secondary effects are as follows.

Variation 1	Variation 2
想定される付随的効果は以下の通りです。	Kyō mo shōjin shima shou.
そうていされるふずいてきこうかはいかのとおりです。	そうていされるふずいてきこうかはいかのとおりです。
Sōtei sa re ru fuzui-teki kōka wa ika no tōridesu.	Sōtei sa re ru fuzui-teki kōka wa tsugi no tōridesu.
The anticipated side effects are as follows.	The expected incidental effects are as follows.

Positive Response	Negative Response
幅広い効果が期待できそうですね。	副次的効果が楽観的すぎます。
はばひろいこうかがきたいできそうですね。	ふくじてきこうかがらっかんてきすぎます。
Habahiroi kōka ga kitai deki-sōdesu ne.	Fuku ji-teki kōka ga rakkan-teki sugimasu.
We can expect a wide range of effects.	The secondary effects seem too optimistic.

Conversation example person A	Conversation example person B
主要施策の効果予測を行いました。想定される副次的効果は以下の通りです。	副次的効果も重要ですね。これらも考慮に入れて進めましょう。
しゅようしさくのこうかよそくをおこないました。そうていされるふくじてきこうかはいかのとおりです。	ふくじてきこうかもじゅうようですね。これらもこうりょにいれてすすめましょう。
Shuyō shisaku no kōka yosoku o okonaimashita. Sōtei sareru fukujiteki kōka wa ika no tōridesu.	Fuku ji-teki kōka mo jūyōdesu ne. Korera mo kōryo ni irete susume ma shou.
We've predicted the effects of our main measures. The expected secondary effects are as follows.	Secondary effects are important too. Let's proceed while taking these into account.

Cultural Context

Consider both positive and negative side effects. Overlooking potential negative impacts may be seen as short-sighted.

本提案の具体的な実施手順を示します。

ほんていあんのぐたいてきなじっしてじゅんをしめしします。

Hon teian no gutai-tekina jisshi tejun o shimeshimasu.

We present the specific implementation procedures for this proposal.

Variation 1	Variation 2
本提案の具体的な実行手順を示します。	Kyō mo shōjin shima shou.
ほんていあんのぐたいてきなじっこうじゅんじょをしめします。	ほんていあんのぐたいてきなじっこうじゅんじょをしめします。
Hon teian no gutai-tekina jikkō tejun o shimeshimasu.	Hon teian no shōsaina jikkō purosesu o teiji shimasu.
I will show the specific implementation steps for this proposal.	I will present the specific implementation steps for this proposal.

Positive Response	Negative Response
実行計画が明確で進めやすそうです。	実施手順が複雑すぎます。
じっこうけいかくがめいかくですすめやすそうです。	じっしてじゅんがふくざつすぎます。
Jikkō keikaku ga meikakude susumeyasu sōdesu.	Jisshi tejun ga fukuzatsu sugimasu.
The clear action plan seems easy to implement.	The implementation procedures are too complicated.

Conversation example person A	Conversation example person B
プロジェクト実行計画をまとめました。本提案の具体的な実施手順を示します。	手順が明確で分かりやすいです。これに沿って進めていきましょう。
ぷろじぇくとじっこうけいかくをまとめました。ほんていあんのぐたいてきなじっしてじゅんをしめします。	てじゅんがめいかくでわかりやすいです。これにそってすすめていきましょう。
Purojekuto jikkō keikaku o matsumemashita. Hon teian no gutaiteki na jisshi tejun o shimeshimasu.	Tejun ga meikakude wakari yasuidesu. Kore ni sotte susumete iki ma shou.
We've compiled the project execution plan. I'll show you the specific implementation steps for this proposal.	The steps are clear and easy to understand. Let's proceed according to this.

Cultural Context

Be prepared to explain the rationale behind each step. Illogical or inefficient processes may be questioned.

競合他社の動向を踏まえた戦略調整案です。

きょうごうたしゃのどうこうをふまえたせんりゃくちょうせいあんです。

Kyōgō tasha no dōkō o fumaeta senryaku chōsei-andesu.

This is a strategy adjustment proposal based on competitors' trends.

Variation 1	Variation 2
ライバル企業の動向を踏まえた戦略調整案です。	Kyō mo shōjin shima shou.
らいばるきぎょうのどうこうをふまえたせんりゃくちょうせいあんです。	らいばるきぎょうのどうこうをふまえたせんりゃくちょうせいあんです。
Raibaru kigyō no dōkō o fumaeta senryaku chōsei-andesu.	Raibaru kigyō no ugoki o kōryo shita senryaku shūsei-andesu.
This is a strategy adjustment proposal based on the trends of competitors.	This is a strategic adjustment plan based on the trends of competing companies.

Positive Response	Negative Response
市場状況をよく考慮していますね。	競合分析が不十分に思えます。
しじょうじょうきょうをよくこうりょしていますね。	きょうごうぶんせきがふじゅうぶんにおもえます。
Ichiba jōkyō o yoku kōryo shite imasu ne.	Kyōgō bunseki ga fu jūbun ni omoemasu.
It considers the market situation well.	The competitive analysis seems insufficient.

Conversation example person A	Conversation example person B
市場分析の結果をまとめました。競合他社の動向を踏まえた戦略調整案です。	競合分析が詳細ですね。この情報を活かして戦略を練り直しましょう。
しじょうぶんせきのけっかをまとめました。きょうごうたしゃのどうこうをふまえたせんりゃくちょうせいあんです。	きょうごうぶんせきがしょうさいですね。このじょうほうをいかしてせんりゃくをねりなおしましょう。
Shijō bunseki no kekka o matsumemashita. Kyōgō tasha no dōkō o fumaeta senryaku chōsei-an desu.	Kyōgō bunseki ga shōsaidesu ne. Kono jōhō o ikashite senryaku o nerinaoshi ma shou.
We've summarized the results of our market analysis. This is a strategy adjustment proposal based on competitors' trends.	The competitor analysis is detailed. Let's use this information to refine our strategy.

Cultural Context

Ensure your competitor analysis is current and comprehensive. Outdated information may weaken your proposal.

本計画の採算性について検証しました。

ほんけいかくのさいさんせいについてけんしょうしました。

Hon keikaku no saisan-sei ni tsuite kenshō shima shita.

We have verified the profitability of this plan.

Variation 1	Variation 2
本企画の収益性について検証しました。	Kyō mo shōjin shima shou.
ほんきかくのしゅうえきせいについてけんしょうしました。	ほんきかくのしゅうえきせいについてけんしょうしました。
Hon kikaku no shūeki-sei ni tsuite kenshō shima shita.	Hon purojekuto no shūeki-sei ni tsuite kenshō shima shita.
We have verified the profitability of this plan.	I have verified the profitability of this project.

Positive Response	Negative Response
財務面での裏付けがあり安心です。	採算性の検証が甘いです。
ざいむめんでのうらづけがありあんしんです。	さいさんせいのけんしょうがあまいです。
Zaimu-men de no uradzuke ga ari anshindesu.	Saisan-sei no kenshō ga amaidesu.
The financial backing is reassuring.	The profitability verification is not rigorous enough.

Conversation example person A	Conversation example person B
事業計画の財務分析を行いました。本計画の採算性について検証しました。	採算性の検証は重要ですね。結果を踏まえて判断していきましょう。
じぎょうけいかくのざいむぶんせきをおこないました。ほんけいかくのさいさんせいについてけんしょうしました。	さいさんせいのけんしょうはじゅうようですね。けっかをふまえてはんだんしていきましょう。
Jigyō keikaku no zaimu bunseki o okonaimashita. Hon keikaku no saisan-sei ni tsuite kenshō shimashita.	Saisan-sei no kenshō wa jūyōdesu ne. Kekka o fumaete handan shite iki ma shou.
We've conducted a financial analysis of the business plan. We've verified the profitability of this plan.	Verifying profitability is crucial. Let's make decisions based on these results.

Cultural Context

Be conservative in your profitability estimates. Overly optimistic projections may be viewed skeptically.

提案実現に向けたロードマップをお示しします。

ていあんじつげんにむけたろーどまっぷをおしめししします。
Teian jitsugen ni muketa rōdo mappu o o shimeshi shimasu.
We present a roadmap for realizing this proposal.

Variation 1	Variation 2
提案実現に向けたスケジュール表をお示しします。	Kyō mo shōjin shima shou.
ていあんじつげんにむけたすけじゅーるひょうをおしめししします。	ていあんじつげんにむけたすけじゅーるひょうをおしめししします。
Teian jitsugen ni muketa sukejūru-hyō o o shimeshi shimasu.	Teian jitsugen ni muketa sukejūru-hyō o o shimeshimasu.
I will present a roadmap for realizing the proposal.	I will show the schedule for realizing the proposal.

Positive Response	Negative Response
段階的な実施計画が分かりやすいです。	ロードマップが非現実的です。
だんかいてきなじっしけいかくがわかりやすいです。	ろーどまっぷがひげんじつてきです。
Dankai-tekina jisshi keikaku ga wakari yasuidesu.	Rōdo mappu ga hi genjitsu-tekidesu.
The phased implementation plan is easy to understand.	The roadmap is unrealistic.

Conversation example person A	Conversation example person B
長期戦略の実行計画を作成しました。提案実現に向けたロードマップをお示しします。	ロードマップが明確で分かりやすいです。各段階の目標を確認していきましょう。
ちょうきせんりゃくのじっこうけいかくをさくせいしました。ていあんじつげんにむけたろーどまっぷをおしめししします。	ろーどまっぷがめいかくでわかりやすいです。かくだんかいのもくひょうをかくにんしていきましょう。
Chōki senryaku no jikkō keikaku o sakusei shimashita. Teian jitsugen ni muketa rōdomappu o o shimeshi shimasu.	Rōdo mappu ga meikakude wakari yasuidesu. Kaku dankai no mokuhyō o kakunin shite iki ma shou.
We've created an execution plan for our long-term strategy. I'll show you the roadmap for realizing this proposal.	The roadmap is clear and easy to understand. Let's confirm the goals for each stage.

Cultural Context
Ensure the roadmap is realistic and allows for potential setbacks. Overly optimistic timelines may damage credibility.

部門間の連携強化策を提言いたします。

ぶもんかんのれんけいきょうかさくをていげんいたします。

Bumon-kan no renkei kyōka-saku o teigen itashimasu.

We propose measures to strengthen interdepartmental cooperation.

Variation 1	Variation 2
部署間の連携強化策を提案いたします。	Kyō mo shōjin shima shou.
ぶしょかんのれんけいきょうかさくをていあんいたします。	ぶしょかんのれんけいきょうかさくをていあんいたします。
Busho-kan no renkei kyōka-saku o teian itashimasu.	Bumon-kan no renkei kyōka-saku o teian shimasu.
I will propose measures to strengthen cooperation between departments.	I propose measures to strengthen cooperation between departments.

Positive Response	Negative Response
チームワーク向上に期待できますね。	連携強化策が具体性に欠けています。
ちーむわーくこうじょうにきたいできますね。	れんけいきょうかさくがぐたいせいにかけています。
Chīmu wāku kōjō ni kitai dekimasu ne.	Renkei kyōka-saku ga gutai-sei ni kakete imasu.
We can expect improved teamwork.	The measures to strengthen cooperation lack specificity.

Conversation example person A	Conversation example person B
組織効率化のための分析を行いました。部門間の連携強化策を提言いたします。	連携強化は重要な課題ですね。具体的な施策を検討していきましょう。
そしきこうりつかのためのぶんせきをおこないました。ぶもんかんのれんけいきょうかさくをていげんいたします。	れんけいきょうかはじゅうようなかだいですね。ぐたいてきなしさくをけんとうしていきましょう。
Soshiki kōritsu-ka no tame no bunseki o okonaimashita. Bumon-kan no renkei kyōka-saku o teigen itashimasu.	Renkei kyōka wa jūyōna kadaidesu ne. Gutai-tekina shisaku o kentō shite iki ma shou.
We've conducted an analysis for organizational efficiency. I'd like to propose measures to strengthen interdepartmental cooperation.	Strengthening cooperation is a crucial issue. Let's consider specific measures.

Cultural Context

This implies you've considered organizational dynamics. Be prepared to explain how you'll overcome potential resistance.

本施策の社内外への波及効果を予測しました。

ほんしさくのしゃないがいへのはきゅうこうかをよそくしました。

Hon shisaku no sha naigai e no hakyū kōka o yosoku shima shita.

We have predicted the ripple effects of this measure both inside and outside the company.

Variation 1	Variation 2
本取り組みの社内外への波及効果を予測しました。	Kyō mo shōjin shima shou.
はんとりくみのしゃないがいへのはきゅうこうかをよそくしました。	ほんとりくみのしゃないがいへのはきゅうこうかをよそくしました。
Hon torikumi no sha naigai e no hakyū kōka o yosoku shima shita.	Hon shisaku no sha naigai e no eikyō o suitei shima shita.
We have predicted the ripple effects of this measure both inside and outside the company.	I have predicted the internal and external ripple effects of this measure.

Positive Response	Negative Response
広範囲にポジティブな影響がありそうですね。	波及効果の予測が過大評価されています。
こうはんいにぽじてぃぶなえいきょうがありそうですね。	はきゅうこうかのよそくがかだいひょうかされています。
Kōhan'i ni pojitibuna eikyō ga ari-sōdesu ne.	Hakyū kōka no yosoku ga kadai hyōka sa rete imasu.
It seems there will be widespread positive effects.	The prediction of ripple effects is overestimated.

Conversation example person A	Conversation example person B
新規事業の影響分析を行いました。本施策の社内外への波及効果を予測しました。	波及効果の予測は重要ですね。これを踏まえて実施計画を調整しましょう。
しんきじぎょうのえいきょうぶんせきをおこないました。ほんしさくのしゃないがいへのはきゅうこうかをよそくしました。	はきゅうこうかのよそくはじゅうようですね。これをふまえてじっしけいかくをちょうせいしましょう。
Shinki jigyō no eikyō bunseki o okonaimashita. Hon shisaku no shanai-gai e no hakyū kōka o yosoku shimashita.	Hakyū kōka no yosoku wa jūyōdesu ne. Kore o fumaete jisshi keikaku o chōsei shima shou.
We've analyzed the impact of the new business. We've predicted the ripple effects of this measure both inside and outside the company.	Predicting ripple effects is important. Let's adjust our implementation plan based on this.

Cultural Context

Consider both positive and negative impacts, internally and externally. Overlooking stakeholders may be seen as short-sighted.

実施に伴う組織体制の見直し案をまとめました。

じっしにともなうそしきたいせいのみなおしあんをまとめました。

Jisshi ni tomonau soshiki taisei no minaoshi-an o matomemashita.

We have compiled a proposal for organizational restructuring associated with implementation.

Variation 1	Variation 2
実行に伴う組織体制の見直し案をまとめました。	Kyō mo shōjin shima shou.
じっこうにともなうそしきたいせいのみなおしあんをまとめました。	じっこうにともなうそしきたいせいのみなおしあんをまとめました。
Jikkō ni tomonau soshiki taisei no minaoshi-an o matomemashita.	Jikkō ni saishite no soshiki kōsei no sai kentō-an o sakusei shima shita.
We have compiled a proposal for reviewing the organizational structure associated with implementation.	I have compiled a review plan for the organizational structure that accompanies implementation.

Positive Response	Negative Response
効率的な体制づくりが期待できそうです。	組織体制の見直しが大規模すぎます。
こうりつてきなたいせいづくりがきたいできそうです。	そしきたいせいのみなおしがだいきぼすぎます。
Kōritsu-tekina taisei-dzukuri ga kitai deki-sōdesu.	Soshiki taisei no minaoshi ga dai kibo sugimasu.
We can expect an efficient organizational structure.	The organizational restructuring is too large-scale.

Conversation example person A	Conversation example person B
プロジェクト実施に向けた準備を進めています。実施に伴う組織体制の見直し案をまとめました。	組織体制の見直しは重要ですね。案を詳しく見せていただけますか？
ぷろじぇくとじっしにむけたじゅんびをすすめています。じっしにともなうそしきたいせいのみなおしあんをまとめました。	そしきたいせいのみなおしはじゅうようですね。あんをくわしくみせていただけますか？
Purojekuto jisshi ni muketa junbi o susumete imasu. Jisshi ni tomonau soshiki taisei no minaoshi-an o matsumemashita.	Soshiki taisei no minaoshi wa jūyōdesu ne. An o kuwashiku misete itadakemasu ka?
We're preparing for project implementation. I've compiled a proposal for reviewing the organizational structure accompanying the implementation.	Reviewing the organizational structure is important. Can you show me the proposal in detail?

Cultural Context

Be sensitive when discussing organizational changes. Ensure you've considered the impact on all affected parties.

本提案のコスト構造を詳細に分析しました。

ほんていあんのこすとこうぞうをしょうさいにぶんせきしました。

Hon teian no kosuto kōzō o shōsai ni bunseki shima shita.

We have analyzed the cost structure of this proposal in detail.

Variation 1	Variation 2
本提案の費用構造を詳細に分析しました。	Kyō mo shōjin shima shou.
ほんていあんのひようこうぞうをしょうさいにぶんせきしました。	ほんていあんのひようこうぞうをしょうさいにぶんせきしました。
Hon teian no hiyō kōzō o shōsai ni bunseki shima shita.	Hon teian no hiyō kōsei o kuwashiku kentō shima shita.
We have analyzed the cost structure of this proposal in detail.	I have analyzed the cost structure of this proposal in detail.

Positive Response	Negative Response
コストの内訳が明確で判断しやすいです。	コスト分析が不十分です。
こすとのうちわけがめいかくではんだんしやすいです。	こすとぶんせきがふじゅうぶんです。
Kosuto no uchiwake ga meikakude handan shi yasuidesu.	Kosuto bunseki ga fu jūbundesu.
The clear cost breakdown makes decision-making easier.	The cost analysis is insufficient.

Conversation example person A	Conversation example person B
財務面からの検討も行いました。本提案のコスト構造を詳細に分析しました。	コスト分析は非常に重要です。結果を基に予算調整を行いましょう。
ざいむめんからのけんとうもおこないました。ほんていあんのこすとこうぞうをしょうさいにぶんせきしました。	こすとぶんせきはひじょうにじゅうようです。けっかをもとによさんちょうせいをおこないましょう。
Zaimu-men kara no kentō mo okonaimashita. Hon teian no kosuto kōzō o shōsai ni bunseki shimashita.	Kosuto bunseki wa hijō ni jūyōdesu. Kekka o ki ni yosan chōsei o gyō ima shou.
We've also considered the financial aspect. We've analyzed the cost structure of this proposal in detail.	Cost analysis is crucial. Let's adjust the budget based on these results.

Cultural Context

Be prepared to justify each cost item. Vague or inflated costs may be scrutinized.

想定されるリスクとその対応策を列挙します。

そうていされるりすくとそのたいおうさくをれっきょします。
Sōtei sa re ru risuku to sono taiō-saku o rekkyo shimasu.
We list the anticipated risks and their countermeasures.

Variation 1	Variation 2
想定されるリスクとその対策を列挙します。	Kyō mo shōjin shima shou.
そうていされるりすくとそのたいさくをれっきょします。	そうていされるりすくとそのたいさくをれっきょします。
Sōtei sa re ru risuku to sono taisaku o rekkyo shimasu.	Yosō sa re ru risuku to sono taisaku o agemasu.
I will list the assumed risks and their countermeasures.	I will list the anticipated risks and their countermeasures.

Positive Response	Negative Response
リスク管理が徹底されていて安心です。	リスク対応策が不十分です。
りすくかんりがてっていされていてあんしんです。	りすくたいおうさくがふじゅうぶんです。
Risuku kanri ga tettei sa rete ite anshindesu.	Risuku taiō-saku ga fu jūbundesu.
The thorough risk management is reassuring.	The risk countermeasures are inadequate.

Conversation example person A	Conversation example person B
リスク管理計画を作成しました。想定されるリスクとその対応策を列挙します。	リスク対策は重要ですね。定期的に見直しを行いましょう。
りすくかんりけいかくをさくせいしました。そうていされるりすくとそのたいおうさくをれっきょします。	りすくたいさくはじゅうようですね。ていきてきにみなおしをおこないましょう。
Risuku kanri keikaku o sakusei shimashita. Sōtei sareru risuku to sono taiō-saku o retsujō shimasu.	Risuku taisaku wa jūyōdesu ne. Teiki-teki ni minaoshi o gyō ima shou.
We've created a risk management plan. I'll list the anticipated risks and their countermeasures.	Risk countermeasures are important. Let's review them periodically.

Cultural Context
This shows proactive thinking. Be prepared to explain how you'll implement these risk management strategies.

本計画の実現可能性を多角的に検討しました。

ほんけいかくのじつげんかのうせいをたかくてきにけんとうしました。

Hon keikaku no jitsugen kanō-sei o takaku-teki ni kentō shima shita.

We have examined the feasibility of this plan from multiple angles.

Variation 1	Variation 2
本企画の実現可能性を多面的に検討しました。	Kyō mo shōjin shima shou.
ほんきかくのじつげんかのうせいをためんてきにけんとうしました。	ほんきかくのじつげんかのうせいをためんてきにけんとうしました。
Hon kikaku no jitsugen kanō-sei o tamen-teki ni kentō shima shita.	Hon purojekuto no jitsugen kanō-sei o takaku-teki ni kentō shima shita.
We have considered the feasibility of this plan from multiple angles.	I have examined the feasibility of this project from various angles.

Positive Response	Negative Response
様々な観点からの分析で信頼性が高いですね。	実現可能性の検討が不十分です。
さまざまなかんてんからのぶんせきでしんらいせいがたかいですね。	じつげんかのうせいのけんとうがふじゅうぶんです。
Samazamana kanten kara no bunseki de shinrai-sei ga takaidesu ne.	Jitsugen kanō-sei no kentō ga fu jūbundesu.
The analysis from various perspectives increases reliability.	The feasibility study is insufficient.

Conversation example person A	Conversation example person B
プロジェクトの実現性評価を行いました。本計画の実現可能性を多角的に検討しました。	多角的な検討ありがとうございます。これを基に実行計画を立てましょう。
ぷろじぇくとのじつげんせいひょうかをおこないました。ほんけいかくのじつげんかのうせいをたかくてきにけんとうしました。	たかくてきなけんとうありがとうございます。これをもとにじっこうけいかくをたてましょう。
Purojekuto no jitsugen-sei hyōka o okonaimashita. Hon keikaku no jitsugen kanō-sei o takaku-teki ni kentō shima shita.	Takaku-tekina kentō arigatōgozaimasu. Kore o ki ni jikkō keikaku o tate ma shou.
We've evaluated the feasibility of the project. We've examined the feasibility of this plan from multiple angles.	Thank you for the multi-faceted examination. Let's create an execution plan based on this.

Cultural Context

This implies a thorough feasibility study. Be ready to present detailed analysis if asked.

提案内容の法的側面を精査いたしました。

ていあんないようのほうてきそくめんをせいさいたしました。
Teian naiyō no hō-teki sokumen o seisa itashimashita.
We have scrutinized the legal aspects of the proposal content.

Variation 1	Variation 2
提案内容の法的観点を精査いたしました。	Kyō mo shōjin shima shou.
ていあんないようのほうてきかんてんをせいさいたしました。	ていあんないようのほうてきかんてんをせいさいたしました。
Teian naiyō no hō-teki kanten o seisa itashimashita.	Teian naiyō no hō-teki sokumen o seisa shima shita.
We have scrutinized the legal aspects of the proposal content.	I have scrutinized the legal aspects of the proposal content.

Positive Response	Negative Response
法的リスクへの配慮が行き届いていますね。	法的側面の精査が不十分です。
ほうてきりすくへのはいりょがいきとどいていますね。	ほうてきそくめんのせいさがふじゅうぶんです。
Hō-teki risuku e no hairyo ga ikitodoite imasu ne.	Hō-teki sokumen no seisa ga fu jūbundesu.
The consideration of legal risks is thorough.	The scrutiny of legal aspects is insufficient.

Conversation example person A	Conversation example person B
法務部門と協議を重ねました。提案内容の法的側面を精査いたしました。	法的リスクの確認は重要ですね。問題がないか再確認をお願いします。
ほうむぶもんときょうぎをかさねました。ていあんないようのほうてきそくめんをせいさいたしました。	ほうてきりすくのかくにんはじゅうようですね。もんだいがないかさいかくにんをおねがいします。
Hōmu bumon to kyōgi o kasanemashita. Teian naiyō no hō-teki sokumen o seisa itashimashita.	Hō-teki risuku no kakunin wa jūyōdesu ne. Mondai ga nai ka sai kakunin o onegai shimasu.
We've had repeated discussions with the legal department. We've scrutinized the legal aspects of the proposal.	Confirming legal risks is important. Please double-check that there are no issues.

Cultural Context

This shows due diligence. Ensure you've consulted with appropriate legal experts if necessary.

本戦略のブランド価値向上への貢献度を分析しました。

ほんせんりゃくのぶらんどかちこうじょうへのこうけんどをぶんせきしました。

Hon senryaku no burando kachi kōjō e no kōken-do o bunseki shima shita.

We have analyzed the contribution of this strategy to brand value enhancement.

Variation 1	Variation 2
本戦略のブランド価値向上への影響度を分析しました。	Kyō mo shōjin shima shou.
ほんせんりゃくのぶらんどかちこうじょうへのえいきょうどをぶんせきしました。	ほんせんりゃくのぶらんどかちこうじょうへのえいきょうどをぶんせきしました。
Hon senryaku no burando kachi kōjō e no eikyō-do o bunseki shima shita.	Hon senryaku no burando kachi kōjō e no eikyō-ryoku o bunseki shima shita.
We have analyzed the contribution of this strategy to brand value improvement.	I have analyzed the impact of this strategy on improving brand value.

Positive Response	Negative Response
ブランド戦略との整合性が取れていますね。	ブランド価値向上の分析が甘いです。
ぶらんどせんりゃくとのせいごうせいがとれていますね。	ぶらんどかちこうじょうのぶんせきがあまいです。
Burando senryaku to no seigō-sei ga torete imasu ne.	Burando kachi kōjō no bunseki ga amaidesu.
It aligns well with our brand strategy.	The analysis of brand value enhancement is not thorough enough.

Conversation example person A	Conversation example person B
マーケティング効果の予測を行いました。本戦略のブランド価値向上への貢献度を分析しました。	ブランド価値は重要な指標ですね。長期的な効果も考慮しましょう。
まーけてぃんぐこうかのよそくをおこないました。ほんせんりゃくのぶらんどかちこうじょうへのこうけんどをぶんせきしました。	ぶらんどかちはじゅうようなしひょうですね。ちょうきてきなこうかもこうりょしましょう。
Māketingu kōka no yosoku o okonaimashita. Hon senryaku no burando kachi kōjō e no kōken-do o bunseki shima shita.	Burando kachi wa jūyōna shihyōdesu ne. Chōki-tekina kōka mo kōryo shima shou.
We've predicted the marketing effects. We've analyzed how this strategy contributes to enhancing brand value.	Brand value is an important indicator. Let's also consider long-term effects.

Cultural Context

Be prepared to explain your methodology. Vague claims about brand value may be questioned.

実施後の顧客満足度向上シナリオを策定しました。

じっしごのこきゃくまんぞくどこうじょうしなりおをさくていしました。

Jisshi-go no kokyaku manzoku-do kōjō shinario o sakutei shima shita.

We have developed a scenario for improving customer satisfaction after implementation.

Variation 1	Variation 2
実行後の顧客満足度向上シナリオを策定しました。	Kyō mo shōjin shima shou.
じっこうごのこきゃくまんぞくどこうじょうしなりおをさくていしました。	じっこうごのこきゃくまんぞくどこうじょうしなりおをさくていしました。
Jikkō-go no kokyaku manzoku-do kōjō shinario o sakutei shima shita.	Jikkō-go no kokyaku manzoku-do appu keikaku o ritsuan shima shita.
We have formulated a scenario for improving customer satisfaction after implementation.	I have formulated a scenario for improving customer satisfaction after implementation.

Positive Response	Negative Response
顧客視点に立った計画で良いですね。	顧客満足度向上シナリオが楽観的すぎます。
こきゃくしてんにたったけいかくでよいですね。	こきゃくまんぞくどこうじょうしなりおがらっかんてきすぎます。
Kokyaku shiten ni tatta keikakude yoidesu ne.	Kokyaku manzoku-do kōjō shinario ga rakkan-teki sugimasu.
It's good to have a plan from the customer's perspective.	The scenario for improving customer satisfaction is too optimistic.

Conversation example person A	Conversation example person B
顧客体験の改善計画を立てました。実施後の顧客満足度向上シナリオを策定しました。	顧客満足度の向上は最重要課題ですね。具体的な施策を詰めていきましょう。
こきゃくたいけんのかいぜんけいかくをたてました。じっしごのこきゃくまんぞくどこうじょうしなりおをさくていしました。	こきゃくまんぞくどのこうじょうはさいじゅうようかだいですね。ぐたいてきなしさくをつめていきましょう。
Kokyaku taiken no kaizen keikaku o tatemashita. Jisshi-go no kokyaku manzoku-do kōjō shinario o sakutei shima shita.	Kokyaku manzoku-do no kōjō wa sai jūyō kadaidesu ne. Gutai-tekina shisaku o tsumete iki ma shou.
We've created a plan to improve customer experience. We've developed a scenario for increasing customer satisfaction after implementation.	Improving customer satisfaction is our top priority. Let's flesh out specific measures.

Cultural Context

Ensure your scenario is based on solid customer insights. Unrealistic expectations may be criticized.

本提案の市場適合性を評価いたしました。

ほんていあんのしじょうてきごうせいをひょうかいたしました。

Hon teian no ichiba tekigō-sei o hyōka itashimashita.

We have evaluated the market compatibility of this proposal.

Variation 1	Variation 2
本提案の市場適合性を検証いたしました。	Kyō mo shōjin shima shou.
ほんていあんのしじょうてきごうせいをけんしょういたしました。	ほんていあんのしじょうてきごうせいをけんしょういたしました。
Hon teian no ichiba tekigō-sei o kenshō itashimashita.	Hon teian no ichiba tekigō-sei o kenshō shima shita.
We have evaluated the market suitability of this proposal.	I have verified the market suitability of this proposal.

Positive Response	Negative Response
市場ニーズとのマッチングが確認できて良いです。	市場適合性の評価が不十分です。
しじょうにーずとのまっちんぐがかくにんできてよいです。	しじょうてきごうせいのひょうかがふじゅうぶんです。
Ichiba nīzu to no matchingu ga kakunin dekite yoidesu.	Shijō tekigō-sei no hyōka ga fu jūbundesu.
It's good to confirm the matching with market needs.	The evaluation of market compatibility is insufficient.

Conversation example person A	Conversation example person B
市場調査の結果を分析しました。本提案の市場適合性を評価いたしました。	市場適合性は成功の鍵ですね。競合製品との差別化ポイントを確認しましょう。
しじょうちょうさのけっかをぶんせきしました。ほんていあんのしじょうてきごうせいをひょうかいたしました。	しじょうてきごうせいはせいこうのかぎですね。きょうごうせいひんとのさべつかぽいんとをかくにんしましょう。
Ichiba chōsa no kekka o bunseki shima shita. Hon teian no ichiba tekigō-sei o hyōka itashimashita.	Ichiba tekigō-sei wa seikō no kagidesu ne. Kyōgō seihin to no sabetsu-ka pointo o kakunin shima shou.
We've analyzed the results of our market research. We've evaluated the market fit of this proposal.	Market fit is key to success. Let's confirm our differentiation points from competing products.

Cultural Context

Be prepared to discuss your evaluation criteria. Subjective or biased assessments may be questioned.

以上が今回の提案の概要です。

いじょうがこんかいのていあんのがいようです。

Ijō ga konkai no teian no gaiyōdesu.

This summarizes our proposal.

Variation 1	Variation 2
以上が今回の提案の要点です。	Kyō mo shōjin shima shou.
いじょうがこんかいのていあんのようてんです。	いじょうがこんかいのていあんのようてんです。
Ijō ga konkai no teian no yōtendesu.	Ijō ga konkai no teian no pointodesu.
The above is the summary of this proposal.	The above are the key points of this proposal.

Positive Response	Negative Response
包括的な提案ですね。検討させていただきます。	提案の概要が抽象的すぎます。
ほうかつてきなていあんですね。けんとうさせていただきます。	ていあんのがいようがちゅうしょうてきすぎます。
Hōkatsu-tekina teiandesu ne. Kentō sa sete itadakimasu.	Teian no gaiyō ga chūshō-teki sugimasu.
It's a comprehensive proposal. We'll consider it.	The proposal summary is too abstract.

Conversation example person A	Conversation example person B
長時間ありがとうございました。以上が今回の提案の概要です。	詳細な提案ありがとうございます。検討して結果をお知らせします。
ちょうじかんありがとうございました。いじょうがこんかいのていあんのがいようです。	しょうさいなていあんありがとうございます。けんとうしてけっかをおしらせします。
Naga jikan arigatō go zaimashita. Ijō ga konkai no teian no gaiyōdesu.	Shōsaina teian arigatōgozaimasu. Kentō shite kekka o oshirase shimasu.
Thank you for your time. This concludes the overview of our proposal.	Thank you for the detailed proposal. We'll review it and let you know the results.

Cultural Context

Ensure you've covered all key points. Missing crucial information may be seen as poor preparation.

次回の会議で詳細を説明します。

じかいのかいぎでしょうさいをせつめいします。
Jikai no kaigi de shōsai o setsumei shimasu.
We will explain the details in the next meeting.

Variation 1	Variation 2
次回の会議で詳しく説明します。	Kyō mo shōjin shima shou.
じかいのかいぎでくわしくせつめいします。	じかいのかいぎでくわしくせつめいします。
Jikai no kaigi de kuwashiku setsumei shimasu.	Jikai no kaigi de shōsai ni setsumei shimasu.
I will explain the details at the next meeting.	I will explain in detail at the next meeting.

Positive Response	Negative Response
詳細な説明を楽しみにしています。	詳細説明が遅すぎます。
しょうさいなせつめいをたのしみにしています。	しょうさいせつめいがおそすぎます。
Shōsaina setsumei o tanoshimi ni shite imasu.	Shōsai setsumei ga oso sugimasu.
Looking forward to the detailed explanation.	The detailed explanation is coming too late.

Conversation example person A	Conversation example person B
本日はお時間をいただきありがとうございました。次回の会議で詳細を説明します。	承知しました。次回の会議を楽しみにしています。
ほんじつはおじかんをいただきありがとうございました。じかいのかいぎでしょうさいをせつめいします。	しょうちしました。じかいのかいぎをたのしみにしています。
Honjitsu wa o jikan o itadaki arigatō go zaimashita. Jikai no kaigi de shōsai o setsumei shimasu.	Shōchi shima shita. Jikai no kaigi o tanoshimi ni shite imasu.
Thank you for your time today. I'll explain the details in the next meeting.	Understood. I'm looking forward to the next meeting.

Cultural Context
Be prepared for detailed questions. Lack of immediate answers may be seen as unprofessional.

ご意見・ご質問がありましたら、お知らせください。

ごいけん・ごしつもんがありましたら、おしらせください。

Go iken go shitsumon ga Arima shitara, oshirase kudasai.

Please let us know if you have any opinions or questions.

Variation 1	Variation 2
ご意見・ご質問がありましたら、ご連絡ください。	Kyō mo shōjin shima shou.
ごいけん・ごしつもんがありましたら、ごれんらくください。	ごいけん・ごしつもんがありましたら、ごれんらくください。
Go iken go shitsumon ga Arima shitara, go renraku kudasai.	Go fumeina ten ya go shitsumon nado go zaimashita-ra, oshirase kudasai.
If you have any comments or questions, please let us know.	If you have any comments or questions, please let us know.

Positive Response	Negative Response
丁寧な対応ありがとうございます。	質問の回答に時間がかかりすぎます。
ていねいなたいおうありがとうございます。	しつもんのかいとうにじかんがかかりすぎます。
Teineina taiō arigatōgozaimasu.	Shitsumon no kaitō ni jikan ga kakari sugimasu.
Thank you for your thoughtful approach.	It takes too long to get answers to questions.

Conversation example person A	Conversation example person B
提案内容について説明させていただきました。ご意見・ご質問がありましたら、お知らせください。	いくつか質問があります。後ほど詳細をメールで送らせていただきます。
ていあんないようについてせつめいさせていただきました。ごいけん・ごしつもんがありましたら、おしらせください。	いくつかしつもんがあります。のちほどしょうさいをめーるでおくらせていただきます。
Teian naiyō ni tsuite setsumei sa sete itadakimashita. Go iken go shitsumon ga Arima shitara, oshirase kudasai.	Ikutsu ka shitsumon ga arimasu. Nochihodo shōsai o mēru de okura sete itadakimasu.
I've explained the content of the proposal. Please let me know if you have any opinions or questions.	I have a few questions. I'll send you the details by email later.

Cultural Context

Be prepared to respond promptly and thoroughly to any feedback or questions.

本件について、ご協力をお願いいたします。

ほんけんについて、ごきょうりょくをおねがいいたします。
Honken ni tsuite, go kyōryoku o onegai itashimasu.
We ask for your cooperation on this matter.

Variation 1	Variation 2
本件に関して、ご協力をお願いいたします。	Kyō mo shōjin shima shou.
ほんけんにかんして、ごきょうりょくをおねがいいたします。	ほんけんにかんして、ごきょうりょくをおねがいいたします。
Honken ni kanshite, go kyōryoku o onegai itashimasu.	Hon anken ni kanshite, go kyōryoku o onegai mōshiagemasu.
We would appreciate your cooperation on this matter.	Regarding this matter, I kindly request your cooperation.

Positive Response	Negative Response
もちろん、全面的に協力させていただきます。	協力を求める前に、もっと説明が必要です。
もちろん、ぜんめんてきにきょうりょくさせていただきます。	きょうりょくをもとめるまえに、もっとせつめいがひつようです。
Mochiron, zenmen-teki ni kyōryoku sa sete itadakimasu.	Kyōryoku o motomeru mae ni, motto setsumei ga hitsuyōdesu.
Of course, we'll cooperate fully.	More explanation is needed before asking for cooperation.

Conversation example person A	Conversation example person B
プロジェクトの成功には皆様の協力が不可欠です。本件について、ご協力をお願いいたします。	もちろんです。全力でサポートさせていただきます。
ぷろじぇくとのせいこうにはみなさまのきょうりょくがふかけつです。ほんけんについて、ごきょうりょくをおねがいいたします。	もちろんです。ぜんりょくでさぽーとさせていただきます。
Purojekuto no seikō ni wa minasama no kyōryoku ga fukaketsudesu. Honken ni tsuite, go kyōryoku o onegai itashimasu.	Mochirondesu. Zenryoku de sapōto sa sete itadakimasu.
Your cooperation is essential for the success of this project. We request your cooperation on this matter.	Of course. We'll support you with all our efforts.

Cultural Context

This implies you need support. Be clear about what kind of cooperation you're seeking.

進捗状況は随時報告いたします。

しんちょくじょうきょうはずいじほうこくいたします。
Shinchoku jōkyō wa zuiji hōkoku itashimasu.
We will report on the progress regularly.

Variation 1	Variation 2
進行状況は適宜報告いたします。	Kyō mo shōjin shima shou.
しんこうじょうきょうはてきぎほうこくいたします。	しんこうじょうきょうはてきぎほうこくいたします。
Shinkō jōkyō wa tekigi hōkoku itashimasu.	Shinchoku jōkyō wa zuiji hōkoku shimasu.
We will report the progress status from time to time.	I will report on the progress as needed.

Positive Response	Negative Response
定期的な報告を楽しみにしています。	進捗報告の頻度が不明確です。
ていきてきなほうこくをたのしみにしています。	しんちょくほうこくのひんどがふめいかくです。
Teiki-tekina hōkoku o tanoshimi ni shite imasu.	Shinchoku hōkoku no hindo ga fu meikakudesu.
Looking forward to regular updates.	The frequency of progress reports is unclear.

Conversation example person A	Conversation example person B
プロジェクトを開始いたします。進捗状況は随時報告いたします。	承知しました。定期的な更新を楽しみにしています。
ぷろじぇくとをかいしいたします。しんちょくじょうきょうはずいじほうこくいたします。	しょうちしました。ていきてきなこうしんをたのしみにしています。
Purojekuto o kaishi itashimasu. Shinchoku jōkyō wa zuiji hōkoku itashimasu.	Shōchi shima shita. Teiki-tekina kōshin o tanoshimi ni shite imasu.
We're starting the project. We'll report on the progress regularly.	Understood. We look forward to regular updates.

Cultural Context
Set clear expectations about the frequency and method of updates.

添付資料をご確認ください。

てんぷしりょうをごかくにんください。

Tenpu shiryō o go kakunin kudasai.

Please check the attached documents.

Variation 1	Variation 2
添付ファイルをご確認ください。	Kyō mo shōjin shima shou.
てんぷふぁいるをごかくにんください。	てんぷふぁいるをごかくにんください。
Tenpu fairu o go kakunin kudasai.	Tenpu fairu o goran kudasai.
Please check the attached documents.	Please check the attached documents.

Positive Response	Negative Response
拝見いたします。ありがとうございます。	添付資料が多すぎて確認する時間がありません。
はいけんいたします。ありがとうございます。	てんぷしりょうがおおすぎてかくにんするじかんがありません。
Haiken itashimasu. Arigatōgozaimasu.	Tenpu shiryō ga ō sugite kakunin suru jikan ga arimasen.
Looking forward to regular updates.	There are too many attachments to check in the available time.

Conversation example person A	Conversation example person B
詳細なデータを用意しました。添付資料をご確認ください。	了解しました。資料を確認の上、フィードバックいたします。
しょうさいなでーたをよういしました。てんぷしりょうをごかくにんください。	りょうかいしました。しりょうをかくにんのうえ、ふぃーどばっくいたします。
Shōsaina dēta o yōi shima shita. Tenpu shiryō o go kakunin kudasai.	Ryōkai shima shita. Shiryō o kakunin no ue, fīdobakku itashimasu.
I've prepared detailed data. Please check the attached documents.	Understood. I'll review the documents and provide feedback.

Cultural Context

Ensure all attachments are properly labeled and easily accessible.

今後のスケジュールは別紙の通りです。

こんごのすけじゅーるはべっしのとおりです。
Kongo no sukejūru wa besshi no tōridesu.
The future schedule is as per the attached sheet.

Variation 1	Variation 2
今後の予定は別紙の通りです。	Kyō mo shōjin shima shou.
こんごのよていはべっしのとおりです。	こんごのよていはべっしのとおりです。
Kongo no yotei wa besshi no tōridesu.	Kongo no nittei wa betto shiryō no tōridesu.
The future schedule is as per the separate sheet.	The future schedule is as shown in the separate sheet.

Positive Response	Negative Response
スケジュールを確認し、調整いたします。	スケジュールが非現実的です。
すけじゅーるをかくにんし、ちょうせいいたします。	すけじゅーるがひげんじつてきです。
Sukejūru o kakunin shi, chōsei itashimasu.	Sukejūru ga hi genjitsu-tekidesu.
I'll take a look. Thank you.	The schedule is unrealistic.

Conversation example person A	Conversation example person B
プロジェクトの全体像をまとめました。今後のスケジュールは別紙の通りです。	スケジュールを確認しました。タイトですが頑張りましょう。
ぷろじぇくとのぜんたいぞうをまとめました。こんごのすけじゅーるはべっしのとおりです。	すけじゅーるをかくにんしました。たいとですががんばりましょう。
Purojekuto no zentai-zō o matomemashita. Kongo no sukejūru wa besshi no tōridesu.	Sukejūru o kakunin shima shita. Taitodesuga ganbari ma shou.
I've summarized the overall picture of the project. The future schedule is as shown in the separate sheet.	I've checked the schedule. It's tight, but let's do our best.

Cultural Context
Ensure the schedule is realistic and allows for potential delays.

本プロジェクトの目標を達成しました。

ほんぷろじぇくとのもくひょうをたっせいしました。
Hon purojekuto no mokuhyō o tassei shima shita.
We have achieved the goal of this project.

Variation 1	Variation 2
本企画の目的を達成しました。	Kyō mo shōjin shima shou.
ほんきかくのもくてきをたっせいしました。	ほんきかくのもくてきをたっせいしました。
Hon kikaku no mokuteki o tassei shima shita.	Hon purojekuto no mokuteki o tassei shima shita.
We have achieved the goal of this project.	The purpose of this project has been achieved.

Positive Response	Negative Response
素晴らしい成果ですね。お疲れ様でした。	目標達成の証拠が不十分です。
すばらしいせいかですね。おつかれさまでした。	もくひょうたっせいのしょうこがふじゅうぶんです。
Subarashī seikadesu ne. Otsukaresama de shita.	Mokuhyō tassei no shōko ga fu jūbundesu.
I'll check the schedule and adjust accordingly.	The evidence of goal achievement is insufficient.

Conversation example person A	Conversation example person B
皆様のご協力のおかげです。本プロジェクトの目標を達成しました。	おめでとうございます。チーム全体の成果ですね。
みなさまのごきょうりょくのおかげです。ほんぷろじぇくとのもくひょうをたっせいしました。	おめでとうございます。ちーむぜんたいのせいかですね。
Minasama no go kyōryoku no okagedesu. Hon purojekuto no mokuhyō o tassei shima shita.	Omedetōgozaimasu. Chīmu zentai no seikadesu ne.
Thanks to everyone's cooperation. We've achieved the goals of this project.	Congratulations. It's an achievement of the entire team.

Cultural Context

Be prepared to provide evidence of achievement. Vague claims of success may be questioned.

関係部署との調整が必要です。

かんけいぶしょとのちょうせいがひつようです。

Kankei busho to no chōsei ga hitsuyōdesu.

Coordination with relevant departments is necessary.

Variation 1	Variation 2
関連部署との調整が必要です。	Kyō mo shōjin shima shou.
かんれんぶしょとのちょうせいがひつようです。	かんれんぶしょとのちょうせいがひつようです。
Kanren busho to no chōsei ga hitsuyōdesu.	Kankei bumon to no chōsei ga hitsuyōdesu.
Coordination with related departments is necessary.	Coordination with related departments is necessary.

Positive Response	Negative Response
部署間の連携を強化していきましょう。	部署間の調整に時間がかかりすぎます。
ぶしょかんのれんけいをきょうかしていきましょう。	ぶしょかんのちょうせいにじかんがかかりすぎます。
Busho-kan no renkei o kyōka shite iki ma shou.	Busho-kan no chōsei ni jikan ga kakari sugimasu.
Great achievement. Well done.	It takes too long to coordinate between departments.

Conversation example person A	Conversation example person B
次のステップに進むにあたり、関係部署との調整が必要です。	了解しました。調整会議の設定をお願いできますか？
つぎのすてっぷにすすむにあたり、かんけいぶしょとのちょうせいがひつようです。	りょうかいしました。ちょうせいかいぎのせっていをおねがいできますか？
Tsugi no suteppu ni susumu ni atari, kankei busho to no chōsei ga hitsuyōdesu.	Ryōkai shima shita. Chōsei kaigi no settei o onegai dekimasu ka?
To move on to the next step, coordination with relevant departments is necessary.	Understood. Can you set up a coordination meeting?

Cultural Context

This implies potential challenges. Be prepared to explain how you plan to facilitate coordination.

予算内での実施を目指します。

よさんないでのじっしをめざします。

Yosan-nai de no jisshi o mezashimasu.

We aim to implement within the budget.

Variation 1	Variation 2
予算内での実行を目指します。	Kyō mo shōjin shima shou.
よさんないでのじっこうをめざします。	よさんないでのじっこうをめざします。
Yosan-nai de no jikkō o mezashimasu.	Yosan han'i-nai de no suikō o mokuhyō to shimasu.
We aim to implement within the budget.	We aim to implement it within the budget.

Positive Response	Negative Response
コスト意識の高い計画で良いですね。	予算が不十分に思えます。
こすといしきのたかいけいかくでよいですね。	よさんがふじゅうぶんにおもえます。
Kosuto ishiki no takai keikakude yoidesu ne.	Yosan ga fu jūbun ni omoemasu.
Let's strengthen interdepartmental cooperation.	The budget seems insufficient.

Conversation example person A	Conversation example person B
コスト削減の必要性を認識しています。予算内での実施を目指します。	コスト意識は重要ですね。効率的な実施方法を考えましょう。
こすとさくげんのひつようせいをにんしきしています。よさんないでのじっしをめざします。	こすといしきはじゅうようですね。こうりつてきなじっしほうほうをかんがえましょう。
Kosuto sakugen no hitsuyō-sei o ninshiki shite imasu. Yosan-nai de no jisshi o mezashimasu.	Kosuto ishiki wa jūyōdesu ne. Kōritsu-tekina jisshi hōhō o kangae ma shou.
We recognize the need for cost reduction. We aim to implement within the budget.	Cost awareness is important. Let's think of efficient implementation methods.

Cultural Context

This implies potential financial constraints. Be prepared to discuss cost-saving measures.

社内での情報共有をお願いします。

しゃないでのじょうほうきょうゆうをおねがいします。
Shanai de no jōhō kyōyū o onegai shimasu.
Please share this information within the company.

Variation 1	Variation 2
社内で情報を共有していただくようお願い申し上げます。	Kyō mo shōjin shima shou.
しゃないでじょうほうをきょうゆうしていただくようおねがいもうしあげます。	しゃないでじょうほうをきょうゆうしていただくようおねがいもうしあげます。
Shanai de jōhō o kyōyū shite itadaku yō onegai mōshiagemasu.	Shanai de jōhō o kyōyū shite itadaku yō onegai shimasu.
I kindly request you to share information within the company.	Please share the information within the company.

Positive Response	Negative Response
承知しました。速やかに展開します。	情報共有の方法が不明確です。
しょうちしました。すみやかにてんかいします。	じょうほうきょうゆうのほうほうがふめいかくです。
Shōchi shima shita. Sumiyaka ni tenkai shimasu.	Jōhō kyōyū no hōhō ga fu meikakudesu.
It's good to have a cost-conscious plan.	The method for information sharing is unclear.

Conversation example person A	Conversation example person B
本プロジェクトの重要性について、社内での情報共有をお願いします。	承知しました。部門会議で共有し、協力を呼びかけます。
ほんぷろじぇくとのじゅうようせいについて、しゃないでのじょうほうきょうゆうをおねがいします。	しょうちしました。ぶもんかいぎできょうゆうし、きょうりょくをよびかけます。
Hon purojekuto no jūyō-sei ni tsuite, shanai de no jōhō kyōyū o onegai shimasu.	Shōchi shima shita. Bumon kaigi de kyōyū shi, kyōryoku o yobikakemasu.
Regarding the importance of this project, please share the information within the company.	Understood. I'll share it in the department meeting and call for cooperation.

Cultural Context

Be clear about what information needs to be shared, with whom, and how.

具体的な実施方法は検討中です。

ぐたいてきなじっしほうほうはけんとうちゅうです。
Gutai-tekina jisshi hōhō wa kentō-chūdesu.
We are considering specific implementation methods.

Variation 1	Variation 2
具体的な実行方法は検討中です。	Kyō mo shōjin shima shou.
ぐたいてきなじっこうほうほうはけんとうちゅうです。	ぐたいてきなじっこうほうほうはけんとうちゅうです。
Gutai-tekina jikkō hōhō wa kentō-chūdesu.	Shōsaina jikkō hōshiki wa kentō-chūdesu.
The specific implementation method is under consideration.	The specific implementation method is under consideration.

Positive Response	Negative Response
検討結果を楽しみにしています。	実施方法の検討が遅すぎます。
けんとうけっかをたのしみにしています。	じっしほうほうのけんとうがおそすぎます。
Kentō kekka o tanoshimi ni shite imasu.	Jisshi hōhō no kentō ga oso sugimasu.
Understood. I'll disseminate the information promptly.	The consideration of implementation methods is too late.

Conversation example person A	Conversation example person B
方針は決定しましたが、具体的な実施方法は検討中です。	分かりました。検討結果を待っています。何か協力できることはありますか？
ほうしんはけっていしましたが、ぐたいてきなじっしほうほうはけんとうちゅうです。	わかりました。けんとうけっかをまっています。なにかきょうりょくできることはありますか？
Hōshin wa kettei shima shitaga, gutai-tekina jisshi hōhō wa kentō-chūdesu.	Wakarimashita. Kentō kekka o matte imasu. Nani ka kyōryoku dekiru koto wa arimasu ka?
We've decided on the policy, but the specific implementation method is under consideration.	I see. We're waiting for the results of the consideration. Is there anything we can do to help?

Cultural Context

This implies the plan is not yet finalized. Be prepared to provide a timeline for when decisions will be made.

本案に対するフィードバックをお待ちしています。

ほんあんにたいするふぃーどばっくをおまちしています。

Hon'an ni taisuru fīdobakku o omachi shite imasu.

We look forward to your feedback on this proposal.

Variation 1	Variation 2
本案に対するご意見をお待ちしています。	Kyō mo shōjin shima shou.
ほんあんにたいするごいけんをおまちしています。	ほんあんにたいするごいけんをおまちしています。
Hon'an ni taisuru go iken o omachi shite imasu.	Kono an ni tsuite no go kansō o o kikase kudasai.
We are waiting for your feedback on this proposal.	We look forward to your feedback on this proposal.

Positive Response	Negative Response
できるだけ早くフィードバックいたします。	フィードバックの期限が不明確です。
できるだけはやくふぃーどばっくいたします。	ふぃーどばっくのきげんがふめいかくです。
Dekirudake hayaku fīdobakku itashimasu.	Fīdobakku no kigen ga fu meikakudesu.
Looking forward to the results of your consideration.	The deadline for feedback is unclear.

Conversation example person A	Conversation example person B
提案書を送付いたしました。本案に対するフィードバックをお待ちしています。	了解しました。内容を精査の上、来週中にフィードバックいたします。
ていあんしょをそうふいたしました。ほんあんにたいするふぃーどばっくをおまちしています。	りょうかいしました。ないようをせいさのうえ、らいしゅうちゅうにふぃーどばっくいたします。
Teian-sho o sōfu itashimashita. Hon'an ni taisuru fīdobakku o omachi shite imasu.	Ryōkai shima shita. Naiyō o seisa no ue, raishū-chū ni fīdobakku itashimasu.
I've sent the proposal. We're looking forward to your feedback on this plan.	Understood. We'll examine the content and provide feedback by next week.

Cultural Context

Be prepared to receive and act on feedback promptly.

今回の結果を踏まえて、次のステップに進みます。

こんかいのけっかをふまえて、つぎのすてっぷにすすみます。

Konkai no kekka o fumaete,-ji no suteppu ni susumimasu.

Based on these results, we will move on to the next step.

Variation 1	Variation 2
今回の結果を受けて、次の段階に進みます。	Kyō mo shōjin shima shou.
こんかいのけっかをうけて、つぎのだんかいにすすみます。	こんかいのけっかをうけて、つぎのだんかいにすすみます。
Konkai no kekka o ukete,-ji no dankai ni susumimasu.	Konkai no seika o ki ni,-ji no dankai ni utsurimasu.
Based on the results this time, we will proceed to the next step.	Based on the results of this time, we will move on to the next step.

Positive Response	Negative Response
次のステップに期待しています。頑張りましょう。	次のステップに進むのは時期尚早です。
つぎのすてっぷにきたいしています。がんばりましょう。	つぎのすてっぷにすすむのはじきしょうそうです。
Tsugi no suteppu ni kitai shite imasu. Ganbari ma shou.	Tsugi no suteppu ni susumu no wa jiki shōsōdesu.
I'll provide feedback as soon as possible.	It's premature to move to the next step.

Conversation example person A	Conversation example person B
プロジェクトの第一段階が完了しました。今回の結果を踏まえて、次のステップに進みます。	お疲れ様でした。次のステップについて、詳細を教えていただけますか？
ぷろじぇくとのだいいちだんかいがかんりょうしました。こんかいのけっかをふまえて、つぎのすてっぷにすすみます。	おつかれさまでした。つぎのすてっぷについて、しょうさいをおしえていただけますか？
Purojekuto no dai ichi dankai ga kanryō shima shita. Konkai no kekka o fumaete, tsugi no suteppu ni susumimasu.	Otsukaresama de shita. Tsugi no suteppu ni tsuite, shōsai o oshiete itadakemasu ka?
We've completed the first phase of the project. Based on these results, we'll move on to the next step.	Good job. Could you tell me more about the next step?

Cultural Context

Be clear about what the next steps are and why they're necessary.

本施策の効果を定期的に確認します。

ほんしさくのこうかをていきてきにかくにんします。

Hon shisaku no kōka o teiki-teki ni kakunin shimasu.

We will regularly check the effectiveness of this measure.

Variation 1	Variation 2
本取り組みの効果を定期的に確認します。	Kyō mo shōjin shima shou.
ほんとりくみのこうかをていきてきにかくにんします。	ほんとりくみのこうかをていきてきにかくにんします。
Hon torikumi no kōka o teiki-teki ni kakunin shimasu.	Hon shisaku no seika o teiki-teki ni chekku shimasu.
We will regularly check the effectiveness of this measure.	We will regularly check the effectiveness of this measure.

Positive Response	Negative Response
効果測定は重要ですね。結果を共有してください。	効果確認の方法が不明確です。
こうかそくていはじゅうようですね。けっかをきょうゆうしてください。	こうかかくにんのほうほうがふめいかくです。
Kōka sokutei wa jūyōdesu ne. Kekka o kyōyū shite kudasai.	Kōka kakunin no hōhō ga fu meikakudesu.
Looking forward to the next step. Let's do our best.	The method for regularly checking effectiveness is unclear.

Conversation example person A	Conversation example person B
新しい取り組みを開始しました。本施策の効果を定期的に確認します。	効果測定は重要ですね。どのような指標で確認しますか？
あたらしいとりくみをかいしました。ほんしさくのこうかをていきてきにかくにんします。	こうかそくていはじゅうようですね。どのようなしひょうでかくにんしますか？
Atarashī torikumi o kaishi shima shita. Hon shisaku no kōka o teiki-teki ni kakunin shimasu.	Kōka sokutei wa jūyōdesu ne. Do no yōna shihyō de kakunin shimasu ka?
We've started a new initiative. We'll regularly check the effectiveness of this measure.	Effect measurement is important. What indicators will you use to check?

Cultural Context

Be specific about how and when you'll measure effects. Vague monitoring plans may be seen as lack of commitment.

皆様のご協力に感謝いたします。

みなさまのごきょうりょくにかんしゃいたします。
Minasama no go kyōryoku ni kansha itashimasu.
We appreciate your cooperation.

Variation 1	Variation 2
ご協力いただき誠にありがとうございます。	Kyō mo shōjin shima shou.
ごきょうりょくいただきまことにありがとうございます。	ごきょうりょくいただきまことにありがとうございます。
Go kyōryoku itadaki makotoni arigatōgozaimasu.	Go kyōryoku arigatōgozaimasu.
Thank you sincerely for your cooperation.	Thank you very much for your cooperation.

Positive Response	Negative Response
こちらこそ、ありがとうございます。	協力の具体的な内容が不明確です。
こちらこそ、ありがとうございます。	きょうりょくのぐたいてきないようがふめいかくです。
Kochira koso, arigatōgozaimasu.	Kyōryoku no gutai-tekina naiyō ga fu meikakudesu.
Effect measurement is important. Please share the results.	The specific content of the cooperation is unclear.

Conversation example person A	Conversation example person B
プロジェクトが無事完了しました。皆様のご協力に感謝いたします。	お疲れ様でした。チーム全体の努力の賜物ですね。
ぷろじぇくとがぶじかんりょうしました。みなさまのごきょうりょくにかんしゃいたします。	おつかれさまでした。ちーむぜんたいのどりょくのたまものですね。
Purojekuto ga buji kanryō shima shita. Minasama no go kyōryoku ni kansha itashimasu.	Otsukaresama de shita. Chīmu zentai no doryoku no tamamonodesu ne.
The project has been successfully completed. Thank you all for your cooperation.	Good work. It's the result of the entire team's efforts.

Cultural Context

This is typically used at the end of a project or major phase. Ensure it's used in appropriate contexts.

本件に関する質問は担当者までお願いします。

ほんけんにかんするしつもんはたんとうしゃまでおねがいします。

Honken ni kansuru shitsumon wa tantō-sha made onegai shimasu.

Please direct any questions about this matter to the person in charge.

Variation 1	Variation 2
本件に関するご質問は担当者までお願いします。	Kyō mo shōjin shima shou.
ほんけんにかんするごしつもんはたんとうしゃまでおねがいします。	ほんけんにかんするごしつもんはたんとうしゃまでおねがいします。
Honken ni kansuru go shitsumon wa tantō-sha made onegai shimasu.	Hon anken ni kansuru go shitsumon wa tantō-sha made onegai shimasu.
Please direct any questions regarding this matter to the person in charge.	Please contact the person in charge for any questions regarding this matter.

Positive Response	Negative Response
承知しました。不明点があれば連絡します。	担当者の連絡先が不明確です。
しょうちしました。ふめいてんがあればれんらくします。	たんとうしゃのれんらくさきがふめいかくです。
Shōchi shima shita. Fumei-ten ga areba renraku shimasu.	Tantō-sha no renraku-saki ga fu meikakudesu.
Thank you as well.	The contact information for the person in charge is unclear.

Conversation example person A	Conversation example person B
詳細資料を配布しました。本件に関する質問は担当者までお願いします。	承知しました。質問がある場合は担当者に連絡します。
しょうさいしりょうをはいふしました。ほんけんにかんするしつもんはたんとうしゃまでおねがいします。	しょうちしました。しつもんがあるばあいはたんとうしゃにれんらくします。
Shōsai shiryō o haifu shima shita. Honken ni kansuru shitsumon wa tantō-sha made onegai shimasu.	Shōchi shima shita. Shitsumon ga aru baai wa tantō-sha ni renraku shimasu.
We've distributed detailed documents. Please direct any questions about this matter to the person in charge.	Understood. If we have any questions, we'll contact the person in charge.

Cultural Context
Ensure the contact person is prepared to handle inquiries. Lack of response may be seen as unprofessional.

今後の課題について話し合いましょう。

こんごのかだいについてはなしあいましょう。
Kongo no kadai ni tsuite hanashiai ma shou.
Let's discuss future challenges.

Variation 1	Variation 2
今後の問題点について話し合いましょう。	Kyō mo shōjin shima shou.
こんごのもんだいてんについてはなしあいましょう。	こんごのもんだいてんについてはなしあいましょう。
Kongo no mondai-ten ni tsuite hanashiai ma shou.	Kongo no mondai-ten ni tsuite giron shima shou.
Let's discuss future issues.	Let's discuss future issues.

Positive Response	Negative Response
ぜひ一緒に検討したいと思います。	課題の優先順位が不明確です。
ぜひいっしょにけんとうしたいとおもいます。	かだいのゆうせんじゅんいがふめいかくです。
Zehi issho ni kentō shitai to omoimasu.	Kadai no yūsen jun'i ga fu meikakudesu.
Understood. I'll contact if there are any questions.	The priority of future issues is unclear.

Conversation example person A	Conversation example person B
一定の成果を上げることができました。今後の課題について話し合いましょう。	良いアイデアですね。会議の日程を調整しましょう。
いっていのせいかをあげることができました。こんごのかだいについてはなしあいましょう。	よいあいであですね。かいぎのにっていをちょうせいしましょう。
Ittei no seika o ageru koto ga dekimashita. Kongo no kadai ni tsuite hanashiai ma shou.	Yoi aideadesu ne. Kaigi no nittei o chōsei shima shou.
We've achieved certain results. Let's discuss our future challenges.	That's a good idea. Let's schedule a meeting.

Cultural Context
Be prepared with specific discussion points. Open-ended discussions without clear objectives may be seen as inefficient.

本提案のメリットをご説明します。

ほんていあんのめりっとをごせつめいします。

Hon teian no meritto o go setsumei shimasu.

We will explain the benefits of this proposal.

Variation 1	Variation 2
本提案の利点をご説明します。	Kyō mo shōjin shima shou.
ほんていあんのりてんをごせつめいします。	ほんていあんのりてんをごせつめいします。
Hon teian no riten o go setsumei shimasu.	Hon'an no chōsho o go shōkai shimasu.
I will explain the benefits of this proposal.	Let me explain the advantages of this proposal.

Positive Response	Negative Response
メリットについて詳しく聞かせてください。	メリットが誇張されているように思えます。
めりっとについてくわしくきかせてください。	めりっとがこちょうされているようにおもえます。
Meritto ni tsuite kuwashiku kika sete kudasai.	Meritto ga kochō sa rete iru yō ni omoemasu.
I'd like to discuss this together.	The benefits seem to be exaggerated.

Conversation example person A	Conversation example person B
新しいアプローチを提案します。本提案のメリットをご説明します。	興味深い提案ですね。デメリットもあれば教えてください。
あたらしいあぷろーちをていあんします。ほんていあんのめりっとをごせつめいします。	きょうみぶかいていあんですね。でめりっともあればおしえてください。
Atarashī apurōchi o teian shimasu. Hon teian no meritto o go setsumei shimasu.	Kyōmibukai teiandesu ne. Demeritto mo areba oshiete kudasai.
I'm proposing a new approach. Let me explain the benefits of this proposal.	That's an interesting proposal. Please also tell us if there are any disadvantages.

Cultural Context

Be prepared to address potential drawbacks as well. Presenting only positives may be seen as one-sided.

実施後の評価方法を決定しました。

じっしごのひょうかほうほうをけっていしました。

Jisshi-go no hyōka hōhō o kettei shima shita.

We have decided on the evaluation method after implementation.

Variation 1	Variation 2
実行後の評価方法を決定しました。	Kyō mo shōjin shima shou.
じっこうごのひょうかほうほうをけっていしました。	じっこうごのひょうかほうほうをけっていしました。
Jikkō-go no hyōka hōhō o kettei shima shita.	Jikkō-go no hyōka kijun o kakutei shima shita.
The evaluation method after implementation has been determined.	I have determined the evaluation method after implementation.

Positive Response	Negative Response
評価基準が明確で良いですね。	評価方法が適切ではありません。
ひょうかきじゅんがめいかくでよいですね。	ひょうかほうほうがてきせつではありません。
Hyōka kijun ga meikakude yoidesu ne.	Hyōka hōhō ga tekisetsude wa arimasen.
Please tell me more about the benefits.	The evaluation method is not appropriate.

Conversation example person A	Conversation example person B
プロジェクト計画の最終調整を行いました。実施後の評価方法を決定しました。	評価方法の詳細を共有していただけますか？
ぷろじぇくとけいかくのさいしゅうちょうせいをおこないました。じっしごのひょうかほうほうをけっていしました。	ひょうかほうほうのしょうさいをきょうゆうしていただけますか？
Purojekuto keikaku no saishū chōsei o okonaimashita. Jisshi-go no hyōka hōhō o kettei shima shita.	Hyōka hōhō no shōsai o kyōyū shite itadakemasu ka?
We've made final adjustments to the project plan. We've decided on the evaluation method after implementation.	Could you share the details of the evaluation method?

Cultural Context

Ensure the evaluation methods are objective and measurable. Subjective criteria may be questioned.

本日の会議の議事録を添付しました。

ほんじつのかいぎのぎじろくをてんぷしました。

Honjitsu no kaigi no giji-roku o tenpu shima shita.

The minutes of today's meeting are attached.

Variation 1	Variation 2
本日開催された会議の議事録を添付ファイルにてお送りいたします。	Kyō mo shōjin shima shou.
ほんじつかいさいされたかいぎのぎじろくをてんぷファイルにておおくりいたします。	ほんじつかいさいされたかいぎのぎじろくをてんぷファイルにておおくりいたします。
Honjitsu kaisai sa reta kaigi no giji-roku o tenpu fairu nite ookuri itashimasu.	Honjitsu kaisai sa reta kaigi no giji-roku o tenpu shiryō nite ookuri shimasu.
I am sending the minutes of today's meeting as an attached file.	I will send the minutes of the meeting held today as an attached file.

Positive Response	Negative Response
議事録を確認させていただきます。	議事録が不完全です。
ぎじろくをかくにんさせていただきます。	ぎじろくがふかんぜんです。
Giji-roku o kakunin sa sete itadakimasu.	Giji-roku ga fu kanzendesu.
It's good to have clear evaluation criteria.	The meeting minutes are incomplete.

Conversation example person A	Conversation example person B
お疲れ様でした。本日の会議の議事録を添付しました。	ありがとうございます。内容を確認し、必要があればコメントします。
おつかれさまでした。ほんじつのかいぎのぎじろくをてんぷしました。	ありがとうございます。ないようをかくにんし、ひつようがあればこめんとします。
Otsukaresama de shita. Honjitsu no kaigi no giji-roku o tenpu shima shita.	Arigatōgozaimasu. Naiyō o kakunin shi, hitsuyō ga areba komento shimasu.
Thank you for your hard work. I've attached the minutes of today's meeting.	Thank you. I'll check the content and comment if necessary.

Cultural Context

Ensure the minutes are accurate and comprehensive. Mistakes or omissions may be seen as careless.

今月の目標達成率をお知らせします。

こんげつのもくひょうたっせいりつをおしらせします。
Kongetsu no mokuhyō tassei-ritsu o oshirase shimasu.
We will inform you of this month's goal achievement rate.

Variation 1	Variation 2
今月の目標に対する達成率についてご連絡いたします。	Kyō mo shōjin shima shou.
こんげつのもくひょうにたいするたっせいりつについてごれんらくいたします。	こんげつのもくひょうにたいするたっせいりつについてごれんらくいたします。
Kongetsu no mokuhyō ni taisuru tassei-ritsu ni tsuite go renraku itashimasu.	Kongetsu no mokuhyō ni taisuru tassei-ritsu ni tsuite go renraku shimasu.
I will inform you about the achievement rate of this month's goals.	I will inform you of the achievement rate against this month's goals.

Positive Response	Negative Response
進捗状況が把握できて助かります。	目標達成率が低すぎます。
しんちょくじょうきょうがはあくできてたすかります。	もくひょうたっせいりつがひくすぎます。
Shinchoku jōkyō ga haaku dekite tasukarimasu.	Mokuhyō tassei-ritsu ga hiku sugimasu.
I'll review the meeting minutes.	The goal achievement rate is too low.

Conversation example person A	Conversation example person B
月次報告をさせていただきます。今月の目標達成率をお知らせします。	報告ありがとうございます。前月比ではどうなっていますか?
げつじほうこくをさせていただきます。こんげつのもくひょうたっせいりつをおしらせします。	ほうこくありがとうございます。ぜんげつひではどうなっていますか?
Tsuki-ji hōkoku o sa sete itadakimasu. Kongetsu no mokuhyō tassei-ritsu o oshirase shimasu.	Hōkoku arigatōgozaimasu. Zengetsu-hide wa dō natte imasu ka?
I'd like to give you the monthly report. I'll inform you of this month's goal achievement rate.	Thank you for the report. How does it compare to last month?

Cultural Context
Be prepared to explain any shortfalls and present plans for improvement.

新しい業務マニュアルを作成しました。

あたらしいぎょうむまにゅあるをさくせいしました。
Atarashī gyōmu manyuaru o sakusei shima shita.
We have created a new work manual.

Variation 1	Variation 2
業務効率化のため、新たな業務マニュアルを整備いたしました。	Kyō mo shōjin shima shou.
ぎょうむこうりつかのため、あらたなぎょうむまにゅあるをせいびいたしました。	ぎょうむこうりつかのため、あらたなぎょうむまにゅあるをせいびいたしました。
Gyōmu kōritsu-ka no tame, aratana gyōmu manyuaru o seibi itashimashita.	Gyōmu kōritsu-ka no tame, atarashī gyōmu manyuaru o seibi shima shita.
To improve work efficiency, I have prepared a new business manual.	To improve work efficiency, we have prepared a new work manual.

Positive Response	Negative Response
マニュアルを早速確認します。ありがとうございます。	マニュアルが複雑すぎます。
まにゅあるをさっそくかくにんします。ありがとうございます。	まにゅあるがふくざつすぎます。
Manyuaru o sassoku kakunin shimasu. Arigatōgozaimasu.	Manyuaru ga fukuzatsu sugimasu.
It's helpful to understand the progress.	The new manual is too complicated.

Conversation example person A	Conversation example person B
業務効率化の一環として、新しい業務マニュアルを作成しました。	お疲れ様でした。全社員への周知方法を検討しましょう。
ぎょうむこうりつかのいっかんとして、あたらしいぎょうむまにゅあるをさくせいしました。	おつかれさまでした。ぜんしゃいんへのしゅうちほうほうをけんとうしましょう。
Gyōmu kōritsu-ka no ikkan to shite, atarashī gyōmu manyuaru o sakusei shima shita.	Otsukaresama de shita. Zen shain e no shūchi hōhō o kentō shima shou.
As part of our efforts to improve operational efficiency, we've created a new work manual.	Good job. Let's consider how to inform all employees.

Cultural Context

Ensure the manual is clear, comprehensive, and user-friendly. Complicated or unclear instructions may cause frustration.

部門間の連携強化にご協力ください。

ぶもんかんのれんけいきょうかにごきょうりょくください。

Bumon-kan no renkei kyōka ni go kyōryoku kudasai.

Please cooperate in strengthening interdepartmental collaboration.

Variation 1	Variation 2
部門間の協力強化にご協力ください。	Kyō mo shōjin shima shou.
ぶもんかんのきょうりょくきょうかにごきょうりょくください。	ぶもんかんのきょうりょくきょうかにごきょうりょくください。
Bumon-kan no kyōryoku kyōka ni go kyōryoku kudasai.	Busho-kan no renkei kyōka ni go kyōryoku kudasai.
Please cooperate in strengthening cooperation between departments.	Please cooperate in strengthening cooperation between departments.

Positive Response	Negative Response
もちろん、積極的に協力させていただきます。	連携強化の具体的な方法が示されていません。
もちろん、せっきょくてきにきょうりょくさせていただきます。	れんけいきょうかのぐたいてきなほうほうがしめされていません。
Mochiron, sekkyoku-teki ni kyōryoku sa sete itadakimasu.	Renkei kyōka no gutai-tekina hōhō ga shì Sa rete imasen.
I'll check the new manual right away. Thank you.	Specific methods for strengthening cooperation are not shown.

Conversation example person A	Conversation example person B
組織の効率化を図るため、部門間の連携強化にご協力ください。	承知しました。具体的にどのような協力が必要ですか？
そしきのこうりつかをはかるため、ぶもんかんのれんけいきょうかにごきょうりょくください。	しょうちしました。ぐたいてきにどのようなきょうりょくがひつようですか？
Soshiki no kōritsu-ka o hakaru tame, bumon-kan no renkei kyōka ni go kyōryoku kudasai.	Shōchi shima shita. Gutai-teki ni dono yōna kyōryoku ga hitsuyōdesu ka?
To improve organizational efficiency, please cooperate in strengthening interdepartmental collaboration.	Understood. What specific cooperation is needed?

Cultural Context

Be specific about what kind of cooperation is needed. Vague requests may be ignored or misinterpreted.

来週の研修スケジュールをお知らせします。

らいしゅうのけんしゅうすけじゅーるをおしらせします。

Raishū no kenshū sukejūru o oshirase shimasu.

We will inform you of next week's training schedule.

Variation 1	Variation 2
来週の研修予定をお知らせします。	Kyō mo shōjin shima shou.
らいしゅうのけんしゅうよていをおしらせします。	らいしゅうのけんしゅうよていをおしらせします。
Raishū no kenshū yotei o oshirase shimasu.	Raishū no kenshū nittei o otsutae shimasu.
We will inform you of the training schedule for next week.	I will inform you of the training schedule for next week.

Positive Response	Negative Response
研修の準備を進めておきます。	研修の内容が不明確です。
けんしゅうのじゅんびをすすめておきます。	けんしゅうのないようがふめいかくです。
Kenshū no junbi o susumete okimasu.	Kenshū no naiyō ga fu meikakudesu.
Of course, I'll cooperate proactively.	The content of the training is unclear.

Conversation example person A	Conversation example person B
人材育成プログラムの一環として、来週の研修スケジュールをお知らせします。	了解しました。参加者リストも併せて共有お願いします。
じんざいいくせいぷろぐらむのいっかんとして、らいしゅうのけんしゅうすけじゅーるをおしらせします。	りょうかいしました。さんかしゃりすともあわせてきょうゆうおねがいします。
Jinzai ikusei puroguramu no ikkan to shite, raishū no kenshū sukejūru o oshirase shimasu.	Ryōkai shima shita. Sanka-sha risuto mo awasete kyōyū onegai shimasu.
As part of our human resource development program, I'll inform you of next week's training schedule.	Understood. Please also share the list of participants.

Cultural Context

Ensure all necessary details (time, place, required preparations) are included. Missing information may be seen as poor planning.

本プロジェクトの成果報告会を開催します。

ほんぷろじぇくとのせいかほうこくかいをかいさいします。
Hon purojekuto no seika hōkoku-kai o kaisai shimasu.
We will hold a results presentation meeting for this project.

Variation 1	Variation 2
本企画の成果報告会を開催します。	Kyō mo shōjin shima shou.
ほんきかくのせいかほうこくかいをかいさいします。	ほんきかくのせいかほうこくかいをかいさいします。
Hon kikaku no seika hōkoku-kai o kaisai shimasu.	Hon purojekuto no kekka hōkoku-kai o jisshi shimasu.
We will hold a results reporting session for this project.	We will hold a results report meeting for this project.

Positive Response	Negative Response
成果報告を楽しみにしています。	成果報告会の準備が不十分です。
せいかほうこくをたのしみにしています。	せいかほうこくかいのじゅんびがふじゅうぶんです。
Seika hōkoku o tanoshimi ni shite imasu.	Seika hōkoku-kai no junbi ga fu jūbundesu.
I'll prepare for the training.	The preparation for the results presentation meeting is insufficient.

Conversation example person A	Conversation example person B
皆様のご協力に感謝いたします。本プロジェクトの成果報告会を開催します。	楽しみにしています。成果に加えて今後の展望も聞かせてください。
みなさまのごきょうりょくにかんしゃいたします。ほんぷろじぇくとのせいかほうこくかいをかいさいします。	たのしみにしています。せいかにくわえてこんごのてんぼうもきかせてください。
Minasama no go kyōryoku ni kansha itashimasu. Hon purojekuto no seika hōkoku-kai o kaisai shimasu.	Tanoshimi ni shite imasu. Seika ni kuwaete kongo no tenbō mo kika sete kudasai.
Thank you all for your cooperation. We'll hold a results presentation meeting for this project.	Looking forward to it. Please tell us about future prospects as well as the results.

Cultural Context
Be prepared to present concrete results and address any shortcomings. Overly positive reports without acknowledging challenges may be seen as dishonest.

Variation 1	Variation 2
	Kyō mo shōjin shima shou.

Positive Response	Negative Response

Conversation example person A	Conversation example person B

Cultural Context

Made in United States
Troutdale, OR
01/29/2025

28460081R10290